HEAVEN'S FRACTAL NET

William J. Jackson

HEAVEN'S FRACTAL NET

Retrieving Lost Visions in the Humanities

INDIANA
University Press

Bloomington & Indianapolis

This book is a publication of
Indiana University Press
601 North Morton Street
Bloomington, IN 47404-3797 USA

http://iupress.indiana.edu

Telephone orders   800-842-6796
Fax orders   812-855-7931
Orders by e-mail   iuporder@indiana.edu

Library of Congress Cataloging-in-Publication Data

Jackson, Bill, date
   Heaven's fractal net : retrieving lost visions in the
humanities / William J. Jackson.
      p. cm.
Includes bibliographical references and index.
   ISBN 0-253-34279-1 (alk. paper) — ISBN 0-253-21620-6
(pbk.: alk. paper)
   1. Fractals. 2. Religion and science. 3. Science and the
humanities. I. Title.
   BL265.M3J33 2004
   291.1'75—dc21

                                                      2003012245

1 2 3 4 5 09 08 07 06 05 04

FOR ROSELLE, MARCIA, AND ROSE

Everybody pieces together what they have as they go
with the help of the beauty which pulls on the soul
and a sense of fractal wholeness we don't understand,
and none of us is ever fully (un)composed.

CONTENTS

ACKNOWLEDGMENTS

Grateful acknowledgment is made to the following sources for permission to reprint material in this book:

"Fractals," *Poetry* by William Aiken. 165, no. 1 (October 1994): 19. Copyright © 1994 The Modern Language Association. Reprinted with the kind permission of The Modern Language Association.

Excerpts from *The Divine Comedy,* by Dante Alighieri, translated by H. R. Huse, Harcourt. Reprinted with the kind permission of the publisher.

Excerpts from *The Divine Comedy* by Dante Alighieri, translated by John Ciardi. Copyright © 1954, 1957, 1959, 1960, 1961, 1965, 1967, 1970 by the Ciardi Family Publishing Trust. Used by permission of W. W. Norton & Company, Inc.

Excerpts from *Steps to an Ecology of Mind* by Gregory Bateson. Reprinted with the kind permission of Mary Catherine Bateson for the estate of Gregory Bateson.

Excerpts from *Mind and Nature* by Gregory Bateson, copyright © 1979 by Gregory Bateson. Used by permission of Dutton, a division of Penguin Putnam, Inc.

Excerpts from *The Wholeness of Nature: Goethe's Way toward a Science of Conscious Participation in Nature* by Henri Bortoft. Copyright © 1996 Lindisfarne. Reprinted with the kind permission of Lindisfarne Press.

The Legends of the Baal-Shem by Martin Buber, p. 19, The Balkin Agency. Reprinted with the kind permission of The Balkin Agency.

International Journal of Bifurcation and Chaos, Leon O. Chua, ed., vol. 1 no. 1 (1991) 1. Reprinted with the kind permission of Leon O. Chua.

"Visage of War" by Salvador Dali. Copyright © 2003, Artists Rights Society (ARS), New York/ADAGP, Paris. Reprinted with the kind permission of Artists Rights Society.

Excerpts reprinted by permission of the publisher from *The Open Work,* by Umberto Eco, translated by Anna Cancogni, pp. 25–26, Cambridge, Massachusetts: Harvard University Press, Copyright © 1989 by the President and Fellows of Harvard College.

African Fractals: Modern Computing and Indigenous Design by Ron Eglash, fig 2.2, p. 25; fig.2.3, p. 27; fig. 2.7, p. 35; fig. 2.9, p. 37. Copyright © 1999 Rutgers University Press. Reprinted with the kind permission of Ron Eglash.

Excerpts from *The Unexpected Universe* by Loren Eiseley, Harcourt. Reprinted with the permission of the publisher.

Excerpt from *The Selected Writings of Ralph Waldo Emerson* by Ralph Waldo Emerson, pp. 24–25. Copyright © Random House, Inc. Reprinted with the kind permission of Random House, Inc.

M. C. Escher's "Rippled Surface" and "Whirlpools." Copyright © 2003 Cordon Art B.V., Baarn, Holland. All rights reserved. Reprinted with the kind permission of Cordon Art B.V.

Photograph of St. Patrick's Cathedral by Etienne Frossard. Copyright © Etienne Frossard. Reprinted with the kind permission of Etienne Frossard.

Wholeness Lost and Wholeness Regained: Forgotten Tales of Individuation from Ancient Tibet by Herbert V. Guenther, p. 64. Copyright © 1994 by State University of New York Press. Reprinted with the kind permission of State University of New York Press.

"Noah's Ark" by Janice Dyar Harrell. Reprinted with the kind permission of Janice Dyar Harrell.

"Civilization's Thin Veneer," by Vaclav Havel, pp. 32–35. *Harvard Magazine*, July–August, 1995. Reprinted with the kind permission of *Harvard Magazine*.

Central Africa, Democratic Republic of the Congo, Kuba people, clothing panel, 20th century, raffia plain weave, raffia embroidery, 27 × 26 inches. IMA82.62. Permission for use of the image by the Indianapolis Museum of Art, Helen Adams Bobbs Fund.

Melanesia, New Guinea, Trobriand Islands, canoe prow, wood and pigment, h: 12 inches, w: 21 inches, D: 1–3/4 inches. IMA 72.93.5. Permission for use of the image by the Indianapolis Museum of Art, Daniel P. Erwin Fund.

"Creation" by Arnold Jacobs, Iroquois. Copyright © Arnold Jacobs. Reprinted with the kind permission of Arnold Jacobs.

Excerpts from Jung, Carl Gustav, *Two Essays.* Copyright © 1966 by Princeton University Press. Reprinted by the kind permission of Princeton University Press.

Revisioning Environmental Ethics by Daniel A. Kealey, p. 70. Copyright © 1990 by State University of New York Press. Reprinted with the kind permission of State University of New York Press.

Philosophy East and West 43, no. 3 (July 1993): p. 481. "Indra's Postmodern Net" by David Loy. Copyright © University of Hawai'i Press. Reprinted with the kind permission of University of Hawai'i Press.

The Postmodern Condition: A Report on Knowledge by Jean-François Lyotard, trans. By Geoff Bennington and Brian Massumi, p. 60. Copyright © 1984 University of Minnesota Press. Reprinted with the kind permission of University of Minnesota Press.

Figure reprinted from *Pathophysiology: The Biologic Basis for Disease in Adults and Children,* by K. L. McCance and S. E. Huether, p. 941, illus. A and B. Copyright © 1994 by Mosby, Inc. Reprinted with the kind permission of Elsevier Science.

Excerpt from *A Thomas Merton Reader* by Thomas Merton, p. 506. Copyright © Random House, Inc. Reprinted with the kind permission of Random House, Inc.

Auriculotherapy Manual, 2nd edition by Terry Oleson, 1996. "Musculoskeletal Points" © Terry Oleson. Reprinted with the permission of Terry Oleson.

Illustrations from *The Beauty of Fractals: Images of Complex Dynamical Systems* by Heinz-Otto Peitgen and P. H. Richter. Reprinted with the kind permission of Heinz-Otto Peitgen.

Excerpt from Russell, Jeffrey Burton, *A History of Heaven: The Singing Silence.* Copyright © 1997 by Princeton University Press. Reprinted by the kind permission of Princeton University Press.

"Peaceful Border between Three Countries" image by Manfred Schroeder from *Fractals, Chaos, Power Laws* by Manfred Schroeder. Copyright © Manfred Schroeder. Reprinted with the kind permission of Manfred Schroeder.

Excerpt from *Cosmic Ecology: The View from the Outside In* by George Seielstad. Copyright © 1983, The Regents of the University of California. University of California Press. Reprinted with the kind permission of the publisher.

"Spirits of the North" illustration, © 2003 Sally Smith. Represented exclusively by Applejack Licensing Intl. of Vermont. Reprinted with the kind permission of Applejack Licensing Intl. of Vermont.

Excerpts from "Blue Mountain Constantly Walking," from *The Practice of the Wild* by Gary Snyder. Copyright © 1990 by Gary Snyder. Reprinted by permission of North Point Press, a division of Farrar, Straus and Giroux, LLC.

Excerpts from *Selected Writings of Gertrude Stein* by Gertrude Stein, edited by Carl Van Vechten. Copyright © 1946 by the Estate of Gertrude Stein. Used by permission of the Estate of Gertrude Stein.

Excerpts from *The Universe is a Green Dragon: A Cosmic Creation Story* by Brian Swimme. Copyright © 1984 by Bear and Company. Reprinted with the kind permission of Bear and Company.

Excerpts from *The Universe Story* by Brian Swimme. Copyright © 1992 by Brian Swimme. Reprinted by permission of HarperCollins Publishers, Inc.

Excerpt from *A Barfield Reader: Selections from the Writings of Owen Barfield,* G. B. Tennyson, ed. Copyright © 1999. All rights reserved, and reprinted by permission of Wesleyan University Press.

Thai Airways International Ad. Courtesy Thai Airways International.

Gaia: A Way of Knowing: Political Implications of the New Biology by William Irwin Thompson, ed., p. 8. Copyright © 1987, Lindisfarne. Reprinted with the kind permission of Lindisfarne Press.

Figure from *Modern Biology* by Albert Towle. Copyright © 1989 by Holt, Rinehard and Winston, reprinted by the kind permission of the publisher.

Centuries, Poems and Thanksgivings by Thomas Traherne, ed. Herschel Maurice Margoliouth (1958), excerpts from pp. 98, 111, and 143. Oxford University Press. Reprinted by permission of Oxford University Press.

Notes on Love in a Tamil Family by Margaret Trawick, p. 11, Copyright © 1990, The Regents of the University of California. University of California Press. Reprinted with the kind permission of University of California Press.

Excerpts reprinted by permission of the publisher from *On Human Nature* by Edward O. Wilson, Cambridge, Mass.: Harvard University Press, Copyright © 1978 by the President and Fellows of Harvard College.

The Butterfly as Companion: Meditations on the First Three Chapters of the Chuang-Tze by Kuang-Ming Wu, p. 379. Copyright © 1990 by State University of New York Press. Reprinted with the kind permission of State University of New York Press.

HEAVEN'S FRACTAL NET

INTRODUCTORY REFLECTIONS

Little Alps and Big Alps,
Again and Again

There is in all visible things an invisible fecundity, a dimmed light, a meek namelessness, a hidden wholeness. This mysterious Unity and Integrity is Wisdom, the Mother of all, *Natura naturans*.

—Thomas Merton[1]

The method is only the way and direction laid down by a man in order that his action may be the true expression of his nature. If it fails to be this, then the method is nothing more than an affectation, something artificially pieced on.

—Carl G. Jung[2]

The Spirituality of a Fractal Sensibility: Toward Whole Networks of Scales

Fractals are beautiful, intriguing, luminous images of subtle organic order.[3] They have recently attracted much attention and are now being used in a growing variety of attempts to understand natural processes.[4] Fractals open up our abilities to recognize patterns that expand and enrich us both aesthetically and in other ways. To some, fractals seem to be evidence of an underlying Universal Intelligence. This book explores that possibility, and others.

Fractals are patterns in which the whole is reflected in the parts, a property called "self-similarity." The first fractals I ever saw were probably the self-similarities in a painting of the Alps which my father had brought home from Switzerland after completing his service in the U.S. Army in World War II. My brothers and I would roughhouse early Saturday mornings while our parents slept, and sometimes we knocked the painting down from the wall and looked at it. Fractures in the craggy peaks of the mountains, the slopes of chalets, and the angles of fir tree boughs made different-sized triangles that reflected one another. But I did not consciously recognize the pattern. Years passed, and after I left the

1

Midwest for the mountains of Vermont, I saw other deep patterns in nature and in perceptions. Now, when I look out at the Alps, I consciously see both the mountains and the fractal nuances. "So what?" you may ask. This book draws on different realms of knowledge to explain why fractals matter.

Fractals may be the simplest of the beautiful and pervasive patterns at work in nature's creativity. The basic facts of fractals are easy to understand, though if you pick up any mathematical treatment of them you'll see how quickly they can become complex, expressed in highly sophisticated formulas and geometrical descriptions.[5] Whatever the source of order in the universe may be, fractals are one of its ubiquitous modes of operating. Appearing in endless variations depending on conditions and the elements involved, they are what nature relies on when it needs efficient shapes to survive, work, build up, break down, distribute, organize, or enliven with order. For example, whenever it is necessary to maximize a surface area while minimizing mass, the evolutionary process selects fractal structure, as in the branching forms of nerves, lungs, and trees.[6] Fractals suggest infinity, recursiveness, and repetition of a principle of order on different scales. Take some time to look through the examples of fractal forms on the next two pages and elsewhere in this book.

When is fractal-like geometry used in the humanities? (The humanities are the endeavors which address the question of what it means to be human.) This book will offer many illustrations of when and where fractals have been used; the examples span many centuries and cover the globe. Artists and writers have often used fractals when modeling the textures of the natural world, when trying to convey spiritually meaningful structures of experience, and when depicting vision, order, abundance, well-being, belonging, consciousness, social relatedness, and natural contexts.

This book explores a wide range of fractal-like patterns across many systems. It does not dwell too extensively on any one but discusses the fractal-like qualities of many—Dante's *Divine Comedy* and Buddhist philosophy, a Hindu temple and a Sufi verse, reiterated actions, designs of paintings and drawings, cosmic patterns carved in stone, and many more. The examples I touch on are not meant to be exhaustive but are merely suggestive of the many instances of fractals in nature and culture which have often gone unnoticed, even when they are right under our noses. Each one configures a "cosm" that reflects in some manner other cosms, and to some extent they relate to the macrocosm that all cosms ultimately originate from and exist within.

It is worth noting here that "fractal" means not only a fixed visual image in space but also a process enacted in time which traces a fractal pattern. This usage of the term "fractal" is becoming

As Mandelbrot has noted, fractal geometry is not just another technical chapter of mathematics. It can help ordinary people see their world in new ways. It suggests infinity in the dynamic cosmos. In its beauty, humans can find openings to a realm beyond and a musiclike order within. Based on images from Benoit B. Mandelbrot, *The Fractal Geometry of Nature* (New York: W. H. Freeman, 1982).

part of common parlance. For example, in an interview entitled "Werewolves, Fractals, and Forbidden Knowledge," American theater director Mac Wellman said, "I think theatre has an ethic and value all of its own, which has to do with presence, with being alive, with enacting oneself and enacting others. The theatre has a fractal quality, too, it can repeat at infinite depth. It's close to religion."[7] Wellman's use of the term "fractal" stresses repetition and infinity. These are some qualities of fractals, but not all. In fact, Wellman could have used the term "recursive," but didn't, probably because "fractal" is more vivid. Many cultural patterns seem to have some qualities of fractals, but fall short of being full-fledged fractals, strictly speaking. Ron Eglash, in his book *African Fractals,* has explored fractal qualities and cultural patterns.[8] He listed the essential qualities of geometric fractals:

1. Recursion. Fractals are generated by a mathematical process of return—the output of one stage is input for the next, making repeated patterns, with variations.
2. Scaling. The overall shape of the whole is found on smaller

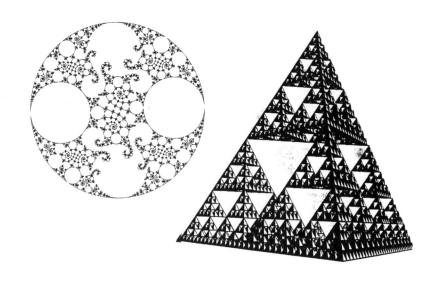

Recognizing fractal patterns and relationships in a variety of forms helps us conceptualize part/whole relationships at various levels of existence. Based on images from Benoit B. Mandelbrot, *The Fractal Geometry of Nature* (New York: W. H. Freeman, 1982).

scales within it. A classic example is a fern frond with smaller fronds, which in turn have smaller fronds.

3. Self-similarity. Recognizable patterns replicate the whole, not necessarily perfectly but at least recognizably, on at least three levels of size. Individually and jointly, the parts resemble the whole.

4. Infinity. This concept, too mind-boggling for everyday logic to grasp, is necessary in fractals, which can trace infinite length within a finite boundary.

5. Fractional dimension. Though the mathematics are beyond the scope of this book, we can see that a fractal is neither a straight line (with one dimension), a flat plane (with two), or a solid volume (with three); yet it may be a line that covers a plane, or a

surface that fills a volume. It has a fractional number of dimensions: between one and two, or between two and three.

Fractals can depict a crumpled sheet of paper, or rough textures like tree bark or the details of a coastline: lines or surfaces with many facets and scales of measurement.

Some of the examples discussed in this book will be full-fledged fractals in the strictest sense, but some will be fractal-like, or fractal-related, with only some of the qualities listed above. Some images will be recursive, some will be composite, some will suggest infinity, some will juxtapose scales, and so on. I will call images with only some fractal qualities "semi-fractals." It is my view that semi-fractals are often capable of spurring the imagination to see further depths in them, even when they are actually self-similar on only a couple of levels of scale. When we recognize the whole replicated in the part, we naturally imagine again the part with further wholes inside it. Thus some patterns and processes are not, literally speaking, fractals, but they suggest fractal possibilities.

I am not a mathematician, but a historian of religion. In my forays into new areas of study I look to thinkers such as Rabindranath Tagore and Octavio Paz, Mircea Eliade and Gregory Bateson. I find affirming resonance and support in the overlapping human life traditions of depth psychology, perennial philosophy (worldwide wisdom traditions), and comparative religion.[9] Once one is familiar with these traditions one can explore uncharted territory, following one's deepest hunches, with the backing of long human experience condensed into recognizable patterns.

Having opened the issue of religion, perhaps I should say a little about it. There are many ways to define the term "religion." One of the word's possible Latin roots has to do with relinking—relinking to the sacred, which in some traditions is a oneness which is vivid in the web of life. The following characterization by psychologist C. G. Jung (1875–1961) usefully highlights some important aspects of the religious or spiritual enterprise in human history:

> Religions are psychotherapeutic systems in the most actual meaning of the word, and in the widest measure. They express the scope of the soul's problems in mighty images. They are the acknowledgment and recognition of the soul, and at the same time the revelation and manifestation of the nature of the soul. No human is separated from this universal basis; only an individual consciousness which has lost the connection with the whole soul is caught in the illusion that the soul is a tiny, circumscribable region, suitable as the object of some "scientific" theory. The loss of the wider connection is the fundamental evil of neurosis.[10]

Comparative religion examines the various styles of religious systems and the kinds of wider connection they offer. Readers unaccustomed to comparative religion may at first find it difficult to think on the large scale that allows the consideration of whole worldviews. I use examples from around the world, from different fields and traditions and from both culture and nature, to illustrate an underlying principle. Some traditional concerns of religion are love, dedication, commitment, and overall orientation,[11] hence cosmic sensibilities. Religions are often concerned with a vast interrelated consciousness, the nature of the soul and God (or the sacred named in other ways), and humanity in relation to the infinite and eternal. It is my contention that fractals can help us reconsider perennial religious questions about nature's order and human needs in a new light.[12]

My goal is to reflect on the graceful roughness of nature and the often-ignored cosmic aspects of cultural expressions, not to invent a world which is not there but to highlight connections and traits which call out to us with a mysterious charm. This book represents not the usual academic analysis (though sometimes that is a part of it) but an interdisciplinary weaving of observations that reflect on wholeness, exploring the wrinkles which nuance it. You ask, "What wholeness?" I answer: the wholeness of a painting, a mountain, a person, a worldview, a cosmos. A snowflake, a grain of sand, a DNA molecule, a salmon, an island ecosystem. Each poem and infant, flea and temple has its own integrity as well as its own relations with the surrounding world. Contemplating wholeness as it is found embodied in different scales means fluidly following the clues that emerge, speculating on meanings and suggesting potentially useful implications.

I share Italo Calvino's high estimation of the values of lightness, quickness, visibility, exactitude, and multiplicity,[13] and I hope this exploration embodies some of them in a useful way. But what is the best pattern to use in presenting an exploration of patterns? I think the most appropriate is fractal-like. My ideas and findings are not confined to a conclusion at the end but are spread throughout the book, reiterated and illustrated in a variety of ways—in artistic images, historical and biographical references, and passages of poetry and philosophy.

When I integrate a quotation into the flow of discussion, without stopping to comment specifically on it as a separate point, think of it as a note in an improvised music of ideas, a strand in a synthesis. (You can always look in the endnotes for details of the quotation's source.) My goal is often to weave separate voices which are basically in harmony into a flow. If you are open to the possibility of deep coherence, it is likely you will recognize it when it appears. Even if at first you cannot quite picture how, for example, "Mind" can be considered a term for the unity of the whole cosmos, considering things *as if* a spiritual oneness among human beings exists, and imagining a single consciousness behind the variety of forms and processes in the universe, may help you reach a new understanding.

Philosophy and theology are disciplines that ask about the universe as a whole. Both are eclectic and inclusive, as they must be to discuss the All, the One, and wholeness. Fractals are models of whole-part relationships. I philosophize about specific examples as they are found in nature and culture around the globe. I have also noted some ironies in thinking about these philosophical issues. For example, how complex the attempt soon becomes when we try to understand the simple, and how torn apart we sometimes feel when we try to grasp the whole! But fractals can help us, delight us, inspire us—they can even help heal us. I can honestly say that fractals are opening a new phase of possibilities in philosophizing about culture and spirituality. Jean Cocteau (1889–1963) sensibly and humorously liked to say, "Since these mysteries are beyond us, let us pretend to be the organizers of them."[14] We can now freshly observe fractals which were already there and benefit from them.

The assumption of perennial philosophy is that the same basic timeless truths are expressed again and again in various times and cultures, in different language and with certain nuances elaborated depending on the conditions. In the view of the enduring philosophy and in light of the reality of life's flow, ownership of one idea by one thinker is an illusion. Each view is indebted to others; all are interdependent. The ideas assembled here are meant to suggest possibilities for contemplation and experience, not doctrine for obedient belief. My attitude, here and in all creative work, is the experimental "Let's try it out and see what happens." It would be self-defeating to hide behind negative presuppositions and refuse to experiment.

In the history of ideas, in comparative religion, and in the study of literature, one examines, compares, and relates statements from various cultures, scriptures, and literatures. So it should be no surprise that many examples are cited in this work. These quotations, stories, images, verses, paintings, and architectural structures are the traces with which I work. When I cite specific instances and comments, I am documenting points in the flow of discussion. When I weave ideas and follow their flow, I am often trying not to dissect or object to them but to affirm and display them—to make a mosaic or video of ideas. As the *Tao Te Ching* says, "It is wise not to confine oneself to oneself." Thus I quote many vivid voices. In fact, the whole point of the book is to make a "mind web" of intertextuality; that is, a weaving of strands, of connections of like-minded views. I do not insist on my own singularity; I want to make one net of the seeming many.[15] This text humbly reflects the larger text: the universe as a text of wholeness without a context (except eternity), a context of all other texts, our cosmic context.

As a historian of ideas, I am cognizant of traditions which speak of a greater reality behind nature, such as Tao, Brahman, or God. But a rational and searching probe inquires into nature to see if in its intrinsic order it explains itself. A view of Tao, Brahman, or God allows stability and connectedness in everyday life, but without a fresh look no new idea emerges—uncertainty and instability are parts of the creative process. We ask new questions, we have new instruments (such as computers), and we explore new answers (such as fractals). Fractals in their various diagrams and organic structures and video animations suggest a vision (of the whole in the parts) which seems related to a spirituality found in all parts of the world over many centuries. They imply interrelatedness or Oneness, mutual interpenetration, and sharing of one nature, one consciousness. The realization is simple, yet it has many ramifications and varieties.[16]

Standing Back and Learning Lessons from Fractal Beauty and Fractal Unity

In this book my intention is to reawaken a vision of cosmic connectedness by using concepts from science, art, literature, and religion. The reason we need to awaken this vision is that it pictures actualities more accurately, portraying the kind of universe we live in and our relations to it. Our age, somewhat disenchanted with old formulations of the realm of the spirit and the term "God," can learn other ways to conceive of the implicit unity some call "the sacred," in part through revisioning traditional spiritual literature by way of the implications of the study of nonlinear or dynamical systems. Chaos science (which significantly overlaps with fractal geometry) and other disciplines that are based on observations of the processes of the cosmos and its complex dynamical systems can be valuable resources in the study of the humanities. Sciences which appreciate the regularities of nature can help those who work in the humanities to see universals and can remind modern humans of important realities. Recent scientific research has gone beyond the old categories of order and symmetry to delve into diversity and unpredictability. The humanities have yet to absorb the significance of the way humans fit into the workings of the cosmos—the humanities in modern times have too often ignored "commonality and pattern as a unifying factor in the interpretation of creativity."[17] Fractals, like the subtle order of the universe denoted by the traditional terms Tao (in China) and *rita* (in India), show ways the template of the cosmos intrinsically wants to go, inclinations of space, energy, matter, life, and mind.

I believe chaos science imagery can be a useful conceptual tool and metaphor for looking into a variety of levels of existence for insights about patterns. Each level has its own traits and integrity and each is integrally related to other levels. Fortuitously, the human scale is rather elastic. As a five-foot-tall "material girl" or boy, one is bound to one scale. But with five senses and the mental powers of creative imagination, the human delves into the whole spectrum of nature's levels, from quark to molecule, from earth's core to distant galaxies, from anthills to the aeries of eagles. Learning from nature, therefore—from organic processes, biology, or animal behavior (or from other systems that offer patterns)—is an exercise in expanding possible understandings. As Owen Barfield wrote, influenced by Goethe, "Love is of man, but wisdom is of nature, and . . . the secret . . . is to stand aside and let the wisdom of nature herself speak through [one]."[18] To be open to the voice of the earth is to learn to tell the story of the universe. Of course, to those who live in poverty and those who live far from a pleasant breeze in the leaves of trees, all this may sound like so much foreign rhetoric.

Those who show how we can learn from nature include Lao-tzu and Aristotle, Dogen and da Vinci, Goethe and Thoreau, Paul Valéry and Pierre Teilhard de Chardin, Gregory Bateson and Aldo Leopold, Loren Eiseley and Konrad Lorenz, Annie Dillard and Barry Lopez.[19] It is necessary to learn from nature to succeed in a variety of fields. Craig Holdrege's book *Genetics and the Manipulation of Life: The Forgotten Factor of Context* points out that our ignored context is the universe around us, the ecosystems of which we are members.[20]

Perhaps *Homo sapiens* is distinguished by its greater capacity for nonlinearity. Other creatures are more bound by linear instinct, but humans have access to higher-order thinking and the freedom of wisdom, which involves a deeper understanding of wholeness. An example of the difference between linear and nonlinear thinking is this: in normal logic, one plus one equals two. In life processes, one plus one may equal three, as when two lovers have a baby. Consequences are proportional to actions in linear thinking, but in nonlinear thinking they are not. The whole is more than the sum of its parts—interrelations produce a rich give-and-take that is self-organizing, self-renewing.

Although Aristotle was immensely important to Western thought, his (and others') limited linear logic and hostility toward paradox (which reflects dynamical conditions) has contributed to unfortunate consequences, including the one-sidedness of rationalism.[21] Arthur Koestler found in his studies of men of science that scientific genius is a curious mix of skepticism and credulity. Both aspects remain active in the exploration that leads to discovery—there must be both freedom of imagination and strictness of rigor. The creative mind keeps the matrices of thought fluid, fresh, and uncluttered, and the levels open to each other, in order to try out an array of possible combinations. New combinations are born in this freedom of exchange, some of the improvised connections survive, and, returning by stages to critique and correct these findings, the creative mind is free and inspired to ask new questions, to relate diverse elements to reveal new patterns.[22] The mind does well to appreciate the freedom of fluid subtlety: "Air finds its way everywhere, water passes through everything."[23] Neutrinos even breeze through solids—a strange truth which John Updike's whimsical poem "Cosmic Gall" strikingly conveys. French essayist Paul Valéry wrote that nature only builds with fluids, and Mihaly Czikszentmihalyi documents the ways in which "flow" creates optimal conditions for thriving and growth in his book *Creativity: Flow and the Psychology of Discovery*.[24]

Scientists such as Benoit Mandelbrot tell us that the construction of models is crucial to discovery. "To understand nature one must be able to make forgeries that look realistic. That proves you have identified something of the essential structure of these shapes." Can we not say the same of a historian who distills the most likely story into a narration of events; an artist who reflects people's moods, situations, landscapes; an anthropologist who reconstructs a culture; and so on? Mediators must translate complex realities into clear usable models. These mock-ups and metaphors are not reality, but they reflect some of reality's complexity with helpful and suggestive accuracy. Mandelbrot explains that Euclidean geometry is often called cold and dry because it deals with abstract forms like circles, planes, and cones. The actual shapes of clouds, mountains, and tree bark are unlike those forms. Between the chaotic roughness and the abstract geometric forms, fractal geometry is neither fully chaotic nor extremely smooth.[25] This book is an artifact of discovery that traces some lines among fractal images and their meanings. It is an appreciation of the functional elegance of nature and mind. It is often said that Americans have a healthy respect for things that work. Nature is a treasury of success stories—viable forms. For seventy million years the shape of the starfish has "worked," has suited the living being to its ocean environment, shaped by the behavior of the ocean, the atmosphere, and the world. We can all respect such fitness and learn from it.[26]

On the one hand, fractal images constitute lenses for visualizing[27] a vague turbulence, such as wind on a sheer curtain, fish

HEAVEN'S FRACTAL NET

swimming in a tank, plumes of fire flaming in a fireplace, or music playing softly in the background. On the other hand, fractals are neatly detailed and precisely symmetrical, like the universe the explorer faces, like the patterns the thinker uncovers when he or she follows elusive hints and notes interfaces and relations among dynamical forces. Fractals are especially useful in imagining, allowing us to conceptualize a network with different scales, thus keeping alive in us a playful sense of possibilities—a willingness to see connections which linear models rule out.

Possible connections are ignored unless one is in the frame of mind which seeks to observe, enjoy, or utilize them. It usually takes some time to see how the various parts of a multifaceted project might fit together. For twenty-five years I have been an enthusiastic collage maker; my compositions (like my writings) include found objects. I like to juxtapose ancient images and new ideas. As a comparativist, I collect many examples to illustrate the principles which concern me; as a collagist I piece together selected elements, arranging them in new patterns to reveal further possibilities, parallels, interconnections.[28] Some of the artworks used to illustrate fractals in this book are collages composed by me. I firmly believe that working with patterns actively and experimentally teaches us in ways words cannot.

The "heaven's net" in this book's title refers to the Chinese saying "Though heaven's net has wide meshes, nothing escapes it." In our age the net is becoming a dominant model for thinking; the web of knowledge is not rigid but flexible, the networks of interconnected systems are apparent to us everywhere. The "strands" which make up this book are intended not to trap anything too fixedly or to leave us stranded in some tight corner, but to reveal aspects of the subtle net, the unity that makes the universe one, loosely holding all—to bring out our partness with, not nightmarish apartness from, the cosmos at various levels.[29] The fractal-like web of wholeness (to use a Native American image) is not a web of conspiracies but a web of invisible sharing, of mutual give-and-take, that is secret, elusive, only glimpsed at times, but that has far-reaching implications for consciously knowing and appreciating what is beyond the limited grasp of conventional thought. In my view the networks of life and existence can be thought of as a fractal-like network of relationships, with each part reflecting the other parts. More on this later.

This book contains good news for anyone seeking meaning, good news regarding the mutuality of lives participating in cosmic processes. Nothing is discrete in the universe; the coherence of the cosmos includes us. The view I present is not bleak but bright and vibrant—human vitality and meaning are enfolded in the universe's very life and gist. I have drawn on the insights of Goethe,

C. G. Jung, Brian Swimme, and many others. As physicist-philosopher Fritjof Capra said, we live in an "interconnected world, in which biological, psychological, social, and environmental are all interdependent."[30] We are only now beginning to fathom some implications of that community of levels of being. This age of interrelations manifests a growing sense of subtle unity: Burst a bomb and you and others reap unseen fallout; poison water and eventually you yourself wither. Go to the hospital and you'll see how oxygen and blood, lungs and brain, nerves and senses are interdependent. Modern corporations show how nations are entangled. Recent physics conceptualizes the subatomic interrelatedness of all.[31] Genetic studies show that all life forms have similar DNA in each cell (and the structure of DNA is spirals within spirals within spirals). This book is a series of integrative ruminations, reflections on fractal modes of interrelatedness.

We human beings were happy enough in other times and circumstances to build a sanctuary with a semblance of solidity—rock shrines in traditional forms, brick sanctuaries for the spiritual self to retreat to, cathedrals, temples, mosques, pagodas, stupas—places in which one can rest and recenter oneself. But our age demands more and more reflections of the co-inherence of living communities, more and more acceptance of varieties of simultaneous actualities. Our sense of the whole cannot come merely from our own historically conditioned cultural worldview or from linear causality; we must learn from what we share with all others in the web of life.[32] Of course, we've been trained to see difference, but it is important now to begin to learn to appreciate and celebrate similarity. For a child of colonialists to say there are no universals (to impose on other people) is enlightenment; for an observer of the universe and living beings to say there are no universals is absurdity. Common factors of human experience link us to universalities of ancient environments; continuities across time link us to the origins of the universe. Interactive complex adaptive systems involved in sunshine and water, air and earth thrive and share life under dynamical circumstances. We are parts, participants in larger wholes. The sooner workers in the humanities realize this, the better.

The basic fact is that long before humans appeared there was already a deep order in the universe. "Order for free" is an economics-based metaphor that is used by some who study evolution, and it signifies a forgotten truth.[33] The order in the universe is a mystery of consciousness. The mystery before and behind the cosmos has been called by many names: Tao, Ein Soph, Brahman, God, the Numinous. Early Taoist sages emphasized the ineffable aspect of the ultimate, yet appreciated the whole-system qualities, and for convenience's sake named the unnamable "Tao" (meaning

"Way," which to ancient Chinese suggested something like what science today calls the mystery of "order for free" in the universe). Let us use that term for the moment. Tao convulses in the primal whole start, the gradual dawn of order's constellations, known as the "Big Bang" or the "Flaring Forth," and pulses in the afterwaves of each part. Each beginning is fraught with far-reaching trends, and the flowing grains and distinctive textures are already there in the nature of things before we arrive to inspect them, suffer them, or surf on them. One primordial originating event of the universe sprouts forth as four laws: gravity, electromagnetism, and laws for the strong and weak nuclear interactions.[34] The enduring structures of cosmic interactions, the scales and intensities of things, are set. A cosmic coherence generates vast elegant varieties of possibility—all from the One, a "system of systems" evolving with self-similarities at various levels.[35] The whole is vibrant with fractal unities and fractal sensibilities, including reverence and praise in the face of beauty.[36]

The best minds have seen inseparable unities—time and space unified, matter and energy as transformations of each other—and we know that every level (subatomic, organismic, ecological) involves networks of mutuality, so why have so many young people been given the impression that nothing is connected? Why do they get the idea that all is in senseless disarray and random mess? Perhaps it is easier to market dark attitudes of alienation, to ride a bandwagon of chronic complainers hawking absurdity, but that is a one-sided view of the human condition. Health, endurance, and survival may seem irrelevant until one is very ill or dying. This book suggests that paying attention to unity, higher consciousness, and the depths of existence is highly rewarding.

Hidden Links: Elvish Sightings of the Power of the Unconscious

This book begins with a trust, a faith in the "unconscious" processes of nature—the deep intelligence of metabolic processes, organic balance, healing sleep, cellular responses. Perhaps an old story from Norse mythology can help dramatize these unsung forces of wisdom:

At one time the monstrous wolf Fenrir easily broke two massive chains which had been forged by Thor with his magic hammer. The great warrior Thor was unable to protect the heroes of the realm of the Norse gods, Asgard. He tried to bind Fenrir but failed. However, Frey, who spent his time in woods and fields observing seasonal cycles of dewy night and bright day, learned of the amazing power inherent *in little things*. He knew that small acts incessantly performed in darkness and silence are able to bring forth births of great significance. Where Thor's heroic muscle and big magic hammer failed to overpower Fenrir, the overlooked hidden and weak could prevail. Frey sought out in the caverns and obscure recesses of earth a race of tiny beings, the elves, who tirelessly worked with nimble silent fingers to forge a set of chains.[37] They knew how to make something that would work, something that could last a long, long time.

What did they use to make these mysterious chains down below in the jeweled dusk? Strange items. The sound of a cat's footfall, the beards of women, the roots of stones, the sinews of bears, the breath of fish, and the spittle of birds. At first these sound like nonexistent things, but each has a subtly hidden power: though we never see a bird's spit, nests are held together with that secret substance (the Chinese use it to make bird's-nest soup). Though usually women have no long beards, they do have a subtle "down" and a masculine side, an animus, and a great strength of enduring energy. The sinews of bears are tough, but bears are light on their feet and can catch fish with their paws. And so on. When these negligible strands were braided together (how often hidden power has to do with minute linkings and imperceptible secretions, like those used by snails to make ridges in their spiral shells), they formed an unbreakable bond that could restrain the monster Fenrir, with his catastrophic snarl. These elves represent the subtle, silent, and miniscule processes of nature, wisdom beyond human rationality and calculative scheming. They can also stand for the "underground" powers in the unconscious, the healing touch of Tao, the wholeness of spirit. This book is about the subtle powers in the mindlike processes of *nature* as well as in human experience, language, and the creativity of *culture*.

In earlier times, we humans did not have so great a need to find a unity. It was enough in earlier times to worship the sacred in the familiar way. In our time we need to inquire further into links and underlying patterns. Our global age intensifies the need for more knowledge about deep themes, interconnectedness of nature and culture, similarities in religions, and possible cooperation between science and the humanities. Now models provided by fractals enhance our conceptual and geometrical vocabulary. These models deserve respect for their ability to help us better understand the modes of thought which can more fully grasp concepts related to wholeness.

The strands of this book are explorations of experiential fractals and sensibilities of infinity.[38] In them, I present arrays of fractal-like images and allusions found in religion, culture, and literature. To anyone who may read this and, encountering new ideas or wild language, accuse me of getting too rowdy, I plead that it's the age we live in that is rowdy. I'm only responding to

African textile made by the Kuba people, Zaire. This clothing panel is a raffia plain weave with raffia embroidery. This traditional geometric pattern seems to assert, "Life is like this, intricate and well ordered, symmetrical on a large scale, yet varied, unpredictable, with larger motifs holding similar smaller ones: diagonals within a rectangle, rectangles in diagonals. We weave and discover life's weaving as we go." Indianapolis Museum of Art, Helen Adams Bobbs Fund.

and celebrating the kind of universe I sense we inhabit, not only with asides and lists of examples and further sources, but also with riffs, rants, and raps, probes of imagination. These riffs do not try to be pentagons of perfect machinery systematized defensively down to the last jot and tittle, but seek to be sketches that musically vamp out rhapsodic explorations. They offer scenarios to consider, a stream of nonlinear collections of wonders, a picaresque for mind and heart. If you miss a point the first time around, don't worry—it will probably reappear before long in new forms. In some cases I refer to fractal-related matters rather than to fractals per se, and to areas not strictly considered parts of the humanities. This book freely casts a wide net, hoping to catch larger interrelated concepts and to suggest openings of interest.

Alfred North Whitehead predicted that when science and religion someday settle into a more viable relationship with each other, their mutual power will shape the human future. Already those who know some of both are making useful contributions, but this field is hard for many people to grasp as it emerges. I hope this book about fractals and spirituality and philosophy will contribute ideas to those who work in the humanities, ideas which will help in thinking fractally and developing a fractal sensibility.

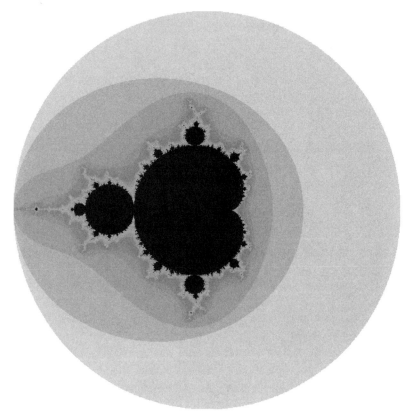

Illustration in black and white of the Mandelbrot set. The concept of the Mandelbrot set was developed by the pioneering mathematician Benoit Mandelbrot from his study of Julia sets, which are associated with iterated functions. It has been described as seedlike, containing an infinite number of fractals. Courtesy of Michael Frame, Mathematics Dept., Yale University.

I feel confident that fractals have the potential to help people in many fields consider new angles on their work and expand their conceptual vocabulary of self-expression. Fractals can offer tools to contemplate and represent such themes as matters of scale, relational dynamics within wholes, and the balance of enduring structures and chance energies that make adaptive configurations.[39]

In my view, human life is necessarily very resilient. Things are not lost once and for all, but can be (and are being) rediscovered in different scales and styles and ages. Renewed inspiration which is truly profound typically comes after one becomes greatly disillusioned, hits rock bottom, and then rises up again. Vaclav Havel saw our need for recovery when he said, "We must discover a new respect for what transcends us: for the universe, for the earth, for nature, for life, and for reality. Our respect for other people . . . for other cultures can only grow from a humble respect for the cosmic order and from an awareness that we are a part of it, that we share in it. . . . It is also essential that the Euro-American cultural sphere—the one which created this civilization and taught humanity its destructive pride—now return to its own spiritual roots and become an example to the rest of the world in the search

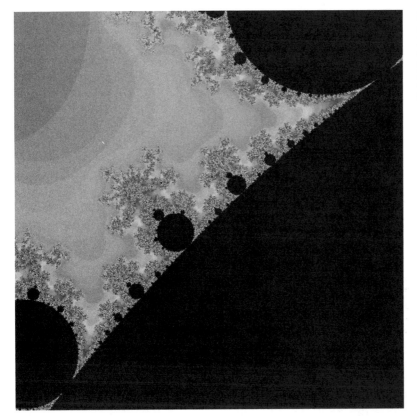

Each Mandelbrot set opens to galaxies of Mandelbrot sets. Courtesy of Michael Frame, Mathematics Dept., Yale University.

for a new humility."[40] This new humility will require humans to get a better sense of their size in the universe. This fractal transcendence of scale reveals humans to be not so small that they are meaningless and not so great that they form the only standard.

I hope this brief introduction is sufficient to serve as an overall synopsis or quick-sketch cartoon to open the parts of the whole work which follows. On the other hand, I am hoping that you may be able to open the book almost anywhere and begin, because I have tried to reflect the whole in the parts as well.

I am fortunate to have learned from conversations with and feedback from insightful scholars in a number of fields. My thanks to Benoit Mandelbrot of Yale and IBM, Anders Nereim at the Art

How many sizes of the same shape can you find in this fractal image?

Institute of Chicago, Raima Larter and the Nonlinear Systems Interest Group at Indiana University–Purdue University at Indianapolis, Bill Durbin at Washington Theological Union, and David Breed of Maximum Entropy, Inc., Chicago, and to others with whom I have discussed fractals and culture. These include IUPUI students and colleagues who read portions of early drafts of this book, such as Johnny Russell, Brian McKenzie, and Professor Richard Turner. Thank you for your encouragement. I am grateful for a residency at the Bellagio Research Center awarded by the Rockefeller Foundation. It helped me carry this project forward (within sight of the Alps) at a crucial time in February–March 2000 after a series of setbacks and interruptions, and I am grateful for that. Fellow residents there, such as Oscar Chase of New York University's School of Law, were very helpful. While in Italy I met F. David Peat in the medieval village of Pari in Tuscany, and I am grateful that he generously shared his time and ideas with me. A sabbatical from my usual teaching duties in the Department of Religious Studies at IUPUI gave me the time I needed to explore my topic in depth, for which I remain very appreciative. I am also grateful to have received an Indiana University Arts and Humanities grant which helped support the visual aspects of this publication. My thanks also to Peter-John Leone, Linda Oblack, Shoshanna Green, and others at Indiana University Press who helped make this book a reality. I am grateful to Kate Babbitt for editorial suggestions, and to Michael Frame of the Department of Mathematics at Yale for useful mathematical comments and bibliographic information. Michael Frame helped me be more aware of questions of vocabulary. Historians of religion read different literature than scientists, so religious and philosophical words they take for granted need to be defined for a scientific audience. Questions are also raised by terms which have strict meanings for mathematicians and physicists, but may be suggestive metaphors when applied in another field. I have tried to be careful in using such terms, but inevitably I do not use some as literally as a mathematician would. Words often have a life of their own beyond any single person's control. They are employed because they seem useful, and sometimes they capture the imagination and open up new vistas beyond their coiner's original view.

HEAVEN'S FRACTAL NET

STRAND ONE

THE WEAVE OF THE NET

Reason has done violence to natural forces which seek their revenge. . . . To heal the damage done . . . religious and magical practices [developed]. . . . This is why the medicine-man is also a priest; he is the saviour of the body as well as of the soul, and religions are systems of healing for psychic illness. This is especially true of the two greatest religions of man, Christianity and Buddhism. Man is never helped in his suffering by what he thinks for himself, but only by revelations of a wisdom greater than his own. It is this which lifts him out of his distress.
— C. G. Jung[1]

Retrieving Heaven's Fractal Net from the Waters:
Sensibilities of the Cosmic in World Religions

When I was growing up in Middle America I used to hear a haunting song on the radio called "The Big Hurt," in which Toni Fisher sang of pain that lasted all night long, and wondered when her heartbreak—the "big hurt"—would end. At the time I didn't know what the song was referring to, though the words seemed quite simple and accessible. Now the point seems clear: it is about the sadness of things that go terribly wrong in life, the pain of hopes dashed. The point resonates onward. People hurt so much that they don't care to go on sometimes. Society, with its many ills and injustices, hurts. The whole planet hurts when it is disrupted at large-scale levels—when the ozone is torn, when oil is spilled into the ocean, when Chernobyl melts down, when the events of September 11, 2001 cause shock waves . . . A main cause of the "big hurts" today is a misreading of the universe and our place in it.

The problems and tragedies stemming from the ways we misread the nature of the universe (or "epistemological crises," to use a fancy term) have already been well defined by Gregory Bateson and many others. Bateson, who combined scientific rigor with philosophical exploration, wrote, "The unit of survival is organism plus environment. We are learning by bitter experience that the organism which destroys its environment destroys itself. . . . The monstrous atomistic pathology . . . of wrong thinking in which we all live can only in the end be corrected by an enormous discovery of those relations in nature which make up the beauty of nature."[2] Our disastrous misreadings divide the mind from the body and the sacred from nature; we forget that we humans are parts of a living world and lose a sense of the unity of the biosphere and humanity. We do not realize that the ultimate unity is aesthetic and biospiritual rather than simply logical. We have failed to see how our knowing "is a small part of a wider integrated knowing that knits the entire biosphere or creation."[3] There is a serious fracture between mind and matter, between intellect and flesh and blood, in the outlook of many modern human beings.

One might ask: Why do we need a bridge between matter and mind if we have been getting along without one? Because we hurt. Perhaps the project of investigating nature objectively that was undertaken by Descartes, Newton, Bacon, and others has been successful in providing more control, but it has also contributed to the way moderns see matter as dead and separate and the mind as something like a ghost in a body-machine. The result is that humans see the world of nature as a mere commodity for the clever to exploit technologically—dead pounds of minerals and gallons of salable waters and so on—instead of as a community of life which humans participate in and owe their very life to. Materialism, scientism, and extreme individualism have often allowed us to exploit the resources of earth while blinding us to the "pattern that connects," to use Bateson's phrase.[4]

If "consciousness is very heavily dependent on having a learning system that can represent the world more or less as it is,"[5] and if, as recent research suggests, the world is a participatory system of living systems that is finely and intricately patterned at all levels, then we need greater respect for the mutual "interexistence" of our human selves with others. Experiencing "interexistence" is as different from one-sidedly imposing clever constructs as riding a dolphin is different from putting a grid over a terrain.[6] Recent interest in wholeness and dynamic systems, in the "holographic universe," holotropic consciousness, and environmental concerns (especially among the young) are hopeful signs.[7] The reason we are exploring fractals here is related to these matters. Fractals are beautiful, useful, and enduring; they pervade nature and culture, and they can teach many lessons.

What Are Fractals, and What Is Their Relation to Nature?

> Fractals lie at the heart of current efforts to understand complex natural phenomena. Unravelling their intricacies could reveal the basic design principles at work in our world.
>
> Only recently, there was no word to describe fractals. Today, we are beginning to see fractal features everywhere. Tomorrow, we may look at the entire universe through a fractal lens.
> —Ivars Peterson[8]

"Fractal" is a term coined by mathematician Benoit Mandelbrot[9] to denote a geometry of nature which traces inherent order in chaotic shapes and processes, using lines so intricate they are more than one-dimensional and surfaces so rough they are more than two-dimensional, to articulate a whole new way of considering and describing structure and form in nature. Fractals begin to delineate the intricacies of nature in ways Euclid's geometric shapes could not—patterns in clouds and ferns, tree bark and bud clusters, the branching of rivers and contours of coastlines, stock market statistics and traffic flow, and so on. This breakthrough in modeling patterns, which gives us new ways of perceiving natural order, stems initially from preverbal pattern recognition but is grounded in mathematics, and models of fractals are made vivid with computer-generated graphics.

Fractals are used to mathematically describe nature's rough irregularities and underlying patterns.[10] Leon Chua reminds us that when one looks closely at turbulent smoke, the rush of water, or the dust of rubble, one finds that beneath the chaos there is

> a much finer structure of immense complexity, a geometric labyrinth of endless convolutions, and a surreal landscape of enchanting beauty. The bedrock which anchors these local and global bifurcation terrains is the omnipresent nonlinearity that was once wantonly linearized by the engineers and applied scientists of yore, thereby forfeiting their only chance to grapple with reality.[11]

Strong words, coming from an engineer! He is saying that people stuck in linear mindsets give up their "only chance" to come to terms with reality and wander off in delusions. I contend that humanity, like the basic nature of the cosmos, experiences personal "bifurcation terrains" (to use Chua's terminology)—splits cutting humans apart, to put it simply—and that "grace" (which Bateson defines as the integration of all the fragmented levels of existence which make life a warring multitude instead of a whole) is the healing, the goal of the universal quest, the unifying holder, and the ultimate rest.[12] Fractals can usefully model the partness and wholeness of our situation, suggesting more accurate ways to picture our realities of relating and belonging. They can help us

Just as spirals on all levels and scales of existence metaphorically bespeak cycles of time—the universe whirling onward—so fractals can suggest the creative pulse of life. Courtesy of H.-O. Peitgen and P. H. Richter, *The Beauty of Fractals: Images of Complex Dynamical Systems* (Berlin: Springer-Verlag, 1986).

make the rediscovery Bateson alluded to above, of the relations in nature which are involved in beauty.

Fractals have the characteristic of self-similarity (another Mandelbrot term). A shape is self-similar if it can be viewed as made up of pieces, each of which is a reduced copy of the whole shape. The whole is reflected in the details of the parts, which cohere and form clusters that together constitute the whole organic shape. The "cosms" depicted by fractal mathematics and computer-generated images range from micro (molecular scales revealed by electron microscopes) to macro (patterns of galaxies). The visual depiction of fractals reveals beautiful patterns as the principle of wholeness-in-parts is recursively played out in harmonious distributions in organisms, in landscapes, and in many systems with feedback

HEAVEN'S FRACTAL NET

mechanisms. Fractal patterns, with their rhythmic echoes of themes, are like a visual music.[13]

We live in a nonlinear world, though for practical purposes our minds are trained in often thinking in straight little lines. Though we live in a "piggyback" world of interdependence, we are in the habit of thinking of the human self in isolation. Fractals, like metaphors from other aspects of chaos science which help us see dynamic nonlinear patterns, stimulate us to conceive of our situations in ways that are more complex and to be better aware of subtle mutualities and the cohesion of underlying orders, to discover infinity submerged amid the finite processes.

In the processes of nature, whenever evolution needs a unified surface or tissue or organic pattern which gives an area for cohesion or circulation, a network for communication, a structure of expansive surfaces (to catch sunlight or absorb oxygen, for example), fractals in their many varieties are the form of choice. A fractal system can absorb and withstand vibrations and impacts better because of its interlinked network; these shocks need not be dealt with all at once by one large linear surface, but can be handled on a multitude of levels and scales. The intake of oxygen by lungs, the "watersheds" of mountains and valleys, the absorption of nutrition by blood vessels all are fractal processes with important functions because a large impact—a flow of one thing striking another—would bounce back, jam up, and overflow. For example, the ever-finer fractal branches of a circulation system allow the distribution of blood or air or water to ever-finer levels. Fractals mediate difference. We find this not only in nature but in culture. The effect of the fractal net image of infinite reflection in Buddhism, as we shall see, absorbs antagonistic inequalities to promote equanimity, as does Christianity's "golden rule": Do unto others (recognizing that in the Spirit you are self-similar) as you'd have them do unto you.

The recursive image of nets, including fractal networks, can serve as a symbol or archetype which, ideally, promotes spiritual vision, compassion instead of vengeance or aggrandizement. In this model, one thing which stands for many, or manyness united harmoniously, can absorb rough treatment. As structures such as hierarchical networks, branches, and nested forms are the ways nature improvises to circulate and regenerate energies when necessity arises, so too in culture fractal-like forms promote a flow of higher consciousness, leading to integrative and transcendent experiences. We need to respect, and take to heart the lessons derived from, the regularities of nature. A balanced understanding involves not only diversity but also universal behavior.

In my view, the promising fractal concept is not a reductionist vision like social Darwinism, Marxism, Freudianism, or any other reduction of motivation in human behavior to political, economic, nutritional, racial, genetic, sexual, or other factors. These modes explain a greater system in terms of a lesser level, with the result that the greater is diminished in the oversimplified description; ascribed motives do not correspond to the richness of reality and insufficient justice is done to the actual case. Fractal patterns involve depth by implicating the level of infinity and holism.[14] They visually evoke a sense of infinity and interrelation in the imagination, offering images useful in thinking about configurations of wholeness. For seekers of deep understanding who are unsatisfied with shallow linear explanations of complex nonlinear systems, this is a great advance. Though fractal geometry is suggestive of nature's complexity, it is not a complete replication of it.

Fractal geometry is a fitting metaphor for elusive order in the cosmos. Fractals bring out visual beauty, a dimension which is a deepening rather than a shallowing mode in human experience, intimating inner harmonies of order. Visual representations of fractal patterns are an extension of our imagination of nature's ways, enhancing our pattern-recognition talents. In terms of unities and units, the whole is repeated in the details which make it up, yet the totality is more than a static assemblage of separate pieces lumped together. Fractal models can stimulate the search for deeper principles in hard-to-read behaviors and help those of us locked into diachronic historical views to imagine more fully the synchronic patterns of wholes.

Fractals, like all things which extend to encompass wholes rather than partial aspects, have a certain irony about them, like trickster cycles in the world's literatures (such as Native American tales of Raven or Coyote or the Two Brothers who play ball). Grab a soldier and the army has you in its grip; approach a Brahmin and you are tangled up with all the gods; open a Hindu text such as the *Bhagavad Gita* and you find the Vedic (pre–*Bhagavad Gita*) past and Puranic (post–*Bhagavad Gita*) future brought together in a nutshell.

The universe is recursive and our understanding of natural processes involves recursion. Fractal-like repetitions in the various levels of the physical world happen on different scales—of behavioral imitations, systemic influences, recapitulations, and so forth. On the microcosmic physical level, "The behavior of the electron is enfolded in plasma, the behavior of plasma is enfolded in the electron,"[15] as wool is implicit in knitting and knitting is implicit in wool (the fibers naturally lend themselves to being twisted into threads and woven together). In nature, as in music, motifs echo dominant themes in multiple variations. The galaxies danced forth by the hundred billion, each with its hundred billion stars, and all existence roars out from the same origin, sharing marks of a common source. As Ilya Prigogine (the Nobel Prize–winning scientist who has made great contributions to systems theory) said, there is no one "fundamental" level, subatomic or galactic, but all are "God's tinkertoys." Fractals help us envision the relations and harmonies we share with larger life processes, the biospiritual realities greater than our individual selves; fractals help us visualize the possibilities of the music of transcendence.[16]

I do not claim that fractal descriptions fit all the patterns in nature or the realities we study and face in life.[17] But they do point to a kind of order discoverable in nature and in the mind, and cultures manifest cascades of recursive and mutually reflective eddies in song lyrics, music, verse, stories, voices, ideas, and visions. This kind of part-whole, nature-culture order has been explored only sketchily,[18] although significant contributions have recently been made to this research.[19] Fractals seem a promising metaphor for explorations of the humanities, because they give us more models to help visualize some kinds of elusive complexity. Fractals also expand our understanding by helping us approach nature for our learning and approach life processes for our ideas about living systems. My appreciation of organic models, natural processes, and patterns of the cosmos in studying religion and literature flows from a hope of learning by focusing on nature's order more than from admiration of the latest advances of science per se. Though powerful, the most recent scientific findings by themselves are not what drives this search.

Mandelbrot chose not to define "fractal" too narrowly.[20] The word is rooted in the Latin *frangere,* or fracture (implying a whole which must exist before it can be broken into parts, just as chaos science implies orders hitherto hidden). He characterized fractals in a way that left them open-ended, able to be used in many applications: "Fractals are visually complex mathematical objects similar in shape and structure over an infinite range of scale, arising from iterated application of a simple rule. Nature is visually complex and has material shapes and structures that are similar over a finite range of scale. . . . Fractal geometry points to a symmetry of pattern within each of the meldings, branchings, and shatterings of nature."[21] Only recently has the number of fractal systems found in nature been recognized (Dietrich Stauffer's figure of one thousand[22] is now considered a vast underestimate). Fractal images help remind us both of nature's rocklikeness and nature's idealikeness, interactions between form and substance. Fractals suggest pattern and flow, what Emerson called reality's "sliding surface." Both sides, idea and matter, are in our lives, as we shall see. "Clay lies still, but blood's a rover," A. E. Housman remarks in "Reveille," suggesting we embody a dynamic symmetry.[23]

On this topic of nature's self-similarities, the Nobel Prize–winning physicist Murray Gell-Mann, writing about beauty and elegance, pointed out that

> There's a quotation from Newton . . . lots of other physicists have made the same remark since—that nature seems to have a remarkable property of self-similarity. The laws—the fundamental laws—at different levels seem to resemble one another. And that's probably what accounts for the possibility of using elegance as a criterion. We develop a mathematical formula, say, for describing something at a particular level, and then we go to a deeper level and find that in terms of mathematics, the equations at the deeper level are beautifully equivalent. Which means that we've found an appropriate formula. And that takes the human being, human judgement, out of it a little. You might object that after all we are the ones who say what elegance is. But I don't think that that's the point. One way to describe what's going on is to say that nature apparently resembles itself at different levels.[24]

Nature's self-resemblance is apparent in many ways; clouds can be rounded like mountains, sand dunes can have waves like oceans or ridges like seashells, blood is watery and salty like the sea, lungs look like trees, and rivers branch upward to springs and downward to deltas.

The experience of perceiving fractal beauty and meaning is engaging and intriguing. Noticing self-similarities on different scales is a revelation of something there but not noticed, something elusive, able to trick and elude detection. We sense something is there, perhaps, but we do not at first focus on the exact principle involved or know how to name it. Once we catch it, it dawns on us again and again in new epiphanies of order—in fir trees, ferns, clouds, water, cracks of mountains, wrinkles and whole faces, flowers (such as Queen Anne's lace), vegetables (such as broccoli, cauliflower, or asparagus), and so on. We look for the parts that look like the whole, and the parts find us, and so do the parts within parts—in structures of music, poetry, architecture, and narrative.

Perceptions of the cosmic[25] constitute a central and pervasive aspect of religions. Where mathematics deals with calculations of the finite and infinite, religion deals with experiences of the cosmic, depth sensibilities of overflowing fullness, the endless and eternal, the abyss of emptiness. The following are a few representative examples which I have culled from the religious literatures of the world. They illustrate some fractal-like sensibilities of the cosmic found in the utterances of poets, seers, and spiritual teachers who needed to depict what they had observed about the nature of consciousness long before the term "fractal" was ever coined. While these examples do not have the mathematical precision of

Mandelbrot, who made a true breakthrough in "naming the whirl-wind" with algebraic formulas and in plotting the patterns with computer imaging, they are self-similar imagistically, and are suggestive forerunners of the concept of fractals. I consider these historical examples to be glimpses of order intuited and remembered, attractive and somehow conveying truth and beauty.

Nets Work

> Let the thread of my song not be snipped while I sing.
> —*Rig Veda* II.28.5[26]

The net is an ancient invention,[27] provoked into existence by reflective thinking and in turn provoking thoughts by its very existence. The spider weaves a web and catches prey; primal humans weave a net and catch birds and fish and other creatures. Ancient forms of nets and fabrics, knitted and knotted, renewed over the generations, are like the fabric of traditional life and lore. A single textile woven of many strands, the archetypal net constitutes a model for all the many kinds of cloths of cultures and fashions which come later. Origin stories of nets, such as the following Norse myth, can be instructive:

> Loki, the capricious trickster, had angered the gods by causing the downfall of the summer sun god Balder, and so he had to run and hide. In the hills, he hid in a hut with doors in all four walls where he could be ever watchful. For fun he spent his days shifting his shape, often becoming a leaping salmon in the cascading waterfalls and streams. One day he sat at his fire thinking through the algorithms of ways the gods might use his own vulnerability to trap him, and he invented the trick it would take. Foolishly yet wisely, Loki made strings by twining linen fibers and crafted them into a well-woven web for catching fish. As he tied the final knot, the gods, sent by Odin on his throne, discovered Loki by his hut. Loki flung the net into the fire and leaped into the water and swam away. The gods noticed the ashes of the linen net, and from that pattern of delicate strands the poet Kvasir discerned the trick with which to catch the Loki-fish. Loki tried to escape by swimming deep and leaping high, but Thor caught him with a net in midair.

Thus Loki had outsmarted himself. Tricksters' acts can be revelations; they can open up parallel patterns and kindred strategies. This is the "trick" of original thinking. The subtle remains of the first net taught the subtle-minded gods how to catch the sneak, and they restrained him—at least until Ragnarok, when chaos will return. We too, through images from the ideas of traditions and seekers, can retrieve the traces and learn to weave anew the visions of heaven's fractal-like net, the often unseen unity underlying the networks of existence.

Fractal illustration. Courtesy of H.-O. Peitgen and P. H. Richter, *The Beauty of Fractals: Images of Complex Dynamical Systems* (Berlin: Springer-Verlag, 1986).

The Strength of Strings No Heart Can Hope to Hum: Fractal-Like Images from Literatures of the World Religions

Time has been kind to the net image; it is as coherent and useful, as sparkling with waterdrops of freshness, as it was two, four, or ten thousand years ago. The net, which is used to survive in a protein-seeking web of life, lends itself to many symbolic uses. The image suggests the interconnected, intercollected realms of Mind—the connective unconscious, to play upon a term from depth psychology. It suggests the knitted links of deep structure, as jade has markings, wood has grain, and physical processes have attractors, patterns holding together in dynamic circuit. The web or net, as we shall see, often serves to indicate the sheer fact of interconnectedness.[28] And many fractal images offer ways of picturing possible networks and patterns.

In ancient Asian literature, fractal-like images of the mysterious oneness of the universe sometimes take the form of descriptions of a cosmic net. There is, for instance, the mention of heaven's vast and subtle net in chapter 73 of the *Tao Te Ching* (sixth century B.C.E.): Tao, Heaven's net, "covers the whole universe. And though its meshes are wide, it doesn't let a thing slip through."[29] All of existence interconnects, mutually entwined in the net of the nonpersonal sacred mystery, Tao.

The net of the Vedic sky god Indra (*Indrajala*) figures in the *Atharva Veda* (1000 B.C.E.). "Great is thy net, brave Indra, Lord of a hundred powers; thine the mighty match for a thousand. Holding them, with his host, therewith hath Indra slaughtered Dasyus a hundred, thousand, myriad, one hundred millions. This world so mighty is the net of Sakra, of the Mighty One. With this, the net of Indra, I envelope all those men with gloom."[30] In both Taoist and Vedic scriptures, the net stands for law or the connective principle of retribution against the wrongdoer and inescapable participation in a system of give-and-take; the net suggests a universal binding and an infinite mesh pattern interlinking all.

Indra brings order out of chaos by conquering the serpent Vritra; like Yahweh, he wields lightning; while Yahweh commands angels, Indra commands *devas*, "shining ones." The Veda uses Indra's original far-reaching power to explain the likenesses found among various levels of existence: "His form is visible everywhere we look, for He is *the Model of every form*. Indra moves in a multiform way with his illusory powers, because his Bay Horses are yoked, ten times one hundred."[31] This statement brings out the kindred quality of the features of the whole; existence is intuited to be one whole system. Implicit in the Vedic view of the cosmos was a well-formed creation reflecting a well-formed creator. (Taoism depicts this sense of likeness too; creatures and creation are "chips off the old block" of the One, the Tao. They share in the flowing grain of life like the lines in wood.) In the *Brihadaranyaka Upanishad*, there is a suggestion that the *devas* are a state of consciousness. "With how many gods [*devas*] does the brahmin priest on the right protect the sacrifice?" "One." "Which is that One?" "Mind. Mind is endless, endless are all the gods, and in that way he wins endless realms."[32] The Indian philosopher Sarvepalli Radhakrishnan commented on this verse, saying that by way of the mind we meditate and that the mind is infinite on account of its modifications. Or, as Allen Ginsberg wrote in his poem "Eclogue,"

> Hail to the Gods, who are given Consciousness
> Hail to Men Conscious of the Gods![33]

Back and forth, one containing the other, divine Mind in all. In the *Bhagavad Gita,* Lord Krishna says, "All that exists is woven on me, like a web of pearls" (VII.7). The encompassing net expressed one vast reality and gave human life a higher context of meaning.

This Hindu vision of the infinite sees the one reality as inclusive and all-pervasive, and it sees all living beings as masks of the One. Each sacred place is a center of the universe in harmony with the other centers, and all external sacred places are symbolic of the sacred Self in the heart. The same sacred Self is in deities, in the inner sanctum of the temple, and in the sacred place where the shrine is located. In India the networks of sacred places to which pilgrims travel are reflections of the sacred already present within. This self-similarity of sacred connecting with sacred has an overall quality of fractal-like processes.

In the *Avatamsaka Sutra,* Mahayana Buddhism extends the metaphor of the net of Indra, developing it in the direction of cosmic interpenetration. There is a tradition that the teaching of the interconnectedness of all in the universe—which the *Avatamsaka Sutra* expounds—was the very first teaching of the Buddha. According to legend, people failed to grasp this profound truth, so the Buddha simplified the message, making it all the more clear.[34] In T'ang dynasty China (618–907), Hua-yen Buddhism found inspiration in the *Avatamsaka Sutra,* which vividly described the interrelations of all beings as the mutual reflections of gems in a vast net:

> Far away in the heavenly abode of the great god Indra, there is a wonderful net that has been hung by some cunning artificer in such a manner that it stretches out infinitely in all directions. In accordance with the extravagant tastes of deities, the artificer has hung a single glittering jewel in each "eye" of the net, and since the net itself is infinite in all dimensions, the jewels are infinite in number. There hang the jewels, glittering like stars of the first magnitude, a wonderful sight to behold. If we now arbitrarily select one of these jewels for inspection and look closely at it, we will discover that in its polished surface there are reflected all the other jewels in the net, infinite in number. Not only that, but each of the jewels reflected in this one jewel is also reflecting all the other jewels, so that there is an infinite reflecting process occurring.[35]

Thus the net image arrives at a clearly fractal configuration of the totality reflected all in one and one in all. The recursiveness of the whole and the quality of infinity make the image all-encompassing and intricate. Mind is like that, and fractals help us see how. Fractal images and zooms within their scales are like snapshots of Indra's net, vivid visualizations of mutualities, connectivities, and subtle relationships. They help us visualize in many ways how the whole can be found reflected in the parts. David Mumford, Caroline Series, and David Wright's recent book *Indra's Pearls,* which discusses fractals generated by circles, gives examples of this richly reflective and generative quality.[36]

The image of Indra's vast network of jewels in the *Avatamsaka Sutra* symbolizes the awareness that although everything which participates or co-inheres in the net may be different in size and value, yet because of mutual reflections and interrelationships nothing is separate. At each warp and woof every single mirrorlike pearl participates by reflecting all the others. Beings have no separate existence but participate all together. In the Zen view, "emptiness" (*ku* [Sanskrit: *sunyata*]) means a net of temporary knottings, the fact of interdependence, the truth that nothing exists separately. The ego's sense of an independent selfhood is illusion; the ego is doomed because all is interwoven.[37] (In Hindu traditions, too, release involves cutting the heart's "knot," releasing bonds of twisted strands of fate, freeing the tangle-obscured light of liberation.)

The net, sharing characteristics with the night of scattered stars, is a poignant image of existence. In traditional narrations, a net caught the Buddha-to-be when he emerged from his mother's womb at birth, and a net of jewels also hung down between the rooms he passed through when he was leaving his family home to discover ultimate reality. The net is an image of "interdependent co-origination," an important concept in Buddhist analyses—each thing is part of an interconnected network of meshes, "and each mesh has its place and responsibilities in relation to other meshes."[38] The Buddhist writer Buddhaghosha, who lived around the same time as St. Augustine (c. 400 C.E.), pictured the minuscule parasitic animals inhabiting our bodies and argued that we do not freely own our bodies, since they are occupied by and in symbiotic relations with other life forms. An American Buddhist, Gary Snyder, also writes of the net as depicting the food chain on earth and observes that in the Avatamsaka philosophy all things and creatures in existence

are necessary and illuminated. From one standpoint, governments, wars, or all that we consider "evil" are uncompromisingly contained in this totalistic realm. The hawk, the swoop, and the hare are one. From the "human" standpoint we cannot live in those terms unless all beings see with the same enlightened eye. The Bodhisattva lives by the sufferer's standard, and must be effective in aiding those who suffer.[39]

Another corollary of the net image is that one does not take credit in an individualistic manner for one's work. The creativity of the universe flows through each person, and the net of relations and inspirations and energies we all depend on is immense.

From the examples above, net and web images may sound characteristically Hindu or Buddhist.[40] It is true that Hinduism and Buddhism are famous for ideas related to this central concept that "All is One" and karmic interconnections mean that mutual respect is called for in a world of such interdependence. But similar ideas are also at home elsewhere. An example from Native American traditions is Chief Seattle's reply to the American president who offered to create a reservation for the tribe:

> Why should I [murmur at the] fate of my people? Tribes are made up of individuals and are no better than [th]ey. Men come and go like the waves of the sea. A tear, a tamanawus, a dirge, and they are gone from our longing eyes forever. Even the white man, whose God walked and talked with him, as friend to friend, is not exempt from the common destiny. We may be brothers after [all]. We shall see. . . . Every part of this country is sacred to my people. Every hill-side, every valley, every plain and grove has been hallowed by some fond memory or some sad experience of my tribe. Even the rocks that seem to lie dumb as they swelter in the sun along the silent seashore in solemn grandeur thrill with memories of past events connected with the fate of my people, and the very dust under your feet responds more lovingly to our footsteps than to yours, because it is the ashes of our ancestors, and our bare feet are conscious of the sympathetic touch, for the soil is rich with the life of our kindred.[41]

People around the world have rediscovered this principle again and again. In Christian traditions, "The kingdom of heaven is like a net cast," according to the Gospel of Matthew[42]—a web of living souls. Poet Robert Frost's statement that "men work together whether they work together or apart" is like James Baldwin's observation that

> Each of us, helplessly and forever, contains the other—male in female, female in male, white in black, and black in white. We are a part of each other. Many of my countrymen appear to find this fact exceedingly inconvenient and even unfair, and so, very often, do I. But none of us can do anything about it.[43]

The American naturalist John Muir also noticed this spontaneous co-involvement of each with all: "When you try to pick out anything by itself you find it hitched to everything in the universe."[44] We co-create and interplay our existences in inevitable mutuality; all are related in interlinking unity, all are harbored in each, each is sheltered in all. Even those who deny their participation rely on others for their existence, and though they resist any sense of wholeness, they make an impact on the whole. The wealthy may ignore any ecological links, yet they will get sick from the germs of the poor who work for them, and suffer upsets when have-nots explode in rage.[45]

But the image of the net, which enables us to see depths of complexity in each simple part, is not meant to be merely a visual model for observers who imagine the well-joined curiosities of the cosmos. It is not just another M. C. Escher artwork to hang on the wall for decoration. In the world's wisdom traditions the idea of the net calls upon humans to play their parts well. Through conscious participation in lives, in love, and in service, people are encouraged to know themselves by co-creating a better world. We could say the "net result" of the image is the arrival at "good." The original meaning of "good" (from the Sanskrit *gadh*) is linked to this point. It involves actions: to gather together, to join, to fit together as a network does. Buddhist virtues of cheerfulness, friendliness, compassion, and nonviolence are matched by similar ideals in other spiritual traditions. As I suggested in the introduction, religion at its best is a relinking. To play one's part in reflecting the whole in an age of alienation and dysfunction is a great challenge. Fractals offer a variety of visual images to help the faltering imagination picture anew the meanings of wholeness and participation.

Because of the holographic nature of the cosmos, with each being co-evolving, interpenetrating, relationally embedded in, and co-inhering with others, the postmodern bumper sticker, "Practice random acts of kindness and senseless acts of beauty," if taken literally, is a paradoxical request for the impossible. Why? In the Indra's-net world of experiential fractals, with all in one and one in all, "random" practice is impossible because nothing is random and nothing is senseless. (I am using the word "random" in the sense of haphazard, outside of all order, meaninglessly disorganized.) In such a sensitive web all works together and every chance encounter reveals connectivities, every "act of beauty" heals, makes whole. The *bodhisattva* (in Mahayana Buddhism, one who has vowed to help all beings) has a compassionate gaze which may turn anywhere, because each angle gives equally good access. ("Everyone in the house has the best seat," as composer John Cage put it. Conversely, preconceived notions of negativity make the malcontent resentful even when all is well.) Some kind acts may be more necessary or meaningful, so there are priorities, but none are meaningless, disconnected, alien to the whole and its parts. "Random" and "senseless" are concepts that belong to those locked into a fragmented worldview, while indiscriminate kindness and beauty belong to a world of wholeness and *karuna*, the term for Buddhism's principal virtue, compassionate love.[46]

The *Avatamsaka Sutra* deploys other cosmic images than the

net; Sudhana's vision of Vairocana's tower reveals how "within the tower there are hundreds of thousands of towers, each one as exquisitely adorned . . . and each one, while preserving its individual existence, at the same time offers no obstruction to all the rest."[47] This alternate image of the cosmos is another way to picture each as open to all. This image is different from St. Augustine's (in *The City of God*), of statues in different parts of a temple, each one able to see only one angle of the whole structure.[48] It is more fractal-like—a tower with many recursive towers within towers.

The cosmic sensibility of the all reflected in the smallest often turns up in Zen Buddhist poems: "How nice it is! No speck of dust / That doesn't contain / All the Buddhas / From every direction."[49] So emptiness and next-to-nothing dust are both full. And truth can appear before us in the way things are already happening: "Splendid! / Falling autumn leaves / Flowers in bloom / Each the exact / Appearance of Dharma."[50] Other images suggest infinite scales, even though only a few are mentioned: "At the tip of each hair on millions of lions / are seen [dancing] millions of lions," goes the verse of a Buddhist poet. D. T. Suzuki quoted this verse and commented on it:

> The reference to the numberless lions on the tip of each hair of a lion symbolizes the Kegon philosophy of infinity. According to this, each object holds in it all other objects, infinite in number, not only summarily "all in one and one in all," but there obtains also individually a state of universal "interfusion." This may lead us to think that the universe is utter confusion. But we must remember that confusion implies individuality and assumes a state of things in which each is resisting the others. Kegon, however, holds that each individuality retaining itself as such at the same time allows all others to enter it without there being any "obstruction" (*muge*) between them.[51]

The image suggests a number of scales, the massive scale of millions of lions, the smaller scale of one lion, the yet smaller scale of one lion hair, and the millions of mini-lions, which suggest starting the series all over again. The Zen verses below also show a cosmic sense of connectedness.

> Up and down the pavilion,
> a light lights lights.
>
> In the busy traffic,
> a man meets
> men.[52]
>
> One moon
> shows
> in every pool;
> In every pool
> the one moon.[53]

Traditional Chinese drawing depicting meditation and the consciousness achieved by the sage. C. G. Jung observed, "This picture portrays the spiritual state of the yogi who is about to rid himself of his ego and pass over into the more complete, more objective state of the self . . . *sat-chit-ananda,* the epitome of being and not-being, the ultimate goal of the Eastern way of redemption, the priceless pearl of Indian and Chinese wisdom, sought and extolled through the centuries." *The Spirit in Man, Art, and Literature,* trans. R. F. C. Hull, vol. 15 of *The Collected Works of C. G. Jung,* ed. Herbert Read, Michael Fordham, and Gerhard Adler (New York: Pantheon, 1971), 126.

Inside the eye
of a flea's flea:
Five Mount Sumerus.[54]

These poetic statements from Japan display a sensibility of infinite relatedness, a vision of all points suffused with the "floating glory" of the Zen orientation, based on the invisible Oneness net of experiencing *satori,* an awakening to cosmic consciousness.[55] Other forms of Buddhism, including Tibetan, also celebrate the enlightened Buddha Mind. The fifth Dalai Lama once looked up at the stars and said, "Her tender flesh is near but her mind I cannot measure." Matter appears before us, reflected in our eyes, but the mysterious spirit hides beyond. The fractals of vision and consciousness involve level after level of revelations and concealments.

The Hindu text *Yogavasishtha,* composed in the thirteenth to fourteenth centuries, does not specifically use the net image but depicts a sensibility of the universe of consciousness in a similarly infinitely whole-in-parts fashion, with macrocosms enclosed in microcosms, intelligent power of Mind throughout the interconnected networks of the multilayered cosmos:

This universe is like a ripe fruit appearing from the activity of the *chit* (consciousness). There is a branch of a tree bearing innumerable such fruits. There is a tree having thousands of such branches. There is a forest with thousands of such trees. There is a mountainous territory having thousands of such forests. There is a territory containing thousands of such mountainous areas. There is a solar system containing thousands of such territories. There is a universe containing thousands of such solar systems. And there are many such universes contained within what is like an atom within an atom (which is making up the fruit, with which we started). This is what is known as *chit* or the subtle sun which illumines everything in the world. All the things of the world take their rise in it. Amidst all this incessant activity, the *chit* is ever in undisturbed repose.[56]

Here consciousness is depicted as infinitely mirrorlike, with levels composed of other levels in the universe, subtler than the subtlest, vaster than the vastest. In the Upanishadic vision, spiritual "consciousness" (*chit*) is all-pervasive and eternal, formless and changeless, simpler than the simplest thing and more complex than the most complex thing. In the Hindu worldview, consciousness does not consist of the brain's synapses firing. It is a way of indicating the eternal substratum behind all, the source of "order for free," informing all with reflected intelligence and exquisite patterns, findable but secret. This is not so different from the intent of the net in the Buddhist texts we just examined. Consciousness is the central reality for the Hindu tradition, from Rig Vedic times onward. It is the eternal witness of changes in time. In Rig Vedic imagery, two birds perch in the tree of life. One eats as the other, the eternal witness, looks on. The bird that eats ultimately gets indigestion. It gets caught up in the process of grabbing at pleasure and loses its way. Like Adam and Eve, it eats the wrong fruit and has to pay with the loss of the Eden of freedom. But the bird who is simply looking on with awareness, unentangled in the pleasures, always abides in paradise—the light in the heart never dies, the *atman* or Self is inherently eternally free. After all the tasting and indigestion, the mistakes, the tragedies, and the purifying sufferings comes the realization that the whole drama was *lila*, the "good king's jest"; the eternal truth of consciousness was always right there in one's awareness, and one keeps looking on. Behind the forms of existence, the infinite invisible intelligence of *sat* (Being), *chit* (awareness), and *ananda* (bliss) is the ground. In the Hindu view, this eternal source of existence appears illusorily as duality, generating the relative world of change. Consciousness in this view, means *atman* wholeness in each of the parts.

In the long history since the emergence of the human being, seers and shamans, mystics and priests have expressed the intuition that life, including human life, has always been an appendage to something vaster—be it consciousness, or *chit,* or Tao. This intuition is not anthropocentric, because humans are not at the center of it; it is at the center of humans. What makes the human unique is depth of consciousness in the instrument of mind and heart, embodied soul and life. Before humans arrived on the scene, some of the depths of the universe, with its complexity and elegance, its subtlety and majestic beauty, its vastness and order, were not known by creatures. As Brian Swimme reminds us, "The universe shivers with wonder in the depths of the human."[57]

Western thinkers and visionaries also have left writings of their observations and descriptions of fractal-like cosmic views—visions of the whole world, the universe, solar systems in divine context. For example, Aristotle described something suggestive of self-similarity when he noted that if one scrutinizes anything closely one finds a similar system within it.[58] He doesn't explicitly mention a third scale, but the imagination may picture it anyway. Mystics and artists, poets and philosophers have often looked closely at things and have used images which are sometimes reminiscent of self-similarity in their writings and art to suggest the vision of cosms within cosms, especially the macrocosm within the human microcosm. Origen, the mystic and church father of the second and third centuries, wrote, "In you is another world in miniature. . . . In you is a sun, a moon, and the stars too."[59]

The Roman philosopher Plotinus (205–270) developed an influential view of the importance of contemplation, asserting that all of nature contemplates, that action is the natural side effect of contemplation, and that the whole life of the universe, with all its interconnectivities, is knowable only by contemplation. The concept of the interpenetration of existences found in Plotinus's work has many important implications. Eco-ethics, for example, finds several relevant points in the thought of Plotinus, including the idea of the interpenetration of all in each and each in all, which Plotinus referred to as *nous,* or Intellect.

> This contemplative vision at once reconciles the Deep Ecology principle of equality with the principle of value hierarchization. At the deep, common level of Nous, all are one and all are Nous; but in the more outer levels of phenomenal emanation each can be categorized "according to their nearness to the first principles." Value differentiation can never negate the fundamental insight of equality, however, as well as the ethical principle which flows from it: never treat anything as a means only, for nothing is devoid of intrinsic value.[60]

In his departure from the action/contemplation dialectic that shaped so much of Western thought, Plotinus has much to offer us today.

Many Christian thinkers envisioned the reflection of the whole in the soul. Gregory Palamas, for example, wrote, "Man, this greater world contained in a lesser, is the concentration into one whole of all that is, the recapitulation of all things created."[61] The literature of mystics around the world, from Taoist to Sufi to monk to yogi, offers many similar examples of this thought. Blaise Pascal's seventeenth-century response to the fractal universe he perceived and experienced around him was to feel humbled. Consider the following passages, which reveal his poignant perceptions. Pascal, a scientist and a mystic, admitted that man's imagination

will sooner exhaust the power of conception than nature that of supplying material for conception. The whole visible world is only an imperceptible atom in the ample bosom of nature. . . . It is an infinite sphere, the center of which is everywhere, the circumference nowhere. In short it is the greatest sensible mark of the almighty power of God, that imagination loses itself in that thought. . . .

Let [a man] examine the most delicate things he knows. Let a mite be given him, with its minute body and parts incomparably more minute, limbs with their joints, veins in the limbs, blood in the veins, humors in the blood, drops in the humors, vapors in the drops. Dividing these last things again, let him exhaust the powers of his conception, and let the last object at which he can arrive be now that of our discourse. Perhaps he will think that here is the smallest point in nature. I will let him see therein a new abyss. I will paint for him not only the visible universe, but all that he can conceive in nature's immensity in the womb of this abridged atom. Let him see therein an infinity of universes, each of which has its firmament, its planets, its earth, in the same proportion as in the visible world; in each earth animals, and in the last mites, in which he will find again all that the first had, finding still in these others the same thing without end and without cessation. Let him lose himself in wonders as amazing in their littleness as the others in their vastness. For who will not be astounded at the fact that our body, which a little while ago was imperceptible in the universe, itself imperceptible in the bosom of the whole, is now a colossus, a world, or rather a whole, in respect to the nothingness which we cannot reach? He who regards himself in this light will be afraid of himself,[62] and observing himself sustained in the body given him by nature between those two abysses of the Infinite and Nothing, will tremble at the sight of these marvels; and I think that, as his curiosity changes into admiration, he will be more disposed to contemplate them in silence than to examine them in presumption.

For in fact what is man in nature? A Nothing in comparison with the Infinite, an All in comparison with the Nothing, a mean between nothing and everything. Since he is infinitely removed from comprehending the extremes, the end of things and their be ginning are hopelessly hidden from him in an impenetrable secret; he is equally incapable of seeing the Nothing from which he was made, and the Infinite in which he is swallowed up. . . . Through failure to contemplate these Infinites, men have rashly rushed into the examination of nature, as though they bore some proportion to her . . . with a presumption as infinite as their object.[63]

The last proceeding of reason is to recognize that there is an infinity of things which are beyond it. It is but feeble if it does not see so far as to know this. But if natural things are beyond it, what will be said of supernatural?[64]

Pascal's sense of scaling recognized the webbed scheme of things in the cosmos, and he humbly admitted when his intellect was out of its own depths. A "depth detector" such as Pascal's inhibits arrogance. Pascal did not presume that the isolated ego-driven human individual was the be-all and end-all, standing at the pinnacle of the crown of creation. Pascal's sense of the infinite and the depths of nature kept him sensitive to his own limits. He knew he was aware of only a little of the vast interconnected networks always linking and surrounding us.

Today strings and strands, nets and webs are more important than ever. Superstring theory employs the enduring power of the image of threads, lines entwined, as a way to conceive of networks of existence.[65] The great advances in genetics were predicated on an ability to visualize and understand the threads of DNA. It seems that humankind is on the brink of the ability to manipulate gene recombination in DNA strands—a micro-level change that has the potential to affect both the individual and societal levels.[66] And in addition to the vast media system with its TV networks and other powerful electronic connections for communication, there is the information revolution of the World Wide *Web,* the Inter*net,* which is yet another level of "Indra's net." The Web brings the world into each home and office, knots and all. Ancient Taoist, Buddhist, and Vedantic philosophers would say the Internet merely mirrors on a small scale the versatility and Flexible Flyer freedom of deep consciousness.

Fractal-Like Recursive Patterns in Traditions: Envisioning Heavens and Hells

> Concepts develop through time. Some concepts die; others narrow down; others stagnate. The concept of heaven opens. It opens up in the cosmos in ever-widening circles and opens down in the human character into the deepest self.
> —Jeffrey Burton Russell[67]

Fractal images are involved in the depictions of heaven and hell in various traditions, but before discussing them I want to pose some questions which may reveal why I consider this a significant topic. Have modern people lost the art of thinking about ultimate things, highest visions, ideal perfections, truth and beauty? Only a few ever had it to a great degree, but they—including Plato, Plotinus, and Dante—provided light for the reflections of others, and their gracefully articulated ideas inspired many imaginations. In this day of technological control, conveniences, and slick synthetic surfaces, perhaps some kinds of beauty—for example, Buddhist and Christian visions of ultimate meanings and heavens, the beauty and systems involved in the highest visions—have become more remote. When the "better angels" of secular man's nature are gone, isn't that when images fueling demonization, with its unconscious urges to hateful acts, sometimes flare up in senseless violence, erupting out of civilized rationalizations?[68]

Infinity, scales, and recursive patterns naturally help the religious imagination envision ideal hidden realms. A number of religious traditions feature recursive structures of cosmic likenesses at varying scales in the hierarchic levels of existence. In some stories and systems, divine doings in heaven are recapitulated on a smaller scale among lesser beings on earth. We can see one example of this in Islamic tradition in the *hadith* (anecdote) about the origin of the Kaaba, which begins with the angels in heaven questioning the wisdom of God in making man the authority on earth. God says, "I know something you don't know," and, realizing they have offended God by their presumptions, the angels start circling the vast heavenly throne in repentance. God has mercy on them and tells them that instead of making such wide circles they can circle a small symbolic cube with gems set in it. (According to tradition, every day 72,000 angels go into this cube and never come out.) On earth, later, Abraham and his sons build the Kaaba after the archetype of the celestial cube. To this day, pilgrims on the *hajj* circumambulate the Kaaba in the Arabian holy city of Mecca. They circle it, as observers say, like millions of stars in the wheeling galaxies. Hence we find a similar pattern played out on several levels: angelic, earthly, planetary. The same circularity unites the different participants on different levels in similar actions. The long-enduring tradition knows something you don't know and expresses it in images which baffle yet open to more.[69]

Similar features are also evident in a color painting of the Temple on the Mount in Jerusalem by Israeli artist Menachim Nachshon. The artist's composition suggests phylacteries on different scales: unseen are the small ones tied to worshippers' arms and foreheads for prayer (inside the temple); next, the smaller temple (though larger than the homes on the hillsides), shaped like a phylactery; and then the similarly shaped immense temple reaching toward heaven. In the painting the eternal light is swirling down into the temple and praise is swirling up, out from the temple like great streams of incense. Swirl-shaped *shofars*, or ram's horns, are sounding the announcement that the Messiah has come. The bands from the smaller templelike phylacteries are rising up in incenselike swirls toward the eternal in the heavens above.

Another image of levels of existence, this one also from Judaism, concerns *hitlahavut*, or spiritual ecstasy. Martin Buber suggests that this ecstasy is not a sudden sinking into the eternal:

> It is an ascent to the infinite from rung to rung. To find God means to find the way without end. The Hasidim saw the "world to come" in the image of this way, and they never called that world a Beyond. One of the pious saw a dead master in a dream. The latter told him that from the hour of his death he went each day from world to world. And the world which yesterday was stretched out above his gaze as heaven is today the earth under his foot; and the heaven of today is the earth of tomorrow. And each world is purer and more beautiful and more profound than the one before.[70]

Recursive Patterns in Dante's **Divine Comedy**

> This is my Father's world and to my listening ears
> All nature sings and round me rings
> the music of the spheres.   —Maltbie Babcock[71]

Perhaps the most magnificent work of art about heaven and hell is Dante Alighieri's *Divine Comedy*.[72] Inspired by vision and tradition, the creative writing is simultaneously nuanced with spiritual autobiography, philosophy, and the poet's art. Dante (1265–1321) narrates a pilgrimage through the levels of afterlife experiences. I will sketch briefly some highlights of one motif especially relevant to a recursive sensibility in Dante's imagery. This masterpiece depicts the medieval Christian view of the afterlife in great detail. At a number of levels in the *Divine Comedy*, patterns shape the structure and give it unity. Throughout, Dante used the three-line unit (*terza rima*) to narrate his journey through the three realms—hell, purgatory, heaven. Each unit reflects the three realms beyond the world, and each rhyme makes a small circle in its rhythm of returning sounds—interlinkings within larger interlinkings.

Another artistic means of shaping and unifying the whole structure symbolically is the image of Dante's upward gaze at the close of each of the three books. John Ciardi suggests that each of these endings shows the ascending soul's starward gaze. Stars, "God's shining symbols of hope and virtue,"[73] guide the soul's spiral journey toward transcendence. At the end of the *Inferno,* the first book of the *Divine Comedy,* the poet states, "My guide and I started on that hidden way to return to the bright world . . . until I saw through a round opening the beautiful things that heaven bears and came forth to see again the stars."[74] And at the end of the *Purgatorio:* "I came back from the most holy water born again, like young plants renewed by their foliage, pure and prepared to mount the stars."[75] And the end of the *Paradiso:* "I wanted to see how the human image was conformed to the divine circle and has a place in it but my own wings were not enough for that except that my mind was illumined by a flash (of grace) through which its wish was realized. For the great imagination here power failed; but already my desire and will (in harmony) were turning like a wheel moved evenly by the Love which turns the sun and the other stars."[76] This motif unites the whole circular motion in a vision of circling lights.

The cosmic motif suggests that existence is all one flow—circular light and love. The circle—circular shapes and processes, from the nine circles of hell to nine circles of light in heaven—is a central image throughout the three books. There is a harmony of similarities on this structural level, because both heaven and hell are part of the same creation. Hell's circles writhe with horror, while the circles of heaven glow brightly with bliss and love. Even the eternal torments of the *Inferno* still remind readers of the Creator's dominion over the wholeness of existence. We will return to this central motif of circles in a moment.[77]

There is a quality of infinite reiteration in Dante's vision of hell's punishments. In each of Dante's encounters with historical figures, the sin that caused damnation is dramatically reiterated in the form of punishment. For example, an adviser who caused a son to rebel against his father has to move in a circular groove, holding his own severed head. "Thus is the law of hell observed in me," his doomed head continually declares, dramatizing the "decapitation" he caused—the death of the head of a household—in his own plight.[78] In other cases too, the heinous acts performed in life are reiterated throughout eternity in symbolic form.

In the *Paradiso* especially, many things are done in circles, presumably because the circle is the form of perfection. John Ciardi commented on the interconnections depicted on this level:

> Dante does not see Heaven through any use of his own powers: it performs itself to him at a level his feeble intellect can grasp; for every one

of the souls that shows itself to Dante is telepathically connected to every other, because all are directly connected to the mind of God. The heavenly souls do not use language: they communicate through their common existence in the mind of God. . . . Out of God's love, as they are joined in the body of God, they send visions down to Dante.[79]

While we cannot go extensively into all the details here, we can indicate a few of the many circles in heaven Dante sees. In canto 8 of the *Paradiso*, Beatrice looks even lovelier to Dante than before; they are up where bright souls shine like stars: "And as within a flame a spark is seen, / Or in a choir a single voice is heard / To come and go while others hold their song: / Even so within that light were other lights / Revolving in a circle fast or slowly / According as they had eternal vision."[80] Rings of glowing souls are also seen in the opening lines of canto 10, where he asks the reader to look up and see "the lofty wheels of heaven." In canto 27, he is shown "The order of the universe, which holds / The

The Vision of the Sixth Heaven. Engraving by Gustave Doré for Dante's *Divine Comedy.* The composite winged creature is made up of angels. In Doré's engravings smaller shapes or figures often make up similar larger shapes.

The Creation of Fish and Birds. Engraving by Gustave Doré. Notice the similarities of curves in the composite shapes: clouds and waves, curves of the serpent, curves of the flocking birds, waves and rocks.

centre quiet, while the rest revolves, / Here begins, as from its starting point. / Now in this heaven there is no other where / Except Divine Intelligence, where burns / The love that turns it, and the power it sheds; / Light and love enclose it with one circle."[81] In canto 31, the saints together form a snow-white rose—another symbol of perfection. The flower gives way to the garden, the garden to the kingdom, the kingdom to the empire; in this poetry one image lifts off to the next. Some of the engravings by Gustave Doré (1832–1883) illustrate the recursive qualities of circles of light: an angel of light made of other glowing angels, and so on. Dante's unwavering inspiration led him to reiterate in countless ways the motif of roundness, circlings, rings of light, round gems, garlands, and spheres.[82] Through these stimulating images of perfect love, blissful realization, and liberating vision in heaven's heights, Dante extends the reader's sense of wonder, justice, and divine beauty. The sky is the promise and fulfillment of transcendence; not avail-

HEAVEN'S FRACTAL NET

able in hell, it fills heaven in abundance. (As an unknown American poet wrote, "Heaven is / no heaviness.") Dante's light touch graces the *Paradiso*. I have only mentioned a few of the more obvious patterns here; a more extensive exploration would reveal many more.[83]

Each generation has poets who write of the perennial states of human experience—joy, suffering, despair—heaven, purgatory, and hell. The American poet Emily Dickinson (1830–1886) often wrote of heaven, sometimes with recursive nuances and infinite resonances. In some verses she depicts quick changes of levels of personal being and worlds of experience.

> And then a Plank in Reason broke,
> And I dropped down, and down—
> And hit a World at every plunge
> And finished knowing—then—[84]

The infinite network of internested "cosms" as a glimpse of wonder (suggested also by Blake in "Auguries of Innocence," which begins with the line "To see a world in a grain of sand"[85]) has also inspired hellish nightmare images of being trapped in a mesh of hopeless despair, such as that depicted in a story by Jorge Luis Borges, entitled "The God's Script."

The narrator relates he dreamed one night or day (a distinction with no meaning for him) that he was in prison and saw a grain of sand upon the floor. Indifferent to that grain, he fell back asleep and dreamed he awoke to find that there were two grains of sand. Sleeping more he dreamed there were three. And he dreamed there were four. And the sand grains kept multiplying on and on until the whole prison was filled and the narrator was dying beneath the heap of sand. Then he became aware he was dreaming and exerted himself to wake up. But he found it was useless to be awake because the sand was still suffocating him. Then someone's voice told him: You didn't wake up to real wakefulness, but to a dream you already had. This dream is actually contained inside another dream, and so on, endlessly, just as there are infinite sand grains. The voice concluded that the path the dreamer would have to follow back to real wakefulness is without an end, and that he will not live long enough to ever really wake up.[86]

"Every man finds room in his face for all his ancestors. Every face an *Atrium*." Ralph Waldo Emerson, journal, Jan. 13, 1850, in Bliss Perry, ed., *The Heart of Emerson's Journals* (New York: Dover Publications, 1958), 247. Cartoon courtesy of the Los Angeles Times Syndicate.

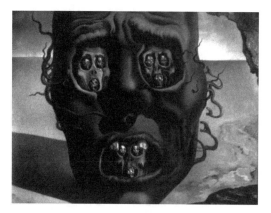

Maybe only a cosmic orphan could experience alienation of such enormous proportions; could soulless matter envision such an endless abyss of dead ends? Even exquisite, self-torturing horrors betray a deep reality; an infinite regress of dreams seems cosmic. Both Buddhism and Christianity have parables suggesting that miserable cosmic orphans may realize they are prodigal sons and return home after their wanderings in self-exile.[87]

Art, like dreams, is a language of the soul or psyche. Dali's painting *Visage of War* shows a nightmarish fractal, a tormented head full of tormented heads full of tormented heads. Courtesy of the Museum Boijmans Van Beuningen, Rotterdam, and Artists Rights Society, New York. © Copyright 2003 Artist Rights Society (ARS), New York/ADAGP, Paris.

In traditional visions, heaven, purgatory, and hell are in a sense unified, coexisting spheres of possible existence and experience, and participation in one or another of these realms is inevitable. The individual is not atomistic but is context-dependent, like a fractal part of a whole, and is, like a fractal, divisible into parts. The images of the realms cause the psyche to wonder how much freedom and self-creation is possible for people of various ages, backgrounds, and places in society.

Tamil Correspondences, Levels, and the Thread of Unity

As I listened . . . a pattern emerged.

—Margaret Trawick[88]

Interrelated likenesses of a less linear and more subtle sort, with the whole again repeated in the parts, are seen by some in connections among levels of existence. Gregory Bateson has argued that "life depends on interlocking circuits of contingency, while [shortsighted, overly purposive] consciousness can see only such short arcs of such circuits as human purpose may direct."[89] Human organisms are part of larger interactive systems—society and culture, biological ecosystems, planetary systems—levels which are all interrelated and systemic. Bateson sees the experiences of religion, music, poetry, art, philosophy, meditation, and contact with nature and children as potentially helpful in bringing out the connectivities, the relations among the levels. The suffering we feel in our self-conflicted, alienated state can drive us to seek the grace of integration and a peaceful unity. The traditional cultures which the alienated left behind offered in some form a wholeness in which people realize that their lives are connected.

A sense of all-in-one, one-in-all resemblances and kinship informs one aspect of Margaret Mead's view of activities in a society: "The way in which people behave is all of a piece—their virtues and their sins, the way they slap the baby, handle their court cases, and bury their dead"—all have similar styles within the logic of the cultural system and its habitat.[90] While this is only a general rule of thumb summarizing her detailed work and that of other anthropologists, it indicates a simplified quality of the whole.

For a long time, the American anthropologist Margaret Trawick closely studied a Hindu family living in Tamil Nadu, South India. The series of interconnected levels of existence she found appear to reveal a kindred relationship:

> As I listened to Themozhiyar, and as I listened to Mahadeva Iyer, a pattern emerged in the picture of the world that each man was drawing for me. The trees, the mountains, the medicines, the households and the poems that they spoke of all had certain distinctive things in common. They were linked through an extensive network of metaphors. They all fit a common framework, and it was one that I had never seen before I came to Tamil Nadu. The large hard mountains encompassed the fertile paddy land as men guarded their women. The eyes blossomed, the breasts wept, and the fields breathed forth their powerful spirits rhythmically. All living hardness softened, all softness melted, and all fluid substance was sublimated into power, into spirit, into new life. Hard consonants contained and were animated by the soft breathing spirit of vowels. The bones of the saint melted with love for God, releasing his soul to join the invisible, passionate cosmic dancer [Lord Shiva]. The tough barky tree poured its life forth in the form of a tender fruit, consummated in ripening, in sweetening, in being consumed as the body of a ripe woman is softened and loosened and consumed as she pours her life into others, as a man's member weakens and diminishes as it pours forth its spirit, its feeling and fluid seed into a new generation. These were the forces turning the world in which Mahadeva Iyer and Themozhiyar lived. All the things they said were arranged around these forces. It had just been a matter of time, of collecting a large enough number of seemingly unconnected bits of information, before I began to see the interlocking patterns in which they all fell.[91]

Time is needed to notice the repeated motifs of softening and flowing because profound reflections reach down into the unconscious rather than merely being satisfied with a surface account. Some suggest that pattern recognition originates in the genetic level of our makeup.[92]

Trawick presents two similar fractal-like line drawings. One is a *kolam*, a traditional auspicious design drawn by women on the threshold in the morning, and the other is a graphic representation of the complex Tamil family relations—the "ideal pattern of bilateral cross-cousin marriage"[93]—made by an anthropologist. They are rather similar. Some *kolams* are strikingly fractal-like. Perhaps human experiences involve multiple mandalas of learning and natural processes which cannot be fully separated and yet should not be jumbled together, either. In any case, fractals help us envision holistic paradigms; they are lenses which may help us better consider systems. Their visual richness and musical ap-

Kolam designs, South India. Hindu house-wives make these rice powder patterns early each morning on the thresholds of their homes as auspicious signs.

pearance suggest their usefulness as reminders of the moments when holistic pattern recognition opens eyes to fitness, poetic justice, and irony.

The Mandelbrot set "gives a metaphor for the interior complexity of all things, for the more you 'fly' your computer into the set [or focus your eyes on different parts of it], the more it opens out to receive you"[94] as you adventure through the fractal realms of wholeness. Without such connectivities as those which Trawick saw in Tamil Nadu's nature and Tamil lives and culture, one is stuck in one level, looking at unconnected bits or alienated from a swirling world of elements whose cohesiveness one cannot conceive. Grasping meaning always involves perceiving wholes, as Herbert Guenther has remarked.[95] The self-reflexivity or recursiveness of the dynamics of wholeness (the way any part has its own wholeness, which is related to a larger wholeness) implies that human experience is an integral aspect of cosmic wholeness. One experiences wholeness through inner affinity, sensitivity, vulnerability, opening to and relating to that which is experienced. It is when a sense of wholeness escapes one that meaning is lacking. A resistance to glimpsing wholes, an avoidance of resonating with them, for whatever reason, ensures a narrow view. A hunger for wholes ensures a challenging quest in this vast "uni-verse."[96] Jumping to conclusions simplistically can be a hazard in an age of hurry; not seeking depth ensures triviality.

Some of the perennial concepts are useful in visualizing the whole: the way of Tao, the nature of *Paramatma* (the "Higher Self," similar to Emerson's "Oversoul"), the "Buddha Nature," and so forth can widen our views of the ultimate. As physicist Richard Feynman has observed, "Perhaps a thing is simple if you can describe it fully in several ways without immediately knowing you are describing the same thing."[97] The interface between simplicity and complexity is like the interface between chaos and systematic order.

Hidden simplicity, with its infinite potential, has a long history of staying elusive. This is a very significant point. It has taken the 2,300 years which have elapsed since Euclid lived to begin to decipher further the geometry of nature. It is said that although the Tao appears to be negligible, yet it is inexhaustible—the infinite subtlety of cosmic Tao rides on elusive simplicity. What other work has matched the *Tao Te Ching* for brevity and depth, simplicity and vastness? What other work has presented a unified systems theory, suggesting wisely the patterns of how things work on many levels of natural existence? Its proverbs and total vision will not soon be obsolete; on the contrary, more and more translations and applications of it keep appearing.

The basic network of unity, the "implicate whole,"[98] may be the real crux of what is reflected by the concept of self-similarity in fractal networks. Similarities in nature show that it's all one system ("system" has to do with oneness, consciousness, energy; universe means "one turning"). There is a cosmic kinship, elusive and subtle, offering clues through likenesses to what holds it all together.

The relations among the parts, the affinities, self-similarities, bonds, repulsions, and hidden likenesses, are the strands of the net which humans have glimpsed again and again since ancient times. In the *Brihadaranyaka Upanishad,* a character in a story seeks to know "the one *sutra,* the 'thread' of spirit along which all things are strung together." In the Hindu worldview, this strand of connectivity is *chit,* consciousness, the *antarjyoti* or inner light, the controller of worlds and beings that is "central control" distributed throughout the universe. The sutra is said to be *vayu,* the breath of life, abiding as earth yet in the earth without earth knowing. The earth is the body of this string of consciousness which runs throughout everything—waters, fire, space, heaven, the directions, all beings, speech, hearing, mind, knowledge, and seeds. The string is the "unseen seer," the unknown knower, the elusive, the mysterious, pure consciousness.

These ideas from the Upanishad are akin to the view of Heraclitus, an ancient Greek philosopher of process and polarities: "The wise is one, knowing the plan by which it steers all things through all," he wrote.[99] One way to access the All, and the consciousness behind the one stream of existence guiding the All, is to contemplate interconnections and likenesses in systems today, in other words to delve into physics and the life sciences and into systems study. As Mary Catherine Bateson rightly says, "Cybernetics . . . makes poets of us, as does any formal system that allows the recognition of similarity within diversity."[100] This similarity is often worth considering in the fractal lens as self-similarities reflecting in a larger whole. Natural beauty evokes the shadows of meaning with the echoes of unity; it is a suggestion of the infinite, fitness of levels, features joined with grace. Though metaphor found in human culture is of great importance in human life (there is a great exuberance of connections in the brain for just that reason), the principle involves more than just humans. As Gregory Bateson and Mary Catherine Bateson have argued, "Metaphor is not just pretty poetry, it is not either good or bad logic, but is in fact the logic upon which the biological world has been built, the main characteristic and organizing glue of this world of mental process."[101] Metaphoric relations expressed, or "syllogisms in grass," as Bateson calls them, are the dominant mode of communicating the interconnection of ideas and related patterns in all preverbal realms of existence. Grass dies, men die, men are (like) grass; water flows, men can flow, men are (like) water. It is not just by chance that a frog has "hands" and so does man. A lowly piece of coal can smuggle in its dark recesses the "flaming wine of the sun"[102] from a forgotten age—in fact we all do, according to current physics, cosmology, and chemistry. We recapitulate and hold in coded form in every cell of our bodies, in subtle memory traces, evidences of long cosmic evolution.

Dogen's Interactive Fluid Zen "Net-aphor"

> From heaven it descends and to heaven it ascends—
> The soul of man is thus similar to water;
> and then it comes back down to earth again
> and then yet again, changing forever and ever.
> —Johann Wolfgang von Goethe[103]

The cosmic sensibility we find in the writings of Dogen, a thirteenth-century Zen master from Kyoto, suggests new meanings when considered in the light of the discussion above. Gary Snyder has suggested that in Dogen's "Mountains and Waters Sutra" we are offered a vision of the nested hierarchies and the webs of the actual nondualistic world in which we live. All creativity and new thinking comes from the novel juxtaposition of levels which before had not disclosed correspondences and connections, so at first the new seems wild:

> All beings do not see mountains and waters in the same way. . . . Some see water as wondrous blossoms, hungry ghosts see water as raging fire or pus and blood. Dragons see water as a palace or a pavilion. . . . Some beings see water as a forest or a wall. Human beings see water as water. . . . Water's freedom depends only on water. . . . Now when dragons and fish see water as a palace, it is just like human beings seeing a palace. They do not think it flows. If an outsider tells them, "What you see as a palace is running water," the dragons and fish will be astonished, just as we are when we hear the words, "Mountains flow." . . . It is not only that there is water in the world, but there is a world in water. It is not just in water. There is a world of sentient beings in clouds. There is a world of sentient beings in the air. There is a world of sentient beings in fire. . . . There is a world of sentient beings in a blade of grass. . . . All waters appear at the foot of the eastern mountains. Above all waters are all mountains. Walking beyond and walking within are both done on water. All mountains walk with their toes on all waters and splash there.[104]

In Psalm 114 of the Old Testament we find the images of mountains skipping like rams and hills like lambs, the earth trembling at the presence of the eternal—the Lord who "turned the rock into a pool of water, the flint into a fountain of waters." Elements seem to be distorted transformations of each other, sometimes with interchangeable qualities; eternal fountain and eternal flame stand for each other; the river of life and the lake reflecting the sky, the flow of lava, the drift of iceberg, the jet stream. A mountain of ice becomes a vaporous cloud of steam, the solid-seeming tree goes up in smoke. Nature reminds us: Don't get too fixed, no man is an island, even stone is not just stone. The humpback whale transmits its raga melodies of varied rising and falling notes, and they are transmuted creatively into new songs as they are sung again through time and the waters, naturally, fluidly. The Sufi poet Rumi also sang of flow.[105]

Dogen wrote much later than Chuang-tzu, a Chinese sage whose fluid thinking shows a musiclike freedom of consciousness among many scales and levels of existence and who finds macrocosms in microcosms. He fluidly illustrates his vision with a few simple metaphors: "Now if water has not accumulated to sufficient depth, it does not have the power to carry a large boat. Pour a cup of water into a depression, and a mustard seed will be as a boat in it; but put the cup into the water and it will stay put, because the water is too shallow for the size of the boat."[106] The sage plays with scales in many ways. *K'un* ("biggest-smallest") is a fish and infinity; awareness is the biggest-smallest. Most beings stuck in relativity feel outranked: a one-legged hopping insect envies the centipede, who envies the snake, who envies the wind, who envies the eye, who envies mind.[107] Man's music is part of earth's music, and earth's music is part of heaven's music.

But for this wise Taoist poet, "To know that the universe is but as a miniscule tare-seed, and the tip of a hair is as big as a mountain—this is the relativity of standards."[108] Chuang-tzu also writes, "There is a kingdom at the tip of the left feeler of the snail . . . and there is a kingdom at the tip of the right feeler of the snail."[109] This is literally true, if one looks through an electron microscope: each feeler tip has its own elaborate structures, if only we can zoom in close enough to see them. Chuang-tzu subtly saw and intuitively grasped the microcosmic systems, as Aristotle had. A modern commentator on Chuang-tzu explains how the possibility of meaning depends on the viewer's flexible openness to a fertile sense of similarities:

> The meaning matrix is the universe itself, where a living experience has polythetic meaning. . . . Metaphor is the humus out of which our fantasies and creations grow. . . . The universe is itself metaphorical, alive with its power ceaselessly to move us from one realm of meaning to another. As soon as one realm is entered, it suggests another realm. . . . Such suggestion may not be a smooth transition, but a jarring contradiction provoking revolt. The revolt is an "imaginative leap," an innovation, a new vista, a new world.[110]

Language itself sometimes reveals this process. The Chinese word *ch'i* originally meant "ears of wheat or corn arranging themselves in rows (similar heights, colors, shapes and the like), waving in the sunny breeze. Then it came to mean arranging or mixing things in a meaningful pattern."[111] Metaphor collapses difference and distance, giving pathways, models, conceptual ways and means to explore, experiment with, and use to understand. "The Cosmogenetic principle states that vast webs of pathways exist potentially at every place in the universe."[112] When the creative juices are flowing humans are inspired to select and weave the potential connections in fresh, exciting, and fitting ways which have some chance of appealing to other minds and enduring in their regard. "Flow" brings many benefits.[113]

In our times it is no longer just Zen masters and commentators on Taoism who ask us to relax our rigid brains and jaded senses to become more flexible and free and appreciate inherent patterns

Fractal geometry image. Courtesy of Clifford A. Pickover, *Chaos in Wonderland: Visual Adventures in a Fractal World* (New York: St. Martin's, 1994).

and self-reflections at different scales and levels. These spiritual concerns and the perceptions of new science sometimes converge. James Gleick, a science writer, gives us glimpses of intricate patterns by describing fractals as looking like "grapes from God's own personal vine," as he tries to do justice to the new views that are being realized in recent discoveries. Only cosmic metaphors can begin to do justice to the phenomena we are trying to approach. Gödel, Escher, Borges, Luhmann, and others have begun to make paradoxical views seem like a mainstream reality. A physicist can now suggest that we envision "a universe in which each atom, rock, and star drinks of the same boundless waters of creativity. Nature is a symphony in which new themes, harmonies, and structures are ever unfolding. These structures and processes remain in constant communication with each other and engage in a dance of form. Life swims in an ocean of meaning, in an activity and coherence that blur the distinctions between the animate and inanimate, between thought and matter."[114] This vision beckons us to experience an ocean of beauty that dissolves "psychosclerosis"[115] (a humorous term for the hardening of the opinionated psyche, the diminishment of sensitivity, the coarsening that too often follows infancy's freshness[116]). Adults habituated to a deadening rigidity, having killed wonder, go on to build walls through which mountains, rivers, stars, and wind can't penetrate. Spiritual paths, with their uplifting music and creative poetic vision, can sometimes offer ways out of this sad impasse.

"Love Is Strange": Water as an Embodiment of Cosmic Possibilities

Though chaos studies and fractal geometry may seem strange at first, they are just siphoning a little of the water which runs freely in the common rivers of life, revealing life's complex simplicities. Geometry teachers in high schools report that fractal images stimulate students to learn more about math and art and computers. Fractals help reawaken wonder in a process in which the cosmos (having evolved human eyes) is inspired by itself, envisions itself, and recognizes its own deep majesty with the help of human perception.[117]

Artists and poets often show us how individual life is a journey of confluences and intertwinings. Poet James McGrath spoke for them: "I travel upon the heartline of past and present, weaving in the sun pollen of who I am today, wading in the rain puddles of having too much to say because I must always speak from four directions."[118] Many identify with this experience of joining together strands of experience—family, profession, ideas, feelings, sensations, places, and people. Poets, artists, story-tellers, and mystics often speak for the four directions, bringing strands together, conceiving wholes and delivering them. Some eccentric scientists, such as quantum physicist David Bohm, seek wholeness and explore brilliant intuitions.

The naturalist Loren Eiseley reminds us that "each man deciphers from the ancient alphabets of nature only those secrets that his own deeps possess the power to endow with meaning. . . . The golden alphabet, in whatever shape it chooses to reveal itself, is never spurious. From its inscrutable lettering is created man and all the streaming cloudland of his dreams."[119] Creativity involves swimming in the fluidity of this potential generative power of mind and life on this planet which humans share.[120] Perhaps for many this sounds strange, not matching their outlook or aspirations. Fractals reveal some of the truth which is proverbially stranger than fiction.

Maybe it is in the interests of convenience and conformity that well-meaning people neglect to tell their children that life *is* strange. Maybe we even hide from that sometimes uncomfortable fact ourselves, wishing life were simpler. I remember that when I was growing up certain songs were banned from the radio—Mickey and Sylvia's "Love Is Strange," for example. On an unconscious level, maybe, it was condemned not for being "dirty" but because it was a fearful revelation, that truly *love is strange.* Einstein wisely said that explanations should be made as simple as possible but not more simple than that. We need to be careful not to screen out the coincidences, correspondences, side effects, and dreams as too weird to belong in the world we would like to see. Paradox reveals life's depths. Fractals depict paradoxes well because they show how the part is not separate from the whole, and how the infinite is enfolded in the finite, and they help us expect life's nonlinear dynamics.

The study of religion, replete with works that focus on points in isolation, can deepen human understanding by helping us pay some attention to common patterns which appear to be self-similar across many different levels and systems. Some dialogues and experiments have already begun on this point.[121] Both a rigorous scientific analysis and an artistry of views able to see and call attention to internal connections of wholes are needed to move freely across the vast net. I do not know which is more startling: the accuracy of the ancient insights of poets and artists who intuited patterns in the cosmos and the nature of consciousness or the expanded vision of some recent scientists who have a poetic view of the nature of things and a sense of the holistic patterns of consciousness.[122] But in any case, both coincide to jump-start our awareness of basic truths which have been forgotten or long hidden.

Perhaps the findings of timeless poets and the latest science

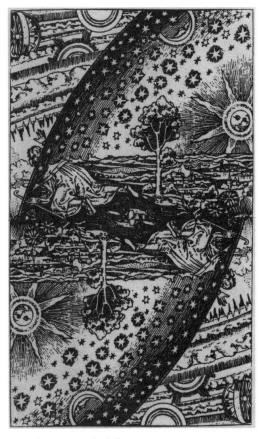

Ezekiel's Vision of Wheels of Light, a traditional image of the state of wonderment in beholding cosmic mysteries. (I have made a mirror image of the original to make it self-reflective. "As above, so below," as the old proverb goes.)

Anonymous seventeenth- or eighteenth-century German woodcut.

are symbolically resolved in the realm of music, a level of patterning where math and feelings, technical skill and unconscious wisdom intermingle. At the end of Plato's *Symposium,* Plato lets the musicians in to "disturb" the order of the banquet with the sounds of their music. He used a nonlinguistic medium to relativize and revitalize the verbal arguments of different sides, to dissolve rigid biases that cause individuals to invest their all in one view and become blind to other equally relevant possibilities. Sending in the musicians humanizes the overly opinionated, making them more congenial to life, more willing to accept its sometimes "strange" complexities.

French anthropologist Claude Lévi-Strauss wrote that music holds the key to the progress of various human disciplines.[123] Perhaps he meant—and I think this is true—that the music of each era enacts a new way of thinking, and if practitioners of other disciplines can catch some of the rhythm, excitement, daring, the thrust of the zeitgeist moving the new music, they may also try new ways and improvise the changes needed for the age in which they live.

Between Plato and Lévi-Strauss, many others, including even the revolutionary German astronomer Johannes Kepler (1571–1630), whose ideas prefigured Newton's, have also pointed to this timeless idea. *"Musica nihil aliud est quam omnium ordinem scire,"* wrote Kepler: "Music is nothing other than knowing the order of all things."[124] Kepler was seeking, with his original thought, to freshly grasp the order of the spheres; even if orbits are not circular, reiteration of an ellipse is also a cyclical rhythm. As the works of Bach can hold as much permanent substance (geometric structure, deep organic and cosmic patterns, laws of harmony and rhythm) as any form of discursive thinking, so too pictures of fractals, mathematicized and computerized sections of cosmic infinity, can embody and suggest deep truths to the perceiving mind. And as one thinker said,

> Because great music is a creation of the agile human mind, we cannot fully understand it until we understand ourselves better. And this is where we find the most exciting potential. . . . If fractals are good models for music, and music is almost a pure creation of the human mind, maybe we can use fractals to model many other aspects of our thought processes. If we get to that point, fractals' contributions to cognitive science will make them one of the most important tools to come along in quite a while.[125]

While it is true that fractal geometry does not pretend to be a panacea, as Benoit Mandelbrot wrote, nevertheless fractals may help us approach the vast and complex fields of religious symbolism and philosophical thinking with a more appropriate sense of scale, systemic patterning, and self-similarity. They remind specialists of ultimate contexts by showing ways of picturing wholes. They help us visualize relationships of parts belonging with each other and to the same whole system. They also help expand our vocabulary and our repertoire of idea-scenarios, so that we have not only Euclid's simple shapes and logic's mechanistic procedures and unrecognized mythic images in the back of our minds, but also organic life processes, nature's self-unfolding geometry—models congenial to life and congruent to understanding.

This is why a paradigm shift to fractals matters. The ladder was a pervasive image in medieval thought: a linear vision that was useful for representing sequential unidirectional activities and arrangements, especially hierarchies. Another image is the building—the bricks or stones of the church, or of knowledge, or of law, or of doctrine. Both ladder and building are static. Today the web, network, fabric, tissue, and other nonlinear images are more accurate: dynamic organic interconnections, with parts which make up, and are made up of, the whole. Wholistic, simultaneous, interrelated aspects are well represented by fractals. Fractals are a great aid in conceptualizing the configurations of net dynamics in forms which more accurately model reality. Ladder building blocks are static and centralized; in a net you change one part and all adjusts, fluid, dynamic, decentralized. Hence strands of fractal enigmas (puzzling but meaningful images), which reflect both problem and solution, hidden and revealed, are suggestive reflections of many situations.

We can enumerate a number of categories from the examples discussed in this strand, depending on which qualities are stressed. For example, (1) images of mutual interpenetration, such as Indra's net and Margaret Trawick's Tamil examples, showing interrelatedness and the pervasive nature of consciousness; (2) sacred images of the cosmic holding of all things, such as a cosmic tree whose branches contain all life, or a circle of circles; and (3) infinite regression, such as the nightmarish hell in Borges's story, or an image less ominous, but nevertheless mind-boggling, as in images of infinite internestedness.

If fractals lead us closer to the actuality, they are an important first step toward livable complexity, the elegant health of the justifiably simple. If fractals, through their visual music, help us pay attention to wholeness, they can be therapeutic conceptual tools, a partial remedy for a wholly fractured age. If fractals are considered aesthetically, as a loose network of Mind suggestive of a rhythmic play of energy as seen in arts and poetry, not as imposed by a dictator using a geometry of regimentation, they can help heal with the creative rhythms of delight and freedom. "Healing comes . . . not because one is whole . . . but from a consciousness

Cracked Idea

We're held together
believe it or not
by all our fractures;

most unity has never
been blatant in parts.
We're all held together

in slivers that sever
what is from what's not;
related by fractures

in all our endeavors
we learn from what smarts.
Wound up together

chained takers and givers,
the sellers and the bought,
are glued by fractures.

Relationships hover.
Lines unite every spot.
We're held together
by all our fractures.

Upper image in collage
courtesy of Clifford Pickover, ed., *The Pattern Book:
Fractals, Art, and Nature*
(Singapore: World Scien-
tific, 1995).

    Lower image courtesy
of Benoit B. Mandelbrot,
*The Fractal Geometry of Na-
ture* (New York: W. H. Freeman, 1982).

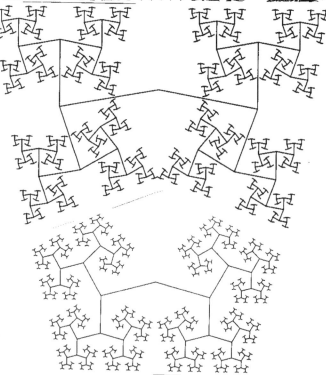

breaking through dismemberment."[126] In a sense fractals offer a convenient revisualization, a beautiful vision of wholeness, a postmodern representation of the intrinsic creative order of consciousness, called Tao, *rita, maat,* and *logos* by earlier civilizations. With our presuppositions we call the order "deep structure," "antichaos," "nonlinear systems," "simplicity/complexity," and "fractals."

Yeats wrote, "Nothing can be whole or sole which has not been rent."[127] The good news is that our hurt and tornness qualifies us for reintegration. The fractures or fragmented aspects of our torn and splintered lives may find in the graceful contours of wholeness expressed by fractals a way to make us grateful again for the incredible richness of being. And our sometimes frantic busy-ness may also learn a relaxing lesson: that one thing done well at any given time is enough, because it is inevitably part of a larger multiscale whole, and is complete in itself as well.[128] Each thing is complete, and the fully complete always eludes us. The Chilean poet Pablo Neruda (1904–1973) wrote, "I'm nothing but the empty net. . . . In my net, at night, I awakened naked, / the only catch, a fish trapped in the wind."[129] Fractals trace our shapes and then escape. Every dip of the net of fractal seeing can bring up interesting catches—structural possibilities for the ways of the whole and the parts. And these visions of fractal wholeness promise to help us adapt and make the best of our "breaks." Fractals help us picture organic belonging to the world of nature, and help us conceive of the inner world of our own nature. As we shall see in the following strands, fractals can help us orient ourselves in the midst of infinity and offer some relief from the "big hurt" I mentioned at the beginning of this strand.

SHIPSHAPE EARTH AND OTHER FRACTAL HOLDING PATTERNS

Those honor Nature well, who teach that she can speak on everything, even on theology.

—Blaise Pascal[1]

Cosmic Images of Wholeness: Fractal-Like Functions in Spiritual Traditions

What are some of the ways we can characterize fractals, wherever we may happen to find them, and how are we to fathom their significance? What are some philosophical and religious applications of fractals, and what are the implications of fractals and related images for finding fulfillment in human life? In this strand we tease apart some of these fibers.

Though "fractal" comes from a Latin word for fracture, the study of fractals is really concerned with wholes, just as chaos science is concerned with order. The study of fractals in the natural world reveals hidden implicit wholeness, orders hitherto undiscerned. A tangle of roots or a density of branches, when seen and photographed with a "fractal eye," subtly displays patterns that are usually ignored.[2] Researchers are exploring simple and complex configurations which were already there in nature for millions of years, seeing them freshly through fractal eyes.

With these patterns we can entertain a flow of ideas—consider and conceive possibilities, mull over and meditate on them, invite the unconscious to help us envision them—we can be at play with inspiration. They entrance us and take us out of time; they free us from a rigid mindset. We can experience infinity "Mandelbroting" and "Pascaling," "Eschering," and "Borgesing"[3] in the imagination, simplicity generating complexity through variably repeated iterations. As we look at the scales of fractal patterns, we see how smaller worlds are embedded in larger ones and mountains are scattered in microcosms. Consider Zen master Dogen's fluid view of some of the scales of existence:

> There are mountains hidden in jewels; there are mountains hidden in marshes, mountains hidden in the sky; there are mountains hidden in mountains. There are mountains hidden in hiddenness. An ancient Buddha has said, "Mountains are mountains and rivers are rivers." The meaning of these words is not that mountains are mountains but that mountains are mountains. Investigate mountains thoroughly. When you investigate mountains thoroughly, this is the work of the mountains. Such mountains and rivers of themselves become wise persons and sages.[4]

What is the point of this light-hearted free-form fantasy on fractal-jagged massiveness? One Buddhist theme in the text is that if you go deeply into anything you find its interdependence with all else, including your own existence. The paper this is printed on is made of trees logged from the mountains; civilizations built in valleys are possible because of the surrounding mountains. Another point has to do with close observation: a close-up of most surfaces shows how many textures have ridges and peaks, mountainlike elevations. As mountains are made up of smaller mountains, so waves are made up of smaller waves and cloud masses are made up of smaller self-similar shapes. Rough old "sage stones" rise from smooth waves of sand in Japanese gardens, offering shapes for contemplation.

The study of fractals is an apt science for the poets and artists who seek to better understand the play of infinity and the principle of wholeness in the form of patterns in nature.[5] Fractals are like "snapshots" of Indra's net, a suggestion of the kind of structural complexity in play throughout the universe. (By play I mean the activity which is delightful to observe, energies in graceful motion, in the whole dance of existence; "play" is the word used for the actions of a game, the performance of music, and the exploratory learning of a child. In Hinduism play [lila] is the divine drama, the existence of life all around us as divine sport.) Fractal images are like diagrams or mosaic mandalas of the systemic complications held together by an underlying simplicity of principle. They are visible and useful in imagining the structures of networks and the dynamics of mutual interpenetration and co-belonging of all living organisms in their communities and environments. D'Arcy Wentworth Thompson described the continuum of life:

We see that the successive chambers of a spiral Nautilus or of a straight Orthoceras, each whorl or part of a whorl of a periwinkle or other gastropod, each additional increment of an elephant's tusk, or each new chamber of a spiral foraminifer, has its leading characteristic at once described and its form so far described by the simple statement that it constitutes a gnomon to the whole previously existing structure.[6]

A gnomon is the part of a parallelogram which remains after a similar parallelogram is taken away from one of its corners—a recursive pattern of subtraction. Nature expresses ideas of number—the mathematical possibilities of multitudes of designs—in such iterations. In its rifflike clusters of variations on themes, ever-proliferating patterns, evolution seems to go on trying out new possibilities. Think of the many kinds of flowers, the many possible configurations of leaves and branches. Consider nature, exploring with computer program–like algorithms of possibility, with playful jazzlike exuberance, generating cycles, combining new points, arriving at surprises. Imagine the fractal-like potential of Goethe's image of an original ur-plant (the mother of all plants, as it were), a form of life flowing with variations into many forms adapted to the differing conditions of the earth, full of the generative source of kinship.

The approach I follow is in tune with Goethe's science: "Nature and nature's phenomena, not theories about the phenomena, are at [its] center and its center of gravity."[7] Fractals help because the concept represents actualities which are very old, related to the structure of Mind and patterns which are basic and go back to the beginning. Fractals represent what survives in the structures and processes of nature, what is perennial or timeless, like enduring wisdom. I am interested in the ways in which the ancient, the timeless or ever-timely, offers essential clues to our understanding of some religious visions.

What we call the Mandelbrot set existed "as soon as nature began organizing itself by means of simple physical laws, repeated with infinite patience and everywhere the same."[8] Because of this, experiences resonating with it have been recorded throughout history. For example, a vision of infinity glimpsed by the English mystic Thomas Traherne (1636?–1674) caused him to describe nature in the following way: "The world is a mirror of infinite beauty yet no man sees it. It is a Temple of Majesty, yet no man regards it. It is a region of Light and Peace, did not men disquiet it. It is the Paradise of God."[9] Fractals help us see again the child's view, infinite and gemlike clustering in each thing seen, views that are subtly hidden by adult habit. Animated tapes of zooms into the Mandelbrot set in color are especially stimulating in opening our eyes.

Fractals open up possibilities for us to contemplate harmonies

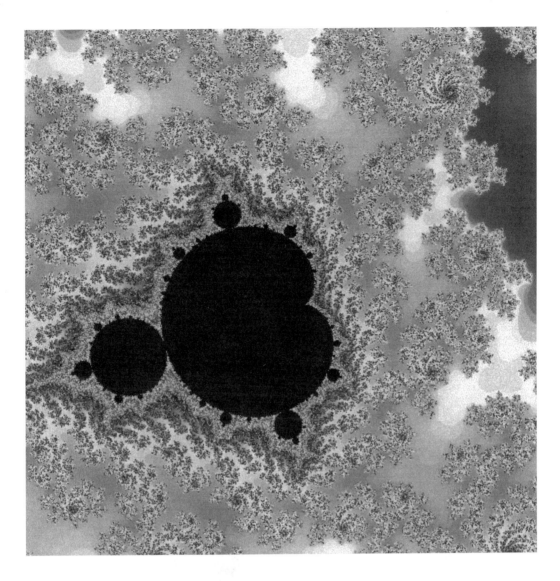

too long ignored. Look at the fractal galaxies twining their way through time, look at DNA with its spirals made up of spirals made up of spirals. Perhaps our increased ability to discern nuances of these patterns signals a reopening of the ancient human quest expressed in the "myth of invariance."[10] This is the old story of human wisdom based on cosmic harmony, the music of the spheres and ancient ordering principles which for so long served to orient human life.

Mandelbrot set. Courtesy of Michael Frame, Mathematics Dept., Yale University.

Geometry That Spans Levels of Existence: Reflections of Wholeness

> Every grain of sap contains the full value of the whole tree.
> —Maharishi Mahesh Yogi[11]

They say there is no Strait Line in Nature; this is a Lie . . . For there is Every Line in Nature. But I will tell them what is Not in Nature. An Even Tint is not in Nature.

—William Blake[12]

It may be useful to discuss in a few ways just what "self-similarity" entails, to bring out nuances and suggest implications. We are discovering that fractal patterns, chaos forms, and "power laws" all involve self-similarity.[13] Molecules, cells, organisms, societies, cultures, planets, and galaxies are all examples of structures on different scales. In the mineral world, levels of scale can be seen in subatomic particles, atoms, molecules, flakes, rocks, boulders, mountains, and ranges. Reflections of wholeness are found in the smaller parts which compose the cosmos in level after level of sizes. The exploration of fractals amounts to a rediscovery of the repeated cycling of the same theme and of the simultaneous distribution of the totality among the constituent parts. Self-similarity often displays an inherent lack of smoothness or expected consistency; anomalies, "strange sets," and paradoxes are involved in

The Sierpinski Arrowhead, a pattern showing "scale invariance" or simple self-similarity. Courtesy of Benoit B. Mandelbrot, *The Fractal Geometry of Nature* (New York: W. H. Freeman, 1982).

HEAVEN'S FRACTAL NET

self-similar patterns. Many levels of existence can be taken for granted until disaster erupts—volcanoes show the earth is alive and dynamic; cancer shows that the order of cell division can be disturbed; pollution can mar harmonies of breathing; war wrecks the placidness of normal life. Gregory Bateson suggested looking for clues to the understanding of one level of existence on another level: for example, using biological processes to understand cultural processes. Though Bateson didn't use the term "self-similarity," it is related to the principle which in pattern recognition and thought processes makes metaphors, poetry, and correspondences of levels possible.

Self-similarity, in more precise and concise language, is the display of "invariance against changes in scale of size," a quality of many natural processes and patterns. Self-similarity is "one of the decisive symmetries which shape our universe and mold our efforts to comprehend it."[14] This is a symmetry consisting of likeness at different scales, not just a mirroring symmetry. Fractals are a family of shapes revealing a widely distributed organizing principle in nature. Delicate structures underlying complexity, intricate recursive shapes, patterns reiterated like lacework, certain mandalas, and organic and artistic microcosms of a variety of shapes exemplify fractals and semi-fractals. By forming model images of whole and parts they give us glimpses of what the total weave is like.

"Enhanced dimensionality" (which is perhaps another name for depth[15]) characterizes these forms: "The fractal dimension indicates the degree or detail or crinkliness in an object, how much it occupies the space between the Euclidean dimensions."[16] The Euclidean dimensions limit visualization to certain simple sets of possibilities; fractals transcend those limits to show more fidelity to the actual "un-smooth" complexity that exists in nature. This lifelike quality of fractals, which allows for more variety and dynamism in orders beyond the oversimplified, is very important. In culture too there are aspects which are sometimes ignored and swept under the rug because of depth and complexity; fractals help us begin to think about them.

We can see the stars and think about them in part because of our fractal eyes, with their light-excitable cells, and our fractal-veined brains, with their cortexes made up of honeycomb-like columns of nerves with branching synapses. It takes one to know one, as the saying goes; one kind of order encountering, noticing, meshing with another kind of order is what we mean by experiences of beauty and meaning. John Briggs, an investigator into fractals, has said, "For me, the most important instrument of thought is the eye. It sees similarities before a formula has been created to identify them."[17] This point underscores what Benoit

Fractal illustration.
Courtesy of H.-O.
Peitgen and P. H.
Richter, *The Beauty of
Fractals: Images of
Complex Dynamical
Systems* (Berlin:
Springer-Verlag,
1986).

Mandelbrot, the discoverer of fractals, has been saying for years—
that fractal geometry helps scientists realize how important the
observing human eye is in science. The organic structure of vision
corresponds with the organic structure of nature. Consider how
our brain and retinal cells function. As the French poet Paul Valéry
says, "The universe is built, on a plan the profound symmetry of
which is somehow present in the inner structure of our intellect."[18]
When we look at something we are actually also examining the
nature of our own eyeballs with their photoreceptive rods and
cones, and the nature of light, and the nature of the brain, as well

as the thing seen; all these examinations are simultaneous and usually about two-thirds unconscious. Hence, we are partly submerged mutual feedback systems (and this has implications for beauty)—we see and echo, project and replicate and appreciate—we are part of a rhythm, participating in mutually reflecting and generating patterns. The intricate networks of blood vessels in our bodies may have resulted from a few basic formulas generated by a configuration of shapes nested one inside the other, which is another way of saying that they are "based on self-similarity."

In a dynamic system's processes there is "an unending, filigreed entanglement, an unceasing bargaining for even the smallest areas," with details of minute whole-system-parts distributed in small-scale replication of the total process.[19] The intricacies of fractal images show the borders where the transitions from order to disorder interact to work out a coexistence in our restless vital systems. They illustrate our own embeddedness in the larger interrelated systems around us. We can observe how fractal processes involved in the yin and yang interfaces of "out there" and "in here" become second nature to us. For example, as we rush to work, we become like the traffic. As we watch television, we absorb the values of the programs we watch. Our original fresh baby vision is changed by the strains and stresses of life.

Fractals imply patterns which possess similar kinds of detail, the whole and the parts not only replicated at different levels of magnification but united, each with the other, in the relations and rhythms of parts and wholes. Contemplating fractals, which demonstrate relations of echoing and mimicking in mirror play, may teach, through implications, needed lessons of wholeness and partness, just as listening to classical music is able to influence our sense of harmony and help in the processes of healing.[20]

It is said that "each life-form [including human] in its own fractal way reflects the dynamical system of nature as a whole."[21] When some mathematicians first scrutinized fractals, they called them "monsters of uncompromising irregularity" because of their own impoverished categories of analysis. Their sensibilities were not complex or subtle enough to prepare them to befriend such "monsters." Benoit Mandelbrot pointed out that "these monsters are the very substance of our flesh"; they order the ways we see and think.[22] It is wiser to learn to befriend and embrace this kind of exquisite complexity and reflexivity than to harden one's stance against it and call it names to keep it at bay.

Fractals provide a kind of visual language, adding to our resources for understanding living systems, providing spatial concepts for focusing on certain kinds of order in realms where we need better theories and models.[23] They confirm with models, examples, formulas, principles, and names what is already there in deep experiences of nature. They give body and name and principle and clarity to rhythms, arrangements, and relationships. For example, a fractal model can help crystallize patterns in a story, a piece of music, or a painting; it can provide a key to thinking about family relationships, or characters' relations in stories, or the way trees branch and waters cascade. Fractals can help us conceptualize and configure intuitive enjoyments already there in our lives, helping bring out camouflaged meanings, potential orders, structures in macrocosms, microcosms, and the "middlecosms" in between.

Let's consider one specific example of how fractals can help us conceptualize subtle processes in human life. The social psychologist J. Richard Eiser, in an interdisciplinary discussion of behavioral and attitudinal change in his book *Attitudes, Chaos, and the Connectionist Mind*, uses such terms as "the fractal mind," "phase space," and "attitudes as attractors." Although strictly speaking "phase space" is a mathematical abstraction representing a state of a system, rather than a physical space, Eiser uses the term metaphorically in developing his model, to help us picture a human situation, conditions in the human psyche:

> Fractal shapes and surfaces are very often excellent "solutions" to particular "problems"—how to trap the maximum amount of sun and rain if we are talking about the surface area of blades of grass in a field and how to maximize potential processing capacity if we are talking about the convoluted surface of the human cortex, contained within the skull. . . . When represented as an energy landscape in phase space, the dimensionality of thought is fractal. . . . Thought falls within a space in which we can discover infinite complexity if we make finer and finer distinctions. It falls also within boundaries . . . about which we can make broad and simple statements if we use more inclusive levels of categorization. . . . [We can picture attitudes as attractors which change only under certain circumstances.] Even a shallow slope is impossible to walk up if it offers no friction. . . . We need to assume . . . as a fundamental theoretical requirement that the slopes on our phase-space maps are less than completely smooth. . . . We need to find extra contours and indentations, extra length and surface area, and hence a greater effective dimensionality. We need the slopes to be fractal.[24]

When the slopes of attitude have a "fractal texture," it means that even small previous experiences which relate to the next attitude which might develop are able to offer some traction by way of their self-similarity. This observation has important implications for the possibility of change: the way mental processes are structured gives clues to help those stuck in problematic ruts, such as harmful habits, addictions, and neurotic compulsions.

Another example of fractal concepts' usefulness in grasping situations is found in photographer Michael McGuire's book, *An*

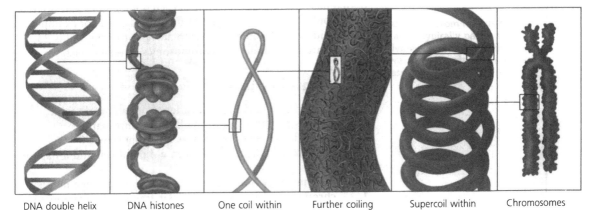

| DNA double helix | DNA histones | One coil within supercoil | Further coiling within supercoil | Supercoil within chromosome | Chromosomes |

Eye for Fractals. McGuire discusses how simplicity and complexity are complementary. A dynamic relation or creative tension runs between these polar extremes, the simple and the complex, an electricity-like current that enlivens systems and reflections. "I wouldn't attempt to grasp that complexity," McGuire said of a scene that included extensive tangled vegetation and a huge mountainous terrain, "without having a conviction of the underlying simplicity."[25] Artistic "faith" involves choosing the holding power of a simplicity that is adequate but not oversimple. An artist's intuition is trained to grasp wholes—how can one function creatively except by eliciting patterns of meaning? The photographer explains that

> In the fractal world dimensions are tangled up like a ball of twine, and objects are neither two dimensions nor three but somewhere in between. In fact, fractal geometry has come to be known as a *geometry between dimensions.* Depending on its wrinkling or fragmentation, a fractal object may be any one of an infinite number of possible fractional dimensions.[26]

Through increasing awareness of brokenness we discover a greater sense of wholeness.

Fractals involve holism in dynamic ways. Think of the spirals of spirals of spirals in DNA. Disturb one part of the DNA and the change shows up on other levels—birth defects, for example. Self-organization of systems is a quality associated with consciousness—sentience, organic intelligence, the ability to grow into coordinated systems and respond to conditions. Researchers have studied a mature carrot and found that any of its cells—any cell type, whether it be leaf or root—can divide and continue in the process of organogenesis or morphogenesis and re-form an entire,

DNA structure composed of spirals made of spirals made of spirals. Illustration from Albert Towle, *Modern Biology* (Austin, Tex.: Holt, Rinehart and Winston, 1989). Courtesy of the publisher.

normally organized carrot. In every cell of living creatures DNA (with the exception of mature red blood cells, which have no nuclei) is coded wholeness of parts. On a level not seen on the surface, there is self-similarity, self-symmetry.[27] It would seem that consciousness (meaning Tao, *atman,* "order for free") is like that— the totality is able to regenerate or heal to some extent through the parts. Some plants, such as the begonia, dramatically reproduce the whole plant from any part; plant a leaf and a whole new begonia grows. Stem cell research also delves into these issues of a wisdom of wholeness found in individual cells. The reflection of subtle light in the power of reproduction and in the resilience of healing bespeaks a wholeness of life, a wisdom of Tao or consciousness.[28] In Taoism this mystery of the subtle principle of the whole which vitalizes is said to work through return; it is a subtle energy which cycles, reiterating patterns again and again. In Vedanta, consciousness is a pervasive light of intelligence that reflects, and is ever full and undisturbed.

"Fractal images have led to a growing contemplation of our reality as a place made up of folded worlds within self-similar worlds—that is, of worlds folded in between dimensions." The conjecture is that things as we know them evolved through long, intense interaction with all else, within the same "holistic dynamical system called life."[29] We share a rootedness in a fractal universe, a kinship with four billion years of evolving life. One way of conceiving of the sacred is as the wholeness implied in the hidden way all things are interconnected (and this conception is a basic tenet of the ancient belief system of the shaman). Similarity of parts implies a recursiveness of the whole played out again and again in a feedback process. The artist and architect connect levels of self-similarity and self-difference, rhythms and contraphonal differences that suggest the holistic patterns and dimensions in the cosmos. Take, for example, St. Patrick's Cathedral in New York City; its self-similar spires reach up on several scales.

The holism of the new aesthetic also brings out new and old relationships between observer and observed—the mutuality of the human participating in what is known by experience—a point which mystics, poets, and artists intuited long ago. Goethe, for example, developed a mode of understanding nature's wholeness which included this.[30] It is true that reductionist science has accomplished great feats, solved subtle problems, and developed amazing technology, but it has its limits. In the twentieth century, thinkers became more aware that the observer is inextricably involved in what he or she witnesses; humans are part and parcel of the dynamic systems they study.[31] Old presuppositions about the human ability to objectively analyze a pattern or a process into its various constituent parts sometimes fail to take into account how

St. Patrick's Cathedral, New York City. The spire shapes repeat on several scales. Courtesy of Etienne Frossard, Brooklyn, N.Y.

the parts are dynamically and integrally connected to each other and therefore have unpredictable effects on the overall process. They also sometimes forget that the observer affects what is observed and vice versa. The observer cannot pretend to exclude himself or herself from what he or she observes. This is now a basic understanding in cutting-edge physics, psychology, and other fields: one's presence, one's decisions and probings intrude into what one is describing. Sometimes this is important and sometimes not. The difference depends in part on the degree of chaos in the system. Not all dynamic systems are chaotic, and among those which are, chaos comes in a variety of degrees. The significance of the disturbance caused by the observer may vary, but obliviousness to the mutuality of observer and observed may lead to a problematic onesidedness.

Examples of Fractals and Related Patterns in the Literatures of Spirituality

If patterns exist at various levels of the physical world, including the mineral, animal, and vegetable realms, and if human systems of perception (nerves, the photoreceptive rods and cones of the eye, and branching dendrites in the brain) partake of these same patterns, then we should be able to find instances of such patterns not only in observations of nature but also in experiential realms of human life. We should see the elegant network of being implicit in the ancient artworks daubed on cave walls showing shamanic trance experiences of entoptic cells, in religious visions, in literary depictions, in story, in folklore, and in a variety of artistic expressions.

And we do. Some aesthetic structures and literary symbolism in Africa,[32] India, and elsewhere anticipated the patterns which today we call fractals, long before computers and chaos science came into existence. Self-similarity was noted by philosophers such as Aristotle, as I mentioned before. Mystic poets both ancient and modern have often suggested such a vision with their images of all in one and one in all. For example, in our time, American poet Robinson Jeffers wrote in his poem *De Rerum Virtute,* that he believed that the first living cell on earth experienced in itself echoes of the future reverberating. He believed, the poem continues, that this first cell of life felt a trajectory, and an intimation of the great creatures that would one day live on earth, as well as the forest of the future with its green leaves, and the ocean where whales would one day swim. The poem states Jeffers's belief that it is not by random chance that the earth generated her brood of living forms, but that earth is able to feel and to choose what develops in time. Jeffers asserts that the great galaxy around us, the "fire wheel" within which we living creatures find ourselves "pinned" is a vast stellar whirlwind in which our own sun is just a single grain of dust, or even a mere electron. He further says the universe in which the giant atom of earth exists, has a life which it fulfills, and has a course on which it is intent—it is not mere dead matter and blind force but a mysteriously conscious way, an impressive display of fertile majesty.[33]

Jeffers reminds us of the awe involved in seeing our star in a larger "whirlwind," our own lives pinned at some point to the flowing galactic firewheel. The planetary system as a "giant atom" pattern is an idea that occurs to modern man naturally, and it involves correspondence on different scales. The poet asserts that the humble form of the first cell had intimations of a long unfolding of future lives inherent in its potential. The planet is full of feeling, choosing, intending, because there is consciousness in one and all. It is natural for human beings to feel awe when facing the stars. A poet like Jeffers is able to articulate such feelings with great eloquence.[34]

Divine visions of the sacred as containing the world or cosmos, as systems-encompassing, as cosms of pattern-holding, are found in the world religions. Vishvadhara, Lord as Holder of All in Hinduism, and the globe-holding Christ child carried by St. Christopher across a raging stream are examples. Such images show the religious imagination depicting the divine power of pervading and holding the universe: "He's got the whole world in his hand," as the African American spiritual says. Worlds within a world, macrocosm in microcosm: these are images of order that inspire the aesthetic sense, and the scales involved inspire reverence and stir a sense of dependence on providence. Examples of an organic shape that holds larger scales within itself include Vedic and Epic images of cosmic systems on the tip of Garuda's feather[35] and of the universe seen in the mouth of the divine child who eats sand (Lord Krishna). In the songs of Lord Rama, whose mere bow-tip holds all the sacred rivers of pilgrimage, and the images of cosmic Lord Vishnu, who has endless cosmoses coming and going through the pores of his skin, we see images of all in one—cosmic visions. In India there are old prayers to the tulasi plant, which is sacred to Vishnu: "I bow to you, tulasi, in whose root abide all sacred waters, in whose stalk are all *devas,* and in whose head or leaf are all Vedas (Hindu revelations)." Yggdrasil (the cosmic tree of Norse mythology) and Meru (the cosmic mountain of Indian myth) are also images that hold the whole universe in a nutshell; in them all the levels of existence are symbolically related in organic unity.[36]

In Vaishnavism, for example in the songs of the late-fifteenth- and early-sixteenth-century South Indian composer Annamacharya, the supreme being's vast body extends everywhere, and each pore in his being "is studded with millions of universal eggs with their creators . . . destroyers . . . gods . . . sun, moon, winds, stars

Starburst Mama, collage by the author. The dark-lined drawing, which I have placed in a background frame of "Venus statues" (fertility images from thirty thousand years ago), follows a pattern suggested by Elaine Carty. Carty, a professor of nursing and midwifery in British Columbia, Canada, has observed the similarities in the birthing process: the womb, the baby's head, the cervix, the vagina all form the rounded arches of birth. Carty conceived of the design as an emblem for a midwives' group. The cross on the baby's head represents the fontanelle.

and mountains . . . all fill this gigantic body in countless numbers. The universal eggs which fill the body of Brahman comprise those universes that are already manifest and those yet to manifest. Brahman hides within itself the possible Brahmandas [potential eggs of the Creator] also."[37] Cosmic patterns of seedlike or egg-holding infinite potential may be somewhat comparable to the self-generative holographic cosmos sometimes envisioned by postmodern science. In his book *In the Beginning,* John Gribbin describes the vast cosmos as alive, conceiving baby cosmoses in dense deep wombs of black holes; these baby cosmoses in turn may then breed new black holes, new cosmoses, and more black holes, and on and on. Wombs and babies are age-old images for the power of generation, and the egg is a deep image in the symbolism of life and life's seemingly infinite generative possibilities.[38]

Artwork at Bread and Puppet Theater Museum, Glover, Vermont. How many ways can you make a face of faces? The features—eyes, mouth, nose—can each be vaguely or explicitly facelike. There can be faces in the eyes, the hair, the ears, the jewelry. This face of faces could represent the single face of a family, a village, a nation, or the whole human race. Though strictly speaking the image is not a fractal because it lacks a third scale of faces within faces within faces, it generates possibilities in the imagination, with recursive parts reflecting the whole.

Mystics often describe divine pervasiveness, spiritual reality, as the master of each and all levels and scales whichever way one turns. The North Indian saint Tukaram, for example, sings to Lord Rama, "I see your lotus feet here, there, everywhere. In every mote of dust I find your presence. Yet, Lord of Life, I also see that you are vaster than space, more capacious than the oceans."[39]

The north Indian poet Tulsidas, author of the *Ramcharitmanas,* a scripture written in Hindi, celebrates Lord Rama's infinity in various ways. Every hair on Rama's body is one of "the countless spheres of creation," and words can never fully express his reality, his life and activities. In the all-inclusive story of God, the "eternal *Ramayana* [the epic of Rama] is far wider than the empirical *Ramayana* and can cover any eventuality." The deep cosmic meaning of the Rama image can manifest in many ways, places, and times: the world has a "thousand million *Ramayana*s that cannot be measured. . . . Rama is infinite, his excellences are infinite, the extent of his stories is boundless," according to Tulsidas's vision. "As Rama the Lord is Infinite so are His stories, His fame, and qualities." Tulsidas tells the reader that even a million Seshas (Sesha is the cosmic serpent of infinity and eternity, on which Lord Vishnu is often pictured reclining) cannot tell the acts of Rama; they are beyond comprehension. The Rama visible in this world is only a small part of his total Reality. His acts are ineffably wonderful.[40] For Hindus the divine is boundless. It is all-pervasive consciousness, rich with forms and multiple replicas of the whole, and it is formless and hidden beyond the observable universe.

Other images suggesting fractal scaling in Hinduism include the rules for constructing the traditionally designed recursive clusters of temple towers or *shikharas,* which follow the fractal idea of an identical architectural motif repeated on a diminishing scale.[41]

The *Taittiriya Upanishad* depicts the rising scales of potential *ananda,* or bliss, in the following manner:

> Say there is a noble youth well read in the Vedas, fleet of foot, firm, strong and having a world full of wealth—that's the measure of a single unit of human bliss. Now a hundred times that human bliss is a measure of the bliss of a heavenly musician and of a Veda-knowing sage without desires. And a hundred times that bliss is a measure of the bliss of the Fathers enjoying celestial life. A hundred times the bliss of the Fathers is the measure of the bliss of the *devas* who are endowed with heavenly bodies, having won the merit of doing their duties. A hundred times that bliss is the bliss of the thirty three gods who live on sacrificial offerings. One hundred times that bliss is the bliss of Indra. One hundred times that bliss is the measure of the bliss of Brihaspati. A hundred times that bliss is the measure of Prajapati's bliss. A hundred times Prajapati's bliss is a measure of the bliss of Brahman.[42]

The down side of this expansive spiritual geometry comes later, when the world-weary are tired of time dragging on downhill, age after age, and disenchanted with the multiplication of cycles

The carved stone ceiling of the Adi Nath temple in Ranakpur displays crystal-like diamond-shaped patterns which symbolize the unfolding of the primordial vibration of existence. This mandala, which is used to contemplate consciousness, was made in the thirteenth century. Courtesy of Adi Nath Temple Publications, Ranakpur, Western India.

in the *yuga* system. (*Yuga*s are the ages which recur in the long cycles of time in the Hindu worldview. *Kritayuga* is the golden age of peace and wisdom. *Tretayuga,* the next age, is a time of gradual decline, and the next, *Dvaparayuga,* is an age of even further decline. *Kaliyuga,* the present time, is the age of discord and disintegration. A whole cycle of the four *yuga*s is a *mahayuga* of 4,320,000 years, equaling one day in the life of Brahma, the creator. Brahma's life is 315,360,000,000,000 human years long. A new Brahma's life cycle begins when the old one's ends. It is a rather fractal-like view of time-cycles made of cycles made of cycles, on a few different scales.) But the Upanishadic verse "When fullness is taken from fullness, fullness remains full" characterizes a property of consciousness which is ever expansive and full of potential generativity.[43]

Buddhist Images and Other Examples from Spiritual Traditions

> Veil after veil will lift—but there must be
> Veil upon veil behind. —Sir Edwin Arnold[44]

Buddhist traditions also convey a sense of consciousness and existence with visual images. The Buddhist *Avatamsaka Sutra* depicts Sudhana's vision of Vairocana's tower in this fashion: "Within the tower there are hundreds of thousands of towers, each one as exquisitely adorned . . . and each one, while preserving its individual existence, at the same time offering no obstruction to all the rest." All are miraculously visible to all. In the *Diamond Sutra,* another cosmic image is used for teaching. There it is said that "If one filled with the seven treasures as many galaxies as there are grains of sand in the Ganges, and offered them—would there be so much merit that no grasp is possible? Take a galaxy for every particle of dust in this vast galaxy and grind it to atoms—will the heap of atoms be very great?"[45] This breakdown into manyness—not merely a heap or galaxy—admits of no inventory; there is no seizing; one cannot reify the metaphor, for the division is too vast to number. A lesson about how many astounding numbers and how much merit may be involved is thus taught by imagining a multiplication of astronomical proportions. Such recursive iterations stun the mind as they are intended to do.

In some teachings found in popular literature, the Buddha shows an ability to play freely with scales of existence to convey a sense of relativity:

> I consider the positions of kings and rulers as that of dust motes. I observe treasures of gold and gems as so many bricks and pebbles. I

Collage of Buddha in Mandelbrot sets, by the author. Meditators sitting before a sitting Buddha image cultivate receptivity to the peace they see there. Thus, there is self-similarity on different scales. The first image, inspired by the memory of the Buddha's original serenity, and the many images of various sizes which followed are parts of a whole. And then many people over the years have sat to reach a similar state of awareness, and have succeeded to different degrees. They imitate the peaceful sitting Buddha and find their own tranquility. This continuum can be visualized as a fractallike pattern over vast stretches of time and space.

look upon the finest silken robes as tattered rags. I see myriad worlds of the universe as small seeds of fruit, and the greatest lake in India as a drop of oil on my foot. I perceive the teachings of the world to be the illusion of magicians. I discern the highest conception of emancipation as a golden brocade in a dream, and view the holy path of the illuminated ones as flowers appearing in one's eyes. I see meditation as a pillar of a mountain. Nirvana as a nightmare of daytime. I look upon the judgement of right and wrong as the serpentine dance of a dragon, and the rise and fall of beliefs as but traces left by the four seasons.[46]

If we consider the Buddhist narratives, going back to the first popular teachings in the form of *jataka* stories (tales of the Buddha's previous lives), we could take them all together as a kind of literary fractal. The Buddha's life and teachings seem to be fractalled into these animal fables. *Jatakas* show similar themes and values—a life thrust of altruism and compassionate self-sacrifice made again and again on different scales and levels of existence (plant, animal, human, royal) and so they are fractal-like, making a whole which is reflected in all the parts.

In the Western world, the Christian mystic Julian of Norwich wrote of her visions of Jesus: "He showed me a little thing, the quality of a hazelnut, in the palm of my hand, and it was as round as a ball. I looked thereupon with eyes of my understanding and thought: What may this be? And it was answered generally thus: it is all that is made." Julian could see the macrocosm in the microcosm, having deeply incorporated the meaning of Jesus's life, experiencing "the divine image as the innermost possession" of her own soul.[47]

We saw in Strand One of this book in the nightmarish story by Borges that that which is honey-sweet order to one person can be bitter chaos and horror to another; the same abyss means panic to the fearful and freedom to the skilled flier. The horror of infinity can be experienced as surely as the splendor of infinity. Some people experience "fractal panic." That is, they are uncomfortable with the subconscious implications of fractals. If there is an infinite order, they worry, does my "freedom" mean infinite choice, or is everything decided? Am I straining against God's or nature's will? Is all of existence just a recursive paisley nightmare, fate determined and guarded by dualities, life caught in a net of predetermined limits? Where is each individual's precious uniqueness if systems and patterns pervade all of existence? Am I not only my brother's keeper but, curiously, also my brother's mirror image, almost his clone, destined to live through curiously similar scenarios? People may feel taken out of their ego-centered selves. They may feel their separate identity, which they have built up by denying contradictions, start to unravel; they may fear losing control, ending without autonomy. Interdependence seems to call for togetherness, reciprocity. This may seem horrible to those to whom individualism is ultimate. But noticing structures which include oneself can also have an obverse side—one can feel free, liberated, released. One can understand one's identity within a context of higher consciousness, with a pervasive light in a world of mutual reflections. Rather than being something to fear, an awareness of the whole patterns of which we are parts may help us find meaning, fulfillment, and creative freedom. Awareness of the attractors which capture our attention can be liberating, because such concepts give us more options to work with. For example, the *Gandavuha Sutra* of the *Avatamsaka Sutra* assures Buddhists that "Having realized that this world is like a dream, and that all Buddhas are like mere reflections, that all things are like an echo, you move unimpeded in the world."[48]

The Sufi poet Rumi (c. 1207–1273) dramatized love's fluid freedom and the intellect's limits in a series of recursive comparisons:

> The Intellect says: "The six directions are limits:
> there is no way out."
> Love says: "There is a way:
> I have travelled it thousands of times."
> The Intellect saw a market and started to haggle;
> Love saw thousands of markets beyond that market.
> Lovers who drink the dregs of the wine
> reel from bliss to bliss:
> The dark-hearted men of reason
> Burn inwardly with denial.
> The Intellect says: "Do not go forward;
> annihilation contains only thorns."
> Love laughs back: "The thorns are in you."
> Enough words! Silence!
> Pull the thorn of existence out of the heart! Fast!
> For when you do you will see thousands
> of rose gardens in yourself.[49]

In this dialogue of observations, the scales of the heart's wonder expand—thousands of journeys of exuberant joy, thousands of markets, thousands of rose gardens. Logic by itself may generate fear and denial that reduces the possibilities of human experience to a fraction, a thorny withered stump. But the psyche seeks fractal wholeness, expressed in the sensibilities of open-ended love. That is, the Self at the heart of each life's psyche seeks the all-inclusive wholeness, seeks to realize oneness experientially, to know its own wholeness and its identity with the self-similar parts. Language such as "integration in the One," "merging with the Spirit," finding one's "Buddha Nature" has been used in various cultures to talk about this urge. Jungian psychology and other therapeutic approaches in our times also use this kind of concept.

Why do we find something like fractal geometric patterns reflected in the intuitions of Zen masters, in the vision of consciousness described in the *Yogavasishtha,* and in mystic poets such as Rumi? Are these patterns sign of the eyes of consciousness opened by vision, perceptions banged awake by the infinite made manifest, notes that memorialize "scales falling from eyes," the ability to see natural beauty and depth, sacred subtleness?

Pascal was struck by this wonder. So was Goethe and other scientists and poets. Darwin said that each organic being "must be as a microcosm—a little universe formed of a host of self-propagating organisms, inconceivably minute and as numerous as the stars in heaven."[50] The dissolving of the ego and the compulsion to dominate, the feeling of personal boundaries being transcended by participating in larger entities, the expansion of conscious awareness—mystics have sung of these experiences for ages. And modern views of nature reveal this possibility as well. In *The Voice of the Earth* Theodore Roszak discusses how on all scales, from the infinitely large to the infinitely small, "nature opens out before us like a Chinese box puzzle: a seemingly endless nesting of systems within systems." Furthermore, as Roszak notes, examination reveals that every system is cradled within other, larger systems. Nothing is context-free; cells making up the tissues of the body are themselves small systems, and the tissues also obviously exist within a larger system—the body as a whole. The body also is not a separate unit but thrives within an ecosystem which is populated by microbes, plants, insects, reptiles, mammals, and various natural forces. The human organism also integrally participates in a society and a culture, and as Roszak points out "both [are] the immaterial creations of the mind that draws upon the body. If we accept the Gaia hypothesis, we must locate all ecosystems within a biospheric system as big as the planet."[51] It is undeniable that the self-organizing earth also has her life within a larger system of systems. To ignore these contexts is to lose touch with a far deeper reality than the passing fashions and distractions that occupy so much of our lives.

One Example of Cosmic Sensibility: Mysterious Life in the Hold of Shipshape Earth

The Incredible String Band composed and performed a song in the 60s about a huge ship which is actually the world, a ship that has been sailing for a long time, suggesting that humans are the "mariners" on a great adventure. Buckminster Fuller popularized the idea of the earth as a cosmic spaceship that contains all lives. This archetypal image nicely captures both the journey quality of life and the long story of cosmic evolution, the "immense journey,"[52] as Loren Eiseley called it. The universe story is a voyage of discovery, unfolding creativity, and adventure too vast for any one person to know. Yet each person has the whole story of the universe configured in his or her physical makeup. The tale is inscribed, the memories curled up in every cell. The DNA coiled in each cell is like a long-journeying ark—in coded form, the memory of the succession of lives that went before is curled up in each of the latest passengers. People share the ark of DNA with all others, riding with them on that serpent's back, traveling up that spiral staircase. Though our existence is wrapped in that ribbon, its presence is so subtle we usually aren't even aware of it. But each cell of every living creature from the very beginning is a "Noah's ark" holding experiences and strategies of survival.

The ship has been used as an image of a microcosm containing the whole for a long time. In the *Taittiriya Brahmana,* a part of the Vedic literature of Hinduism, it is said that eternal Brahman—the all-pervasive pure being-consciousness-bliss which forms the background of every-thing—contains all beings as if they were in a boat. That is, it is of the nature of consciousness, of its very essence, that all beings and the "thirty-three shining ones" (*devas*) and all other things that exist are contained within the depths of the heart of one who realizes it. Another image of the whole and its parts, the cosmic contained in a vast vehicle, is the ancient Egyptian cosmic boat of the eons. This ship of the seasons and the ages held creatures, such as a bull and serpent, representative of different aspects of time or processes of the universe, such as the motions of planets and constellations in the heavens and the revolving cycles of the years and the eons.[53]

"Noah's Ark" by Janice Dyar Harrell, North Vernon, Indiana, framed by Mandelbrot set arcs from H. O. Peitgen and P. H. Richter, *The Beauty of Fractals: Images of Complex Dynamical Systems* (Berlin: Springer-Verlag, 1986) Courtesy of the artists.

The early Christian church identified with nautical images, in part because in Greek the letters of the word *ichthys,* fish, are an acronym for "Jesus Christ, son of God, savior." Persecuted Christians met under the sign of fishes and the crosslike anchor; the apostles were fishers of men; the church was a boat, a body of people holding together, afloat on the sea of time's changes.

Hindu stories in verse and song tell how Krishna, the avatar of Vishnu who embodies love, is a pilot of a boat who saves the fearful passengers (after playing some tricks on them). (The meaning of those stories is not so different from the point of Delacroix's painting *Christ Asleep during the Tempest.*) Old classics, such as Murasaki Shikibu's *Tale of Genji,* Homer's *Odyssey,* and Sebastian Brandt's *Ship of Fools,* as well as modern books such as Rimbaud's *Drunken Ship* (often considered the greatest example of French lyric poetry in the nineteenth century), Herman Melville's *Moby Dick,* William Golding's *Rites of Passage,* and Katherine Anne Porter's *Ship of Fools,* explore the idea of a ship at sea as a microcosm

The prow is enlivened by the nature of water; it reflects the waves it rides. Canoe prow, wood and pigment, c. 1900–1950, Trobriand Islands, Papua New Guinea, Melanesia. Indianapolis Museum of Art, Daniel P. Erwin Fund.

of the human condition in the swirling cosmos which is beyond human control. We can begin to see how in the psyche many memories of and ideas about ships come together to form an archetype, an attractor that has captured much attention over the centuries.

Dreams and shamanic journeys are sometimes understood through the image of the boat. Dreams are creative microcosms of whole situations experienced by the psyche. As Thomas Moore says, "The dream is the ark of Noah where the many animals . . . abide with us during time of blindness, when we fail to see the invisible within a world taken literally."[54] In dreams a mysterious inner stranger who is usually hidden from us pilots us through refreshing images we need to experience. The shaman's drum functioned for many generations as a kind of ark of sound used for carrying multitudes on the journey to the realm of trance, the realm of spirits and life forces. Floating on that drum-ark, tribal peoples contacted the sacred source of healing power and brought it back.

It is clear by now that the theme of the boat as microcosm is like a fractal we can fly in many directions (think of the animated Mandelbrot set); it easily takes us from the highest conceivable levels of being to the ground level of ordinary folk, the fishermen at work with nets and their wives calculating numbers. The vessel of life and consciousness (awareness on various scales), generative and expansive, is civilization in a seedpod, outlasting the waves of the floods, planted again and again, efflorescent again and again. The idea of the boat, fractal-like, contains possible boats on many scales, adaptable to many situations.

Folklore also plays with the boat image. Icelandic verses present a mathematical puzzle:

> Twelve boats have I offshore;
> In every boat there are twelve men;
> And every man, he kills twelve seals;
> Into twelve strips each seal is flayed;
> Into twelve lengths each strip is cut;
> Two men sit down to share each piece—
> Work it out yourself, O King![55]

The imagery moves toward smaller scales at five different levels.

The voyage continues. To stand at the prow, facing a horizon of water and sky, evokes in the helmsman the abyss of eternity, the mystery of the infinite, awareness sailing into transcendence. M. C. Escher, an artist whose art reflects a fractal-like sense of infinity in a number of ways, wrote, "Deep, deep infinity! Quietness. To dream away from the tensions of daily living: to sail over a calm sea at the prow of a ship, toward a horizon that always recedes; to stare at the passing waves and listen to their monotonous soft murmur; to dream away into unconsciousness."[56] To the sailor of infinity—the not-so-grounded thinker—the German poet Friedrich von Schiller called out a friendly warning:

Thou sail'st in vain—Return!
Before thy path, INFINITY!
And thou in vain!—Behind me spreads
INFINITY to thee!
Fold thy wings drooping,
O Thought, eagle-swooping!
O Fantasy, anchor!—The Voyage is o'er
Creation, wild sailor, flows on to no shore![57]

We might think of our own skeptical age with the help of a parable: Naive reductionist man sails out with arrogance and logic to make his fortune. Encountering the nonlinear ocean and the sky's boundlessness, he feels he is in over his head and retreats from his myopic, overly purposive enterprises before the nonhuman undertow capsizes him. He learns to feel included in the infinite whole and to follow the mysterious patterns he discerns, realizing the inherent self-similarity in the cosmos. He learns to live more congruently with the biospiritual ecosystems surrounding him. He learns to cooperate, blending in with terrains and weathers, a partner in the earth's ventures. He understands that arrogance of the pilot spells self-defeat. Thinking about this image evokes journey metaphors from African American spirituals—"I know I'm on a long long journey, sing halleluia!"

As I have suggested, when taken together, the many images of life as a boat in various cultures, life as a fragile craft balanced on uncertain waters, form an archetypal idea, a whole fractal-like boat of many boats of various kinds and sizes. Each example has its own nuances, but they may be all imagined as aspects of a whole fractal archetype or "attractor" in the common life of human psyches and in the whole span of human history. At least this seems true in the realm of imagination—the psyche. In the strict realm of mathematics it may seem like a wild idea: life's journey as a ship made of many cycles of time, and cycles in the lives of creatures on various scales.

In this strand we have considered many examples of fractal-like imagery found in various traditions and in the works of individual poets and mystics. "Blake and Fractals," by J. D. Memory, can serve as a conclusion:

The Trehan Bahow Mirror, an ancient Celtic design. Courtesy of George Bain, *Celtic Art: The Methods of Construction* (New York: Dover, 1973).

William Blake said he could see
Vistas of infinity
In the smallest speck of sand
Held in the hollow of his hand.

Models for this claim we've got
In the work of Mandelbrot:
Fractal diagrams partake
Of the essence sensed by Blake.

Basic forms will still prevail
Independent of the scale;
Viewed from far or viewed from near
Special signatures are clear.

When you magnify a spot,
What you had before, you've got.
Smaller, smaller, smaller yet,
Still the same details are set;

Finer than the finest hair
Blake's infinity is there,
Rich in structure all the way—
Just as the mystic poets say.[58]

LIKE FATHER, LIKE SON

... created in the image of God.
—Genesis 1:27

To be human is to be semi-divine, carrying the image of the divine.
—Seyyed Hossein Nasr[1]

Imitatio Dei: Self-Similarity Following Sacred Patterns

Can people escape traditional models of behavior and be autonomous? Is it possible? Is it desirable? For most of human history, patterns of behavior have been learned by imitating admired relatives, culture heroes, or deities. This strand examines some examples of these reiterated actions as fractal-like patterns found in all cultures, from ancient and traditional cultures to current popular culture.

In the world religions (Hinduism, Buddhism, Taoism, Judaism, Christianity, and Islam, for example), we often find teachings that encourage people to imitate at the human level the archetypal cosmic figures. On a humble scale ordinary people can emulate great ones—a Taoist can become more and more sagelike, an ordinary Hindu can imitate some of Lord Rama's righteous actions,[2] a Christian can learn from the story of Jesus to live his or her life for others. They thus come to exhibit similarities at various scales of realization. Each member of a tradition, at varying degrees, at different times of life, behaves in accordance with the ideal which overarches all, or diverges from it.

Similarities reveal systemic integrity in a network at varying levels of scale of actualization. The term "self-similarity," which points to fractal-like situations of mutuality of persons within larger fields of nature, society, and spiritual worldviews, seems useful in grasping some religious concepts. For example, in early Christianity the concepts of one God for the world, one bishop for the flock, one church to show the way to salvation of the soul, and one husband as head of the family show a modeling of hierarchically related authority on different scales. This pattern argues that the line of command from greater to lesser status was the correct orthodox way to salvation. I realize that this use of the term "self-similarity" is not mathematically as precise as when it is used to describe, say, a Sierpinski gasket (a full-fledged diagrammatic example of fractal geometry), so it may be more accurate just to say "similar."

The comparative study of religion, at least in part, consists of exercises in pattern recognition. Fractal geometry, illustrated by photos from nature, works of art, computer images generated by mathematics, and examples from architecture and literature, adds new dimensions and vocabulary to the process. It alerts the visual and conceptual faculties to some of the kinds of patterns which are found in nature. Scientists such as Brian Swimme tell us that everything is the product of the same ultimate origin, flaring forth from the fireball, and everything is processed by some of the same forces (for example, gravity, time, sun and moon cycles, and laws governing the nature of fluids). And, because mind and nature share similar structures, the similarity of patterns has meaningful implications.[3] It is not a coincidence that we find many variations similar to some archetype or original, like the echoes of a voice under a bridge. To some, repeated reflections or echoes may be an example of emptiness and confusion;[4] to others, they mean rhythms of life, infinite abundance.

Self-Similarity in Structures of Ancient Religious Systems

The examples above show that the recognition of similarity reveals profound and intriguing aspects of great world religions. Inquiry into similarities can also be useful in cross-cultural studies that examine the structures of religious orientations to the environment and practices such as rituals. Perhaps the term "family resemblance" would be useful in religious studies to indicate where, in different orders of religious traditions—illiterate tribal religions and universal religions with scriptures, archaic religions and modern ones, classical religions and postmodern ones—there is great distortion or difference yet some underlying pattern, connection, or theme.

Similarities are of great concern to the influential scholar of comparative religion—Mircea Eliade, for example. In *The Sacred and The Profane: The Nature of Religion,* Eliade shows how religious people experience some places as sacred, connected with higher realms; they are microcosmic representations of the cosmos, locations where the power behind the cosmos is contacted. In such places, for religious people, everything is fraught with more significance, freighted with more connections, meanings, consequences. Eliade writes that "the religious experience of the non-homogeneity of space [that there are certain special sacred centers, e.g., Jerusalem] is a primordial experience homologizable [comparable or similar] to a founding of a world," which means that these locations share similarities with a cosmic archetype.[5] They replay again and again in individual lives, in annual rituals, and in cycles of history a reflected aspect of the origin; they reenact the original all-important acts. A hierophany (an eruption or revelation of holy power in a religious tradition) reveals a sacred center of space, and that special place organizes surrounding space; it is the same process as originating a whole world. The break in ordinary space allows a world to be built, an axis for future orientation, a specific configuration of reality. (In this sense "world" means a whole way of life.)

Wholeness is an organizing principle expressed in the way religions orient human life in the center of sacred space. Eliade remarks that to construct an altar to Agni, as Vedic people did, is to reproduce on a microcosmic scale a representation of the whole creation; water represents the primordial waters, clay the earth, walls the atmosphere, and songs proclaim that the cosmic region has been created, that the new earthly territory has been claimed.[6] Taking possession of the territory is an act similar to, though on a different scale from, conquering original primordial chaos and organizing the universe. For traditional people, the momentous always involves the totality in synecdochal format—a part is used to represent the whole. In my view, fractal studies and related endeavors may involve a rediscovery of the cosmic on new scales and in new terms, and so they have far-reaching implications. Religion has given so much attention to nineteenth-century science and twentieth-century politics that it has forgotten the art of envisioning the cosmic as the basis of spiritual understanding. When religions are solely accountable to modern scientific reason, they lose the ability to contemplate depth and feel awe at mystery.[7] Constructive and artistic energies that were formerly used to sculpt, paint, and build churches now go into designing advertising campaigns and programming computers. This is not to say that all scientists lack awe, but only that our age is still struggling to formulate the relationship between the human being and the mystery of the origin.

The need to grasp the cosmic whole—to encompass it some-how and hold it—and the need to play a part in the whole by organizing life according to that authoritative original configuration have been concerns of prime importance to traditional peoples. Zulus, who call themselves "the people who came from the sky," say that the High God has a village in the heavens and that people have modeled their villages on that. In his book *African Fractals,* Ron Eglash shows settlement patterns and other cultural artifacts that are fractals. Aboriginal art from Australia often features ovals within ovals. Some Native Americans still build initiation lodges with walls, roof, and floor representing the six directions, repeating the cosmogony on a smaller scale. In my view all of these repetitions of a pattern over the generations, of various sizes and nuances, form a fractal-like process in time.

Human thinking in patterns of wholeness is pervasive in religious activities all over the world. Imagine a series of concentric circles: "Palestine, Jerusalem, and the Temple severally and concurrently represent the image of the universe and the Center of the World. This multiplicity of centers and this re-iteration of the image of the world on small and smaller scales constitute one of the specific characteristics of traditional societies."[8] The temple copies celestial architecture (as does the Kaaba in Mecca). This acknowledging of several scales of similarity is a kind of order around which people have perennially organized and lived out their lives. To resonate among two or more scales of self-similarity—altar, temple, capital, nation, earth—makes them seem memorable and inevitable; an infinite livable relationship between the humble on earth and the divine above and beyond. The multiple copies at each level, necessary for a pattern to qualify as a fractal, are caused by the ever-changing circumstances in time, since nothing is ever static, but is always more or less attaining to the ideal.

Traditional people find and accept divinely ordained order to subdue the energies of chaos and make sense of life. But humans never conquer chaos by imposing their structures; they only "hypnotize" it for a while. The cycles of consolidation and decay in history always bring change, new challenges. Traditional people experience the invasion and destruction of the city or the temple as the return of the original chaos, as the dragon of origins. The flood of destructive forces must be fought with warrior strength and divine help. People repeat the victory of the gods when they succeed in defeating invaders—they identify with the original divine events, though the historical scale differs from the cosmic one.[9] It is the same ultimate system, the same archetypal actions, just on a different scale. This kind of experience forms an atemporal archetypal moment in historical time—an incarnating of repeated patterns of the whole distributed among the parts—and people perennially gravitate toward it as the order always known. Religious people may experience these repetitions as the cosmic shudders of eternity, the orgasmic crescendos outside of time. It is not a mechanical rhythm like that of a clock or metronome but a climax of yearning, a melting of time and difference, a sharing in the transcendent sacred being. It is a blissful culmination outside of historical time. It expresses, if we use modern science's paradigm for origins, the momentous explosive energy of the original fireball and burst of inspiration and creation, the fullness of wholeness. What seems like periodic decline and renewal to historians is experienced by religious people as return to original procreation, chaotic potency, immersion in much-needed wholeness. In that return to the power of the origins, the meaningless fragmentations are all lost and dissolved in rejuvenating paroxysms of pervasive divine order. Or, if the experience is one of conflict interpreted religiously, the paroxysms may be of sacrifice and dissolution to follow divine injunctions—of death to find fullness of life.

The initial conditions set the trend, as both chaos science and tribal peoples have grasped[10]—the whole is found at the auspicious beginning, the totipotency, the embryonic stage. This insight is shared across cultures and across time. Traditional Chinese thinking asserts that the subtle energy *ch'i* is abundant in the early morning atmosphere; Hindu yogis say *prana*, the life force, is most abundant after deep sleep, in the predawn hours before day begins. Religious people are drawn to experience the original time, to taste the primordial or celebrate the most significant earlier events; the most significant holiday in the West is still Christmas. This pattern shows a reach for wholeness, a paradigmatic return, a search to be captured by the momentous source, to be made whole with it. Many indigenous cultures understand this: by reenacting and reciting what happened at the most powerful point, the origin, they attempt to capture the world whole. They try to engage the whole expansive system and duration, to be like the first beings and continuous with generations of celebrants over the centuries. Wirikuta pilgrims in the American Southwest, pilgrims to the Holy Land or Mecca, and Seder celebrants all revitalize their roots by returning to and sharing in origins. The power of endless iteration in time can only come from a biospiritual[11] vision-story deep enough and reflective enough to fulfill archetypes endlessly. These old rituals concerning center and origin are fractal-like attempts to tap into the plenitude of the all-containing beginning.[12] Performers of rituals repeat the traditional patterns at many different scales of meaning and intensity, from being dimly aware and going through the motions, to experiencing great depth of fulfillment and rich understanding. Even in one person's lifetime a number of scales are involved in ritual practice—life is usually not static.

Traditions, like living creatures, have a self-regenerative power of fertility and multiplication. When healthy, they continuously self-replicate, cycle after cycle. Here is an image from a modern woman's dream depicting this line of ongoing life:

> I once dreamt I was telling stories and felt someone patting my foot in encouragement. I looked down and saw that I was standing on the shoulders of an old woman who was steadying my ankles and smiling up at me. I said to her, "No, no, come stand on *my* shoulders for you are old and I am young." "No, no," she insisted, "This is the way it is supposed to be." I saw that she stood on the shoulders of a woman far older than she, who stood on the shoulders of a woman even older, she stood on another soul, who stood on the shoulders. . . . [13]

In this image, the chain of people of increasing age is recursive, and in its infinity suggests being part of vast and continuous processes in the same venture. It dramatizes well the necessary information, encouragement, and wise energy that sometimes connects generations. The continuity of links through time, the perpetuation of memories and transmission of lifeways, form the order of living traditions. When these traditions are working well, it is only fitting that people yearn to feel a part of them as a way to fulfillment and self-transcendence. The satisfaction of belonging to community and tradition is well represented in visual patterns surrounding daily life: village arrangements, women's artworks, and children's games.

Traditional religious societies continue to follow patterns of return to origins in public celebrations, making contact at their center of the world, and reenvisioning the beginning of time in social events such as harvest rites, New Year's festivals, and solstice celebrations. As Mircea Eliade noted in *The Sacred and the Profane,* a person in traditional societies is not truly human unless he or she recapitulates the original actions, activating the archetypes of sacred depth; without these reiterations of the beginning a human is not fully alive.[14] In later times, these ritual patterns seem to be internalized in the contemplative lives of mystics. Mystics experience individual return to the original condition before time when they practice meditation, focusing on the transcendent light in the human heart, feeling that they are at the center of the cosmos. For example, Chuang-tzu tells stories of sages in meditative trance who go back to the origins. Other contemplative traditions in the East and West express this sense of return to the center of the cosmos or the beginning of time.[15] These religious practices of symbolic return, public and private, share affinities and display "family resemblances."

Following the Ultimate Likewise:
The Taoist Sage as Self-Similar to Tao

> Man follows the earth. / Earth follows the universe.
> —*Tao Te Ching*[16]

The philosophical Taoism that flourished in China several centuries B.C.E. (and has continued to influence Chinese thought ever since) taught that sages are followers of the Tao. Sages harmonize with the Tao and find their similarity with it until they realize their oneness with it. Lao-tzu's *Tao Te Ching* describes the processes of life, the patterns of the cosmic Tao. Lao-tzu suggests that people can live like that mysterious formless model: acting without ostentation, keeping to the lowly through humility, using the power of patient returning, experiencing creative quietude, and so on. The sage or leader follows observable nature; nature follows the way of heaven; heaven follows the ineffable principle of the whole, Tao:

> The Tao is great.
> The universe is great.
> Earth is great.
> Man [the human being] is great.
> These are the four great powers.
> Man follows the earth.
> Earth follows the universe.
> The universe follows the Tao.
> The Tao follows only itself.[17]

The person becomes great by following the rhythms of the earth to grow food, hunt game, prepare for winter. The earth follows cosmic laws, spinning in sunshine and moonlight; cosmic patterns are under the sway of mysteriously elusive Tao, which curves, bringing returns, and which is the hidden original being. Tao is a nebulous, fluid, protean power, spontaneous and nurturing. Confucius, who took this Taoist view for granted, concerned himself with proper relations on the social level. He taught that the north polar star is in place and stars revolve around it; likewise, the ruler at the center of the earth, sitting in a reverent state of mind and facing south, need not command ostentatiously—he will have a flawless reign, full of dragon-power vitality. *Li* is the principle of doing the right thing and performing the appropriate rites, all invisibly ordered by a harmony already in existence before human life appeared on the scene. At their best, person and society find congruence with cosmic order: different scales, same harmony.

In his "Bull Mountain Parable," the Confucian thinker Mencius (c. 371–c. 289 B.C.E.) taught that *jen*, humane nature or human-heartedness, is inborn, but that the inborn natural virtues, if disturbed and ruined, are similar to a logged-off mountain which has been devastated by destructive impacts. The result is a blighted life, one in which natural health, virtues, and talents are destroyed by traumas and abuse.[18]

Mencius wrote of the similarity of ruler and domain as a kind of osmosis of leadership or flow of influence: "If the prince is a man of Humanity (*jen*) then nothing exists in his state that will not be Human. If a prince is a man of Justice, then nothing exists in his state that will not be Just." The prince's influence flows through the whole hierarchy of society in this vision of the ideal. In the Chinese vision of the way things work, in the interwoven network of lives, like naturally follows from like, whether creatively or destructively. Mencius noted that there is a slight difference between man and animal and that some disregard this difference. He says the true person takes great care of the difference. Similarity to beasts—in other words, catastrophic beastliness—is natural if one loses one's sense of the good, of humanity, and of justice; one then lives in degradation.[19]

Mencius uses the example of a deformity. If a person has a crooked finger, he will go to great lengths to fix it; he does not want to embody a glaring difference. If one is unaware that one's mind is different, and is not embarrassed, one is called ignorant of properly similar things.[20] All learning is intended to regain the mind that has strayed,[21] to be at home in childlike natural similarity to the basic norms of traditions. That is, the Confucian ideal is to find consonance with inborn humanity, which is a larger potential that the best people nurture by following the natural way of heaven. In ancient China, therefore, people traditionally found their place in larger orders of society and the cosmos. Some of these ideas are very old, but they are continually being forgotten and recalled. For example, Goethe in the nineteenth century wrote, "Each creature is but a patterned gradation [*Schattierung*] of one great harmonious whole."[22] This resembles the fractal-like view of Taoists and Confucianists. Even in our age of great differences and pride in individuality, problems cause us to search for common ground and mutually agreeable solutions.

Hinduism and the Following of Divine Patterns

> *Tat tvam asi.* Thou art That.　　—*Chandogya Upanishad*[23]

In Vedic literature, many statements assert the imperative to recapitulate what the *devas* or "shining ones" did at the beginning of time or to reiterate the sacrifice of Indra, the original hero, who overcame the watery monster Vritra. Whether one is building a house or a place of worship, organizing a society, or anointing a king, "We must do what the Gods did in the beginning."[24] "Thus the Gods did; thus men do."[25]

The Upanishadic vision, *advaita vedanta,* offers another early envisioning and practice of self-similarity. The *atman,* or spiritual self, is the ultimate consciousness at the heart of all. One's affinity with others in the cosmos is determined by the same Self found in all. The spiritual Self in each being, *atman,* is a vision of spiritual togetherness, self-identification with the One—One in all, all in One. In this view, all living beings have the *atman* consciousness at their core and are parts or micro-instances of the ultimate Self, which is spiritual consciousness, Brahman.

In the Hindu classic *Manava Dharma Shastra (Manu's Code of Law),* there is an injunction: "Think of these similarities—the Teacher is the image of Brahman [the ultimate]; the Father is the image of Prajapati [the Father of creatures]; the Mother is the image of the earth [nature]; the elder Brother is the image of one-self."[26] This is a description of kindred beings who share corresponding likenesses on different scales. In this symbol system, individuals participate in greater archetypal beings, cosmic figures, and transpersonal identities. Both the *Manava Dharma Shastra* and the *Bhagavad Gita* teach that the great people follow *dharma,* the principle that orders the universe and gives individuals the roles they play in life, and ordinary people follow the standard set by the great ones. When this is not the case, ominous portents in nature bode ill, as disorder infects one level after another.

In Buddhism, which grew out of Hinduism and carried the ideas of karma, *samsara* (the ocean of births and deaths), and nirvana to other lands, we can find more examples of sharing similarity. The Dalai Lama, for example, said, "True compassion develops from the recognition that everyone does not want suffering and does want happiness, just like us."[27] In sacred Tibetan Buddhist places, self-similarity is sometimes architecturally depicted; for example, within a large stupa or dome-shaped monument there may be smaller stupas, and on each of the smaller ones 108 yet smaller ones may be depicted.[28]

Judaism and Patterns of Likeness

> Let us make man in our image, after our likeness.
> —Genesis 1:26

There is a rabbinic saying to the effect that every time a man or woman walks along the street, an invisible choir of angels goes before him or her, singing, "Make way for the image of God."[29]

This image of a fanfare for the common person's participation in divine glory is intended to remind humans of their high destiny. In the Judaic tradition, God is good, and God expects the creatures formed in his image to be good, though free will is also a part of the whole picture.[30] It takes three levels of holy beings to bring this out: the Supreme Being, the mediating angels, and the humans walking down the street.

The Talmud teaches that God is approachable because man is made in God's image, though the two exist on vastly different scales of being. "Though he was necessarily apart from His creatures by reason of His infinite majesty, and absolute perfection, there was a firm and secure connecting link between them, because man had been created in His image."[31] This connection separated humans from the animals and raised them toward divinity, helping them cross the line dividing them.

One of the key principles of rabbinic ethics is the imitation of God.[32] God is holy, and the chosen people, who are a sign to nations, must likewise be holy—"whatever He does He commands Israel to perform."[33] The good Jew should be a worthy part of the ideal Israel and the ideal Israel should pattern itself on God's goodness. "Israel is the retinue of the King and his duty is to imitate the King."[34] This Talmudic teaching is one of many which show that one can only glorify God by resembling him. The teaching is direct: "Be like Me" is a Talmudic commandment. The various stages of each life and differing degrees of people's goodness make for different scales of self-similarity in the whole of the community and over centuries of history.

Judaism symbolically teaches lessons of self-similarity using nonhuman life as well. There is the story of a tree which offered food, water, shelter, and a place to rest to a tired man. The tree was blessed by the thankful man: "I cannot bless you to have shade, sweet fruits, water at your root—you already have these blessings. So I will bless you this way: May all your saplings be like you." This is the blessing of self-similarity of the good[35]—may all the smaller-scale versions of you, and their seeds, and so on ad infinitum, share your goodness. All the possible attempts to live up to this ideal form of helpfulness and generosity form a spectrum from great successes to dismal failures, and together they form a kind of conceptual fractal.

Another Talmudic comment concerns the special love involved in humans' knowing their divinity. "Beloved is man, for he was created in the image of God; but it was by a special love that it was made known to him that he was created in the image of God, as it is said 'For in the image of God made He man.' "[36] This is a way of saying, "Don't think you're separate, evil; you are part of God." The Talmud presents a vision of God as infinitely flexible, able to fill heaven and earth, to speak from between the two staves of the Ark and to address humans from the space between two hairs; God can zoom to variable scales in relation to the levels and proportions of the universe, now bigger than the cosmos, now the size of a pore or smaller.[37] This is like the infinite consciousness described by Hinduism, subtler than the subtlest, greater than the greatest.

For human beings, models of behavior, whether they are followed consciously or unconsciously, are like recursive patterns— think of peer pressure, social customs, professional expectations and fashions. Think of education, sacraments, stories of heroes, and other guides people emulate. All play the game of follow the leader. Activating growth toward deeper and larger-than-life archetypes is part of the creativity and coercive power of religion. Sometimes parables, myths, and wisdom stories set up schemes with which we judge ourselves, by means of possible similarities between ordinary people and legendary heroes. For example, if the Hindu mythical musical figures Narada and Hanuman sing off-key and thereby mangle melodies, terrible repercussions follow. In Judaism, if a great rabbi mispronounces certain words at prayer, disastrous effects result. This shows that the great have a great responsibility, but also warns ordinary people to be careful, reminding them that their actions also have consequences.[38]

Imitation of Christ: Christianity and Similarity

Jesus was a sailor when he walked upon the water . . .
And when he knew for certain only drowning men could see him
He said all men shall be sailors then until the sea shall free them.   —Leonard Cohen[39]

The earliest known sculpture of Jesus is a well-carved statue of the youthful shepherd whose hair curls much like the wool of the lamb he carries on his shoulders. Visually, spirals of different sizes on different surfaces are patterns of similarity; texturally kindred qualities are shared by both youth and lamb. Jesus, God become man, mediator and savior, son of God and son of man, is a shepherd, and the sheep share their lives with, and have some likeness to, the shepherd, though he exists on a different level.[40] Because of the kinship between the Son of Man and humble men and women, there is hope for the Christian; love unites persons and the Divine Person.[41] Thus, in Christianity, the expansive self is the soul related to others through *agape*, love, the mode of Jesus' life expressed in the golden rule, mutual love. The vision of reciprocity is not just of an atomistic individual soul, but of a mutual coming together of believers in the mystical body of Christ.

Collage of ink drawings of the earliest sculptural images of the Good Shepherd on a fractal background. Good Shepherd image by Roland H. Bainton, *Behold the Christ* (New York: Harper and Row, 1974).

The sacraments illustrate the correspondence between human and divine features. An early defender of the Church, Tertullian, wrote of membership in the church, "By baptism man recovers the likeness of God." Thus, humans gain fellowship with the divine by having their spiritual births of water and the spirit. In communion one takes in the nature of Jesus, interiorizing the holy body in the form of the consecrated host.

Christ is the second Adam and is also God. *The Imitation of Christ,* a great spiritual classic in Christianity, depicts a way of participating in Jesus' nature and destiny—to suffer, to be loving, and to please God. *The Imitation of Christ* appeared in 1418 and became a work of popular devotion, the most widely circulated book in Christendom aside from the Bible. Possibly written by Thomas à Kempis (c. 1379–1471), a German monk, the *Imitation* is anti-intellectual, affirming that it is better to feel pious compunction than to know how to verbalize, define, and rationalize. A key teaching of Christianity is to "love your neighbor as yourself"; since you are on the same scale, treat your fellows as similar to, not other than, you. On another scale, to love God with one's whole being makes this human-level love more possible. Devotion to God can thus spur compassion toward fellow beings.[42]

The first great interpreter of Christian teachings, the convert Paul, taught in his epistles that the follower of Jesus could rise from the dead with him in mystical rebirth to share his spiritual nature, transcending death. To be a member of the mystical body of Christ is to transcend the body's alienated apartness, joining a larger-scale wholeness. "Become imitators of me, even as I am of Christ," Paul advised.[43] Of course Jesus himself said, "Be perfect even as your Father in heaven is perfect" and "pick up your cross and follow me." The statement "Wherever two or three gather in my name, I am there" asks its hearer to visualize a network of people of faith in clusters, united together in a larger whole, by the name. Paul wrote of larger whole as the "mystical body"[44] of Christ.

"The kingdom of heaven is in the heart" is another teaching which evokes a cosmic mystery. The images Jesus uses to teach the traits of the kingdom of heaven have to do with such qualities and processes as germination, scale, multiplication, worth, and holding power: a man sowing good seed, a grain of mustard seed which has the great potential to expand from tiny to vast, leavening, treasure, a net which can gather all kinds of sea creatures, and so forth.[45] The term "kingdom of heaven" means not only a place where souls go after death but also the state one is in when God rules one's inner life. But this also is not a simple matter. C. G. Jung wrote of the Christian belief in a fractal-like God, with wholeness in the one God, in the three Persons, and in humans:

> "Since the Holy Ghost is the Third Person of the Trinity and God is present entire in each of the three Persons at any time, the indwelling of the Holy Ghost means nothing less than an approximation of the believer to the status of God's son. One can therefore understand what is meant by the remark 'you are gods.' The deifying effect of the Holy Ghost is naturally assumed by the *imago Dei* stamped on the elect."[46]

But in Jesus' images of the kingdom of heaven, the qualities of a hidden treasure, a generative power, a condensed potential to hold and order the many in the one, the traits are noticeably fractal: "Jesus' life and ministry resembled an earnest [a token] for the future. In this sense the kingdom was already present in fractal fashion: small in scale but true to character. . . . Whether viewed from near or far, the kingdom reveals a striking similarity."[47] Jesus' archetypal parables planted seeds which grew in people's lives to varying degrees of fulfillment. And some of his other teachings, such as the command to forgive a brother seventy times seven times, have an almost fractal-like quality—they suggest something beyond our usual dimensions.[48]

An important part of the formative theologian Augustine's (354–430) method of interpreting scripture was the rule of reading figurative speech in an expansive spirit of *caritas*—the movement of the soul toward God and neighbor in love, forming a larger network of life. Poetic language was thus understood not literally but in an evocative, love-awakening mode. This mode expands the self, relating one to a larger spirit and others around one in heart-felt kinship—the fellowship of God's children. Augustine shaped the cognitive recognitions and experiential realizations of the Christian ideal for many generations. His views were reiterated, shaping Christian thought for twelve hundred years, until the Protestant Reformation and Luther's development of a more literal approach.

Christian mystics of medieval times and later also developed understandings which linked the human and divine in experiences of imitation and similarity. Thomas Traherne, an English mystic, wrote,

> The Image of God implanted in us, guided me to the manner wherein we were to Enjoy, for since we were made in the similitude of God, we were made to Enjoy after his Similitude. Now to Enjoy the Treasures of God in the Similitude of God, is the most perfect Blessedness God could Devise. For the Treasures of God are the most Perfect Treasures and the Manner of God is the most Perfect Manner. To enjoy therefore the Treasures of God after the similitude of God is to Enjoy the most Perfect Treasures in the most Perfect Manner . . . and my Desires [were] so August and Insatiable that nothing less than a Deity could satisfy them.[49]

Enjoyment of godlike awareness of the bounty of being re-quires a childlike quality of wonder. But Traherne evokes the joys of mature wisdom as well. He summed up his view: "The Laws of God command you to live in His Image, and to do so, is to live in Heaven."[50] The lives of Francis of Assisi (c. 1181–1226) in Italy, John Chapman ("Johnny Appleseed," 1774–1845) in America, and

Mother Teresa (1910–1997) in Calcutta exemplified such a Christ-like life.

Mystics of other traditions also encouraged this expanded cosmic sense of reality, which allowed people to follow in the footsteps of God, to transcend their narrow limits. For example, in *Poemandres* (attributed to the mystic Hermes Trismegistus), the reader is told,

> "[C]ontemplate God to have all the whole World to himself, as it were all thoughts, or intellections. If therefore thou wilt not equal thy self to God, thou canst not understand God. For the like are intelligible by the like. Increase thy self unto an immeasurable greatness, leaping beyond every Body, and transcending all Time, become Eternity, and thou shall understand God: If thou believe in thy self, that nothing is impossible, but accountest thy self immortal, and that thou canst understand all things, every Art, every Science, and the manner and custom of every living thing. Become higher than all height, lower than all depths, comprehend in thy self, the qualities of all the Creatures, of the Fire, the Water, the Dry, and Moist; and conceive likewise, that thou canst at once be everywhere in the Sea, in the Earth. Thou shalt at once understand thy self, not yet begotten in the Womb, young, old, to be dead, the things after death, and all these together; as also, times, places, deeds, qualities, quantities, or else thou canst not yet understand God."[51]

To realize the being of God, one must explore all that would be found in the experience of God. One must expand the vessel of one's being, expand sympathy and awareness. A narrow outlook cannot know the infinite.[52] Besides its usefulness in picturing the realization of cosmic potential through such experiential practices, the concept of self-similarity is also relevant in the ethical question "What if everyone acted the way I am acting—would it be good or disastrous?" and in the injunction to expand one's sympathies and visions to better comprehend reality, vast and various. While it may seem that these behaviors entail parallel similar actions, not action across scales, it could also be argued that there are many scales involved, from heroic sacrifice to minor inconvenience, from highest vision to tiny glimmer of insight, among the members of a society, and in the moments of the individual's life cycle.

All at Once and Once and for Allah: Islamic Patterns of Similarity and Apocalyptic Style

Allah's divine oneness, which was of paramount importance in Muhammad's revelation, inspired a new oneness on the human level—solidarity among the Arab tribes of sixth-century Arabia. The values given in the Qur'an and the example of Muhammad's life became paradigms for the immense Islamic civilization. Each of its outreach missions—invasions, conquests, colonizations—extended, if not always the whole religion, at least some of its trappings.[53] "La ilaha illa'Llah"—there is no god but God. Allah is God—divine heavenly power. Earthly power in Muslim society expresses Allah's dominion, the accomplishment of Allah's will on earth. The word "islam" means "submission."

Traditionally the self-stated Islamic mission is to form a world society that has submitted to God's will. Some followers of Islam are willing to use political and social means to accomplish this goal, including war against foes of the Muslim enterprise. "Since Allah is, in essence, power . . . it is not surprising that earthly power should be seen as a way of expressing and strengthening Allah's dominion."[54] Thus, in Islam, there are self-similarities among the cosmic Lord, Allah; the community's collective religious identity; and the ruler, the family, and the individual. The revelation, the Qur'an, which is chanted to echo in believers' memories, is the pattern-setting authority.

Islamic sensibilities are intimately tied to the formation of thought processes that are similar to the contents and structures of the Qur'an. The Qur'an is known, interpreted, and followed in varying degrees or scales by the 1.3 billion Muslims around the world. One aspect of this sensibility involves a fragmentary break from the linear outlook. The Qur'an itself is a nonlinear collage of passages. "The rejection of linearity involves a rejection of narrative," Norman O. Brown suggests.

> In fully developed Islamic theology, only the moment is real. There is no necessary connection between cause and effect. Time does not accumulate. The world is made up of atomic space-time points, among which the only continuity is the utterly inscrutable will of God, who creates every atomic point anew at every moment. . . . The apocalyptic style is *totum simul* simultaneous totality, the whole in every part.

It may not be necessary to point out here that "the whole in every part" is one of the chief characteristics of fractal structure; this simultaneity instead of linear progression creates a special quality in the Qur'an. Brown goes on to explain, after citing a great Islamicist and a literary theorist,

> It does not matter in what order you read the Qur'an: it is all there all the time. . . . The bewilderment is part of the message [as is the case in *Finnegans Wake* as well]: "through the windr of a wondr in a wildr is a weltr as a wirbl of a warbl is a world."[55]

This enactment of what I call the *principle of shattering* in the movement of the language itself brings alive the effect of the meaning. Language shattered into facets, like fractals, reveals the power of Allah, a power far beyond mere men, who must submit to Allah's divine will. The believer's sensibility is shaped in a pattern similar to the all-in-one and all-or-nothing power in the Qur'an's structure. The nonlinearity and all-at-once and once-and-for-all quality of the Qur'an helps explain the urgent apocalyptic sensibility of Islamic extremists at their wits' end, ready to sacrifice all in this world at any moment for access to a future world that promises to be much greater. It also helps us understand the sincere following of conscience by the world's many millions of devout Muslims and the experiences of the infinite found in the lives and writings of sufis such as the great Persian poet Jalal-ud-din Rumi.[56]

Of a sudden thou didst lavish grace upon thy servant:
I saw no cause for it but thy infinite kindness.[57]

Horrific Similarity: Profanely Playing God

We have considered how some spiritual teachings exhort seekers to become Godlike, emulating the virtues of the supreme being. Reversals of *imitatio dei*—demonic usurpations of the role of God—are reported in the news of our time and have probably always been part of the human story. Several examples will suffice to illustrate this behavior. Zlatko Dizdarevic, journalist and author of the book *Sarajevo: A War Journal*, interviewed a sniper who was being held in a Sarajevo prison. The sniper told him, "I am happy to kill a child when he is with his mother because there is something fantastic in the face of the mother."[58] One can probably see a transfiguration of the mother's face as her reason for living vanishes, she realizes that all her care and love have ended, and she loses her will to live. The sniper's pleasure in his malevolent act is like the thrill gamblers in Dubai experience when they hear a crying child on a racing camel; the more the child cries, the faster the camel runs, and the more likely it is that the terrified child will die in the process. The watching gamblers find it exciting, according to journalists who have witnessed such scenes. Humans can experience power they are not meant to know. At the moment it may seem as if the act is free of any consequences; later the actor realizes the cost. For example, young soldiers in Desert Storm, in the giddy arrogance of superior firepower, played with death (setting up corpses in chairs, posing with them for photos as if they were playing cards, for example). Later they required therapy to help them cope with their psychological scars, nightmares, and flashbacks. "God is not mocked," and playing with horror often backfires.[59]

God may be thought of as connectedness, sacred unity, as we

have seen in Bateson's work and elsewhere. The totality of unity (*tawhid* in Islam), the pattern that connects, exists as the sacred and should be thought of as a verb, "not a noun, proper or improper" according to Buckminster Fuller; it is a fluid, subtly floating, graceful process, ever-emerging. It is the ultimate syzygy (technically a conjunction or straight-line configuration of celestial bodies). It is not meant to be thought of as rigidly geometric, in static material terms; it is a flutter or pulse of light like the music of existence, a flow of process, a plasma of the northern lights.

Those who see horrific sights—the murder of a child changing the face of the mother who gave it birth, for example—must pay a psychic penalty, unless they have attained some kind of saintly consciousness.[60] Society puts on trial people who play God, the "mercy killer" nurses and doctors, lynchers, and assassins, because their actions are not commensurate to their status. Executioners designated by the state's legal system stand for something larger than themselves—society, justice—but even they cannot trifle with power. As the old wisdom from China warns, "Who plays with the master's tools cuts his own hand."[61] To usurp the master, Tao, is to step out of bounds, to steal a malevolent taste of transcendence. Power seems to represent easy control, but "uneasy lies the head that wears a crown." In the various systems, the ultimate—Tao or God—is a mysterious infinite all-knowing consciousness; only God or the wholeness of Tao can know what a mother's face looks like when her baby's life is taken. A weak man cannot do this with impunity; he will suffer demonic consequences. Concepts such as karma and retribution express this sense of connection, of one's partness in the web of the whole universe, from which there is no escape.

As a youth, Nathan McCall pulled a gun on someone who had intimidated him for years. He later described the feelings he experienced during that moment—when in a quick act he pulled the gun out, pointed it at the man's chest and fired, he saw a side of the man he had not seen previously. The intimidating fierceness was gone, and there was a surprising look of shock and terror instead. McCall said that at that moment he felt like God, a feeling very powerful and enjoyable, and so pleasant that he wanted to continue shooting. After a number of years went by, McCall read in an article about psychology that others who had killed also felt a very similar orgasm-like thrill at such moments.[62] The urge to feel powerful is unconsciously the urge to experience a freedom, a greater consciousness, an uncanny supernatural marvel—an unconscious wish to feel momentarily "like God." The pseudo-cosmic sensation of a nervous system stimulated by crack cocaine is also a "whole body climax" which exacts a terrible price—loss of humanity. Drugs are fraught with power—shamans use them in therapeutic rituals and others unconsciously use them to get free, to unlearn miseducation.[63]

The words of Texas death-row inmate John Lamb illustrate another kind of fractal-like configuration—a pattern dominant in his personality. His attitude seems configured around a fractal of societal indifference. He paralleled the way people did not care when as a child he was being beaten regularly by an abusive step-father—they did not stop it—and the way people were indifferent to or even glad of the fact that he was going to be executed. He responded with indifference:

> As far as society goes, how can I feel bad? I mean, all these people that say, "Go ahead and kill him" are no different from the people that knew my stepfather was whipping the hell out of me. . . . And they didn't have enough guts to step up and say anything about that, yet they got enough guts to say go ahead and kill me now. So that's how I look at it.[64]

There were many occasions of indifference on different scales, from trivial to serious, in a life whose totality seems one of the self-same indifference.

The issue of humanity's participation in divinity is complex and debatable. In the origin story of the Judeo-Christian worldview the great fall and the order of right and wrong came when the serpent said that God was afraid that if humans ate from the tree they would become like God in knowledge of good and evil.[65] Yet when leaders accused Jesus of declaring himself to be God, Jesus cited the tradition: "In your own Law it says that men are gods."[66] This shows the tension between two teachings which both exist in the tradition. The human is said to be made in the image of God, but the potential ways in which humans share in divinity are deep and complex. The issue comes up in Hinduism also; men should not imitate in their own lives the love relationships Lord Krishna has with the milkmaids (*gopis*), for those relationships represent God and human souls. People are asked to love their souls and to be like the divine in spiritual love. Overstepping the line, in the view of philosopher Simone Weil, has to do with consuming what one should only consider. Vice, depravity, and crime, she says, almost always are attempts to "eat beauty," to eat what one should only look at. Mysterious fascination with great power and the desire for vengeance can devour a soul.[67] Experiences of abuse and violence can self-perpetuate and generate addicts; the situation is like that depicted in stories of vampires—the bitten infect others with the need to bite and drink blood.

To end on a more pleasant note, today's news reports also contain images of playing God in a good sense: giving presents to underprivileged children, performing community service, experiencing the connections benevolently. Love is the greatest fractal of them all, if fractal means the power to hold the many different scaled parts of the whole. "We are ultimately helpless before the archetypal experience of love and we understand little; even its epiphanies are only openings into yet more possibilities of loving."[68] Love is subtly connective, contagious, caught by inspiration, kindled or seeded by its own true being and sweet embrace.[69]

"Sweep the garden—any size," as Zen master Oda Sesso Roshi said. Any scale is enough to hold attention and demand our best; every scale is enmeshed with other scales and larger wholes. One can start anywhere and productively participate in wholeness.

"Otherizing" Kin or Celebrating Oneness

Some scholars do not think unity is as important as difference. C. J. Bleeker is a proponent of this view: "Historians of religion [who] think that the kernel of religion is to be found on [the] level [of *religio perennis,* the perennial philosophy, which stresses common factors and underlying similarities] . . . are greatly mistaken. . . . [Their] ambition should be, not so much to describe the common spiritual good of humanity, but to clarify what is typical, unique, exceptional in the religions."[70]

Which is most important—difference which isolates or sameness which unites? Is it the uniqueness which segments of humanity use to wall themselves off from others that is most important, as C. J. Bleeker suggests above, or is it the connective similarities they share? It depends on one's need; if one is making peace or putting out a fire, the unity is necessary for cooperation. If one is an intellectual provoking thought in a community of armchair philosophers devoted to critical thinking with nothing personally at stake, such as the survival of a group or an endangered species, common traits may seem uninteresting. This is not to say that those who focus on differences are callous or useless; it is more a plea to avoid one-sidedness.

Historian of religion Wilfred Cantwell Smith has suggested that "the future progress of one's own cherished faith, even within one's own community, depends more largely than most of us have realized on the ability to solve the question of comparative religion."[71] The reason for this has to do with the very real necessity of compatibility. Others have argued that the times of dynamic historical development are those when searches for unity are at the forefront of concern. For example, the historian A. Gordon Melvin has described an alternation of dynamic (full of productive activity) and static (more stagnant) historical periods in the history of the West. The era leading up to the year 300 B.C.E. was dynamic; that was the time when Socrates, Plato, and Aristotle saw wholes as prior to parts. The year 700 C.E. was static, characterized by atomism and a materialist philosophy. The era 1250–1300 was dynamic; Duns Scotus and Aquinas had begun to deduce from whole to parts, gaining a sense of systems. The year 1400 was static because of Ciceronian formalism. The year 1650 was dynamic; physics, mathematics, biology, and social thought were each discovering new integrations. Melvin concludes that "after rather unprogressive periods, the stem of the old wisdom of wholeness must be recovered so that a new and greater branch may grow."[72] This return to a concern for larger issues of wholeness at first might seem like regression, but one does not live by crumbs alone.

The boundaries which keep traditions in line are like sacred attractors (to borrow the image of "strange attractors" from chaos science).[73] Origins or initial conditions—the roots of the historical development of the tradition and their thrust in time—partly determine later possibilities. For example, the Palestinian and Greco-Roman roots of Christianity set ground rules, directions, limits to behavior, boundaries within which acceptable decisions are to be made. These patterns show memories, scars from trauma and habits, and they generate reiterations which emphasize the uniqueness, the difference of the trajectory of the tradition. Often religious institutions have officially denied their similarities and have hidden their borrowings, as if ashamed to share in a common humanity.

Power Relations, Peer Relations, and Relations of Subordination

The power involved in translating ideas from one language to another is strong and subtle, and it can be used for good or ill. A translation can bring out kinship or put someone beyond the pale. For example, if one translates the reference to a religious ritual in verse III.69 of the classical Hindu *Manava Dharma Shastra* as "the fire-worship," it sounds quite heathen—some weird adoration of flame which good moderns would never engage in. To alienate, to otherize, one need only emphasize the outlandish. But if the reference is translated as "a symbolic rite focusing on fire as the manifestation of divine power, mediation, spiritual brightness, and mystery," an altogether different response is created. This translation suggests experiences which are more universal, a psychological readiness to take the others seriously, a maturity that brings a willingness to open oneself to treating others as equals, with legitimate rights and reasons of their own. For another example, take the term "Allah." There are times when simply translating this as "God," the same God known to Christianity and Judaism, can usefully remind Westerners of kinship. The prophetic relig-

Visual image of a "strange attractor." Strange attractors' re-iterative paths make fractal patterns. I believe attractor shapes can help us visualize or imagine how cultural archetypes work by reducing their dynamics in time to a pattern in space showing the repetitions with variation. For example, picture the recurrent rhythms of a song; or the image of a goddess, focused on again and again, and the prayers said to her; or the repeated return to an idea of faith or hope. These returns stimulate fantasies or mental impulses around the focal point of the attractor. Orderly human behavior and the natural changes of time usually involve moving from one basin of attraction to another, in different times of the day and successive phases of life cycles. A concept such as "strange attractors" enhances the vocabulary and the conceptualizing faculty of the humanities. Courtesy of J. C. Sprott, Physics Dept., University of Wisconsin.

ions (Judaism, Christianity, Islam) are, historically speaking, members of one family of traditions, though at any given time some defensive people pretend this is not so.

The results are very different once we make the choice to alienate ourselves, or when we are unconsciously moved by forces of habit to keep our alienating stances and to generate self-importance by looking at others askance, as lower, meaner. The arrogation of power by using disinformation to fabricate dissimilarity is an old ploy and can be defensive or offensive. Terms such as "the sacred" or "the holy" are useful in conceptually uniting members of the human race, while terms such as "primitive," "pagans," "idolatry," and "infidels" are presumptuous, as most professional scholars of world religions now recognize. Emerson wrote in "Uses of Great Men" that "the possibility if interpretation lies in the identity of the observer with the observed. . . . Like can only be known by like."[74]

Hatred can utilize the scales of consciousness to symbolically depict one's own importance and the inhumanness and insignificance of an enemy. The rabbi at the funeral of the terrorist Dr. Baruch, who in 1993 opened fire on a crowd of praying Muslims, said, "A million Palestinians are not worth one fingernail of a Jew." Dehumanizing names—"mad dog," "mud-people," "rag doll," "pig," and so forth—make it easier to forget the overwhelmingly basic similarities all humans share. Intentionally dissembling, dissimilarizing, distancing, and emphasizing otherness to one's own advantage inspires people to approach members of other religions in a simple-minded, linear fashion. But the other religions, such as those of Native Americans, often have understandings of the sacred which are very deep and complex—nonlinear. Moderns with egalitarian ideals imagine the caste system of a traditionally organized Hindu village in linear fashion, unable to conceive of its having any intricate, nonlinear aspects.[75] They are also usually unable to see their own caste system of ownership, status, fame, and so forth. Monotheists of prophetic faiths may presume that their faith in God is superior to and very different from the faith of those they label "polytheists." But what if the original intention behind the injunction against idolatry was to keep believers from taking the symbol system as the ultimate reality, to caution against the confusion of literalism? Sometimes those pointing the finger and the sword may have their own "idols," such as a word which alone is God's name, or power, or revenge, or the belief that their group speaks with God's only true voice in the world.

The medieval Christian mystic Meister Eckhart speaks of an irrepressible spiritual intimacy: "Between God and the soul . . . there is neither strangeness nor distance. Therefore the soul is not in the likeness of God but rather it is altogether 'his like'—and the same as he is."[76] In this teaching, spirit is the same as the divine spark. Some people are comfortable with such expressions of unity, while others, such as Muslim legalists, are aghast. Fear is a terrible, often unconscious, power, because it can engender fractals of rage. That is, it can unleash cascades of fury at varying scales and levels, adding up to one huge outrage.

When political fears are roused, "oneness" becomes a battle cry and one's foes become the demonized focus of one's religion. But the well-rounded historian of religion knows the importance of a different side of life, something other than defensiveness. Religious experience is often tied up with vulnerability or brokenness. In archaic and primal religions, extraordinary experiences such as psychosis and illness form part of the shaman's development—by curing him- or herself into a whole being again, the shaman brings knowledge of healing to the community. Without a wound, one lacks sensitivity. "Nothing can be whole or sole which has not been rent," as Yeats wrote.[77] Religious spirit lives at that opening to the sacred unity, feeding on the energy there, turning the chaotic spiritual energy into order, meaning.

Experiential Openness and Resonance

Brokenness may be likened to an open center where microcosm and macrocosm meet and compare notes. When one is open, with the psyche fractured into fractals of past chaos and future order, as it were, one can experience finer levels, and one's micro-scales are attuned. By this I mean that when one is aware of both troubles and hope one is sensitized more fully, and this can occur when one is in a vulnerable state, "broken open." One is then tenderly open to taking things in, a process that becomes impregnated in the unconscious, which is therefore able to give birth to wholes. Buddha taught that "life is *dukkha*," meaning that suffering is built into the natural scheme of things. Buddha also taught that beauty is the whole of the holy life.[78] Realizing the basic nature of suffering impelled the Buddha-to-be to begin his quest for the ultimate beauty. In the Western literature of the grail, the Fisher King could only be healed when the right knight asked, "How were you wounded?" The healing is the wholing. The unknotting and reinvigorating is the renewal of the order arabesqueing through the systems of the cosmos. Through this opening, this wound which we ignore and deny at first, positive archetypes can be activated. When voiced and acted out and shared with others, the deep images cause a vast ensemble of music instead of the cacophony of paranoia, anger, hate, and fear.

When it reaches for the mystery of wholeness, becoming seeks ultimate Being. For example, the Buddhist mantra *Om mani padme hum* means "the gem of eternity is in the lotus" of birth and death, and the climax image in Buddhism—"the dewdrop slips into the shining sea"—can be seen as the temporary soul-drop merging with the sea, or the spiritual sea of consciousness suffused into the drop. Both interpretations are views of the same event—different scales, different spaces that are filled by proportions but are the same intermingling whole.

Mandalas of all kinds are images of a central Wholeness that meditators focus on and imaginatively enter in deep contemplation. Mandalas orient minds to an ordering sacred consciousness, a "something" which is not a "thing," though it is called "the kingdom of heaven within," and the plots of the dramas of this connective consciousness rise up from the realm called the "collective unconscious." It is a connectivity of relations, a dynamic network. And it is an intimate mystery to us, as C. G. Jung has written:

> This is something strange to us and yet so near, wholly ourselves and yet unknowable, a virtual centre of so mysterious a constitution that it can claim anything—kinship with beasts and Gods, with crystals and with stars—without moving us to wonder, without even exciting disapprobation. This something claims all that and more, and having nothing in our hands that could fairly be opposed to it, it is surely wise to listen to its voice.[79]

According to the perennial philosophy, people talk about the One, or "the Simple," in different ways without realizing that they're all trying to indicate the same thing. To the Hindu it sounds Upanishadic, like the nature of *chit* (consciousness); to the Christian and Jew it is "spirit" or *ruah*; to the scientist it is "order

for free" in the universe; to others it is spiritual consciousness. It is reflected intelligence in the order in the brain, in the DNA in a flower seed, in the Milky Way, in a football game or office building.

When process philosopher Alfred North Whitehead advised people to seek simplicity then distrust it, he meant that when you find a holding pattern, don't become too satisfied with it but go on to explore its complexities further. For complexities are held by simplicity just as chaos is underpinned by patterns. Consciousness creates order; where there is order there is a pattern that reveals consciousness. The perennial philosophy does not say that a grain of salt has a human brain, but that a subtle consciousness pervades it and all things in creation. It is like water, which can be still and reflective, and can also be roiled and rippled. Fractal

A Bodhimandala, a traditional Tibetan diagram used for the contemplation of wisdom in a variety of applications. This focus for meditation promotes enlightenment through sincerity, patience, kindness, life lessons, self-control and the mystery of Emptiness. Courtesy of South Indian Art Works.

diagrams are like two-way mirrors in which chaos and order can look at each other and perform a spiral duet of formless potential and musiclike patterns, resolving infinite partnesses in larger wholes. That is, they help us visualize and conceptualize relations of simplicity and complexity.

A Tibetan Buddhist vision of wholeness, presented by Herbert Guenther, suggests that

> the creative dynamics of the whole's, and, by implication, the individual's supraconscious ecstatic intensity presences itself in five gestalts (constituting the complexity of an individual's existentiality).
>
> We must never forget that we as living beings—dynamic systems—are the whole and also are only part of it—"fractals" (endlessly repeated self-similarities). This modern concept "fractal" has already proved its usefulness in many areas and its extension to the old concept of *sku* [a gestalt of both the expression and the expressed] is not at all a farfetched notion. It is a well-known fact that fractals are characterized by *self-similarity* in which a given figure or motif keeps repeating itself on an ever diminishing scale. In *rDzogs-chen* thought, the motif is Being/wholeness that repeats itself in its gestalts (*sku*) that together form the geometrical figure of a centred four, known as a mandala.[80]

Fractals, though simple, are rather magical, like mandalas—they can creatively lead the nimble mind anywhere. They are metaphors to depict such visions of vastness, levels beyond—the cosmic, the infinite—to fathom the "more things" in heaven and earth than "are dreamed of" by materialism, to depict the whole as a taken-for-granted grace, like the elusive self-effacing Tao. Tao is called the perfect simplicity which is the banquet's host but to some doesn't seem to exist. The "uncanny guest" who has lost his respect for, and his gratitude and relation to, the invisible host sees all the "suchness," the unique moments in Indra's gemmed net, as merely random. The hidden self-similarity usually goes unnoticed—in the structures of life, and in the forms of human religiosity—until one is ready to see it.

Resonance with the elements of life, multiple vibrations in harmony, enriches life with depth.[81] Because of resonance, we are more than we know. Because we are coordinated with the cosmos around us, we are greater than individualism might realize. Does the cosmos speak to us? Only insofar as, and in the ways that, embodied beings receive it in their openness and perceive it with their own microcosmic resonance, envisioning its structures and meshing with them. As Plotinus wrote in *On Beauty,* "No eye ever saw the sun without becoming sun-like, nor can a soul see beauty without becoming beautiful. You must become first of all godlike and all beautiful if you intend to see God and beauty."[82] Elsewhere Plotinus says, "all knowing comes by likeness,"[83] and many likenesses, all associations interrelated by kinship, are fractal in their

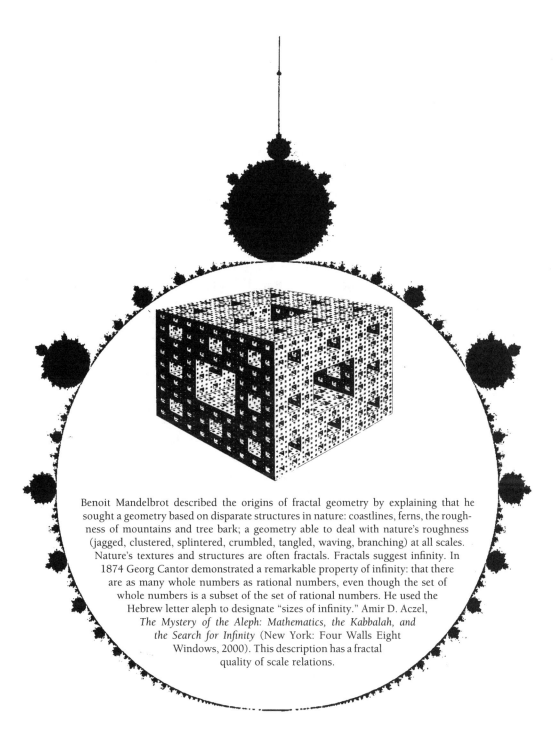

Benoit Mandelbrot described the origins of fractal geometry by explaining that he sought a geometry based on disparate structures in nature: coastlines, ferns, the roughness of mountains and tree bark; a geometry able to deal with nature's roughness (jagged, clustered, splintered, crumbled, tangled, waving, branching) at all scales. Nature's textures and structures are often fractals. Fractals suggest infinity. In 1874 Georg Cantor demonstrated a remarkable property of infinity: that there are as many whole numbers as rational numbers, even though the set of whole numbers is a subset of the set of rational numbers. He used the Hebrew letter aleph to designate "sizes of infinity." Amir D. Aczel, *The Mystery of the Aleph: Mathematics, the Kabbalah, and the Search for Infinity* (New York: Four Walls Eight Windows, 2000). This description has a fractal quality of scale relations.

relations and affinities. It is difference that allows a thing to be separated out and recognized. Information has to do with the registering of distinct differences of data, but knowing is based on seeing similarities, resonances, metaphors, connections. So, it is said, wholeness is known by soul, consciousness is known by consciousness. It is likeness that lets the mind connect the seen thing's qualities with other things in consciousness, allowing recognition with more depth.

Vincent van Gogh wrote to his brother Theo, "We are still far from the time when people will understand the curious relation between one fragment of nature and another, which all the same explain each other and enhance each other."[84] We are closer to this time now. We see that the trunk and limbs of the branching tree, the tributaries of rivers, the lungs, and lightning are self-similar. They are all forking shapes, bifurcating in the same universe. All around us on this round earth we see the rounded mounds of mountains and hills, and on the hills the rounded tops of trees with rounded leaves, under the clouds which are also rounded puffs made of smaller puffs (sculpted by roundness-loving winds from a round sun-ball), surrounded by the blue of the sky. Artists, poets, and mystics have long delighted in such coincidences, and now there are new sciences seeking to understand the wholeness of systems, not just the parts. We can see wholeness better now, including van Gogh's whole contribution.[85] A greater awareness of the possibilities and inevitabilities of pursuing self-similarities in the culture we make and in the lives we live is a valuable benefit reaped from relating fractals to the humanities. It means becoming more aware of ancient natural processes. A sense that the little part participates in the identity of the great whole, and finds its place within that larger rightful context, constitutes what might be called a "fractal sensibility." But that is just a way to communicate something deep by using a term that has recently come to stand for vivid visualizations which conceive anew ancient part-whole relations. The motto of the Paleontological Society, *"Frango ut patefaciam,"* can speak for the many fractal patterns which intrigue us: "I break in order to reveal."

CREATURES OF CREATIVITY, CREATIVITY OF CREATURES

We work in the dark—we do what we can—we give what we have. Our doubt is our passion and our passion is our task. The rest is the madness of art.
—Henry James[1]

Wholeness Thinking in Images:
"The Madness of Art" and Art's Rational Strength

After depression come relief and joy; after pain, pleasure; after storms, sun. Without tears in our eyes there are no rainbows for our souls. From such alternating weathers the artist's soul makes beauty, or at least a work of art.

To learn about creativity can be empowering. Consider African American poet Etheridge Knight, a Midwestern man who was imprisoned for robbery in 1960. Wounded in the Korean War, Knight had become addicted to drugs. In prison, as he read and discovered the freedom in poetry, his imagination took off and he became an imaginer, a creative thinker, a full-voiced poet. He found a new life, new friends, a new destiny. Creativity is contagious, a spark that can kindle inspiration, a river that can break barriers and circulate life energies. In my view, which, I admit, includes imagination as a significant human faculty, "creativity fractals"—self-similar patterns and processes of part/whole elegance—can be seen in nature, and in the work of individual artists, and in ongoing traditions of art.

Soul exuberance is creative. Nature's beauty too involves an overflow. Henry David Thoreau called snowflakes and raindrops "products of enthusiasm, the children of ecstasy, finished with the artist's utmost skill." He also said that "nature perfected herself by an eternity of practice."[2] But if one uses repetition too much, tries to control too much, one is caught up in unpredictable predicaments. Artists make the best use of surprise, knowing it can spur energy. The mind, an integral part of nature's creativity, is rooted in the whole cosmos and the long story of life. Our dreams come like stars in the night, our hands reach toward the future each day, and our hearts give the ongoing drumbeat to the creative present. A thread of richness runs inextricably through it all.

"When we try to pick out anything by itself," naturalist John Muir observed, "we find it hitched to everything else in the universe."[3] That "hitched-ness" is crucial to the vision of mind and creativity we are developing. Overly purposive myopic logic would reduce and cut out the "hitched-ness"—the dynamic relationships—as so much clutter.[4] Creativity requires a broader range of possibilities and dynamisms; imagination draws on more than is known by the overly restricted mind. Einstein said imagination is more important than knowledge in making discoveries. He described how he experienced the sinews of the universe, so to speak, in the muscles of his imagination, to learn (as he put it) "what the Old One thinks."[5] Imagination overcomes obstacles; it hitches and it bridges, and it discovers connections by exercising freedom. It is fueled by feelings and joins the heart to the mind in a feedback loop. It intuits and synthesizes. It fills in gaps by working with an organic sense of the whole, as historian William Irwin Thompson suggests:

> The imaging capacity of the mind is not the epiphenomenal discharge of purer processes of computational logic. . . . The image is a transform of awareness from other dimensions of sensitivity. The song you did not hear you may begin to hum. The bacteria you did not see you may begin to envision. This capacity to think in images and then transform them into other dimensions of reference is vital to art, poetry, and science. High on a peak in the Andes, Darwin's imagination took fire as he saw how "we are all netted together."[6]

Although facts by themselves reduce, images expand dynamically, resonantly webbed with other parts of lived experience.[7] Abstract prose (the kind we see in most instruction manuals) seems thin and superficial; the language of story often feels deep and thick and has a richness associated with life. Myths "name the whirlwind," and art builds stations or installations where the shock of awe can flash. A growing sense of wonder and depth and an openness to possibilities in creativity and self-transformation have provided important advantages in the long story of human evolution.

Stories have probably helped even the most linear-minded moderns survive by keeping them alive to nonlinear realities. For example, the hunter Orion, imagined in the stars, stands for an ancient human story of overcoming the monster (or at least bringing home the bacon); millennia later it's still current. Perhaps the original story of the hunter told by ancient people, and the multitude of versions in all their variations, expansions, and summaries—the whole and the parts—can be thought of as a fractal-like process. There are many tellings, on many scales, from brief to extremely long-winded, all sharing certain similarities.

Gregory Bateson argues that processes in evolution are akin to the mental activities of creatures, because both are part of the processes of "Mind" active in the cosmos—Mind meaning the meta-pattern that connects, the unifying factor in the network of existence. Works created by creative people (poems, art, and music, for example) are marked by mental creativity. For Bateson, the entire nature and purpose of art and poetry is "to exemplify the creativity of mind," and this is "the appropriate fundamental theorem for a science of aesthetics. In creativity, mind is brought together, and this integration is a close synonym of 'beauty.' " Whatever beauty is, it remains a nurturing mystery.[8] Its attractive gracefulness integrates the disparate forms and expressions of Mind or Consciousness, and that fractal trait is inspiring.

Denial of beauty (as when an artist says, "I don't buy into beauty") seems to be a strategy to accomplish a nontraditional effect. Scratch a denier and you may find love for certain kinds of beauty. Although many of us might think of angst-driven Franz Kafka as unconcerned with ideas such as that beauty is the rejuvenating source of vitality, we would be wrong. "Anyone who keeps the ability to see beauty," Kafka said, "never grows old." What quality or identity of beauty makes it regenerative, so that it is always youthful and rejuvenating us?

Think of a landscape of mountains[9]—snow-covered Alps in the distance, rising in zigzags made of smaller zigzags from the shore of the lake at your feet. Beauty often evokes a mysteriously elusive hint of the infinite. By "the infinite" I mean the cosmic—the network of endless orders on all scales: systems of systems smaller and smaller, systems of systems larger and larger, and the beyond. Long-twirling galaxies, planets, networks of terrain and ecosystems, cultures and organisms, molecules and cells, atoms and subatomic systems like strings.

Beauty conjures some shadow or trace, some suggested gestalt or sweet echo, of the infinite's characteristics—self-similarity, proportional harmony, scales within scales, for example. This holds true on the human scale as well, though the connection may be elusive. Imagine the elegance of a profile, unselfconscious silhou-

ette curves that seem as free as a falling leaf's path yet have a
classically functional form; nothing is extraneous, and the graceful
and the playful, the self-similar and the unique are combined.
Beauty suggests and requires fluidity; not just pinpoint focus, but
movement among whole parts (individual features, such as eyes
shaped like lotus petals) to take in the startling loveliness of part
wholes (the profile contours of cheeks and forehead with the eyes).
Beauty evokes wholeness and stimulates resonance; it evokes intuitions of the pleasing congruence of fineness in both seer and
seen.[10]

While a materialist or a literalist or a linear reductionist may
see a grain of sand as a mere grain of sand or a flower as a mere
flower, the poet William Blake saw more, experiencing self-
reflexive recognition in aesthetic perceptions and processes that
revealed the cosmic nature of the parts of the universe and his own
potentially cosmic self. In a flower he saw reflections of his own
creativity, and he was pleased to feel himself as part of the same
cosmic process and humbled to realize he was a small outcome of
such a vast process. Humility is the beginning.[11] Gregory Bateson

has said that " 'things as they are' are always seen, experienced, conveyed, through a creative filter, whether one recognizes it or not." The inner artist of perception, the inner fashioner of selective and associative memory, determines much of experienced reality by noticing and playing with relationships and similarities.[12]

The most crucial aspects of the integration of mind that is beauty involve unconscious processes, the unforeseen epiphany that depends on the ripening of time, the uncontrollable and fortuitous event (which some call "the happy accident") that is beyond one's conscious purpose. (As playwright David Mamet says, no art comes from the conscious mind.[13]) Let's consider some examples.

Singer-songwriter and actor Tom Waits marveled about the ways of creativity—how some things so carefully planned turn out in the end to be meaningless, while other things, quietly accumulated without much awareness during stretches of one's busy life become a treasure rediscovered when they're needed most, giving one's work freshness and bold power.[14] It is as if, in Waits's view, the finest materials involved in composing art depend on the "crude"—by which he means the basic, honest, deep, and unfakable, the real, uninhibited, and rough—those materials edged with the energies of chaos. The refinement of the greatest art may depend on raw materials of experience, blunt truths, images of strong direct expression, vital and vivid memories, wild and weird colors and rhythms. Thus the creative outlook plays its part with open innocence, a readiness to try whatever might work, to use one's consciousness as a clear mirror to reflect all, the largesse of the cosmos. Waits notes that no matter how much a creative musician rehearses and performs his or her music, the music has a life of its own—it doesn't want to stay the same, but continues to change. While it is possible to force music to remain the same, even then to make good music one must respect the inevitable moments when it escapes from one's conscious control.[15] To go with it on a spontaneous ride bigger and more full of surprises than your planning, deciding, and controlling brain, is to improvise onward. Creativity thus enacts something on a number of levels of life observed, enjoyed, retrieved. Creativity is the trickster catching a wave of life; it involves a process of growing, developing with coordinates of which you are not fully conscious, the way a baby grows, from within. (As the codes in DNA form a scenario for an organism's development; the images and urges in the unconscious are potential scenarios for creativity, as C. G. Jung suggested in his studies.)[16]

Psychologists distinguish between primary-process thinking (the chaotic realm of dreams and daydreams, fantasies, highs, altered states) and secondary-process thinking (the logical, the concrete, analytical rationality). Creativity involves a return to primary-process thought, with its streaming images and free associations, while the presentation of creative ideas, the refining and framing of them, uses the skills of secondary-process logic. In physiological terms, "most people produce alpha waves when they are relaxing, and reduce alpha frequency when they are working on a problem. Creative people such as artists and poets produce less alpha when they are relaxing, and increase their alpha frequency when they work on an imaginative problem."[17] Creativity needs algorithms of playfulness and grace, swirlouts from the confining grid of linearity, iterating pathways of fertile abundance's curlicues, relational energies flowing with beauty. Simply put, wholistic envisioning is "more like a web than a ladder," as arts scholar Vishakha Desai puts it.[18] When it is consigned to linear rungs of progression or shunted amid too few possibilities, the mind short-circuits and produces Procrustean results.

As comic and writer Steve Martin recently said, "the creative process in art and science is very similar. You have to forget all the rules and start shaking things around."[19] The too-rigid rule-follower who so carefully keeps everything in its proper place is not prepared for what the process of creativity really involves. *Cogitare* (to think) literally means to "shake together" or to "select among a number" in order to discover new combinations, to play around with multiple possibilities. Experiment and innovation demand open improvisational freedom and fluidity. Discovery requires openness to small impulses and new resources that constantly appear on the horizons of everyday life. If Antonio Stradivari (1644–1737) hadn't taken a walk one day in Venice and if he had not responded with curiosity when he saw a pile of discarded waterlogged oars, he would not have picked up those pieces of wood, dried them, and refashioned them into some of the finest violins the world has ever heard. That moment of recognition, the following of an impulse, and those patient acts of craftsmanship all took clarity.

Through openness to the new possibilities flowing toward us now, where the waters of past and future converge, "creatives" get their "sweet revenge" on all the mishaps of conditioning and injustices of the times. The deepest issues at stake here are beyond economics or conditioning.[20] Carl Andre said, "Culture is something that is done to us. Art is something we do to culture,"[21] and this is true whether we have in mind graffiti artists or Leonardo da Vinci. The artist cultivates art in his or her psyche, and when it appears and impresses other psyches, the process makes a shared fractal of cultural energy that awakens a hidden but somehow lacking aspect of existence, an image of the whole open to experience and conversation. Saying the impact of art involves a shared fractal of cultural energy is a way to describe a subtle process that changes perceptions. "Memes" are usually thought of as little bits of memorable ideas that catch on in a culture, but Leonardo's vision touched many lives, on a variety of scales.

> What would become of mankind if nobody had lucky ideas anymore? . . . Our consciousness is that sack which has . . . in it . . . what chances to fall into it. We never appreciate how dependent we are on lucky ideas until we find to our distress they will not come. A dream is . . . a lucky idea . . . from the dark, all-unifying world of the psyche.
> —C. G. Jung[22]

Child Creativity, Wholeness, Echoes of Eco

Balanced precariously on the anvil of time, some creative people have spoken of cultivating an artist's wise blindness rather than pretending to an arrogant know-it-all expertise. The poet Rainer Maria Rilke, for example, advocated art as a freeing way of life which is primal:

> Not any self-control or self-limitation for the sake of specific ends, but rather a carefree letting go of oneself. . . . Not caution but rather a wise blindness. . . . Not working to acquire silent, slowly increasing possessions, but rather a continuous squandering of all shifting values. . . . This way of being has something naive and instinctive about it and resembles that period of the unconscious best characterized by a joyous confidence: namely the period of childhood.[23]

Like a child at play, the artist swims among possibilities. The artist lives on the lookout for creative permutations, serendipitous new juxtapositions. The artist surrenders hopefully, trusting in the process, at peace with the necessity of going along without knowing much about it. Why? Because a resilient sense of wholeness is there in the innocence of childhood. The word "innocent" means "unhurt"—not fractured, not alienated, but simply present as Being, a natural state of healthy harmony. This child-wholeness is described in early Taoism and in Vedic imagery.[24] The term "neotony" refers to human retention of aspects of infancy throughout life—fresh openness and playfulness are important parts of learning new things. Unless this resilience is cherished and nurtured throughout a lifetime, as traumas, disappointments, and setbacks come, learning becomes very difficult and creative ability is lost. Ashley Montagu is remembered for saying, "The goal is to die young as late in life as possible." A person who remains young in this way loves learning and finds great joy in ideas.

This fresh childlike delight forms a common theme in creativity. Norman O. Brown comments,

The artist is the man who refuses initiation through education into the existing order, he remains faithful to his own childhood being, and thus becomes a "human being in the spirit of all times, an artist." Hence, the artist tree is distinguished by profounder roots in the dark unconscious: "Artists extend much farther down into the warmth of all Becoming; in them other juices rise into the fruit."[25]

The artist refuses to relinquish wholeness, keeps access to wholeness, even if this hold on wholeness may not always be apparent. As Zeus swallows the wise goddess Metis whole and has the goddess Athena spring whole form his head, so the artist swallows the world whole and brings it forth again whole and transformed. As the poet Claudio Rodriguez says, clarity comes to us from far above. Clarity is a gift. Clarity concerns the viable wholeness, the graceful unity of parts. It concerns clear order that can emerge from murky chaos where it lurks.[26]

Umberto Eco, one of the great aesthetic theorists of our time, drew his own conclusions about wholeness and art after careful consideration of the thoughts of Benedetto Croce, John Dewey, and others. Consider Croce's fractal-like ideas about wholeness and art:

Each part of [an artistic representation] throbs with the life of the whole, and the whole is in the life of each part. A true artistic representation is at the same time itself and the universe, the universe as individual form, and the individual form as the universe. Every accent of the poet, as well as every creature of his imagination, encloses the entire destiny of mankind, with all its hopes, its illusions, its pains, its joys, its grandeur, and its misery, the entire drama of reality, incessantly becoming and growing out of itself, in suffering and in pleasure.[27]

The whole in the life of each part, the equivalence of the vast universe and the small artwork, the scales of individual, mankind, and dynamic reality all seem to me to suggest themes relevant to fractals.

Eco notes that although Croce doesn't explain the "mechanism" of this aesthetic experience, he does say that "to give an artistic form to an emotive content is to imprint it with totality, to lend it cosmic inspiration."[28] (Consider that in wisdom traditions the soul is associated with knowing wholes: it is the mirror of consciousness that enables us to know ourselves. "Wholeness marks everything it touches with the indelible seal of Being," as Buddhist scholar Herbert Guenther writes.[29]) Speaking of emotive content imprinted with totality, with cosmic inspiration, is again a way of saying the whole is reflected in the part, the vast and infinite in the tiny.

This sense of "the including whole implicit in ordinary experiences" was something the symbolist school of art put at the center of many works of art. John Dewey argues that "about every explicit and focal object there is a recession into the implicit which is not intellectually grasped. In reflection we call it dim and vague." For Dewey, the dim and the vague are aspects of the whole's "global nature": "At twilight, dusk is a delightful quality of the whole world, it is its appropriate manifestation. It becomes a specialized and obnoxious trait only when it prevents distinct perception of some particular thing we desire to discern." Reflection is able to focus on a part, but "the undefined pervasive quality of an experience is that which binds together all the defined elements, the objects of which we are focally aware, making them a whole." Dewey considers the essence of art to be the fact that it evokes and emphasizes "this quality of being a whole and of belonging to a larger, all-inclusive, whole which is the universe in which we live." In the same way, aesthetic contemplation can inspire religious awe as one realizes divine harmonies. But Dewey admits, "I can see no psychological ground for such properties of an experience save that, somehow, the work of art operates to deepen and to raise to great clarity that sense of an enveloping undefined whole that accompanies every normal experience."[30]

Eco doesn't deny this presence of a whole with which art is involved, but he does note Dewey's failure to explain the psychology of it. Eco's attempt at explanation leads him to systems of information theory—the how of communication and the expansiveness of the "open work." He does not look into the why—why wholeness is involved in experiencing art. (I would say it is because a "borrowed splendor" is at work in the mind, in the psyche's consciousness—awareness is reflected from a deeper consciousness active in the universe from the beginning, a point to which we shall return.) In developing his view of art and "the open work," which can involve more and more participants. Eco also considers Luigi Pareyson's aesthetics:

> The work of art . . . is a form, namely of movement, that has been concluded; or we can see it as an infinite contained within finiteness. . . . The work therefore has infinite aspects, which are not just "parts" or fragments of it, because each of them contains the totality of the work, and reveals it according to a given perspective.[31]

This part-whole concept portrays a fractal perception of Mind's nature which involves an interconnected network and various scales of comprehension:

> The infinite points of view of the performers and the infinite aspects of the work interact with each other, come into juxtaposition and clarify each other by a reciprocal process, in such a way that a given point of view is capable of revealing the whole work only if it grasps it in the relevant, highly personalized aspect. Analogously, a single aspect of the

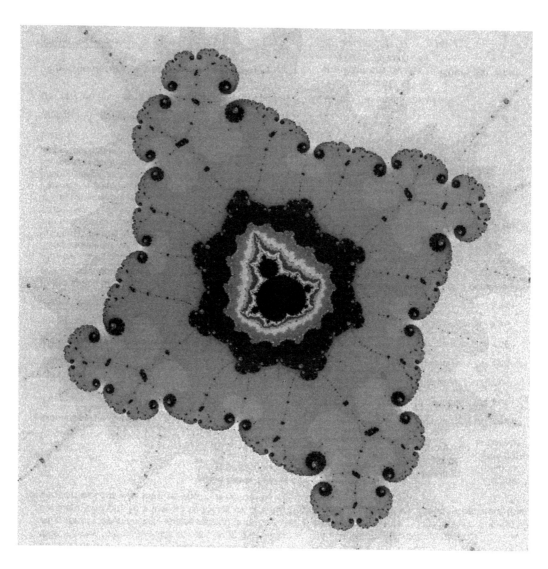

Fractal image. Courtesy of Michael Frame, Mathematics Dept., Yale University.

work can only reveal the totality of the work in a new light if it is prepared to wait for the right point of view capable of grasping and proposing the work in all its vitality.[32]

Eco is ultimately concerned with theorizing about works of art which are dynamic with openness, expanding unending possibilities of interaction with the participating audience. Thus the infinite aspects of art which Pareyson describes interest him. But here too, as with Croce and Dewey, the sense of the cosmic, the vast and open wholeness itself, is a background that is left unexplored. In a sense their concern is with the forgotten background of infinite wholeness.

It takes time to assimilate experiences and develop creative ideas and forms, to experiment with textures and home in on the likeliest way to display the work of art. Creativity demands that

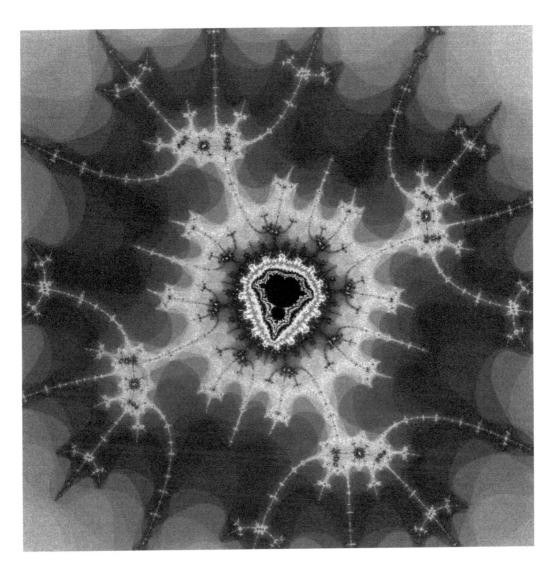

the artist relinquish rational control and enter into other orbits around fascinating points. It draws one toward attractors one doesn't understand, but which one can feel, like a folksong's rhythm. One must at times go with other rhythms which disturb the mechanical routine, allow other cycles to dominate and inspire, to play out possibilities in isolation from prevailing conventions, for these are necessary parts of new growth and creativity, as well as new intellectual realizations. (They are also involved in transformations of identity and developments of relationship.) Speciation, the evolution of new species, involves a return to an earlier chaotic stage of "totipotentiality,"[33] responding to new circumstances, exploring a new way. In the same herd, one animal explores attack as a strategy when being pursued by an attacker, and over the centuries descendants that follow that strategy adapt

Fractal image. Courtesy of Michael Frame, Mathematics Dept., Yale University.

and adapt, becoming eventually buffaloes; another animal explores running away, and its descendants eventually become horses.[34] Artists, who live at the more fluid, adaptable, earlier level of toti-potentiality,[35] are often the first to notice, face, and creatively incorporate the new (whether that involves imagining inventions, responding to the presence of new technology, or bending technology into new art). Humans have a longer period of infancy and childhood than other creatures: they learn through play to take adaptable stances.[36] Because they don't live in that state of flexibility, it is difficult for many humans to learn new ways past a certain age. Music's fluidity can be a lubricant that keeps creative and transformative possibilities open. Music often empatterns the nervous system and mind with changing melodic patterns which are subconscious models. Of course, freedom comes not just from open possibilities but also from creative encounters with challenging limits as well as play that works to maximize possibilities by experimenting within, and ultimately transcending, confinements. Thomas Berry, an ecology-minded theologian, eloquently suggests that we realize Mind in our creative lives and the creative universe around us:

> Empirical inquiry into the universe reveals that from its beginning in the galactic system to its earthly expression in human consciousness the universe carries within itself a psychic-spiritual as well as a physical-material dimension. Otherwise human consciousness emerges out of nowhere. The human is seen as an addendum or an intrusion and thus finds no real place in the story of the universe. In reality the human activates the most profound dimension of the universe itself, its capacity to reflect on and celebrate itself in conscious self-awareness.[37]

By this, I believe, Berry means we do not know of a more complex being than the human, able to fathom the depths of the universe, or a more powerful one, for good or ill. The human seems to have a potentially more expanded consciousness, though this evaluation is not meant to belittle other forms of life.

I do not wish to belabor the issue of consciousness here, yet I feel the need to clarify the question briefly. The reader might ask, "Consciousness? I always thought of consciousness as something which is located only in people, because it means 'self-awareness' and only people, with their large brains, are aware of what they are." In the view I am presenting, "consciousness" means signs of something like "mind" throughout the universe. As Berry said, in the human, the universe becomes aware of itself, but there is another kind of intelligence that has been at work from ancient times which does not seem to depend on humans to organize things— molecules, organisms, galaxies, and so on. Scientifically speaking, there is entropy, but there is also "order for free."[38] In my view, this order results from the dynamic stability of the pervasive consciousness, which in many wisdom systems is understood to be the background to existence, the Being behind becoming. Terms such as "Tao," "Brahman," and "Buddha Nature" have been used for ages to name this formless consciousness. I am arguing for an old tradition which fits with recent findings put forward by the new researchers and thinkers.[39]

When people say they don't believe in "God," they often think the only kind of "God" there is to not believe in is a white-haired, bearded father figure on a throne in heaven surrounded by angels. But to many, "God" means a formless, infinite, eternal consciousness, out of which all emerges and into which all returns. Timeless wisdom, exponents of the perennial philosophy, and some modern thinkers have depicted this consciousness—Lao-tzu's Tao, Vedanta's *Brahman-atman,* the "One" of the Greek philosophers,[40] the Buddha Mind or Luminous Void, the Sufis' *Nur* (Light) and *Tawhid* (Oneness of Allah), Kabir's Ram, Eckhart's Godhead, and the Manitou of Native Americans. It is the Being written of extensively in the comparative writings of Ananda K. Coomaraswamy,[41] the mystery discussed by Tagore and Einstein, the Self of "self-organization" in systems. In Judaism, it is called the Light beyond the sun, the Spirit or *Ruah* that fluttered the waters in the beginning, Ein Soph, the unfathomable depth of mystery beyond Elohim, upon the surface of which humans have written many names. It is Logos in Christianity. In traditional wisdom, it is not just persons who have self-knowledge. According to many traditions around the world the Light of Consciousness is behind all kinds of knowing, and solar imagery has served for a very long time as a reiterative archetype of life.[42]

Consider these lines of Dante: "O Light Eternal, who alone abidest in Thyself, alone knoweth Thyself, and known to Thyself and knowing, lovest and smilest on Thyself."[43] The spiritual Light in each being is what knows, in this view; all else, even powerful persons, only "slenderly know" themselves if they are ignorant of this Light. They act but "they know not what they do."

Consider a Hindu image of this spiritual Self, the mystery known as *Hiranya-garbha*—the "golden-wombed," the egg or seed origin capable of generation that is found in each being. *Hiranya-garbha* is said to be immortal—in humans, in birds and beasts, and in all other living beings. "God," or the original creative consciousness, is thus present and available in subtle formless form in all beings. Love is said to originate from *Hiranya-garbha*'s true nature.

Science-oriented thinkers such as Thomas Berry and Brian Swimme say that if psyche weren't there at the origin, we wouldn't have it now. It is like *atman* going all the way back to the beginning of time. F. David Peat wrote of this issue in his book *Blackwinged Night*. Just as matter-energy[44] was there at the origin and expressed itself in different forms through a process we mythologize as the dance of Dionysus and Apollo, so "protomind" was there already "as a *unity* to matter."[45] Peat points to a neuroscientist and to a physicist who both picture the origin of consciousness not at some point in historical time but as a process of emergence that occurs at the quantum level. Peat discusses other contemporary thinkers who picture space-time and consciousness at the quantum level as emerging from "some sort of eternal Platonic realm of [archetypal] Ideas."[46] This view suggests that various structures shaped by consciousness (e.g., archetypes, scientific theories, artworks, and architecture) "have a deep connection to the structuring principles of nature."[47] Peat notes that forms that we find pleasing, such as in math, music, or natural beauty, have a similar or identical source—they are developed by centers of consciousness, we might say.[48] Rupert Sheldrake pictures consciousness in terms of fields encoded with nature's habits; Ervin Laszlo speaks of quantum fields of memory and information, again trying to explain the Mind and world aspects of the *unus mundus,* and others are reexploring this ticklish area of mind/body, consciousness/matter. ("Unus mundus" refers to the ancient spiritual view that a single realm exists, but through human perceptions, conditioning, and habit it appears as separate entities of mind and matter. In this case, instead of "building a bridge" between mind and matter, we need to realize the original oneness, a point made by Taoism and Vedanta.)

Creativity: Wave upon Wave of Catchable Energies

> Each atom, rock, and star drinks of the same
> boundless waters of creativity.   —F. David Peat[49]

Stephen Jay Gould, who writes of evolution as producing a copious bush of life that branches, splits, and speciates again and again into new forms, described the "wonderfully glorious concatenation of improbabilities leading up to a perfectly sensible result."[50] All kinds of unique conditions and accidents culminate in peacocks and doves, in *Hamlet* and *Seinfeld,* in Aquinas and Monty Python. The universe is always gambling. The final result of a creative process depends on intricate, interacting factors. Creativity often involves withdrawal then return, intimacy then distance, involvement then disentangling, traveling a loopy circuit, combining from different levels, selecting from streams of possibilities, trying out new juxtapositions, like honeymooners with a copy of the *Kama Sutra.*[51]

Thelonious Monk advised jazz musicians, "Don't play like they tell you to play, you play like you want, and in 15 or 20 years they'll catch up."[52] Those who knew him recall how Monk tried out many possibilities in practice sessions with other musicians, without concern for salability or the likelihood of pleasing conventional audiences, satisfying his own quest first and foremost.

Creativity's withdrawals and returns form a rhythm that ensures a constant motion, a fluidity. Restless roving increases chances of finding—stumbling across new possibilities, combinations. Creativity is a flexible catch-as-catch-can state of taking advantage of the instability, the volatility, of the excited nervous system. It is skillfully dancing along with the fluidity already there at play in the materials and process. Creativity thrives poised on the line between order and chaos. Creativity is best explored as a process by which things grow, an ongoing challenge and discovery, falling and recovery, rather than a finished perfection, an unchangeable result. It is passion deftly coping with and overcoming obstacles.

Take, for example, musician Leon Fleischer. He was diagnosed with focal dystonia of the right hand, a neurological disorder which affects localized muscle tissue firmness and function. He would not give up his calling as a musician; he adapted his technique and developed three specialties—performing left-handed piano works, teaching at a conservatory, and conducting orchestras. After several years of this vigorous work in music, Fleischer began to play the piano with both hands again.[53] Given time, his indomitable creativity again and again got the upper hand. The "madness" of art is the sanity that is unexplainable and irreducible, a kiss of the whole, aroused intuitive imagination.[54] The flowing madness of art, obeying higher laws than the ones it breaks, is more holistic and wholesome than the fixations of the night side of reason. Reason can be used to rationalize onesidedness, marginalizing others for being too dissimilar to itself. Reason is good at analyzing parts and demanding coherence, but wholes often elude logic's careful myopia. Perhaps it is true that "the great fault with us all is that we force logic on facts whereas it is facts themselves that create logic," as D. T. Suzuki wrote.[55] Logic is important but it is not the whole story.

Holistic relatedness is the concern of creative spirit. Oliver Wendell Holmes rightly noted that a master of arts is one who, in dealing with an inorganic mass of scattered facts, "shoots through them the magnetic current of his [or her] thought" and causes the disparate bits to "leap into an organic order and live and bear fruit." It is a life-engendering, life-harmonizing, life-accompanying, and reflecting power.

The Way of Art as Opening and Paradox

Art, like creation, opens before us and invites the living to enter a world of worlds to be explored. We create to envision and experience what might be, what is possible but not yet in existence. To "create dangerously," as Albert Camus said: in an untrammeled way without attachments. To create without fears or preconceptions is to renew. The creative process follows desires to let archetypal truth work its way out. Maurice Sendak, an artist renowned for his children's books, said he is often haunted by a weird image during the creative process. Then he works with it, in story and illustration, to embed it in a likely context, to make it rationally feasible. The strength of passionate desires in the creative imagination can expand the limits of myopic reason, revealing more of reality, bringing dawn after dawn of awakening.[56] At the point of awakening, when the mind is still near dream-states, it is more free to explore fresh paths and combinations. In the second half of life especially one can develop this capacity for discovery.[57]

Awakenings of all sorts are like the Vedic vision of the poet rising into the shining world, singing, evoking the *devas* in the bliss-shining heavens, tasting the consciousness shining beyond form, reflecting the unity of a golden man on a golden bird facing a golden sun. Joseph Campbell said that "the revelation of art is not of ethics or a judgement—not even of humanity as one generally thinks of it—but a marvelling recognition of the radiant Form of forms that shines through all things."[58] Art can open ways to vantage points of transcendence.

The strictly rational mind often fails to appreciate paradox when it becomes too locked in linearity. But life is paradoxical, poised between mutually contradictory dynamics. As students of systems and evolution have noted, the autopoietic (self-producing) paradox is part of the reality of the world of life: self-organization involves interdependence, yet each twist of the spiral of life's co-evolution (in which micro and macro changes interact) leads to greater autonomy. (For example, flocks of birds are more free than sea slugs.) Yet more autonomy inevitably involves greater cooperation, more complicated interdependency—both greater freedom and deeper embeddedness. In our world, it is not possible for the individual to be truly isolated; the individual always has relationships of dependency, *befindlichkeit*, contextual belonging. The fact of *hemiolia*, a term which indicates ambiguity of the parts and the whole, is what makes self-transcendence possible: the never fully separate can realize hidden unity. There are often great creative potentials in the tensions of the paradoxical, more than in the homogeneity of consistency. Contradictions reveal Janus-

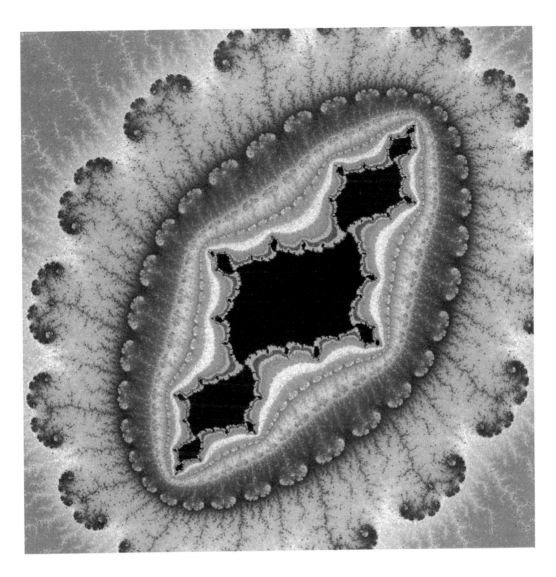

faced truths—the line between them is the threshold between deep phenomena and the flash of quirky insights, new ideas.[59]

Opposites can work well together, and are a necessity, in the overall dynamics of a developing life or work of art. An artist needs reason and imagination, realism and idealism, concept and impulse, earthy emotion and cool abstraction. One beautifully improvised discovery can spur and inspire many others, even among people who seem outwardly unlike the original source. For example, the proper Southern lady who is also one of America's great story-tellers, Eudora Welty, has said that she is inordinately fond of jazz. A Chinese visitor to Gettysburg recalled learning Lincoln's Gettysburg address as a kind of mantra, which gave him hope and strength during the hardships he endured on the Long March.[60]

Aristotle asserts in his *Metaphysics* that if a person rejects the

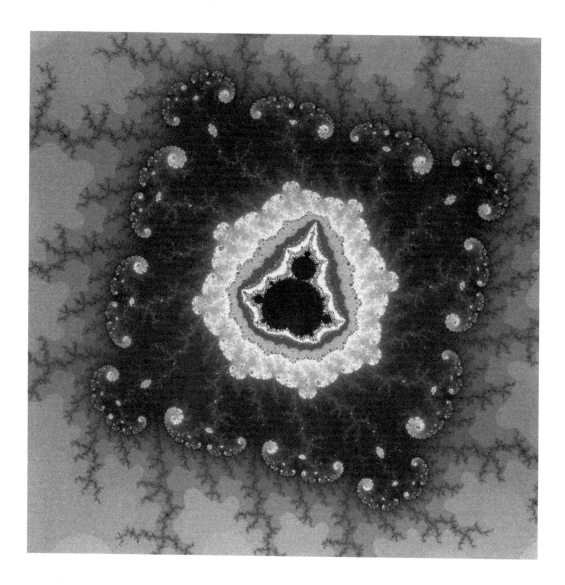

principle of contradiction, he inevitably arrives at the conclusion that "all things are one," which he refuted as absurd.[61] But in the dynamic vision of Buddhism and other wisdom paths, "insight into the oneness of all is the great goal, and only by contradictions can it be attained."[62] As Jung said, "To draw wisdom out of foolishness is the whole of art."[63]

The principle of paradoxicality is the fruitful split up the middle, the interface of whole symmetrical bodies of system, the hidden opening of creative fertility, kept secret and private under covers of forgetfulness and convention but silently fecund. The world of stars and oceans, jellyfish and hummingbirds, toads and roses and birthday parties, is a nonlinear world. Everything loops and feeds back into everything else, changing like teeter-totters of interdependence. Living systems inevitably are dynamic. Understanding them seems to involve paradoxes.

Paradox reminds us that if we go too far, too determinedly in any direction, we forget significant other aspects. We need a balance of tensions to be able to be self-integrated and self-transcendent. The overly simple linear view may be logical but it fails us in many real-life situations because it does not contain enough life to deal with complexity.[64]

A spider's thread between two points is a straight line, a necessary beginning. But one thread does not a whole web make, just as one region, dimension, or quadrant does not make a mandala that diagrams the whole cosmos. A dowser finds a vein of water hidden underground (or so my old friends in Vermont tell me), as an acupuncturist seeks points related to meridian nerves in the body. Dream analysis can reveal situations one's conscious mind ignored. Energy flows have their own way to go, guided by systemic necessities which may involve structures and relations often hidden to linear logic.

As life dances on, a meaning-seeking pattern-discerner, considering nonlinear gestalts, finds hidden principles that are contrary to surface expectations and follows up their implications. Erich Jantsch, an explorer of systems theory, writes of arts conveying a wholeness by embracing opposites. He advocates Dionysian planning in human designs, blending freedom and discipline, involving religious attitude and experience. In physical and biological systems evolution is governed by "order through fluctuation." A dynamic worldview must focus on processes and their interactions, their self-development unfolding with continuous feedback linkage to their own origins. Jantsch finds the Chinese wisdom of Tao useful in discussing his understanding. He believes human life draws its energy from living out, as fully as possible, the various tensions to which it is subjected in the fields of force between such opposites as individual and system, nature and culture, body and mind, instinct and rationality—the edge of chaos.[65]

The nature of the cosmos gives us clues and cues. Wisdom is the ability to understand the innate nature of things and oneself and to act accordingly. The connections, patterns, and rhythms of existence are not always obvious, and yet those who ignore them are "out of touch." Life experience itself is inevitably reflected in our work. "If in manic depression or its gentler variations artists list first starboard and then portside on the blinding swells of the imagination, small wonder that, on returning, they distill paradox into beauty," as the exquisitely eloquent Natalie Angier observes.[66]

What Douglas Hofstadter calls "Strange Loops" occur "whenever, by moving upwards (or downwards) through the levels of some hierarchical system, we unexpectedly find ourselves right back where we started."[67] The Mandelbrot set zooms to perform this amazing circular flight through infinite landscapes. We find ourselves in a place similar to where we began, as we might return to the refrain of a song, except now we have the benefit of other hindsights from our loop of experience, and we're facing in another direction, ready for another foray. We live in such an exquisitely tangled hierarchy of hierarchies, with loops that feed both back and forward, rhythms of return, and patterns of Mind, to assure us that it's possible to keep improvising onward.

Sensitivity to Resonating Nuances and "Chunks"

> In creativity, mind is brought together [from various levels], and this integration is a close synonym of "beauty."
> —Gregory Bateson[68]

The paradox of relations between chaos and order, the graceful working and playing out of their tensions, is what keeps creativity alive and gives it cadence. What John Briggs and F. David Peat, in *Turbulent Mirror,* call the "madness of art" involves a stochastic process of searching among levels of possibly relevant materials. Many "shifts of perspective . . . at various scales" precede discoveries—many attempts and little shifts of seeking, which altogether achieve at last a "major shift of perspective," a new idea. Creations are a record of these mental journeys along the trajectories and of trophies from the highlight moments of good luck and coincidence. Briggs and Peat observe that "the ability to jump from reference plane to reference plane while coupling different planes together appears to depend upon the creator's sensitivity to nuance."[69]

"Nuance" refers to the shades of meaning, complexity, and subtle differentiations, deep richness which the mind cannot neatly label. A talent for nuance is a sense that there are series of ranges of connectable textures or contexts, meaning patterns, intriguing clusters of possibilities: an inspiring impression of tangled reality which the creative person then expresses in some artistic form of communication. As Briggs and Peat have observed,

> A poet unfolding nuance is like an equation iterating on the boundary between finite order and infinite chaos. The creator discovers self-similarities . . . an interlocking series of metaphors, or rather "reflectaphors." A reflectaphor is any creative device (including, in literature, such devices as irony, metaphor, simile, pun, paradox, synecdoche) that relies for its effect on creating in the mind of its audience an *unresolvable* tension between the similarities and differences of its terms.[70]

Uniting playful and poignant cross-references in an organic order that seems to live, forming a little cosmos—such is the work of creativity.[71] Simultaneous clarity and dizziness, expectations fulfilled and surprised, a floating devotion to a floating world of connectivity, eliciting "a reverence for uncertainty," the ability to wonder in openness, tender and supple like the baby Lao-tzu describes[72]—such is the work of creativity, able to live and grow in our world of like-minded stars and black holes, algae and elephants.

George Benson has said that "when Innovators [like Charlie Parker, John Coltrane, or Wes Montgomery] touch their instruments they affect the whole world. . . . It's a slow fire that burns right through the industry, it elevates the music from where it was, it takes it to another place. It's a difference that makes a difference, and change that introduces waves of change."[73] "Chunking" is one way to picture some of the factors involved in improvising. Chunking involves visualizing or imagining an accurate attractor: a pattern or form that has archetypal significance and depth in the psyche. In various arts and disciplines, chunking is possible when the unconscious comes into play. Chunking means one has assimilated the nuances of something—such as piano playing—and made them one's own, so that it has become second nature, so deeply familiar one could do it in one's sleep. By immersing oneself in the nuanced process through practice, one becomes fluent in it, fluid, flowing collaboratively with the possibilities. It has become part of one's unconscious reservoir of possibilities. Preparation is crucial; practice, mental rehearsals, virtual run-throughs, bit-by-bit focused visualizations.

Psychologists use the term "chunking" to describe the process by which we store familiar sequences in long-term memory as a single unit. This "chunk" or bundle then serves as material the skillful practitioner of an art or discipline can wield, play around with creatively along with other chunks. The master chunker can juggle and tentatively arrange a number of chunks together and arrange several clusters of chunks in nuanced patterns. A master chunker improvises playfully with these materials gathered over time. The unseen source of mastery is the imaginative play, which is partly unconscious. It is dreaming and the motivation of the joyful activity of having one's activities jibe successfully with the imagination and the appreciation of others. Think of Wes Montgomery playing guitar all night for the sheer joy of discovery, making his dreams come true and come to life. Or Jimi Hendrix improvising with his guitar at all hours of the day and night. It takes a lot of practice and, as Kurt Vonnegut is purported to have said, creative work enables one's soul to grow.[74] Our psyche weaves together what it feels intuitively belongs together and in this way our psyche gets itself together.

Drawn by the Updraft, Taking Risks Involved in Love

In old stories, beauty is often a powerful attractor stirring great efforts to reach beyond oneself. Consider the knights of the Round Table, who lived lives of dedication and chivalry inspired by beauty.[75] Soul-stirring beauty can stun, make one beholden, inspire one to serve the principle behind the beauty. It can lift one to relate to the mystery. The attractive one makes the beholder want to become more like that beauty, to develop an affinity and find a unity; thus beauty is a mysterious love-instigator. Beauty persuades even the roughest lout to arrange himself in the right order in relation to the wielder of beauty, to cultivate sensitive love like a knight errant. Beauty inspires us to become more nuanced. Beauty's magnificence enshrines actual significance and stirs dedication, loyalty, and deference, leading to self-transcendence.

Risks are involved every time one spontaneously takes off into the unknown. When the dull man sees spontaneous beauty sometimes he tries to dampen it, make it still and sensible like him, because risks mean uncertainty, loss of control, being at the mercy of the contingencies of providence. You might fall if you fly or go off-key if you sing, become obscene if you dream, lose your balance if you dance. Censors insist on sticking to the known, keeping a poker face, bluffing until death. A thaw in the status quo unleashes unknowns, uncontrollable forces. Better, they say, to stay in the illusion of settled safety. To say it's not a time for trying anything new is to say there are many people afraid to improvise and move onward, who instead look back to the (long-ago improvised) answers of the past which have become hardened and who wish to mechanically repeat an earlier era's successes. The spirit of creativity seen in improvisation in jazz and in other forms of music and art can offer courage and hope, faith in the ability to invent new ways, to those who have ears to hear.

Life is more like a web of song than a brick, and the cosmos is more like a Mind than a machine, more an unfolding process, a journey, than a static state. If life is at all like a brick, it is more like a brick in a temporary altar than a brick in a static wall or building. If life is at all like a machine, it is like a soft, intelligent, self-organizing, creative "machine." Life is more a system, organic and responsive; machines are too rigid and nonparticipatory in larger wholes of mysterious origin and creation to serve as good models. (Stephen King may have humanized an automobile in his novel *Christine*, but mechanical devices have their limits.) Just as ecosystems and communities of knowledge coexist like strands of a net, so the depths of existence and intricacies of relations can be better expressed in fractal-like compositions than in Euclidean ones.

In a process that has lasted billions of years, the planet Earth has initiated herself over long eons of changing conditions, educated and healed herself, learned to cultivate life in an atmosphere of interpenetration, and balanced and harmonized herself. We can learn from her creativity, as Brian Swimme suggests.[76] The center of the universe, the center of creativity, the dynamism for fashioning life is everywhere—it is all-pervasive, but the earth is the site that nurtures the potential so it can show what it has to reveal.[77] Complex adaptive systems, whether they are the size of an organism or the size of a planet, share similarities. Because of this, little lives like ours can learn from the cycles and swirls of the warm moist creative earth and her fertile diversity and patient overcoming of obstacles, her partness and wholeness. Human creativity is self-similar to the way Tao is said to work: through undoing knots, through the flow of softness and return, through simplicity and depth of Being. When the natural human craving to experience ever-new creativity is thwarted by regimentation, this craving may manifest in such impulses as obsession with youth and blindness to truly fresh creativity in mature expressions and vibrant lives. Repressing the flow of creative energies can turn them to poison. Eros will burn one way or another; it will kindle either visions of delight or a gleeful pyromania of vengeance. To recognize beauty and its evocations of depth is to honor creativity and share in it, to resonate with it and be a child of the watercourse Way, at home in the universe. In a holistic view protoplasm was ultimately woven out of the "soup" of neutrons (which were undifferentiated in the beginning of the universe); protoplasm's creative potential was enfolded in those neutrons, and the neutrons were loomed in lively lattices of protoplasm in the weaving of creative life's finely nuanced fabric. Hidden intelligence illumines every fractal level; we need only our eyes' deep presence to help us see with more clarity.[78] In the coming decades and centuries, if current trends continue, humans will discover more and more fractal-like structures in the cosmos.

In such a universe, those who look carefully observe deep patterns: "Knowledge is gained by learning; trust by doubt; skill by practice; and love by love,"[79] as Thomas Szasz said, and creativity generates creativity by flowing fractals. Knowing the beauty of the universe as a divine presence has been called the only way the soul can know its Source; unconscious seeking of beauty is said to be at the root of human straying and falling.[80] Beauty is inherent in the process of evolving; it is deeply built in to existence and in-

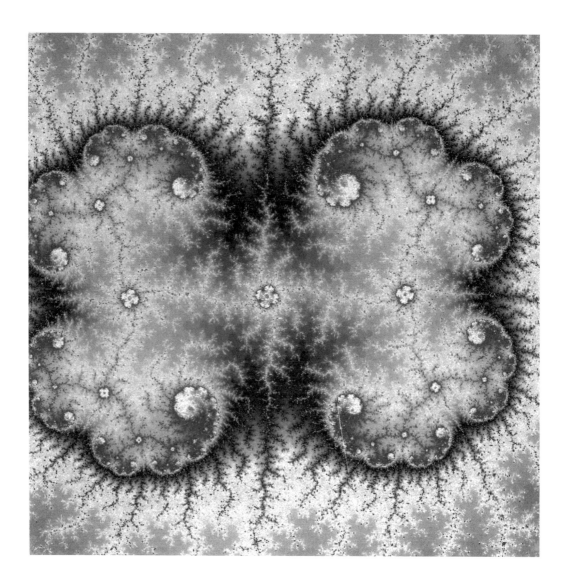

Fractal image. Courtesy of Michael Frame, Mathematics Dept., Yale University.

tricately tied to potentiality in humans. It is a perennial inspiration exciting reverence and gratitude, care and wisdom. French philosopher Simone Weil, who had Christian religious experiences but never converted from Judaism, sang of experiencing

> Fiery stars . . . mute . . . icy . . .
> in the heart suddenly their fire divine.[81]

The imaginative Swiss painter Paul Klee (1879–1940) wrote that "the artist . . . is a creature upon earth and a creature within the universe; a creature on one star among the other stars." By sharing a partship in the universe, recognizing a basic oneness with the world in which he finds himself, the artist, Klee suggests, extends creative forces in nature, abstracting meaning with his personality's own style. "Thus, the artist creates works of art, or participates in the creation of works, which are an image of the creative work of God. . . . Just as children imitate us while playing, so we, in the game of art, imitate the forces which created, and continue to create the world."[82] A Telugu proverb asks, "Will a tiger bring forth an ant?" The answer: No, a tiger will bring forth a small tiger. Similarly, the mysterious source of life brings forth a kindred creative mystery when it gives birth to humanity, creative and mysterious humanity.

ATOM SNOWFLAKE KINGDOM EARTH

Fractals in Literature

> Beginning again and again and again explaining composition and time is a natural thing. It is understood by this time that everything is the same except composition and time, composition and the time of the composition and the time in the composition.
> —Gertrude Stein[1]

Philosophers and Poets on the Signs of Mind in the Cosmos

"Science is spectrum analysis. Art is photosynthesis," as Karl Krauss said,[2] because art is about interrelatedness, catching subtle energies and using them, while science divides things into parts to find the law and get the advantage. Artists are intrigued by things that are mysteriously attractive. Julie Taymor, the director and theatrical designer who created the wildly imaginative costumes for the animals in the Broadway musical *The Lion King,* said in a television documentary about her work, "You always look for beauty because that is the only God-like thing in being human; the attempt to make something that moves the spirit is the only thing that keeps me going."[3] The desire to create art that moves the human spirit, art that exorcises fears and hatreds, art that captures the music of life keeps the creative process in artists active. Singing the poignancy of life keeps the dreamer and the poet in us involved and busy. Art and dreams involve unconscious processes in which symbols spontaneously arise. The unconscious must be expert in fractal wisdom because it can distill a whole constellation of situations into unforgettable and hard-to-fathom images: precise, often surreal, parts which stand for the whole. A genius for the most vivid images gives vitality to literature, visual arts, creative thinking. American sages such as Emerson and Thoreau (and visionaries and philosophers from other cultures, too) expressed some of their more important points using fractal-like images. Today there is an interest in relating concepts from chaos theory and other dynamic systems studies to the realm of literature.[4]

According to a Hindu proverb, blades of grass are weak when considered individually, but when they are braided together into a rope they are strong enough to hold a captive elephant securely. The strands which I bring together here are twisted together into threads, threads twisted together into cords, cords twisted together into rope. All these parts are interwoven to secure the idea that fractal-like images are found in the works of diverse poets and thinkers who observed patterns long before Benoit Mandelbrot coined the term "fractal." In this compilation of reflections on patterns in selected verses from around the world, I explore a fractal-like cosmic sensibility found in a variety of cultures and times. Although many images do not have all five of the qualities of a full-fledged fractal listed in the introduction, they do suggest to the imagination perceptions of wholeness in parts, a sense of infinity, striking similarities of parts of systems, and recursiveness to some degree or other. I call such evocative images which bring fractals to mind "semi-fractals."

Ralph Waldo Emerson (1803–1882), the American philosopher whose many interesting intuitions and important insights still stimulate thinking among creative people, entertained some thoughts on a trait we might now call the fractal-veined oneness of nature. "The unity of Nature—the unity in variety—which meets us everywhere" was the theme which inspired Emerson:

> All the endless variety of things make an identical impression. . . . The fable of Proteus has a cordial truth. A leaf, a drop, a crystal, a moment of time, is related to the whole, and partakes of the perfection of the whole. Each particle is a microcosm, and faithfully renders the likeness of the world.

Emerson thus presents a basic quality of fractals—parts reflect the nature of the whole. What is more, the parts share self-similarities with each other, bonded by kinship in Oneness:

> Michelangelo maintained that to an architect a knowledge of anatomy is essential. In Haydn's oratorios, the notes present to the imagination not only motions, as of the snake, the stag, and the elephant, but colors also; as the green grass. The law of harmonic sounds reappears in the harmonic colors. The granite is differenced in its laws only by the more or less of heat from the river that wears it away. The river, as it flows, resembles the air that flows over it; the air resembles the light which

traverses it with more subtle currents; the light resembles the heat which rides with it through Space. Each creature is only a modification of the other; the likeness in them is more than the difference, and their radical law is one and the same. A rule of one art, or a law of one organization, holds true throughout nature.

Emerson goes on to discuss his view of the reason for, or source of, this unity—the Spirit or Oversoul, which is known in some worldviews as Tao, Consciousness, Mind, or Universal Intelligence:[5]

> So intimate is this Unity, that, it is easily seen, it lies under the undermost garment of Nature, and betrays its source in Universal Spirit. For it pervades thought also. Every universal truth which we express in words, implies or supposes every other truth. *Omne verum vero consonat*. It is like a great circle or sphere, comprising all possible circles; which, however, may be drawn and comprise it in like manner. Every such truth is the absolute *Ens* seen from one side. But it has innumerable sides.[6]

This is quite different from the rather nihilist saying that there is no universal anything, only innumerable sides. Emerson, a great observer and discoverer of connections, went on in this vein to discuss the inseparability of acts and words in the human realm. But our concern here is the fact that the attempt to express self-similarity led Emerson to envision a great interesting fractal-like circle of circles.[7]

Similarly, in his meditation on bones, Emerson's contemporary and neighbor Henry David Thoreau (1817–1862) helps us envision the universal intelligence, Mind in the cosmos, the "meta-pattern that connects."[8]

> The skeleton which at first sight excites only a shudder in all mortals becomes at last not only a pure but suggestive and pleasing object to science. The more we know of it, the less we associate it with any goblin of our imaginations. The longer we keep it, the less likely it is that any such will come to claim it. We discover that the only spirit that haunts it is a universal intelligence which has created it in harmony with all nature. Science never saw a ghost, nor does it look for any, but it sees everywhere the traces, and it is itself the agent, of a Universal Intelligence.[9]

Thoreau felt that if humans kept in closer personal touch with the elevating vital streamings of nature and the Universal Intelligence within both nature and themselves, they would not externalize and dissipate their sense of the sacred. In his words, they wouldn't "build temples up" and thereby "bring themselves down." The way Thoreau described nature's vital streamings helps us see beyond their surfaces to their intricate circuits and elegant coursings within: "These motions everywhere in nature must surely be the

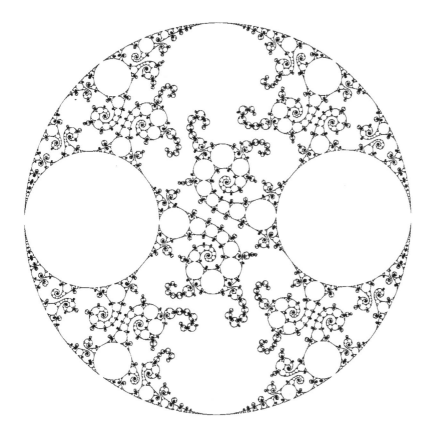

"Self-Homographic Fractal." A fractal image reveals aspects of wholeness; a unity composed of whole parts can offer a field for visual imaginings. A comparativist's ability to shift perspective and juxtapose elements is valuable in many processes, from decision making to problem solving and creative design. It is useful to be able to notice foreground and background, whole and part relationships. A fractal sensibility can help keep a flexible multiple-sided viewpoint while holding on to an encompassing coherence. Awareness of dynamic alternatives is essential to creativity, inventiveness, humor, and freedom. Courtesy of Benoit B. Mandelbrot, *The Fractal Geometry of Nature* (New York: W. H. Freeman, 1982).

circulations of God. The flowing sail, the running stream, the waving tree, the roving wind—whence else their infinite health and freedom. I can see nothing so proper and holy as relaxed play and frolic in this bower God built for us."[10]

Thoreau's perceptive discussion of veins, fingertips like drops of water, and other natural correlations and likenesses shows a subtle and precise poetic intuition at work in playful observation of nature. In his last book, *Faith in a Seed,* he notes that oval or cone-shaped stands of pine trees are often found in hardwood forests and that both the tree and its fruit are cone-shaped. This is but one example of his fractal-like sensibility, a sensibility implied in a line from *Walden,* "The sun is but a morning star," which intimates more and more beyond, as if each part reflects more which is beyond it within a similarity-sharing whole.[11]

American poet Robinson Jeffers (1887–1962) also wrote about glimpsing signs of a single consciousness that enlivens the universe: "We scream and laugh," he writes in his poem "The Beginning and the End," for human beings are "clamorous animals" who seem to have been born with howls, destined to die with groans. Jeffers notes that the stones in the yard seem to prefer silence, but also that each thing in existence has its own kind of awareness; as the cells in a person's body feel and feed and influence each other

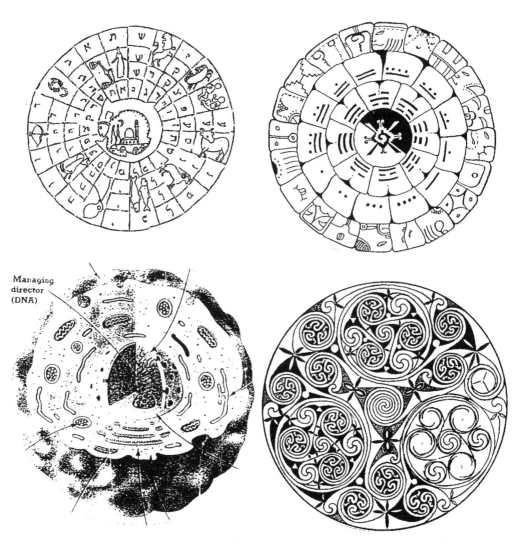

A variety of circular patterns. Upper left: an old image of Jerusalem in the center of a zodiac chart. Upper right: a Mayan diagram of cosmic forces with the basic polarities in dynamic interaction in the center. (This yin-yang-like symbol is known as *Hunab Ku*.) Lower left: a diagram of a cell from a biology workbook for children. Lower right: a circular design from the Book of Kells (800 C.E.), with clusters of spirals in circles. Some Celtic patterns reiterate coils within coils at different scales, dynamically giving rise to each other. Book of Kells drawing courtesy of George Bain, *Celtic Art: The Methods of Construction* (New York: Dover, 1973).

"each unto the all." And as the cells of a person make one total being, all things together "make one being, one consciousness, one life, one God . . ." Jeffers observes that although one may measure a comet's orbit or a hawk's dive in the sky, the human mind can never be calculated. He asserts that rocks and earth and planets and stars and galaxies have their own share of consciousness, and he says that it takes an animal's nervous system to bring this consciousness into focus.[12]

This poet's intuition reflects expansively, suggesting a mystic's vision. He speaks of consciousness as an infinite dimension pervading and reflecting the cosmos. Jeffers envisions the mutual influence of animals, stones, cells, and minerals, all in vital interrelationship. Ecology has confirmed this web of interexistence. A further correlate of this is that in such a universe the creative person is one who "catches the wave" of creative energy that vitalizes and circulates through the whole creative universe.

The knack of glimpsing a consciousness of wholeness in the parts, intuiting self-similarities throughout the whole, shows up in the work of many poets. Russian poet Iosif Utkin's "The Tale of Red-Haired Motl" illustrates this:

> Travel any road,
> Or go to any country.
> Every house is a motherland,
> Or an ocean to itself.[13]

In each house in condensed or subtle form is found the nation or even more—the formless chaotic process of potential—all the streets lined with houses, all the countries dotted with towns and their many streets, all the countries multiplying all these elements, and thus full of the whole, and kindred, self-reflective and similar. The large is in the minuscule, and so one could start anywhere and find cosmic infinity. A suggestive Ashanti proverb puts it this way: "The ruin of the nation begins in the home of its people."[14] As we travel through levels and scales to reach the immensely vast and deep, we see reality as realms embedded in realms nested in realms.

In "Villanelle of the Nuclear Physicists," Adam LeFevre wrote,

> The smallest particle has been split
> We must split it again and again
> until the inside is outside of it.[15]

His poem "The Autopsy" unfolds through images enclosed in images to dramatically illustrate the quest for truth through endless insides. It is a recursive series of openings, surprises. It is not a fractal, yet it shares a quality of ever-new vistas with the movies of fractals that endlessly zoom in on the images within the Mandelbrot set.

> It was up to the doctors.
>
> They unzipped the dead man
> and discovered sleeping, made out of coal.
> They unzipped the sleeping
> and discovered windows made of distance.
> They unzipped the windows

and discovered an oriole, also dead.
They unzipped the oriole
and discovered what they thought were human tears,
but chemical analysis proved it was sea water.
They unzipped the sea water
and discovered footprints.
They unzipped the footprints
and discovered more footprints,
which continued until the wee hours of the morning,
when the doctors unzipped the footprints
and discovered a deep sky,
which they immediately concluded
was the cause of death.[16]

Rainer Maria Rilke is another poet who "unzips" many possibilities to find further vistas and conveys the sense that there is always more and that though large patterns hold—spirals and circlings—there is a basic momentous unconsciousness or ambiguous indeterminacy as well. A confusion of the personally known and the impersonal unknown magnitudes marks the poetry of a great quest.

I live my life in growing orbits
which move out over the things of the world.
Perhaps I can never achieve the last,
but that will be my attempt.

I am circling God, around the ancient tower,
and I have been circling for a thousand years,
and I still don't know if I am a falcon, or a storm,
or a great song."[17]

It was Rilke who reminded us that if we go with an attentive focus to the smallest thing—a grain of sand—we will find a master there. That is, a mystery, able to teach us lessons if we inquire, waits inside the negligible textures and objects we are usually too busy to notice.[18]

Mark Strand's poem "A Piece of the Storm" depicts something vary small and exquisite as both ideal and real, and maybe able to stand for everything—the whole.

A snowflake, a blizzard of one, weightless, entered your room
And made its way up to the arm of the chair where you, looking up
From your book, saw it the moment it landed. . . .

A solemn waking
to brevity, to the lifting and falling away of attention, swiftly,
A time between times. . . .

In the smallness of one flake all the snowstorms that ever melted come to mind and pass, the moment fading into the eternal now. In the same collection is Strand's poem "What It Was":

An endless depth
of smallness; a song, but less than a song, something drowning
Into itself, something going, a flood of sound, but less
Than a sound; the last of it, the blank of it,
The tender small blank of it filling its echo.[19]

Even the inconsequential "insignificant," if it is met with love, provides a start on the path to ultimate significance and real consequences.

This fractal-depicting passage from the center part of Paul Lawson's poem "Any Old Stone" stands for the whole:

Any old stone—you think it can't talk?
Dumb old stone? Ho! Every atom in it talks,
every part of every atom talks. Just listen.[20]

Any old stone knows more than an unconscious human, it would seem—knows how to hold itself together, knows what it wants and how to get it, knows its place of belonging, and so forth. Grains of sand, rocks, snowflakes, and trees reveal common powers to psyches that are receptive. Songs and storms and birds and spirals share certain similarities. Refreshing artworks feature surprising juxtapositions that connect disparate creatures and elements of creation through echoes or reflections or resemblances. How naturally Mark Twain portrays a church on a mountainside, mixing several scales: "A scarred and wrinkled precipice rises. . . . On a tiny bench halfway up its vast wall sits a little snowflake of a church, no bigger than a martin box apparently."[21] A mountain, a church, a birdhouse, a snowflake—all are one in the freely imagining mind.

Poetry can induce ecstasy by confusing the humble and minute with the vast and glorious. Alfred Dorn's celebratory realization of the whole configured subtly and magnificently in any snowflake brings this out:

Here is a snowflake in my hand, like some
White Athens in the palm of history,
A moment's fragile Parthenon. . . .

And I a god who holds it as it dies
To sudden dew. This molecule of world
May be dominion of a subtler nation,
Inviolate to our eyes. If atoms dream,
What kingdom claims this melting star of snow![22]

In eight brief lines, Dorn brings from a crystal of icy form the exquisite greatness of Greek civilization at one of its peaks. The poet is a maker, revealing that atoms may dream, that there are "subtler nations." The poet shows the play of scales by raising questions which freely wander, interconnecting realms of star and dew, molecule, eye, and world.

William Blake is most famous for calling attention to the infinitely large represented in the infinitely small:

> To see a world in a grain of sand
> and a heaven in a wild flower
> hold infinity in the palm of your hand
> and eternity in an hour.

Such similarities often evoke in poets a vaster vision or deeper love. Robert Bly traces the meta-pattern that connects a woman's body and forms of nature to open an experience of the eternal in his poem "Ferns":

> It was among ferns I learned about eternity
> Below your belly there is a curly place.
> Through you I learned to love the ferns on that bank,
> and the curve the deer's hoof leaves in sand.

Woman's body mediates between the disconnected male and the realms of nature and the beyond. Entering the warm split-up-the-middleness of elusive beauty, awakening man traces depths and learns how his longings are involved in cosmic correspondences.[23]

Poet Ruth Whitman's verses adorn a public monument in Boston, visualizing the recursive patterns inherent in the generativity of mothering: "I will be planted again and again. I will awake in the eyes of their children's children."[24] The whole pattern of generation involves the givers of life sharing in the future lives of kin. In a certain sense they are present, again and again.

Some poems express the way personal situations reflect their surroundings on a smaller scale, such as this one by Marie Ponsot:

> . . . hunched in a shell of coat, a blindered hood.
> Alone a long time, I remember sun—
> poor magic effort to undo the fog.
> Fog hoods me. But the hood of fog is sun.[25]

This short poem by Frank Jones expresses the reality of the mountain climber looking out from the vantage point he has gained onto the vista ahead. He thinks he has attained the ultimate, but his belief turns out to be an illusion caused by the part's not fully knowing the whole:

> After the apex, what?
> Why of course, one peak
> after another.[26]

"Creation." Iroquois artist Arnold Jacobs uses self-similar leaf or eye shapes to show the harmony of bird, tree, land, turtle, water, and radiant sun. Copyright © Arnold Jacobs. Used with permission.

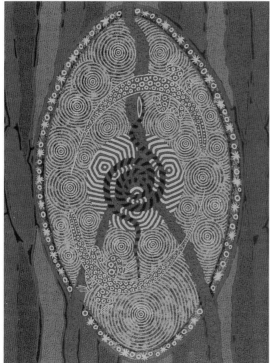

Pirla Warna Warna, by Aboriginal artist Malcolm Jagamarra. Australian Mission to the United Nations.

The letter P, showing coils within coils within coils, on a page of the Book of Kells. About 800 C.E.

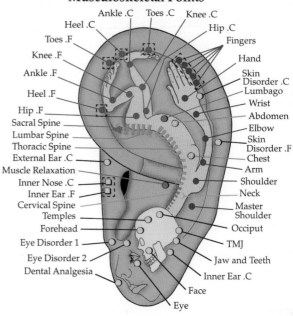

Musculoskeletal Points

Ankle .C   Toes .C   Knee .C

Heel .C   Hip .C

Toes .F   Fingers

Knee .F   Hand

Ankle .F   Skin Disorder .C

Heel .F   Lumbago

Hip .F   Wrist

Sacral Spine   Abdomen

Lumbar Spine   Elbow

Thoracic Spine   Skin Disorder .F

External Ear .C   Chest

Muscle Relaxation   Arm

Inner Nose .C   Shoulder

Inner Ear .F   Neck

Cervical Spine   Master Shoulder

Temples   Occiput

Forehead   TMJ

Eye Disorder 1   Jaw and Teeth

Eye Disorder 2   Inner Ear .C

Dental Analgesia   Face

Eye

The acupuncture points on the ear corresponding to parts of the body, another example of how "the whole is in the parts." From a chart accompanying Terry Oleson, *Auriculotherapy Manual: Chinese and Western Systems of Ear Acupuncture* (Los Angeles: Health Care Alternatives, 1998).

A sense of fractal patterns helps us understand old and new art and architecture better. Detail of an advertisement, showing recursive structures in traditional architecture of Thailand, and postmodern architecture of Sydney, Australia. Courtesy of Thai Airways International.

Fractal image entitled "Peaceful Border Between Three Countries." There is some of the other in each, and this sense of wholeness keeps the three at peace. Courtesy of Manfred Schroeder, *Fractals, Chaos, Power Laws: Minutes from an Infinite Paradise* (New York: W. H. Freeman, 1991).

Merren Parker,
Basking.

Merren Parker,
A Gift from the Sea.

Merren Parker,
Dolphin Spiral.

Merren Parker,
Dolphin Spiral 2.

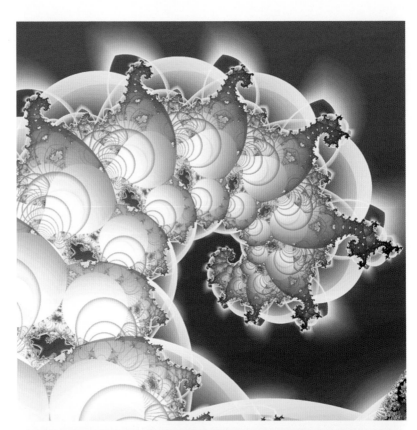

Merren Parker,
Metamorphosis.

Merren Parker,
North and South.

Merren Parker,
Spirals with Phantom.

Merren Parker,
Devourer.

Merren Parker,
The Thinker.

Merren Parker,
Spiral with Eye.

Merren Parker,
Ammonite.

Fractal image
B1SODJ01.PNG.
Courtesy of Paul W.
Carlson, *Mind-Boggling Fractals* CD-ROM.

Fractal image B2TBLJ01.PNG. Courtesy of Paul W. Carlson, *Mind-Boggling Fractals* CD-ROM.

Fractal image C11SDJ03.PNG. Courtesy of Paul W. Carlson, *Mind-Boggling Fractals* CD-ROM.

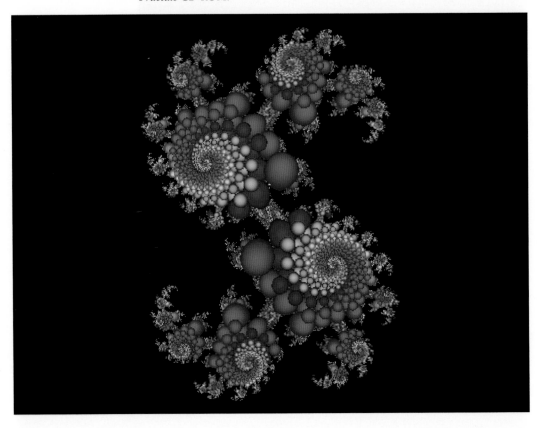

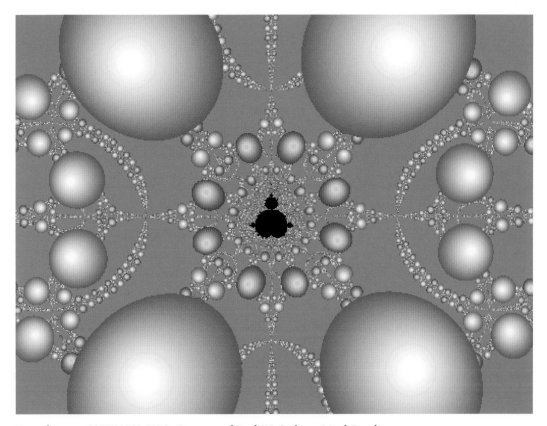

Fractal image C1SPDM03.PNG. Courtesy of Paul W. Carlson, *Mind-Boggling Fractals* CD-ROM.

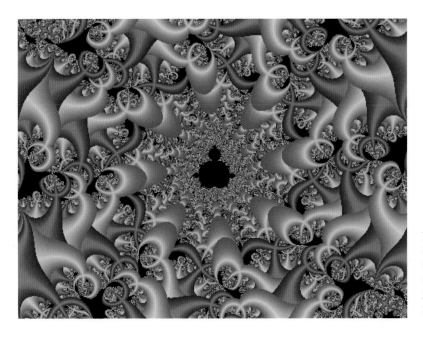

Fractal image C1STKM01.PNG. Courtesy of Paul W. Carlson, *Mind-Boggling Fractals* CD-ROM.

Fractal image C2SODJ01.PNG. Courtesy of Paul W. Carlson, *Mind-Boggling Fractals* CD-ROM.

Fractal image
PSSPHJ02.PNG.
Courtesy of Paul W.
Carlson, *Mind-Boggling Fractals* CD-ROM.

Fractal image
N4STKM04.PNG.
Courtesy of Paul W.
Carlson, *Mind-Boggling Fractals* CD-ROM.

Fractal image CMSQRM03.PNG. Courtesy of Paul W. Carlson, *Mind-Boggling Fractals* CD-ROM.

Fractal image C9RSGJ01.PNG. Courtesy of Paul W. Carlson, *Mind-Boggling Fractals* CD-ROM.

Fractal image CMLEVM01.PNG. Courtesy of Paul W. Carlson, *Mind-Boggling Fractals* CD-ROM.

Fractal image CMPTLM04.PNG. Courtesy of Paul W. Carlson, *Mind-Boggling Fractals* CD-ROM.

Fractal image S2CONJ01.PNG. Courtesy of Paul W. Carlson, *Mind-Boggling Fractals* CD-ROM.

Fractal image C1TBLM04.PNG. Courtesy of Paul W. Carlson, *Mind-Boggling Fractals* CD-ROM.

Fractal image C4STKJ01.PNG. Courtesy of Paul W. Carlson, *Mind-Boggling Fractals* CD-ROM.

Sometimes life seems like a fractal called "Devil's staircase," in which there are steps made of smaller steps, in endless progression. The infinite expanse is straightforward, mountains and rivers without end.

In the works of many mystics we find a connection between innocence and the infinite, between infancy and infinity. The rediscovery of depth vision or fluid wholeness involves a return to states of mind known in childhood. Alfred, Lord Tennyson (1809–1892), who reiterated his own name in solitude as a kind of meditative mantra, spoke of "the inner infinity," which is found in human life and within the innards of nature. The opening of his poem "Vastness" conveys some of the fractal sensibility found in his meditative verse: "Many a hearth upon our dark globe sighs after many a vanished face, / Many a planet by many a sun may roll with the dust of a vanished race."[27] Such reflections on distance, which are fractal-like though not exactly fractals, can heighten our sense of wonder regarding our earthly predicaments.

The Chinese poet Ch'iu-Ti Liu evokes the undividedness of childhood's vision, but he gets us there by listing paradoxes to mull over:

"Devil's Staircase" fractal. Courtesy of Benoit B. Mandelbrot, *The Fractal Geometry of Nature* (New York: W. H. Freeman, 1982).

Separation is pregnant with connections.
Trees are parted by the wind,
And yet are parts of the wind—but Listen!
Your breath touches ten thousand plants
That measure the sky with their own stalks.
You embrace them into a chorus of the Whole:
They belong to your songs, as
Your songs belong to them.
The same way shall you embrace your own roots.
In your memory of swamps trembling with algae,
You will teach your roots to walk into a tree.
A child walks . . . [28]

Thomas Traherne's Treasures of Childhood:
A Mystic's Fractal-Like Paradisal Reflections

When the One self-reiterating continuously flows
the thousand-fold divided arches
firmly fitting interlinked each into the next
then the joy of life streams out from everything
from tiniest point to vastest star
and all strife and every conflict
find eternal peace in God.

—Johann Wolfgang von Goethe[29]

Seventeenth-century English poet Thomas Traherne wrote about how he marveled at the glories of nature in his childhood, when "som thing infinit Behind evry thing appeared."[30] Later in life, the mystic recovered a child-fresh new perception. For most people, the vitality of the original experience is diminished by obsession with finite matters, but the mystic returns to the child's vision at a deeper, higher level and scale on life's spiral. Traherne believed that each person born is given a paradise on the condition that he keep a childlike vision, which is lost through conforming, competing, succumbing to the pressures of existence, exploiting things and people as objects instead of working within the sensitive framework of mutuality the Jewish theologian Martin Buber named *I and Thou*.[31]

Traherne's writings are celebrations of the sense of infinite blessings. He appreciated in detail the endless gifts God had bestowed on him and on all people. In some passages he speaks of the soul's fractal-like nature and the need for a longing vision:

He therfore hath not made us infinit Treasures only in Extent: and Souls infinit to see and Enjoy them: which is to measure and run Parallel with them: but in Depth also they are evry where infinit being infinit in Excellency. And the Soul is a Miraculous Abyss of infinit Abysses, an Undrainable Ocean, an inexhausted fountain of Endles Oceans, when it will exert it self to fill and fathom them.. . . .Unless we expect this with infinit Ardency, we are a Lazy Kind of Creatures Good for Nothing.[32]

Thus Traherne sees the soul as a depth of depths, which may themselves hold further depths, since endlessness is invoked here. In this sense his suggestive images are rather fractal-like.

Traherne recalled how in childhood he saw fresh Eden-like scenes, and he spoke of a childlike return to them as an adult, of regaining youthful vision and enjoying a glorious timeless kingdom again:

> The Corn was Orient and Immortal Wheat, which never should be reaped, nor was ever sown. I thought it had stood from everlasting to everlasting. The Dust and Stones of the Street were as Precious as GOLD. The Gates were at first the End of the World, The Green Trees when I saw them first through one of the Gates Transported and Ravished me; their Sweetness and unusual Beauty made my Heart leap, and almost mad with Extasie, they were such strange and Wonderfull Thing: The Men! O what Venerable and Reverend Creatures did the Aged seem! Immortal Cherubims! And yong Men Glittering and Sparkling Angels and Maids Tumbling in the Street, and Playing, were moving Jewels. I knew not that they were Born or should Die. But all things abided Eternaly as they were in their Proper Places. Eternity was Manifest in the Light of the Day, and som thing infinit Behind evry thing appeared: which talked with my Expectation and moved my Desire. The Citie seemed to stand in Eden, or to be Built in Heaven. The Streets were mine, the Temple was mine, the People were mine, their Clothes and Gold and Silver was mine, as much as their Sparkling Eys Fair Skins and ruddy faces. The Skies were mine, and so were the Sun and Moon and Stars, and all the World was mine, and I the only Spectator and Enjoyer of it. I knew no Churlish Properties, nor Bounds nor Divisions: but all Proprieties and Divisions were mine: all Treasures and the Possessors of them. So that with much adoe I was corrupted; and made to learn the Dirty Devices of this World. Which now I unlearn, and becom as it were a little Child again, that I may enter into the Kingdom of GOD.[33]

Traherne's understanding of the source of the paradisal wealth of infinite beauty is very revealing. It is related to Bateson's meta-pattern that connects. It is the sacred as the unifying relatedness, the relationships which pulse among the parts as the subtleties of living wholeness. His description vividly conveys belonging, participation, co-inherence. Nothing can be valuable in selfish separation; ultimately all must be known and enjoyed in a fractal-like all-in-one, one-in-all experience of togetherness, not isolation.[34]

> That any thing may be found to be an infinit treasure, its Place must be found in Eternity, and in Gods Esteem. For as there is a Time, so there is a Place for all Things. Evry thing in its Place is Admirable Deep and Glorious: out of its Place like a Wandering Bird, is Desolat and Good for Nothing. How therfore it relateth to God and all Creatures must be seen before it can be Enjoyed. And this I found by many in-

stances. The Sun is Good, only as it relateth to the Stars, to the Seas, to your Ey, to the feilds, &c. As it relateth to the Stars it raiseth their Influences; as to the Seas it melteth them and maketh the Waters flow; as to your Ey, it bringeth in the Beauty of the World; as to the feilds; it clotheth them with Fruits and flowers: Did it not relate to others it would not be Good. Divest it of these Operations, and Divide it from these Objects it is Useless and Good for nothing. And therfore Worthless, because Worthles and Useless go together. A Piece of Gold cannot be Valued, unless we Know how it relates to Clothes, to Wine, to Victuals, to the Esteem of Men, and to the Owner. Som little Piece in a Kingly Monument severd from the rest hath no Beauty at all. It enjoys its valu in its Place, by the Ornament it gives to, and receivs from all the Parts. By this I discerned, that even a little Knowledg could not be had in the Mysterie of Felicity, without a great deal. And that that was the reason why so many were ignorant of its nature, and why so few did attain it. For by the Labor required to much Knowledg they were discouraged, and for lack of much did not see any Glorious motives to allure them.[35]

Traherne's descriptive analysis of the interweaving network of qualities, the all-or-nothing characteristics, the embeddedness within a cosmos of living relations, is one which would be valuable for those who have begun to be dissatisfied with purely material motives or selfish behaviors, for those tired of seeking self-satisfaction through merely calculative thinking—if only they did not suffer from a jaundiced eye. Actually, the opening of the "gates of paradise," allowing a glimpse of eternal depth, may not be so rare. An interviewer once reminded Robert Graves of an experience of expanded sensibilities he had had at the age of twelve, which he'd talked about previously. Graves said, "You probably had a similar vision, and you've forgotten it. It needn't be a vision of everything; so long as it's a foretaste of Paradise. Blake had one. All poets and painters who have that extra 'thing' in their work seem to have had this vision and never let it be destroyed by education."[36] The poet and artist may seem odd to conventional people because they have kept their fresh "beginner's mind" or because their lives preserve or rediscover it. They may at times seem antisocial, reclusive, or hypersensitive as they seek ways to keep working out their haunting vision.

An American example of such a person might be the poet Emily Dickinson (1830–1886), who wrote many poems featuring images of and references to heaven, hidden relationships, and freely imagined scales. This one envisions the vast number of the risen at the Resurrection:

> No crowd that has occurred
> Exhibit I suppose,
> The general attendance
> That Resurrection does.

Circumference be free,
The long-subjected Grave
Assert his primogeniture,
The Dust adjust and live

On atoms features place,
All multitudes that were,
Efface in the comparison,
As suns annul a star.[37]

The first stanza envisions the astronomical number of the multitudes appearing on the day of resurrection from the dead—the
greatest get-together ever. In her poetic vision, scale is expandable
and fluidly free. Dust can come to life, "circumference be free"
inclusively, the circular soul and circle of all graves being transcended. If one were to place human features on the atoms so that
each atom beamed with a face, the number of people who have
existed throughout time would blot out that vast multitude, just
as suns can eclipse a mere star. The poet celebrates great awe in
her imagining of all the souls together and employs playfulness in
interchanging scales with a sense of cosmic freedom.

What is the nature of human beings? We could say that the
universe kept trying to evolve a conscious being who would be
like a living mirror in which it could look at itself more as a
whole—a full-length mirror instead of a tiny fragment. It sought
a being with awe, awareness, reverence, and understanding to
celebrate with knowledge and feeling, with rituals of changing
seasons and life and death, the sacred reality of the cosmos. It
gave humans the gift of the ability to be stunned with wonder at
creation's grandeur, the ability to love and appreciate the skies
and mountains, seas and deserts, forests and rivers, flora and
fauna. It evolved humanity as a participatory mirror with a voice
to help sing the sun across the sky, to recognize the rhythmic
solstices and join in the dance. The universe sought a loop of
life lacing back into its source. Humans are born bedazzled into
an amazing cosmos. Johnny Thunder's rock song "I'm Alive!"
says it well. We are astonished, at our healthy best and our peak
moments, at the glory of being. When this astonishment is lost,
we try many ways to regain it, some of them unconscious, negative, and destructive, as when we use drugs. But as Mencius
said, to recover the mind of the child should be the point of education and the goal of life.[38] How does this bedazzlement relate
to the facts of life that involve suffering and decay, the Buddhist
diagnosis that life is suffering caused by craving, and the realities
of violence, horror, destruction? Only with a heart kindled with
appreciation and love for life in all its poignancy can we work
with compassion to relieve pain or bring joy and beauty to others. St. Francis, Mother Teresa, and other inspired souls show us

how to comfort and serve with love. When we see suffering and great need, it is moving to see the human touch—the caring, soothing, consideration, caresses, and motherly love that nurse with gentle strength are so gratifying and so natural. Sympathy that is extended to soothe a fellow soul's aches beautifully enacts fractals of compassion. Yet at times the human touch seems rare; we have built up defenses against the inconvenience and discomfort of feeling our shared human depths. Kind treatment of others comes out of the unspoiled sense of wonder and kinship known as love. Factors of modern life have dehumanized us, mechanized us, shaped us into individuals who see others as objects. Fear makes us shrink away from the personal opening. By "otherizing" fellow humans we become inhumane; we lose the ability to feel what others feel. Ego separates us and offers us agendas that are selfish, dry, mean. So Mencius told the Chinese to regain the child's state. Jesus said, "You must be born as a child again," and Tibetan Buddhism teaches the priority of regaining the "child mind." Thus this view is not limited to any single culture; examples from all over the world speak of this vision of divine glory in the universe.[39]

The soul is partial to the whole. We say partiality exists when there is a special affinity or favoritism. A baby might be partial to the features of her mother. "Partial" also suggests a play on words, as if to say the soul is part of a larger whole and longs for wholeness. What sorts of wholeness? In dreams, one's unconscious configures the whole of one's situation in images. There are social wholes to which we wish to belong and cosmic wholeness known variously as Tao, *atman,* Love, the One, God, and so forth. Consciousness in the soul, the Self, reaches out to larger wholeness as it is able. Fractals, with their infinite reflections of wholeness in parts, depict this. Of course, suffering can also reflect the fractal sensibility, as lines from Oscar Wilde's "Ballad of Reading Gaol" testify: "All that we know who lie in gaol is that the wall is strong; / And that each day is like a year, a year whose days are long."[40] The claustrophobic slow replication of days made up of years, which are in turn made up of long days, produces a sensation of soul-stifling suffocation. We easily imagine seconds which tick like minutes, and minutes long as hours. The soul's seeking of the whole seems to need only freedom to happily iterate itself.

Fractals Everywhere and Voices of Infinity: Other Mystic Poets of Cosmic Sensibility

Muslim mystical poet Mahmud ibn 'Abd al-Karim Shabistari is known for singing of the transcendental reflected in the creation.

In his book *The Secret Rose Garden,* written in the fourteenth century, he told his listeners to find the vast hidden glory of God in each small thing, because the nature of the universe is to scintillate subtly everywhere, reflecting the divine:

> Know the world from end to end is a mirror;
> In each atom a hundred suns are concealed.
> If you pierce the heart of a single drop of water,
> From it will flow a hundred clear oceans;
> If you look intently at each speck of dust,
> In it you will see a thousand beings,
> A gnat in its limbs is like an elephant;
> In name a drop of water resembles the Nile,
> In a barley-corn's heart is stored a hundred harvests,
> Within a millet-seed a word exists,
> In an insect's wing is an ocean of life,
> A heaven is concealed in the pupil of an eye,
> The core in the centre of the heart is small,
> Yet the Lord of both worlds will enter there.[41]

This Sufi poet's vision was informed by the Qur'an[42] and by other Muslim poets who were mystics. The listener to this poem can open up each bit and find infinite wonders and relations.[43] Although strictly speaking the poem is not a full-fledged fractal, it evokes the vast potential hidden in the tiny in many realms of life. The theme of the infinite within the finite is common to fractals and to Shabistari's images. In the world of our experiences, wonder is reflected infinitely—if suns are in each atom, if oceans are in drips, if populations crowd in dustmotes, if a single barley corn holds harvests, if an eye holds heaven, then all bespeak a deep truth, a mysterious consciousness in the heart. Miracles pass us by if we are otherwise occupied; mystic poets are on watch to see the "imprisoned splendor" and are stirred to sing the wonders they find hiding in each little thing. As Lahiji's commentary on this poem asserts,

> Man is the eye of the world, and . . . the world is the reflection of God, and . . . God Himself is the light of this eye. Man is the eye which looks into the mirror and just as the mirror reflects the face of the person who is looking into it, the reflection possesses itself an eye, and in the same time that the eye looks at it also God, which is the eye of man, looks at Himself through man. . . . From one side God is the eye of man; from another, man is the eye of the world, because the world and man are only one, man being its eye. This man is called the perfect man. Since man is a resume of everything that exists, he is a world in himself and the relation that exists between God and man exists between man and the world.[44]

Perhaps we should call this cosmic quality "self-reflectiveness," since "self-similarity" has such specific meanings in the realm of mathematics and geometry.

The Christian mystic St. Teresa of Avila, who lived in the sixteenth century, wrote of the nature of the soul in her book *The Interior Castle*. The soul is a "beautiful castle." It is "the pearl of the East," the "tree of life beside the divine waters of life." In Teresa's vision of life, the divine sun at the center of the soul, when obscured by sin, stops sharing its light with the soul, even though by nature the soul is able to enjoy the presence of God, just as a crystal can reflect the sun. In this view, each soul is a multifaceted translucent gem or crystal, but when the crystal is covered by a thick black cloth, hiding it from the sunshine, it is not irradiated. Radiant souls beam forth in the state of grace. The different mansions of the soul-castle are like facets of the psyche-gem.[45] The light reflecting from the numerous surfaces of the multifaceted gem is something like the net of Indra we encounter in Hinduism and Buddhism. Of course in the Buddhist image of the net of Indra there are reflections of reflections of reflections, and so on . . .

The mystic's taste for infinity, the artist's eye for fractals, the poet's (or scientist's) sense of scales and pattern recursiveness in a continuum of oneness—all are interrelated. They are not to be confused, but they are not to be kept separate either. Traherne and Teresa, Emerson and Bly are not alone in their exuberance—even understated Japanese culture has its exponents of the outburst of gentle cosmic vision exploding and dazzling one wherever one focuses. Zen literature is also awash with a playful cosmic sensibility. "A seed of mustard conceals Mount Sumeru." And "in a handful of water scooped up in my palm the mermaids are seen dancing to their hearts' content." In the experience of *satori* these miracles are everyday occurrences, Zen scholar D. T. Suzuki tells us.[46]

The literature expounding the Buddha Mind has many such depictions. There is an orderly interpenetration of all in all: scoop up water and find a moon in your hands; carry flowers and your clothes are scented with them, as the Zen saying goes. Scales seem interchangeable in one's awakened and expanded perceptions: "Taking up one blade of grass, use it as a sixteen-foot golden Buddha."[47] The moment contains time's variety enfolded (like coded DNA in every cell) and all the Buddhas are present each second: "In one moment variety unfolds / In one moment Buddhahood is complete."[48] This sensibility is part of Western poetry, from Blake's grain of sand to Kelly Cherry's "God's Loud Hand," in which she writes, "If it is not raining, there may be a blue sky like a blessing / being pronounced over a meal, which, / though taken alone, / tastes of life"[49]—the whole is available in the minute sample.

In Zen and Tibetan Buddhism and Tantric yoga, the awakening of the microcosm to its identity with the macrocosm constitutes the goal; connectedness is brought out through symbols, gestures, rites, mantras, visualizations, and poetry. "All is one" has become a cliche in pop culture, usually misunderstood but good for a laugh. ("Make me one with everything," the Buddhist said to the hot dog vendor.) Yet a cosmic sense is found in all the religions. "Whoever saves one life saves the world entire" is a teaching of Judaism, dramatized with an inscription engraved inside a ring at the end of the film *Schindler's List*.

Annie Dillard, an American creative writer who seems to have a rather mystical outlook in some of her writings, neatly brings out a vision of the whole working in each part:

> Thought advances, and the world creates itself, by the gradual positing of and belief in a series of ideas. Time and space are in touch with the Absolute at base. Eternity sockets twice into time and space curves, bound and bound by idea. Matter and spirit are of a piece but distinguishable. And the universe is real and not a dream, not a manufacture of the senses; subject may know object, knowledge may proceed, and Holy the Firm is in short the philosopher's stone. . . . People are reasoned, while God is mad. They love only beauty; who knows what God loves?[50]

This is an attempt at a cosmic sensibility, but it is still somewhat linear in a quirky way—eternity's relation to time seems unnecessarily limited in its double socket. Often the best poems and creative writing are like trickster stories, reminding us not to expect simple linear routines from the depths of existence; the sacred has many loopholes, the better to play around with us. A simple switching of scales or perspectives makes us marvel. Think of Lauryn Hill's song "Everything is Everything" or a poem by Charles Wright which suggests, "All things are found in all things, / Wind in the peach trees, time's dust: it's in light that light exists."[51]

Assertions and denials of participation and uniqueness play games in a prose poem entitled "Fractals" by William Aiken. The poem presents images of daily life being lived and time passing, and its final third goes like this:

> And do not say we live by memory—we do not live at all. The firebush has fractals, bloom and branch repeating its sharp crosses, but not me. House sparrows take a town with pluck and beauty, their fields and back yards spent, yet all the streets to love. Each day, a trowel in my hand, I scratch in the garden like a flicker, my buff body bent, a little red on the secondaries. And do not tell me yesterday comes again, pulling the collar up, smoothing the hair down. Nothing lasts. It all needs repeating.[52]

We know, from repeated experiences, from the repercussions of our actions and the impacts others make upon us, from sharing and incorporating nutrients, love, ideas, and many other things at various levels, that we are interrelated. All the nodes of the net are selves, selves which self-organize and relate to each other. "Atoms and flames, tornadoes and trees, each represents a centered, unseen, shaping dynamism. . . . The whole system of life resembles a self. . . . It organizes all sorts of materials, creatures and energy into a coherent, self-sustaining process," Brian Swimme, a scientist who is also a poet, tells us.[53]

Psychologist and consciousness researcher Jean Huston speaks of mystics as achieving a clearer kind of knowing which, like a hologram, sees each part in reference to the whole. She notes that some kinds of meditation set up a synchronistic firing of cells in the brain, an integrated "macrophasic" wave, with certain cells engaging other cells expansively in a kind of symphony of the creative mind. She believes that some mystics, such as St. Francis of Assisi or St. Teresa of Avila, attain a "holonomy," that is, a knowledge of wholeness, through their participation in a deeper wholeness of human potential, and their experience shows other humans that they too can know deeper patterns of consciousness.[54] Yogis affirm this and practice disciplines of meditation to experience it.

Physiologically, fractals are involved in the cells of the eyes, the synapses of the brain, and the branches of the lungs. Internal harmonies and beauties are involved in human perception of beauty and new experiences. "As the region that helps us take in the new, integrate it with the familiar, and generate from the exercise a novel response, the limbic system is, in a sense, a microcosmic creator,"[55] science writer Natalie Angier notes. The limbic system is also involved in babies' first experiences of bonding and adolescents' first experiences of love. In the near future more research into fractal structures in human physiology, into the experiences of mystics, and into various arts and therapies will continue to bring fruitful new perspectives on human capacities.

The healing arts of wholeness, such as the appreciation of musiclike fractals (visualized harmonies) in exquisite designs and literature, and the promotion of well-being in the web of life help us rediscover the state of grace with nature which is our original endowment: a talent for the art of living. Fractal pattern processes are involved in both pervasive structures in the physical world and extraordinary states of mind. By "extraordinary states of mind" I mean peak experiences, moments of discovery, perceptions of the infinite, and other times of awe. Thomas Traherne wrote, "What a treasure is every [grain of] sand when truly understood! Who can love any thing that God hath made too much? His infinite

Henry David Thoreau wrote of observing an oval group of pines on a patch of ground in a forest of oaks; the conical or oval pines themselves had a regularly and solidly conical outline, and their fruit—pine cones—did so as well, as did the cones' individual seeds on yet a smaller scale. An artist could compose a picture ambiguous yet recognizable: is it a pine cone made of pine cones, or a tree, or a group of trees?

goodness and wisdom and power and glory are in it."[56] Whether one uses the term God or Tao or Mystery or Holy Spirit or Brahman or Allah or Buddha Nature when invoking the vision of the infinite within the parts of existence, one is appreciating the same power. (All names for the sacred are obviously tentative or presumptuous. As an elderly Hindu friend of mine once joked, "What right does any human have to name God, since God is not any human's little newborn baby?")

Notes on Fractal Sensibilities in Various Stories and Verses

Fractal-like details abound in stories and novels. In *Invisible Cities,* Italo Calvino wrote of a traveler who in wild regions desires "a city where the buildings have spiral staircases encrusted with spiral seashells."[57] This image has only two levels of scale, so it is a semi-fractal, not a full-fledged fractal. Similarly, in E. M. Forster's *Passage to India,* the echoing sound in the serpentine Malabar caves is said to sound like "a snake composed of small snakes" vibrating through the dark air.[58] This is a primal sensibility, of things breaking down into smaller constituent versions of themselves, or of being built up from parts that look like the whole.

In some works the structures of the stories themselves or the technique of the writing may include fractal-like patterns or concepts. Let's consider a few examples.

In traditional literature there are elements of plotting that may be approached as fractal-like patterns, or at least recursive motifs. In Valmiki's Ramayana epic of ancient India, for example, Lord Rama is the main hero, but there are parallels between him and the lesser character Sugriva. Some actions also echo like repeated motifs—Rama's father Dasharatha shoots an arrow at a sound and mortally wounds an ascetic by accident, and this act has disastrous effects. Rama shoots an arrow at a golden deer; this too, changes the course of his future. The form of the verses making up this great poem (a rhythmic couplet known as a *shloka*) originates from a hunter's shooting a mating bird and being cursed in a rhythmic utterance by Valmiki. Other arrows, such as the one that kills Jatayu, are also crucial.

A Jewish folktale called "Adam's Diamond" illustrates another point about oneness and manyness. In the story God feels bad about having kicked Adam out of the garden of Eden so suddenly and invites him back for a feast. After enjoying the sumptuous dinner, Adam relaxes and begins to outstay his welcome, not taking God's hint that he might want to go and have a look at the world. God offers him a consolation prize: "Take one of whatever you like from here." Adam looks around at treasures of every kind and sees a huge diamond the size of a watermelon. He thinks he could live for a whole lifetime on the proceeds of such a valuable item. So he picks up the hefty diamond and starts out for the gates of Paradise to make his exit, all the while being followed by an angel. As he is about to pass through the gates, he sees the flaming swords of the cherubim guarding them, and he turns to look back, feeling sorry to be leaving and wanting to change his mind—but now it is too late. Adam walks slowly out of the garden, and when he pauses before crossing a stream, an angel gives him a small shove to get him started. Adam lurches and drops his diamond into the stream. He cries out and the angel says, "Just reach in and pick it up again!" When Adam steps into the stream he sees thousands and thousands of diamonds the same size as his and becomes confused: "Which one is mine?" The angel says, "It doesn't matter. Do you think you're the first one who was ever exiled from Eden and tried to take along a diamond with you? Thousands and thousands of your kind have already passed this way."[59] The image is one of a reiterated action rather than a fractal. If we compare the Hindu story of Indra, the powerful sky god who feels self-important until he sees a long line of ants and is told that each of them in a previous life had been an Indra, we see another shock of disillusionment. Indra's story is also a lesson about realizing the context of vast time, a return of a sense of being part of a larger picture rather than an isolated unique ego. Vastness humbles.

More fractal-like is Nahman of Bratslav's oddly expansive and inclusive story:

> Among all the countries there is one country
> which includes all countries
> (in that it serves as the rule for all countries).
> In that country there is one city
> which includes all cities
> of the whole country
> which includes all countries.
> In that city there is a house which
> includes all the houses which
> includes all the cities of the country
> which includes all countries.
>
> And there is a man who includes everybody
> from that house which
> includes all the houses which
> includes all the cities of the country
> which includes all countries.
> And that man knows all the jokes of the country,
> and of all the countries in the world.[60]

Perhaps this is a way of saying that God's sense of humor includes all humorous situations.

Jonathan Swift (1667–1745) lived during the European Enlightenment, which was characterized by reason. He and his contemporaries, who included Pope, Steele, and Addison in England and Voltaire and Montesquieu in France, satirized the foibles of the establishment. Swift's masterpiece *Gulliver's Travels* displays a playfulness with scale which has precedents in myth, fairy tale, folklore, and fantasy. It carried his ideas to new levels of wild satire, with micro-size Lilliputians and macro-size Brobdingnagians: people who were similar to humans but on a different scale from them. Like Chuang-tzu, Swift was a very free-spirited story-teller who was able to imagine beings the size of insects and beings the size of mammoths.[61] Today we might imagine beings the size of subatomic particles, of molecules, of planets, of solar systems, of galaxies, and so forth. But rather than pursue this tack further, allow me to present a few other examples of recursive structures in works of contemporary culture.

Various films use structures of reiterations, self-reflective images on different scales, or language which plays with recursive ideas. *L'année dernière à Marienbad* (1961; released in the U.S. as *Last Year at Marienbad,* 1962) is a well-known example of the use of hypnotic repetition to weave a story which is fascinating in its ambiguity. In a more recent film, *Groundhog Day* (1993), Bill Murray plays a curmudgeonly character who must repeat the same day over and over again until he gets it right. In *Escape from Alcatraz* (1979), a character describes prison life as a whole made up of countings—the prisoners count the days; the guards count the prisoners; the "king bulls" count the counts.

The images in the film *The War* (dir. Jon Avnet, 1994) might be considered a fractal of homes on the theme: what makes a place a home? The opening shows a disturbed veteran sitting at the site of a burnt-out house and watching it being bulldozed—the sad destruction of the family home. Next in the story comes a tree-house, a home away from home built by children—smaller-scale, secluded and elevated—but it too is destroyed. Then there is a home of hopes and dreams which the veteran bids on and which the family wins in the end—a future home for them. In the end, the veteran, who dies as a result of a mining accident similar to one he experienced in Vietnam, "goes home" on yet another scale. Homes of different levels and magnitudes form the leitmotif in the structural imagery of the story.

In *Beyond Numeracy,* the book of essays by mathematician John Allen Paulos, there is an essay entitled "Human Consciousness, Its Fractal Nature." In it the complexity of human consciousness, which includes logical thoughts, musing, becoming intrigued, or focused examination, all exhibit self-similarities. Paulos notes that "the forward movement, horizontal digression, branching, and backtracking at various levels and scales define this human shape and constitute a fractal in a many-dimensional logical space."[62] The author reviews a fictitious book (entitled *Rucker: A Life Fractal*) whose author suggests through his story that "human consciousness—like endlessly jagged coastlines, or creased and varicose mountain surfaces, or the whorls and eddies of turbulent water, or a host of other 'fractured' phenomena—can best be modeled using the geometrical notion of a fractal. . . . unlimited branching and complexity are characteristic of the notion, as is a

Author's collage of illustrations depicting differences of scale in Jonathan Swift's *Gulliver's Travels*. Original drawings by Charles Brock.

peculiar property of self-similarity, whereby a fractal entity (in this case the book) has the same look or feel no matter on what scale one views it (just the main events or finer details as well)."[63]

Some authors use styles which are not actually fractal but may be reminiscent of some features of fractals. Because of the Cubist-style reiterations in her writing, which are like self-reflective fractured units of language, Gertrude Stein comes to mind first. William Gass observed that Stein configured language in a spatial rather than a temporal manner. He noted that her sense of the process of reading included the way reading itself is often interrupted, and recursive, and continually looping back upon itself. Gass himself, influenced by Stein, wrote a book entitled *The Tunnel* with streams of similar scenes, each rewritten into a variation on the previous one.[64] Writers' influence on each other (intertextuality) in inventing schools of writing is a fractal-like process, but so is readers' performance of their writing; each act goes beyond the structure of the individual pieces and becomes part of a larger self-reflective whole. Alexander Argyros hypothesizes that "narrative is probably self-similar to those innovative processes in nature whose engine is chaos. In other words, the global dynamics of narrative serve as a cultural attractor, a self-adjusting algorithm through which all cultures of which we are aware seem to have spun their cosmos."[65]

One critic of Argyros and others who are interested in the connections between chaos theory and literature asserts that "novels aren't self-organizing systems, that's why we need novelists."[66] I would say that one *can* see a novel as a self-organizing system. One can also see it as a string of paragraphs and chapters, as a genre, as a linguistic product, and so forth. One can refuse to see it as a self-organizing system, but one cannot deny that it can be seen and understood as one by others who may be more imaginative or in other ways more ready to perceive it that way. Someone who is unable to see a text as a system organized by and perceived with energies perhaps sees it as a static entity, a substantial passive entity, a material product. But I would say it is possible to see the text as a process, evolving it as a series of perceptions, synapses flashing, memories accumulating, forms learned, information studied, a series of painful or pleasurable, deep or shallow experiences brought together by the desire to tell a story. Consciousness threads together the pieces into a unity. The center of the vortex may be called "Shakespeare" or whatever, but if the writer is good, then the words gathering in a manuscript day after day self-organize—they form a self-organizing system of which the writer is only partly conscious. The narrative is a process that goes on working out an organic design inherent in words, ideas, concepts. Things begin to "write themselves" if they are allowed; the characters start to take on a life of their own. No doubt this is hard for some to imagine. But the self-organizing system is a flow of process, a process of gracefully growing the stories that the writer learns from the relationships among the parts. Ideas gather around an enduring concept like iron filings on a magnet, or like nutrients assimilated into an organism. Stories often *do* write themselves, as many writers have attested.

Let's close with a dizzying passage from Gertrude Stein. Systems often are vibrant with the sensibilities of repetition; think of the recursive waves of the ocean, similar ridges of sand dunes, layers of fading mountains going out all the way to the horizon. The reiterated respirations and pulsations of all life are similar to hypnotic rhythms of sound and are akin to soothing caressing touches. (They are also akin to the rise and fall of civilizations.) Gertrude Stein's writing often demonstrates how accurate intuitions are concerned with noticing the inevitable, the universal systemic oneness:

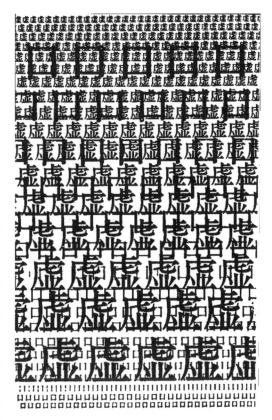

Reiterated Chinese characters for "mouth," "empty," and "lie" form a silent wall of falsehood in this artwork by Seiichi Niikuni. This recursive play with the characters of language is not a fractal.

> There is singularly nothing that makes a difference a difference in beginning and in the middle and in ending except that each generation has something different at which they are all looking. By this I mean so simply that anybody knows it that composition is the difference which makes each and all of them then different from the other generations and this is what makes everything different otherwise they are all alike and everybody knows it because everybody says it. . . .
> Beginning again and again is a natural thing even when there is a series.
> Beginning again and again and again explaining composition and time is a natural thing.
> It is understood by this time that everything is the same except composition and time, composition and the time of the composition and the time in the composition.
> Everything is the same except composition and as the composition is different and always going to be different everything is not the same. Everything is not the same as the time when of the composition and the time in the composition is different. The composition is different, that is certain.
> The composition is the thing seen by every one living in the living they are doing, they are the composing of the composition that at the time they are living is the composition of the time in which they are

living. It is that that makes living a thing they are doing. Nothing else is different, of that almost any one can be certain. The time when and the time of and the time in that composition is the natural phenomena of that composition and of that perhaps every one can be certain.

No one thinks these things when they are making when they are creating what is the composition, naturally no one thinks, that is no one formulates until what is to be formulated has been made.

Composition is not there, it is going to be there and we are here. This is some time ago for us naturally.

The only thing that is different from one time to another is what is seen and what is seen depends upon how everybody is doing everything. This makes the thing we are looking at very different and this makes what those who describe it make of it, it makes a composition, it confuses, it shows, it is, it looks, it likes it as it is, and this makes what is seen as it is seen. Nothing changes from generation to generation except the thing seen and that makes a composition.[67]

Of course, now we have computer programs to correct our grammar to make it more standardized, but a writer such as Gertrude Stein could, as it were, get into the fractal-like potentiality of a theme and spin out the iterations in a creative trancelike unfolding of possibilities. And more than fifty years later, the literary aspects of performance arts and visual arts have not gone very far from her.

Restlessly oscillating improvising consciousness playfully echoes on and on. The chant of the mantra repeated for years,[68] the refrain of the song sung again and again, the reiteration of a motto to keep an idea alive, the droned repetition of techno-music tones at a rave (and also "chill music" to calm one down), recursive cycles of cycles of drumbeat patterns (known as *talas* in South Indian music) that give structure and continuity to a melody—all these are uniquely empowered to form states of mind as they resonate in time, letting listeners transcend their smaller selves and join higher or other contexts. Repeated self-reflective parts can give us a way to the whole.

Nursery rhymes also often echo with hypnotic sounds and revolving images. Some even have fractal-like imagery with visual similarities: "Round the rugged rocks the ragged rascals ran." And "There was a crooked man / and he walked a crooked mile / He found a crooked sixpence / beside a crooked style."[69] And "The shadow of the balusters, the shadow of the lamp, / The shadow of the child that goes to bed— / All the wicked shadows coming, tramp, tramp, tramp, / With the black night overhead."[70] The web of nearby shadows is scary enough to a child, but other ominous shadows approaching in deeper darkness are worse. Each of these various scary images is "all of a piece," meaning that all are parts of one whole.

Of course there are neurotic repetitions, too, and automatisms

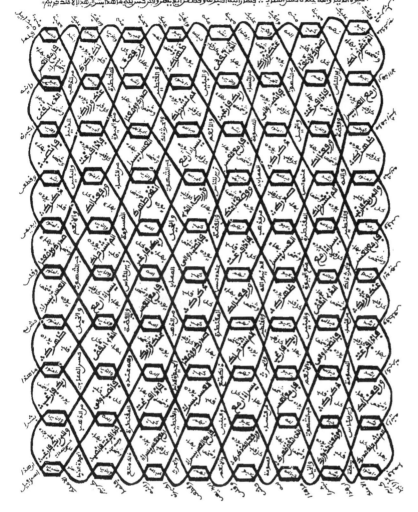

This network of names is written in a Moroccan dialect of Arabic. The names of the four greatest angels in the Muslim worldview are at the four corners. The names of lesser angels are woven into the latticework design. The diagram may serve as a prayer for recitation. This is not a fractal, but it is a visual network.

and wheel-spinning substitutes for genuine traction when engaging in healing or wholeness. Just as there are fractals of sadness—open up fractals of depression and you encounter self-similar memories of other down times and ways to feel bad and people and things you'd rather not mention—there are associated memory networks of self-similar moods on various scales. The power of recursion—of atoms, dust motes, snowflakes, and gems in endless numbers that multiply into kingdoms and cosmoses—won't go away. And the power of reiterative seeking and the meanings found in overviews and underviews that glimpse wholeness won't go away. The cycles of return permeate the flow of everyday life, and arts and dreams shadow and sum up our days in images which

Fractal spiral. Courtesy of H. O. Peitgen and P. H. Richter, *The Beauty of Fractals: Images of Complex Dynamical Systems* (Berlin: Springer-Verlag, 1986).

stand for the whole configuration of self-similar multiscaled parts. (When we see no wholeness or unity, we see no possibility of self-similarity.) In dreams we see a firebird or walls which we cause to fall; we experience an unexpected return of faces we once knew; we find ourselves unprepared for an important event or naked in public. We rehearse and perform, relive and rehearse, forget and recall, rediscovering deep affinities as if for the first time; we return again and again to what we love, like blood always leaving and returning to the heart, in boredom and in awe. Life works out its possibilities through many returns, which the fertile imagination can easily picture as so many fractal reiterations.

ELEPHANTS CARVED IN IVORY

Nature-Culture
Fractal Wholeness

In this strand we inquire how to consider the wholeness of nature and culture. What do we need to learn about wholeness to understand nature-and-culture issues? The inadequacies of old perspectives leave openings and possibilities for new approaches. If we can see fractals "all over the place" because fractals are involved in our own physiology and because the world of nature involves fractal patterns and the nature of consciousness is fractal-like, how does that help us see part-whole relations of man to nature? Can humans be both embedded in nature and unique?

Overlappings of Nature and Cultural Traditions:
Discovery and Invention, Inspiration and Cultivation

> Many social scientists have turned away from a laws-and-instances ideal of explanation toward a cases-and-interpretations one, looking less for the sort of thing that connects planets and pendulums and more for the sort that connects chrysanthemums and swords.
>
> —Clifford Geertz[1]

What fire or light sets man apart from other living creatures? Or is the same Mind behind chrysanthemums and swords (to use

Ruth Benedict's example, discussed in her book *The Chrysanthe-mum and the Sword: Patterns of Japanese Culture*), and if so is that bothness a benefit to human beings? What is the wholeness, the larger structure of which nature and culture are fractal parts?

Whatever sets man apart from other living creatures is impor-tant and needs to be appreciated; but whatever alienates man fa-tally from nature needs to be corrected. We need to recognize the mutuality of natural and social systems. I would like to consider the possibility that, with a fractal-like recursiveness, nature and culture are self-similar to each other, "internested" on different scales and levels.

Let's consider human culture and the world of nature from a few angles, without being in a hurry to draw conclusions. Like a powerful phoenix building an immense nest, a series of Chinese emperors built a wall to keep out the bewildering barbarians of chaos, thereby adding an extruding wrinkle to the earth's surface. This stone scar on the skin of the earth is culture built of and on nature. Like miniature elephants carved of their own ivory, or a musical instrument made from a tortoise shell, culture is processed nature.[2] And nature, for her part, has culturelike processes of her own, if we think of anything which is formed of natural resources to be culture. Caddis fly larvae, tiny creatures living in lakes and brooks, shape small tubes of grains of sand, urged by instinct to heap together bits of matter and use their own silklike secretions to bind them into regular forms that look like human artifacts. (Some spin precise webs or nets between two rocks in a stream to trap food, and perform other engineering feats.) Humans have long fashioned weapons, turning flint, wood, and sinew against the nonhuman world of living rock, trees, and pouncing pumas. Cul-tures transform and consume nature, and nature, through the forces of time and the elements of decay (rain and flood, sun and fire, virus and mold), consumes cultures. Some thinkers like to point out how human systems mimic natural systems and need to be seen ecologically; others take the view that other forms of life thrive by successfully manipulating humans.[3] Thoreau eloquently emphasized how indebted every culture is to the wilderness.[4]

"Great things are done when men and mountains meet," as William Blake wrote;[5] at the edge of mind and the mundane the story of life gets interesting. We can never separate the story of humans from earth, just as we cannot separate tribal people from their landscape because their inner terrain is so ecologically adapted to the outer terrain. The Hani (or Huoyi) people of Yun-nan province in southern China, for example, live lives so inter-twined with water buffaloes and rice terraces on mountain slopes and with the timing of rice planting and harvesting seasons, which are determined by shamanic practices and depend on careful use of water and sun, that their cultural identity, their customs, and their region cannot be separated from each other without causing ecological and cultural disaster. This kind of profound unity has much to teach us.

There is great value in considering the interconnections of nature and culture from several approaches rather than just one. Insights can be gathered and compared from poets, artists, philosophers, creative writers, and naturalists and from thinkers in the fields of ecology, sociobiology, and systems theory. Some cultural anthropologists, such as Leslie White, think of culture as "superorganic," that is, beyond the laws of natural selection. Others, such as Noel Boaz, note that whatever affects reproduction affects biological evolution.[6] Culture makes humans unique. The behavior of other creatures is more fully genetically programmed—ants and doves and chimps follow the same patterns for many centuries. But human culture reinvents itself, with some continuities, across generations, and change seems especially obvious and accelerated in the last century. This human cultural freedom is an answer to a puzzle. Noel Boaz asks, "How could natural selection act to produce a mechanism of human behavior so tenuously connected to human biology?"[7] The value of play in the long childhood of humans and the value of the risks and open explorations involved in learning make the human story a new act in the drama of the cosmos. The advantage of such a great range of adaptability in a small amount of time, Boaz argues, shows how culture can be a mechanism by which behavior can adapt at a fast evolutionary rate. Genetic mutations are the basic engine of evolution in ants, doves, and chimps, but the process is extremely slow. Of course human culture can be so overpowering that people forget important basics. Violent video games and movies and easy access to weapons may make a child forget what fantasy is, and the child may go on a shooting rampage he later regrets. Ignorance of the nature of the mind and feelings and unexamined unlimited individualism and ownership rights may give humans "amnesia."

To have to explain and argue that humans are a part of nature, that we are manifestations of the life of our planet, and that therefore our thinking and culture share patterns with nature, would seem as absurd as having to explain to the sun that it has a relationship to fire. It would be absurd if it were not so urgently necessary in an age when the very nature which gives humans their lives is despised and destroyed. It would be ridiculous and pathetic if this ominous disjunction that exists between man and nature were not so horrifying and deadly. After centuries of the Western venture which might aptly be called "the man apart concept," it is becoming clearer that such an approach is dysfunctional, too homocentric and provincial. Christian theologian Jürgen Moltmann wrote,

> In "the struggle for existence" symbioses between competing organisms have a far greater chance of survival than conflicts of competing organisms. The subject-object relationship of man to nature and the pattern of domination and exploitation do not lead to any symbiosis between human and nonhuman systems that would be capable of survival; they lead to the silencing of nature and to the ecological death of both nature and man.[8]

There are many reasons why human links to nature must be reconsidered and experienced anew. Ecopsychology shows us some of them.[9] Many scientists and science teachers are imparting to moderns a humility at the size of our human part in the total scheme of things, consciously or unconsciously conveying a sense of human apartness and insignificance in the vast cosmos of space-time. Few science teachers have been able to inspire the appropriate wonder at the immensity of the cosmos and a wise gladness at our conscious "partness" within it, our integral participation.[10] The effect has been the dwindling of a sense of hope and meaning among students; hope and meaning somehow often seem incompatible with the knowledge of how vast the universe is and how mindbogglingly deep is time. It is almost as if many adults have no knowledge of the earth after all these generations of their ancestors living here, nothing of enduring usefulness to pass on to the young who need to know.[11]

Even though humans, as Loren Eiseley ironically reminds us, originally fell from the grace of instinct to ape each other in learned behavior in cultural traditions that became "second nature" to them, human beings are still made up of natural systems—mind and nature overlap.[12] Humans never leap out of nature—their veins and metabolic cycles, heartbeats and hungers, artifacts and behaviors, however "free," must still work within limits given by nature. However much they strut and boast, give commands and are comically surprised at unexpected pratfalls, humans remain creatures through and through. Human beings delude themselves with the cover story of progress, and they vaunt technology as a rival to nature, but there is no clear evidence of linear, unmitigated progress in history. Huston Smith writes in his book *Forgotten Truth* that

> nature favors the curves that space itself conforms to; the yin-yang rhythms of turning gyres and waves that crest and fall. . . . Hope, not fact, powers the dream of onward and upward toward the dawning light. If human life is truly natural . . . it is seasonal. Fall and winter are its lot as assuredly as summer and spring. Half the art of living is a talent for dying.[13]

This reminder of the perennial givens of human nestedness in nature brings into the picture life's nonhuman orders, and the fact that what is bitter chaos to one order may be sweet pattern to another.

Emerson saw the situation clearly when he said of man, "So much of nature as he is ignorant of, so much of his own mind does he not yet possess."[14] But it is not the knowing that seeks to overpower nature that reveals to man his own mind, it is the knowing that comes of a sense of mutuality, of participating in a larger whole. Shamans and poets have often had the sanity to assume this embeddedness in nature and have intimated this all along in their songs. In the seventeenth century, the English poet George Herbert wrote,

> Man is all symmetry,
> Full of proportions, one limb to another,
> And all to all the world besides.
> Each part may call the farthest, brother;
> For head with foot hath private amity,
> And both with moons and tides.
>
> Nothing hath got so far
> But man hath caught and kept it as his prey;
> His eyes dismount the highest star:
> He is in little all the sphere.
> Herbs gladly cure our flesh, because that they
> Find their acquaintance there . . .
>
> More servants wait on man
> Than he'll take notice of. In every path,
> He treads down that which doth befriend him
> When sickness makes him pale and wan.
> Oh mighty love! Man is one world, and hath
> Another to attend him.[15]

But such a togetherness with nature is an endangered species of experience wherever man has imposed his own imperatives. If this were not the case, there would have been no need for the United Nations to adopt the World Charter for Nature in 1982, which asserts that "mankind is a part of nature and life depends on the uninterrupted functioning of natural systems." Another word for this togetherness would be coexistence, or better, mutual interexistence; all things interexist.

A respect for the wilderness, an appreciation of the wild, is needed now more than ever. Wild animals are fast, free, unpredictable, and they have an intelligent fierce beauty. They stand for the wild energy that fuels the immense pilgrimage of life's evolution. The "coydogs" (the result of mating between coyotes and domesticated dogs) who laugh in the mountains of Vermont remind us of a cycle. Once dogs were wild, then man domesticated them. When the wild coyote mated with a domesticated dog, a new breed of wild dog was born—the wilderness took back her own to the original state. Gary Snyder reminds us that

> consciousness, mind, imagination, and language are fundamentally wild. "Wild" as in wild ecosystems—richly interconnected, interdependent, and incredibly complex. Diverse, ancient, and full of information. At root it is a question of how we understand the concepts of order, freedom and chaos. Is art an imposition of order on chaotic nature, or is art (also read "language") a matter of discovering the grain, a matter of uncovering the intricate and nonsymmetrical order, of the processes that bring about the natural world? Observation, reflection, and practice show artistic processes to be the latter.[16]

One implication of this is that the less a culture recognizes and respects nature as the source of possibilities, whether out of narcissism or greed, religious fanaticism or atheism, the more precarious will be the life it claims to celebrate and support. Nature is the raw ore mined and refined into cultural objects, as the wilderness is the original wisdom system from which human refinements are derived.

The creative development of human language was a turning point in the history of life on the planet on a par with the evolution of photosynthesis or the migration of living things from the ocean to the land. With it began the weaving of a new level of mind-networking over the planet. It set humans apart from their past, freeing them from thickets of instinct, bringing them into the realm of communicative ideas and creativity. Science writer Loren Eiseley eloquently describes this change:

> Man had broken through that network of strangling vines by the magical utterance of the first word. In that guttural achievement he had created his destiny and taken leave of his kindred. There would be no way of return save perhaps one: through the power of imaginative insight.[17]

By learning to speak, define, measure, and categorize in words, learning what was taught him, man "drifted insensibly from the heart of things. At first, he kept an uncertain memory of his origins in the animal world. He claimed descent from Grandfather Bear or Raven, and on ritual occasions he talked to them or to his mother, the Earth."[18] While they were in trance, shamans soared as birds and swam as if immersed in the spirit world like fish in water. Perhaps they were entranced and enchanted by realizing the nature of their nervous systems and their connections with the unconscious life force in all.[19] Stories like India's *Ramayana* epic celebrate the kindred spirit and friendship humans share with birds, bears, monkeys, and squirrels and sing of the youth of the human race.

With the freedom to invent, build up, accumulate the means to imagine new ways of life, humans could create a new world of their own with comforts and conveniences; little by little, culture became more complex until civilizations were able to forget the wilderness out of which they were constructed. In the river valleys—the Indus Valley and along the Tigris and Euphrates, the Nile, the Yellow River—civilizations first rose, and over the centuries developed economic trade and cultural exchange. "In the end, their cities would lie congregated and gleaming like the nerve ganglions of an expanding brain."[20]

Did humans develop this system of communication, which involves categorizing, thinking, imagining, and envisioning? Or can we say that it was a process of mutual growth, a struggle on the border between faculties and givens, internal rhythms and patterns dancing with self-reflective external rhythms and patterns, mutualities of man and cosmos intermeshed, "interfulfilled," we might say? George Seielstad points out that

> culture mimics a living process. Life evolves by the differential survival of replicating entities, culture by the differential survival of imitating entities. Ideas, thoughts, speculations, and dreams compete for the limited attention a given mind or set of minds can devote to any single topic. Those memes that survive this competition are the ones that excel in terms of longevity, fecundity and fidelity of imitation. Over time these crowd out the others. . . . Humankind is extraordinarily lucky to be involved in both kinds of evolution.[21]

This explanation is helpful in considering the positive aspects of the process, but why are there so many "unlucky" and painful human issues? What happens when market forces hog the limited space with dubious products, forcing out some of the life-supporting memes? Greed can destroy lives, and miseducations and misperceptions can lead to destruction, dysfunction, traumas, wars . . .

Dreams of Reason in the Furnace of Concealed Flame

Perhaps we need to show not only that human life is part of nature but also that the human body is more than a machine—that the brain, for example, can be seen as a computer, yet it may have mysterious creative potentials which a computer does not have. Culture follows the processes of nature at various levels. Ideas survive and evolve, and language, like DNA, encodes information. Both kinds of living systems are fueled by wild energy; there is creativity in both, the ability to wander, search, follow hunches, discover, evolve. All this bespeaks mind, embodied consciousness, mentality, not just machinery.

Modern people often look down on nature, attributing brute qualities to it. They unconsciously project their own values and oversimplify the possibilities of life. Reductionists today, for example, like the nineteenth-century evolutionists, are obsessed with the importance of struggle. They tend to ignore the better qualities of human beings, such as goodheartedness and attraction to wisdom, cooperation and self-sacrifice, motherly caring for the young, and appreciation of beauty. One must also include language and visions of order and meaning which coincide with or harmonize with the processes of the cosmos. Though these play an important part in the total gestalt, old-fashioned evolutionists ignore them. Although society and man are mutually productive of each other, they also ignore how the inner consciousness of the individual in meditation, vision, prophetic revelation, trance, and so on brings up archetypal depths of religious experience. Humans do not live by cutthroat competition alone but are pulled by other, subtler updrafts. They are driven by inborn natural drives, the urgency of *eros* exciting them to reach completion. We cannot ignore how humans are pulled by momentums to generative peaks of richness, with experiences of fulfillment energizing the built-in hard-wiring of mind and branching nerves, with endorphins of earned bliss, such as anandamide.

With faith in the ability of rational, linear science to discover and control the materials of nature, science philosopher Francis Bacon (1561–1626) foresaw a whole new realm of possibilities for human life—a realm not subject to irrational custom, a way of experiment and invention. This realm of technological advance has become so prevalent that many moderns are out of touch with the ultimate sources of their energy and also with the potential dangers of the powers humans now wield, routinely underestimating how missteps can seriously damage delicate balances in the biosphere.

The language of the collective unconscious, with its deep images and archetypal scenarios, forms an ancient fuel and fire that is constantly active in the motivating backgrounds of human life. Human beings are usually only dimly aware of this turbulent depth of images, where things are not rigidly separated as they are in the logical mind. The shadows of the unconscious spring up in reaction to the events of our waking lives, bringing figures from earlier days of the human race, the days of caves and mysteries, the days of developing the wits to use fire to preserve the spark of human life. All the past still smolders in our unconscious, flickering when we sleep at night. The unconscious is a wealth of wisdom which can kindle understanding; it is also a power with which politicians and others seeking wide support may seek to tamper, whether they do so knowingly or not.

It is no accident that so many mythologies and systems use this fire imagery: Vedic hymns to the sacred principle of fire, Agni, the mystic fire of consciousness in the work of Shri Aurobindo, the Zoroastrian praise of fire as sacred symbol, Dante's *Divine Comedy,* and other light-centered systems. We come from a great fireball, according to the story science has been piecing together for decades, and "we all shine on" (as John Lennon's song "Instant Karma" proclaims) similarly with the life inherent in the original gradual dawning and "flaring forth" of suns and fireball earth which became all this.[22]

There seem to be long-term rhythms in history; breakdown then synthesis, multiplications then unifications. In writing about "blurred genres" in his book *Local Knowledge,* Clifford Geertz notes signs that distinctions between the humanities and the social sciences are collapsing. Analogies from the humanities enrich sociological conceptions more frequently than previously. New combinations of fields, interdisciplinary explorations offer rich possibilities in the postmodern age. Theodore Roszak's explorations in ecopsychology in his book *The Voice of the Earth* offer a good example. Another example is sociobiology, a scientific endeavor spearheaded by Edward O. Wilson. Let us consider what Wilson's influential views, and the less well known alternatives to them, might add to the discussion of human culture and the matrix of culture.

Self-Similarities in Evolution and Mental Processes: E. O. Wilson's Mammal Genes and Mammal Society

> The ancient world takes its stand upon the drama of the Universe, the modern world upon the inward drama of the Soul. —Alfred North Whitehead[23]

A comparison of the approach of the pioneering researcher of sociobiology Edward O. Wilson and the views of Gregory Bateson may prove useful in considering ways to think about living systems (such as human culture, societies, and ecosystems) and their fractal processes. According to Wilson,

> Universal human rights [are a primary value] because we are mammals. Our societies are based on the mammalian plan: the individual strives for personal reproductive success foremost and that of his immediate kin secondarily; further grudging cooperation represents a compromise struck in order to enjoy the benefits of group membership.[24]

Wilson believes that "the highest form of religious practice, when examined more closely, can be seen to confer biological advantage."[25] Religion can function in a life-supportive way, giving people practices and beliefs that will help them survive through restraint and mutual aid. Wilson cites Hans Mol's work, which explains religion as conferring advantage on believers. But is all religion so easily reducible? Do the practices of Buddhism, including monkhood, celibacy, self-sacrifice, and the effort to extinguish the sense of a separate self, have personal self-perpetuation as their foremost concern or outcome?

Wilson believes that "the genes hold culture on a leash. The leash is very long, but inevitably values will be constrained in accordance with their effects on the human gene pool. The brain is a product of evolution."[26] Wilson does not (as far as I know) discuss the concept that Gregory Bateson and Humberto Maturana explore—that "evolution and cognition are flip sides of the same coin."[27] This means processes of Mind (or if you prefer, mindlike processes) are involved in the dynamics of both. That is, something like "mind" or consciousness is at work in both selective processes: survival of good ideas and survival of life forms.

Wilson believes the discipline he fathered, sociobiology, "can account for the very origin of mythology by the principle of natural selection acting on the genetically evolving material structure of the human brain." He further believes that "religion is one of the major categories of behavior undeniably unique to the human species."[28] Wilson proposes that the deep structure of religious beliefs can be examined sociobiologically by investigating natural selection at three levels. On the surface we find the selection of rites and customs by ecclesiastical leaders who choose elements for emotional effects in historical situations. At the ecological level, environmental demands test learned conventions, to see whether they function and support life. The third level focuses on cultural evolution and population flux, by which the frequencies of genes change. Wilson thinks religious constraints circumscribe a group and give its members a sense of identity, demanding their allegiance.

> Our hypothesis requires that such restraints exist, that they have a physiological basis and that the physiological basis in turn has a genetic origin. It implies that ecclesiastical choices are influenced by the chain of events that lead from the genes through physiology to constrained learning during single lifetimes.[29]

Wilson concludes that "religious practices that . . . enhance [believers'] survival and procreation will propagate the physical controls that favor acquisition of the practices during single lifetimes. The genes that prescribe the controls will also be favored."[30] Self-propagation by genes seems all-important here—in this view, religion exists with the ulterior motive of perpetuating the genes of the believers. In this view, instead of interdependence it is cause and effect that seems most important: the brain of the believer survives in the world of life because it helps the self-centered genes (which encoded its basic formation) to thrive and multiply.

The genetic level seems fundamental to British geneticist Richard Dawkins. That the self-interested gene should dictate, and not be transcended by, biospiritual wisdom seems to be the highest vision of which Dawkins and some other geneticists are capable. But can the purposive gene, out to perpetuate itself, be the ultimate? The gene's short-sighted purposiveness may not include a larger self-interest, a desire to perpetuate a healthy environment, or a beautiful tradition. It ignores spiritual values, such as caring for the welfare of others, for which the person in whom the genes repose may sacrifice his or her life. Without that religious altruism, many of humanity's greatest spiritual leaders and reformers (such as Buddha, St. Francis of Assisi, Gandhi, Martin Luther King, Jr., and Mother Teresa) make little sense. If it is all simply a matter of selfish genes out for themselves, such figures are simply foolish aberrations from human and natural order.

This brings up an important question: To what should our behavior be self-similar? What are a human's and a society's appropriate scales? Should we follow the "selfish gene" level of activity to perpetuate our own kind? We can learn from a variety of processes—the way nature works can provide unlimited inspiration. To see the gene as an absolute standard seems to involve envisioning life as a machine. Humans are filled with the genius of organic life; they have access to an ocean of adaptive capacities, fluid improvisational resilience, and lightninglike brilliance.[31]

Wilson has been criticized by historian William Irwin Thompson, who contrasts him with biologist Umberto Maturana. Thompson writes that Wilson pursues a biology of the Right—sociobiology in which reality is to be perceived by reductionism, a method of breaking down nature into basic parts like mechanisms in a machine. Wilson emphasizes the gene pool, not the individual; in his view, the system is run by selfish genes, out for themselves, and this view serves the purposes of a technocratic society, in which a sanctified science manages human understanding and creates a supposedly better, more comfortable, life for those members who go along with its premises. (In *The Postmodern Condition*, French philosopher Jean-François Lyotard says much the same thing, that knowledge in our age is in the service of technocracy.)[32]

Wilson waxes quite enthusiastic and optimistic about the powers of science:

Let me give again the reasons why I consider the scientific ethos superior to religion: its repeated triumphs in explaining and controlling the physical world; its self-correcting nature open to all competent to devise and conduct the tests; its readiness to examine all subjects sacred and profane; and now the possibility of explaining traditional religion by the mechanistic models of evolutionary biology. The last achievement will be crucial. If religion . . . can be systematically analyzed and explained as a product of the brain's evolution, its power as an external source of morality will be gone forever and the solution of the second dilemma will have become a practical necessity.[33]

Some of these points, such as science's readiness to examine sacred subjects, seem like wishful thinking. Many scientists routinely exclude many ideas, topics, and possibilities from serious consideration because they feel they already know the answers. They are neither ready nor willing to consider anything but holding fast to their opinions and careers. Of course there are many other scientists who are courageous, conscientious, and open-minded, able to explore extraordinary possibilities.

Wilson continues his assertion of faith in science:

The core of scientific materialism is the evolutionary epic. Let me repeat its minimum claims: that the laws of the physical sciences are consistent with those of the biological and social sciences and can be linked in chains of causal explanation; that life and mind have a physical basis; that the world as we know it has evolved from earlier worlds obedient to the same laws; and that the visible universe today is everywhere subject to these materialist explanations. The epic can be indefinitely strengthened up and down the line, but its most sweeping assertions cannot be proved with finality. What I am suggesting, in the end, is that the evolutionary epic is probably the best myth we will ever have.[34]

But I cannot assume, with Wilson, that his kind of smooth science, which excludes all possibility of sacredness, owns the narrative of the whole universe. There are scientists and thinkers capable of a deeper poetic vision and sense of the sacred, such as Thomas Berry and Brian Swimme, F. David Peat and Gregory Bateson.[35] And others have the creative religious imagination capable of weaving fitting connections among levels of existence, which I find much more promising than Wilson's scientism. They realize that the clash between religion and science does not mean that religion must be eliminated, but that "the clash is a sign that there are wider truths and finer perspectives within which a reconciliation of a deeper religion and a more subtle science will be found," to use the words of philosopher Alfred North Whitehead.[36]

Wilson's reading of the story of evolution is not the only one we have, as William Irwin Thompson reminds us.[37] He points out how Umberto Maturana (for example) explores unities and wholes and focuses on the individual as the true ontological unity (rather than merely a separate entity) in evolution. And rather than taking a mechanistic and atomistic building-block approach to living systems, Maturana has a deep sense of the relational, speaking of "relations of interconnections . . . not . . . separate anatomical entities."[38] Similarly, Gregory Bateson is also deeply concerned with relationality.

Thus, although Edward O. Wilson has doubtless made important contributions to the contemporary discussion of areas of overlap in nature and culture, biology and mind, he also operates within cramping limitations. Wilson is a great authority on ants and knows much more about such topics as how a rational ant would react to the idea of individual rights than about the nuances of religion. He occasionally speaks of the "deep structures" of religion, but from his writing seems to lack a truly profound sense of the nature of religious experiences. It is natural that one's training and experiences allow one to see certain things and not others. He is not so adept at imagining the depths involved in the experience of a shaman, a yogi, a poet-visionary, or a Buddha, or Lao-tzu's experiences of the holistic processes of nature, and this shows up in his mechanistic view of organic life processes and his neglect of self-organizing consciousness on other than genetic levels. His faith in a certain kind of scientistic power leaves little room for levels of consciousness other than on the genetic and social scales. Rightly applauded for his environmental concerns, he nevertheless has a patriarchal utilitarian outlook—he is for biodiversity, so long as useful products can be made from the rainforests.[39]

Wilson assumes he need concern himself only with an old version of the sacred (which no longer works because of science), not recognizing in Bateson's (and others') recent views of the sacred a depth, a subtle unitary reality. Wilson lacks a sense of paradox in approaching processes in conscious systems. He seems to feel that human consciousness can and should be trained to be scientific and that the scientific view is highest and should rule all else. (I wonder what African American culture—or any other culture—would look like if its members followed Wilson's suggestion. I would contend that African American culture enjoys great vitality precisely because of the power of the church, its spiritual center.)

Both Dawkins and Wilson are brilliant in their own fields, and both are exceptionally scientistic. But as Alfred North Whitehead has observed, the extreme specialization and professionalism which are normal in our age are socially dangerous: "The leading intellects lack balance. They see this set of circumstances, or that set; but not both sets together. The task of coordination is left to those who lack either the force or the character to succeed in some definite career. . . . The progressiveness in detail only adds to the danger produced by the feebleness of coordination."[40] Perhaps a lesson to be learned from this discussion is that appreciating larger patterns requires a talent for magnanimity and awe, and life experiences develop that talent in some explorers.

The discoverer of fractals, Benoit Mandelbrot, is a multitalented mathematician with an intuition for whole patterns. In his view, it is necessary that those who are "nomads by choice" explore settled disciplines. They are freer to look at levels of complexity than specialists, and they may see more connections in the whole. I have found the works of "nomads by choice" such as Gregory Bateson, Benoit Mandelbrot, Ralph Abraham, Stuart Kauffman, F. David Peat, and John Briggs to be especially rich and thought-provoking.[41] We need to recognize patterns in nature and culture which are worthy of contemplation, including those emerging concepts of fractal studies which lurked for so long in the margin, hinted at and used in organizing life and culture, but were not articulated. Let us turn to some of these in chaos science to explore further the dynamism in nature and in human nature.

Correspondences: Evolution as Mental Process: Bateson and Systems Theory, Chaos, and Paradox

Is it possible to use any of the postmodern concepts found in physics when we discuss religious traditions and their complex worldviews and *darshanas* (visions, philosophies)? What might be some useful implications of the paradigm shift to chaos science, and the theory of dynamic systems, which includes other influential disciplines as well?

The formalisms, or structures and principles, derived from chaos studies are now being considered in relation to artificial intelligence. A number of researchers working to model symbols and memories have become interested in the complex dynamics of systems which include patterns wandering between "basins of attraction," and other typical chaos science topics.[42] They are finding certain correspondences among levels fascinating, and some of them are conceptualizing in terms of fractals. James Gleick wrote,

> Their fractal structure offered the kind of infinitely self-referential quality that seems so central to the mind's ability to bloom with ideas, decisions, emotions, and all the other artifacts of consciousness. . . . serious cognitive scientists can no longer model the mind as a static structure. They recognize a hierarchy of scales, from neuron upward, providing an opportunity for the interplay of micro-scale and macro-scale so characteristic of fluid turbulence and other complex dynamical processes.[43]

I would suggest that traditional cultural and religious symbol systems and practices be included in this venture. There are various life processes which might be compared: processes in living organisms, processes in social organisms, and processes in human societies and traditions. There are fractal analogues in mental or psychic space (the subjective realm of experience).[44] There are coherences, correlations, echoes, and reflections among the levels of different living systems. Patterns in nature (trees and seashells, for example) carry signs of the order of survival, the power of negentropy (a term used by Bateson and others for the organizing force of consciousness running counter to the law of entropy), and records of their self-organizing growth. James Gleick, the author of *Chaos: Making a New Science,* puts it well:

> Pattern born amid formlessness: that is biology's basic beauty and its basic mystery. Life sucks order from a sea of disorder. . . . A living organism has the "astonishing gift of concentrating a stream of order on itself and thus escaping the decay into atomic chaos." To Schrodinger as a physicist, it was plain that the structure of living matter differed from the kind of matter his colleagues studied. The building block of life—it was not yet called DNA—was an aperiodic crystal. "In physics we have dealt hitherto only with periodic crystals. . . . Compared with the aperiodic crystal, they are rather plain and dull." The difference was like the difference between wallpaper and tapestry, between the regular repetition of a pattern and the rich, coherent variation of an artist's creation.[45]

As scientists looked deeper into what had so long been simplified, the enhanced perception of complexities opened new possibilities of understanding. Depth can reveal graceful beauty, for beauty is a compelling trace of the escapade of life working its way to fullness from decay. Or as William Carlos Williams put it, "Rigor of beauty is the quest."[46]

Bateson suggests that the meta-pattern which connects networks of existence "is primarily (whatever that means) a dance of interacting parts and [is] only secondarily pegged down by various sorts of physical limits and by those limits which organisms characteristically impose."[47] He evokes an image of fluidity, the flow of relations, of aurora borealis–like protoplasm, of synapses firing like lightning, of cascades and smoke billows, and of blood circulating in branching veins. The interaction of multiple centers of awareness can show amazing intelligence—even small centers related to one another can orient themselves in the macrocosm. Think of the monarch butterflies who orient themselves from Leamington (in Canada) on Lake Erie to Mexico each year; the coordinates are mapped and followed in their brains, which are the size of pinheads. It is not fully known what patterns they use; they seem to follow river valleys (which geese follow in their migrations). Perhaps these patterns are the collective consciousness of the whole flock, wisdom in their genes from the long traditions of generations past, the process of their interrelated consensus of memory connected to the cosmos. Some are driven off course by wind and perish at sea or on land where there are no milkweed plants growing. They do not seem to orient themselves by earth's magnetic fields, as whales and salmon do. Group intelligence, sensitivity to the enduring forces in the environment, and memories in cells are all subtly interconnected in the lives that repeat these amazing migrations year after year, going through changes but preserving patterns.

The nature of living systems is a stochastic process of cumulative and integrative development, to use Gregory Bateson's terms.[48] "The evolutionary process must depend upon such double increments of information. Every evolutionary step is an addition of information to an already existing system. Because this is so, the combinations, harmonies, and disorder between successive pieces and layers of information will present many problems of survival and determine many directions of change."[49]

Ants build empires, conduct wars, travel long paths with two-way traffic, build castles—all by instinct. Humans depend on learning that is sometimes at odds with the wisdom in their bones and blood. Bateson explains,

> In the transmission of human culture, people always attempt to replicate, to pass on to the next generation the skills and values of the parents; but the attempt always and inevitably fails because cultural transmission of culture is a sort of hybrid or mix-up of the two realms. It must attempt to use the phenomena of learning for the purpose of replication because what the parents have was learned by them. If the offspring miraculously had the DNA that would give them the parental skills, those skills would be different and perhaps nonviable. . . . Between the two worlds is the cultural phenomenon of explanation—the mapping onto tautology of unfamiliar sequences of events. . . . The realms of epigenesis and of evolution are, at a deeper level, typified in the twin paradigms of the second law of thermodynamics: 1. that the random workings of probability will always eat up order, pattern, and negative entropy, but 2. that for the creation of new order, the workings of the random, the plethora of uncommitted alternatives (entropy) is necessary. It is out of the random that organisms collect new mutations, and it is there that stochastic learning gathers its solutions. Evolution leads to climax: ecological saturation of all the possibilities of differentiation. Learning leads to the overpacked mind. By return to the unlearned and mass-produced egg, the ongoing species again and again clears its memory banks to be ready for the new.[50]

If learned hatreds were to become part of the genetic makeup there would be little hope for the future of war-torn humanity. Fortunately what we learn in our cultural conditioning does not affect our DNA. "Thought and evolution . . . are a shared stochasticism, two systems partly in interaction, partly isolated from each other."[51] Tradition and learning are attempts to transmit wisdom; they provide continuity of culture, custom, and religion. Tradition is designed to help us stave off and survive chaos by means of organized attention, channeled energy, harmonious life. Because the natural world around us has this general systemic structure it is an appropriate source of metaphor to enable people to understand themselves in their social organization.

In Bateson's view, rigor and imagination are the two great complementary poles, the yin/yang dynamic system of mental process, and either extreme by itself is unhealthy, even lethal.

> Rigor alone is paralytic death, but imagination alone is insanity. A sort of freedom comes from what is necessarily so. After that is recognized, comes a knowledge of how to act. . . . Survival depends upon two contrasting phenomena or processes, two ways of achieving adaptive action. Evolution must always, Janus-like, face in two directions: inward towards the developmental regularities and physiology of the living creature and outward towards the vagaries and demands of the environment. These two necessary components of life contrast in interesting ways: the inner development—the embryology or "epigenesis" is conservative and demands that every new thing shall conform or be compatible with the regularities of the status quo ante. If we think of a natural selection of new features of anatomy or physiology—then it is clear that one side of this selection process will favor those new items which do not upset the old apple cart. This is minimal necessary conservatism. . . . In contrast, the outside world is perpetually changing and becoming ready to receive creatures which have undergone change, almost insisting upon change. . . . Always the creature itself must achieve change in its own body . . . acquire certain somatic characteristics by use, by disuse, by habit, by hardship, and by nurture; the acquired must never be passed on to offspring.[52]

Bateson sums up the understanding that mind developed out of nature and that it is all one process of Mind in this way: "If you want to understand mental processes, go look at biological evolution. If you want to understand biological evolution, go look at mental process."[53] We can argue that evolution is a two-way mirror in which creative mind and wild nature look at each other, meet, and dance. Bees and bears, termites and anteaters, and musicians blowing a trumpet made of a human thighbone—all are signs of mind. A cotton plant is nature, a T-shirt is culture—both are temporary weavings, carefully elaborated matter produced by intelligent energy, and both burn to ash in fire.

But we are still faced with questions of Mind in nature and culture; we have further reflections to make about nature and human traditions, how they are unified and how they are dissimilar.

Evidences of Mind in Matter

> How impossible it is, that the world should exist from Eternity, without a Mind.
> —Eighteenth-century American preacher
> Jonathan Edwards[54]

> The harmony of natural law . . . reveals an intelligence of such superiority that, in comparison with it, all the systematic thinking of human beings is an utterly insignificant reflection. —Albert Einstein[55]

> Thought, which science has expelled from its place at the top of the spiral of evolution, reappears at the bottom of it: the physical structure of atoms and their particles is a mathematical structure, a relation. What is equally extraordinary is that this structure can be reduced to a system of signs—and is therefore a language. The power of speech is a particular manifestation of natural communication; human language is one more dialect in the linguistic system of the universe. We might add: the cosmos is a language of languages.
> —Octavio Paz[56]

James Gleick, writing of the new science of chaos, remarked that the idea that most appealed to and excited young research scientists he interviewed was "the spontaneous generation of pattern in the world." Gleick found that "at the pinnacle of the complicated dynamics are processes of biological evolution, or thought processes."[57] Years earlier, Bateson had reached a similar conclusion, as we have seen: processes like those of the mind are active in the workings of nature. Much earlier religious traditions had developed concepts such as "Buddha Mind," *chit,* and others to speak of this subtle cosmic intelligence. Yung Ming, the Sung dynasty Buddhist, suggested, "The one Mind can take in all minds and return them to the One Mind, this is the meaning of Indra's net."[58] In the twentieth century, Sir James Jeans remarked that the world more and more looked more like a thought than a machine.[59] In all of these ways it is observed that "nature [is] constrained. Disorder [is] . . . channeled . . . into patterns with some common underlying theme."[60] Principles empattern nature and human traditions as well. Organic systems, natural or cultural, evolve to survive: starfish, the Iroquois Confederacy, the Pentagon, the Chinese Communist Party. They can generate information needed to live on into new circumstances and then renew themselves.

Some people may have already decided that universal form, evidence of unity, the wholeness of system-generating forces that shape organic life, the oneness of mind and nature, the relations of culture and biology are insignificant. They think that saying that all humans are religious, each devoted to something in his or her own way, is useless. I say universals do matter, since without unity nothing holds. This underlying Mind, if we use that term for the meta-pattern that connects, gives unity, community.[61]

Most people cannot see patterns in their fields of vision and experience unless they have the vocabulary to think about them, the right metaphor to let them pick the patterns out in their distinctiveness, the focus to perceive them. Original thinkers, poets, seers have a more direct experience of images as their source of knowledge; ordinary people follow in the footsteps of an Einstein rather than exploring time, energy, gravity, matter, etc., in a radical way themselves. Thomas Kuhn made this point in his study of paradigm changes in scientific thinking. After a new model succeeds in being accepted, it is taught, and becomes dogma, and it is taken for granted; people begin to think of it as the way things are and always have been, a cut-and-dried habit-hardened "reality."[62] But each vision is makeshift, temporary, and subject to revision as time passes. Emerging now are concepts like fractals and attractors, to be refined in coming years.

Cartoon of a soldier armed with a soldier, who likewise is armed with a soldier. Author's collage of a figure in a newspaper cartoon by J. V. T.

Gregory Bateson explored how evolution is a mental process. It is systemic, and the natural processes of evolution have parallels with other systemic processes, including thinking. Thinking and evolution are akin to each other; they share a pattern which connects. They are similar processes with feedback loops allowing for self-correction. Bateson's daughter, Mary Catherine Bateson, who works on some of the same issues as her father, explains that "the sacred," in this view of things, refers to matters "intrinsic to description" and thus can be recognized as part of "necessity." A mode of knowing which sees a certain sacred quality in the way the biological realm is organized may be more accurate and in tune with wise decision-making than one that sees nature as mere dead matter devoid of spirit.[63] Both Batesons believe the sacred, the aesthetic, and consciousness should not be left out of a theory of human action in the world. Anthropological and ecological order overlap, as Mary Catherine Bateson showed in her book *Our Own Metaphor,* which described a conference organized around her father's work. In this view, the universe is a process which in a certain sense *thinks*.

The universe thinks: at every level it shows thoughts about affinity, forces being drawn together in gravity, love, and other dynamic bonds. Being pervading the basins of space thinks up light clusters, whirling galaxies of stars. On earth the universe has thoughts of fresh air, rainforest oxygen moved by dynamic winds which are spurred by the sun. Stones are ideas of hard stability, endurance. The universe has thoughts of fertility in valleys, dryness in deserts, heights in the Himalayas and Andes and on Kilimanjaro. Imagine how the whole interlinking set of cosmic conditions thinks of life and comes up with forms of energy, some slow (worms), some fast and able to fly (birds), some fierce (tigers), and some huge (elephants and whales). The universe thinks of regeneration in spring; storms wash the atmosphere and germinate new seeds; lightning strikes and weeds the dry forest with fire, an idea of consuming brightness and heat; new creatures are born and old ones die and become earth. The universe goes on thinking and nothing stands still. The ocean of existence mulls things over with its tides.

There is a dynamic richness in this view, a holistic depth. This idea is capable of opening many fresh perspectives for modern people: to better understand natural systems, think of them as ideas. Theodore Roszak further explores this view:

> The systems we see around us in nature are the cosmologically given archetypes of what rises to articulate self-awareness in us as "thoughts." We think because, in some sense that blends the literal and the figurative, the universe "thinks." It conjures up ideas. The historical and hierarchical progression is from natural systems, as old perhaps as the initial cosmological conditions, through the human mind toward the social, cultural, technological systems that make up our portion of life on Earth. At which point, reflecting upon the nature of things, we mirror the ideas that were our progenitors—the great system of the universe that encompasses all the rest.[64]

There are a growing number of works on facets of this theme. For example, Gerald Edelman in his book *Bright Air, Brilliant Fire* asserts that the early development of neural pathways in the brain is governed by Darwinian selection. Living beings carry within them (and in their language) the signs of their long journey of growth and mutation—what some call "prochronisms."[65]

We are mirrors of the universe. A seed from a tree or a man holds the whole universe it its depth of possibility. Gary Snyder, a poet inspired by both Zen and tribal peoples, is profound enough to elude convenient categories of academia. (Is he a nature poet? A student of tribal ways? An anthropologist? A Zen Buddhist philosopher? An ecologist?) Snyder has developed a vision of nature both rigorous and playful over the past half century. In the preface to his *No Nature: New and Collected Poems,* he notes that nature has a way of always being beyond our knowledge. He reflects that ordinary life goes on despite all the whimsical fads and fashions that run through societies, as well as the delusions which sway large populations and the "enabling mythologies"—stories that give a rationale to life's circumstances. Snyder asserts that nature in the wild probably sports a similar goofiness, with amazing varieties of life forms (like zebra fish and Venus flytraps) subsisting somehow on earth's varied terrains. Nature, Snyder reminds us, means the whole physical universe, not excluding city life, industrial developments and toxic products and byproducts, which exist alongside trees and grass. Nature in Snyder's view inevitably eludes our preconceived notions and our attempts to capture it in human theories. He insists that a single fixed entity called "nature" doesn't actually exist (hence the title of his book), and that a sense of knowing the true "nature of things" also is more an illusion in the mind than a reality which humans have fathomed. Snyder suggests we best respect nature by not attempting to trap it, but by admitting it always slips from our clutches, and by seeing that our own innate "nature" likewise shares in wild nature's qualities of fluidity, openness, and an existence which interdepends on certain conditions.[66]

Snyder's poetry and essays reflect the richness of the natural universe and his realizations. Here is an example: "Nature is not a book, but a performance, a high old culture . . . Ever-fresh events / Scraped out, rubbed out, and used, used, again . . ."[67] One can explore the oneness of nature and culture by looking into the "culturelikeness" of nature or the "naturelikeness" of culture. There is a story which may help dramatize the need for this exercise.

Men who deny their emergence from and dependence upon nature are like a reductionist sailor who built a boat to get from port A to port B. It was a linear project to make him some money. But he did not notice that the ocean is a nonlinear system that has undertows, storms, typhoons, cycles of climate, and so on. It is connected with winds and moon, sun and stars. But the sailor, merely concerned with short-term gain, using linear thinking and purposive behavior, concentrated on getting from A to B. And the ocean (or nature or *samsara*) in time always swallows such a sailor in its undertow. We might think of him as a man, a generation, a civilization. No matter how big his boat, he is not going to be master of it all. He is a pilgrim passing through, and he has a part to play. But to assume the right to pilot nature to his own liking is hubris. There is an undertow, an "underTao," a deep-down-under unconscious which it is perilous to ignore and deny. There are overarching realities he cannot dictate to but instead must submit to and cooperate with. A better model for the conscious person in the cosmos might be constant flexible subjectivity adjusting like a moving mirror, a meta-center which embraces and reflects all as a fractal made of a variety of possible fractals.

Relativity and paradox have changed our understanding, and time has undermined systems which tried to live out the rational utopia. The Goddess of Paradox, the Goddess of Spirituality, the Goddess of the Pattern that Connects—as we begin the new millennium these sisters are bringing a loosening of the structures within which the mind is compelled to live. As philosopher Charles Peirce said, on some matters it is good to befriend the "logical vague"[68] in its own terms and on its own scale—to become too crisp about the inherently mysterious or to become fuzzy too quickly is to mislead.

There are some processes in nature which work slowly, like water wearing away stone. The earth had to initiate herself. Time is the wounder and healer, the educator of nature. The experience of evolution is a constant test and reinitiation. Part of learning from nature about nature and ourselves involves trusting the unconscious and growing like a seed, not knowing all we know.[69] Artists and creative thinkers of all kinds know the importance of this—playing, experimenting, taking chances, following a hunch, not knowing exactly why something seems right but staying with it and developing it anyway. This takes a careful, well-trained intuition.

Humans of the modern era live out a bizarre relationship with nature: born of seed and egg, made of cells that are made of particles from the primordial Lightburst, we deny our family relationship with nature, we distance ourselves, as if we suffer from amnesia. Actually we practice many forms of forgetfulness. We've come a long way, from river valley to palace and cathedral spires to satellites, and we've gained digital technology, but we have lost knowledge of valuable "country ways." Unlike many creatures on the levels of life from which we ascended, we fear the dark and avoid our deep background. A look into our organic past shows we have DNA similar to that of all forms of life. But we are not just *de*scendants; we are *a*scendants too, we have a second birth away from earth and toward the spiritual sky. When we obliterate awareness of our origins in the "order for free" emerging in the turbulent universe we act in ways that are crazy and destructive. When we enrich the health of life on earth we sustain our future generations of descendants, who hopefully will continue to ascend. We share the fate of nature. A return to the source is in order. We need to learn to be resourceful in a deeper, wider sense, truly knowing the cosmos out of which we have cultured ourselves.

Nature and Culture in the Relations of Humanity and Land

> Until the human is understood as a dimension of the earth, we have no secure basis for understanding any aspect of the human. We can understand the human only through the earth. Beyond the earth, of course, is the universe and the curvature of space. This curve is reflected in the curvature of the earth and finally in that psychic curve whereby the entire universe reflects back on itself in human intelligence.
>
> —Thomas Berry[70]

In order to explore and visualize some specific examples of correspondences which relate nature and culture, land and man, let's first consider some fractals in nature. I will illustrate some of these patterns from a variety of levels to make them easier to see.

Some plants have a distinct fractal form. Isomorphs such as the Kentucky coffee tree and the compound umbel have branches with self-similar branches with self-similar branches. Other fractals are more subtle and require patient examination to be seen. Ferns (fronds of fronds of fronds), asparagus (little spears making up a larger spear and tiny spears folded into the head), cauliflower, garlic bulbs (which break down into cloves which are like smaller versions of the unbroken whole bulb): the list goes on, making a banquet of stalks, fruits, and vegetables with fractal qualities.

Articles in scientific journals explore the fractal dimension of the wind, fractal river basins, chance and self-organization, fractals

Cauliflowers show self-similarity on several scales, hence are fractals. Photo courtesy of Benoit Mandelbrot, Yale University.

as a way to characterize the aggregate distributions of particles in soils, the fracturing of a chunk of metal, earthquakes. Just enter "fractals" in a bibliographic search and you will generate growing lists of fractal titles. Fractals are involved in animal movements such as the foraging patterns of the albatross, the patterns best suited to the survival of birds in their environment, and the movements of insects in micro-landscapes. M. F. Barnsley's *Fractals Everywhere* offers other examples with illustrations.[71] Waves of sand dunes, ocean tides, cloud shapes; lightning, mountains, and coastlines; indeed, to the observant seeker fractals *are* everywhere.

In the human being, fractal structures exist in the "bile duct system, the urinary collecting tubes in the kidney, the brain, the lining of the bowel, the neural networks . . . the placenta";[72] the heart and lungs display structures of self-similarity on a number of scales. There are billions of neurons in the brain, branching dendrites reaching out like a vast fractal forest. There are many synapses where neurons interrelate—"talk to each other," making up pathways of thought. Muscle tissue is made up of bundles of bundles of bundles of bundles—look at a cross-section and you see myrofibrils bundled within fascicles, fascicles bundled within sacs.

Fractal structures are shared by various forms of organic life, including humans. Leaving aside Eastern traditions on this topic for the moment, let us consider some Western thinking. German philosopher Friedrich von Schelling developed the concept of *naturphilosophe* (natural philosophy, or natural science), which shaped the Romantic movement. J. G. Herder argued that close links between human beings and the geographical places where they live offer proof that human beings are an intrinsic part of nature, not a creature apart.[73] Johann Joachim Winckelmann's *History of Ancient Art* (1849–1873) influenced the German philosophers Herder, Schelling, Goethe, and Georg Hegel, as well as other Romantics. Von Richthofen developed a "special geography" based on the idea that "Every area on the earth, no matter how small, whether a continent, a small island, or a naturally bounded state, a mountain, a river basin or a sea, is examined as a grouping of smaller unit areas."[74] He called the study and description of these units "chorography." Carl Ritter theorized about how structures of countries played crucial parts in determining the development of the people who lived there. He sought to construct a holistic global view and took steps in that direction, developing some of Herder's ideas, seeking laws that unite the diversity of nature with qualities in human life. Earlier thinkers also explored and wrote evocatively of the relations between human beings and the land on which they live and depend.

Today it is recognized more commonly (because of ecological

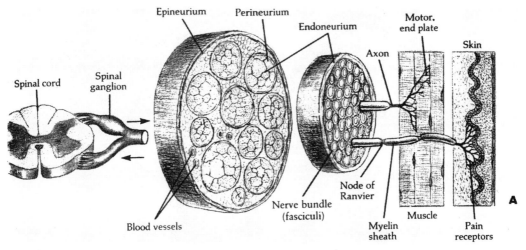

Epineurium Perineurium Endoneurium Motor, end plate Skin

Spinal cord Spinal ganglion Axon Node of Ranvier Nerve bundle (fasciculi) Blood vessels Myelin sheath Muscle Pain receptors

A

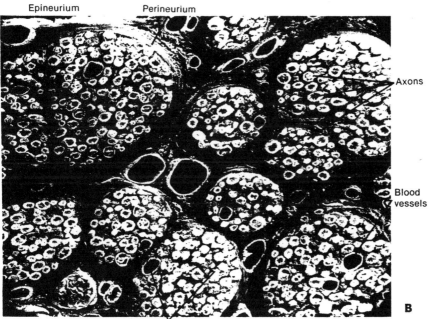

Epineurium Perineurium Axons Blood vessels Endoneurium

B

studies which show interdependence) that the world around us exists also deep within us. A vivid example from Arctic conditions can help us recognize the truth of this fact. Notice the self-reflective images conveyed by the observant and intuitive naturalist writer Barry Lopez in this passage in which he develops a holistic vision of the terrain and fauna of Alaska:

> The land, an animal that contains all other animals, is vigorous and alive. The challenge to us, when we address the land, is to join with cosmologists in their ideas of continuous creation, and with physicists in their ideas of spatial and temporal paradox, to see the subtle grace and mutability of the different landscapes. They are crucibles of mys-

Bundles of bundles of bundles. Reprinted from *Pathophysiology: The Biologic Basis for Disease in Adults and Children*, Kathryn L. McCance and Sue E. Huether, 941, Copyright 1994 Mosby, Inc., with permission from Elsevier Science.

"Spirits of the North," by Sally J. Smith. The "mind" in the universe, and the ecological "landscape" in the living creature, are inextricably entwined. © 2003 Smith/ Applejack Licensing.

tery, precisely like the smaller ones that they contain—the arctic fox, the dwarf birch, the pi-meson; and the larger ones that contain them, side by side with such seemingly immutable objects as the Horsehead Nebula in Orion. These are not solely areas for human invention. To have no elevated conversation with the land, no sense of reciprocity with it, to rein it in or to disparage conditions not to our liking, shows a certain lack of courage, too strong a preference for human devising.[75]

Which shall dominate—land or man? Lopez considers the power of the land to be timelessly beautiful and terrifying: "It penetrates all cultures, archaic and modern. The land gets inside us; and we must decide one way or another what this means, and what we will do about it."[76] Lopez observes how for many centuries Eskimos have accepted the land; their task is to achieve congruence with it. Modern Americans generally accept the view that the land is to be changed, controlled, and exploited. Lopez observes that we avoid the deeper paradoxes of our surrounding landscape, where we find "horror within magnificence, absurdity within intelligibility, suffering within joy."[77] With all the technology and power modern people wield over the earth, we are not strong enough to face those complex knots of life. We are too often concerned with finding ways to impose a desired order and not often enough aware of the deep order already present. The easier life we make often allows us to postpone facing hard truths, but it cannot obliterate that fiery moment forever. I believe a fractal sensibility (an awareness of wholeness in which the parts integrally reflect the whole in which they participate) can help us picture our situation with greater accuracy. In his book *African Fractals* Ron Eglash argues for the mathematical sense of African designs. These patterns show an undeniable beauty and fitness, a fractal wisdom of organization of space.

Perhaps people in the modern age are ready to appreciate the

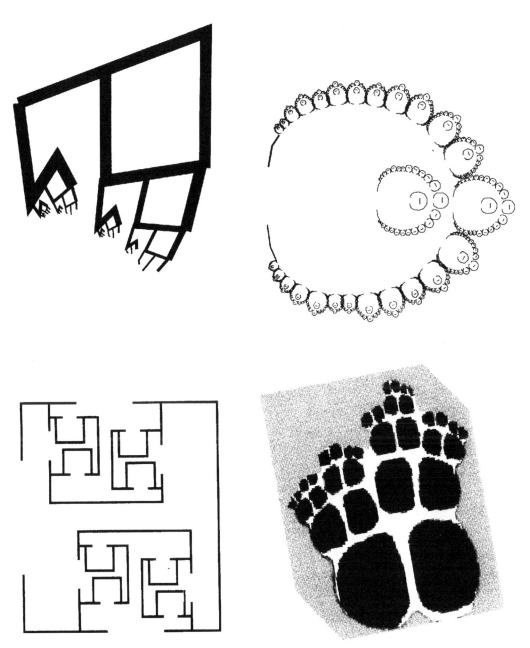

These configurations of space show how Africans organize paths and dwellings in fractal patterns. Clockwise from top: streets of Cairo; a Ba-ila settlement; a Senegalese settlement; a Bamileke settlement. Courtesy of Ron Eglash, *African Fractals: Modern Computing and Indigenous Design* (New Brunswick, N.J.: Rutgers University Press, 1999).

ways of the cosmos more than they have been at some other times in the past. A look at the life of a hero of modern thought might illustrate this.

Descartes Encounters Chaos and Backs Off

The souls of the dead are no bigger than a grain of wheat when they come, yet they too like to have their backs protected from the wind of nothing, the wind of Descartes, and of all who grew thin in maternal deprivation.

—Robert Bly[78]

René Descartes was born in 1596 in La Haye, France; soon after his birth his mother died of tuberculosis. His father feared that the little boy, who grew "thin in maternal deprivation," would die too, but despite his delicate health, he survived.

Descartes was an inquisitive child with contemplative moods, and his father began calling him "my li'l philosopher" even while he was a small boy. From the age of eight he studied at a Jesuit school. In the mornings, because of his delicate health, he was allowed to stay in bed. He would lie there in solitude, thinking, reading classics, brooding, while his classmates were in the classroom reciting their lessons, showing the teachers what they had memorized. Descartes followed this pattern of working in bed like an invalid even as an adult, finding it a fertile place to develop his own ideas instead of simply accepting what everyone else was taught to think.

From 1612 to 1616 Descartes studied law. Then, feeling wanderlust and craving a change of scene, he traveled to Paris, where he met wealthy youths who liked to gamble, finding it an exciting diversion. He was good at games of chance because as a clever mathematician he could figure out the odds and reduce the element of chance as well as or better than others playing the games. But after a while the excitement wore off and he was bored with games of chance, too.

For two years he pursued mathematical questions. Restless, craving action, he joined the army. Partly in response to the religious war which was troubling Europe during this time Descartes developed a method of reasoning which was to become known as Cartesian philosophy, and he worked out the principles of analytic geometry, the basis of modern mathematics, methods of "conducting the reason" and procedures for searching out a certain kind of truth based on visible proof in the sciences. His work in these areas of thought became the basic principles of modern science. The enterprise was so new that the word "scientist" was not coined until two centuries later.

After a few years of life as a soldier and traveler, Descartes settled down. He lived a rather secluded life but corresponded widely with other thinkers. He was afraid his thinking might stir the church to persecute him, so he did not publish much of his work, but friends persuaded him to publish his *Discourse on Method* (the full original title was *Discourse on the Method of Rightly Conducting the Reason and Seeking Truth in the Sciences*). It is significant that, like Copernicus and Galileo, Newton and Pascal, Descartes was celibate. This rational style of truth-seeking ordained a new priesthood, in a manner of speaking, dedicated to a new vision. Whether consciously or not, the subtler powers of thought were fueled by the sublimation of basic energies.

Descartes wrote his meditations in French, the vernacular of the day, rather than Latin. Anyone who could learn and think for himself could explore Descartes's thoughts, while Latin was the language of the authorities, the old knowledge, limited to the elite. (This choice of colloquial expression in the mother tongue has been significant in history, East and West. It has given rise to new literatures and classics, and has been important in waves of religious change. The Buddha spoke a regional language, rather than Sanskrit. Bhakti saints sang and wrote verses in their mother tongues, including Tamil, Hindi, Telugu, and Kannada. Dante chose a dialect of Italian for the *Divine Comedy*. Luther translated the Bible into German.) Descartes's new ideas, written in French, enjoyed the advantage of offering fresh perspectives in everyday language, and they attracted other intellectuals of the day.

In the collective folk memory, often a hero in a particular field is given heightened importance while lesser or previous contributors are forgotten, and such was the case with Descartes. Placing Descartes in the context of previous and subsequent thinkers will help us see his importance. Addison wrote that Descartes, by his intellectual grasp of the heavens, "destroyed those orbs of glass which antiquity had fixed above" and "scorned any longer to be bounded within the straits and crystalline walls of an Aristotelic world." As the inventor of analytic geometry (with Pierre Fermat), Descartes connected algebra and geometry to lay the foundations for modern mathematics. "Cartesian doubt" refers to Descartes's insistence that methodic doubt was necessary to clear the way for fresh thinking. Voltaire, Descartes, Locke, and the other modern thinkers start out with cobweb-sweeping doubt and a "clean slate" (though most now doubt presuppositions can be erased so easily). Descartes is at the root of a subjective and idealistic tradition of thought in modern philosophy, as Bacon is at the root of an objective and realistic tradition. Descartes spoke for the primacy of consciousness, the idea or experience of the mind knowing itself first and foremost, and this was part and parcel of Renaissance individualism. Descartes' famous statement "I think, therefore I am" implies that the explorations of philosophy must begin with the philosopher's own thinking self—the body and the world are less certain. This began a series of epistemological arguments involving other philosophers—Leibniz, Kant, Berkeley, Hume, Locke, and others. Kant tried to turn the tide against secular and sometimes atheist rationalist approaches which originated with Descartes and Bacon, and which resulted in the skepticism of Hume and Diderot. Like Pascal, Kant denied that the intellect was the supreme authority in the arena of transcendental problems. The impact of Darwin's and Spencer's thinking went against Kant's cause, and some of Kant's and Schopenhauer's success in influencing Western thought was taken away by proponents of mechanist materialism. Bergson tried to show a way beyond mechanism with the concept of *élan vital;* the dialectic goes on age after age.[79]

More than one momentous move in thinking can be traced back to Descartes. His statement that "The nature of physical things is much more easily conceived when they are beheld coming gradually into existence, than when they are only considered as produced at once in a finished and perfect state" was momentous because at that time the modern world was becoming self-conscious of the logic which from then on would control its understanding, "the logic of which Darwin's *Origin of Species* is the latest scientific achievement."[80] The concept of evolution was a big paradigm shift for modern Western thinking to absorb, moving from mythological views of creation which included a symbolic representation of wholeness but were static.

Descartes believed there are two entities. There is mind (or soul) which comes from God, and there is dead matter, which is mindless "extension." These two meet uneasily in the will of human beings and make humans act, allowing the mind to know. Descartes's system needs no Creator's continuing actions to explain the universe as it is; his system pictures the universe as capable of reaching this state from any given beginning by means of mechanical evolution.[81] Descartes's dualism of mind and body is problematic, a crude metaphor which is a falsehood the modern world is stuck with and seems unable to get beyond unless moderns rediscover the lost soul. Arguments against the mind/body dichotomy, problematizing the metaphor, calling it into crisis with critical thought, and conceiving of alternatives, have been well made by Arthur Koestler, Ken Wilbur, Gregory Bateson, and many others. Constructive postmodern thinking, organicism, Bateson's *Mind and Nature: A Necessary Unity,* ecology, the women's movement, the men's movement, nonlinear thinking, postcolonialism, dynamic systems theory, and complexity studies all work to understand and undo disasters.

The pale-faced Descartes lounged in his bed,[82] just thinking, alienated from his body, saying, "I think, therefore I exist," not "I breathe, I love, I explore the landscape, therefore I am." The modern outlook is deeply associated with our ability to live in the brain, separated from the body. But man does not live by brooding alone. Moderns get others to do their work for them so their heads won't be bothered with hands-on action and its results: less-educated people have only their bodies. Subordinates without education generally have only their own bodies in the present moment for the experience of living.

A moment in Descartes's life—his encounter with chaos, we might risk calling it—is worth pondering. At the age of twenty-three Descartes envisioned a vortical pattern (a tourbillon or spiral whirl in the solar system) which he thought at the time was an inspired vision, and he wrote about it on a piece of parchment under a title suggestive of divine heights, "Olympica." It was evidently a dizzying experience which felt unusually significant to him at the time, and the original dream led to a couple of other dreamlike thoughts while he was still half asleep. The image Descartes experienced was like a Zen koan. He characterized it as strange, terrifying and ominous, and he puzzled over it as if trying to feel what the momentous-seeming glimpse of the cosmos meant.

This traumatic inner drama happened November 10, 1619, when Descartes was in Germany, intoxicated with the enthusiasm of discovery, making some of his breakthroughs in thinking that would lay foundations for modern science. In this feverish state of excitement, the young mathematician had a dream. He experienced being spun around, as if in a whirlwind, and this threw him off course, disorienting him. As if startled by a bolt of lightning, he opened his eyes and saw sparklets swirling in the space around him in the room. Then he opened a poetry book and read, "What way of life shall I iterate?" As he was being spun around, he began to realize that the course of his life and his grasp of existence were not all in his conscious control; he lost the rigid ego's self-centered illusion of self-determination. The book seemed to suggest that the insight of poetic visualization is deeper, prior to and inclusive of philosophical reasoning. Descartes fell asleep on his left side, and then turned over on his right, having negative associations with the left (feeling that an evil wind was blowing him away) and positive associations with the right (feeling it was the side of the Spirit of Truth, revealing realities) in a binary, linear way. He imposed a rational order on every jot and tittle of the dream, as if to thereby protect himself from its implications.[83] But the way it deeply disturbed him gives us a glimpse of a moment in which his confused conscience was trying to tell him something; it seemed momentarily to put his venture into a relativistic perspective. It must have felt like being whirled in a bewildering flurry, suffering a breakdown of order and then recovering control with a return to focused thinking. He still had a lot to do, and so he hurried past this glimpse of confusion and insecurity. He sought relief from the unease of uncertainty, and quickly chose a static reductionism instead of life's whorl of fluidity. Thus the West postponed a realization of the limits of rationalism—it had three centuries of business to take care of first. Descartes's experience, though significant enough to be remembered, was not useful in his time; it was an answer to a question which science was not yet ready to ask.[84]

"What way of life shall I iterate?" It was a poignant moment for the brilliant mathematician and innovative philosopher, a crisis. What could be smaller than a spiral of light in the cells of the eye? Yet what could be greater than the basic mystery of the dynamic cosmos it reflects? One can feel the binary uncertainty of the unlabeled metaphor in his dream being experienced as reality—it feels like all meaning but can also evaporate, vanish like light fading from the eyes, leaving no meaning. A way of life is a whole; it needs to be a "one" holding many. Yet without wisdom, such as the Hindu and Buddhist insights into self, or the Christian view such as is found in Meister Eckhart's or Thomas Merton's works, for example, the paradox goes unresolved. One hurries on, too conscious to delve into what way of life is to be iterated.

Descartes, Milton, Rossini, and Leibniz all had inspirations while lying down. The West does not have yoga's *padmasana* (upright "lotus position") as part of meditation's methodology—Rodin's "Thinker" ponders with bent spine. If Descartes had had more inspirations while active—perhaps mountain-climbing like Nietzsche—his view might have included the body more integrally, might have been more in tune with the actual dynamics of life's wholeness. The disembodied mind is precariously Faustian. The reclining man's faith in technique, his hope for unlimited progress through scientific technology, his charitable gaze toward whatever seems convenient—none are virtues with long-term results, though they reap great short-term profits. They leave a confusing legacy of false expectations of exploitation and disappointments of disembodied individualism to future generations. The legacy of Descartes's search for "clear and distinct ideas" is great, though often unconscious, like Victorian ideas with steam-engine dynamics in the background, and colonialists in company uniforms with handlebar mustaches, like the mechanical nutcracker device shaped like a soldier in the *Nutcracker Suite*. Jekyll and Hyde and Dorian Gray emerge in the colonialist experiment. A fondness for quick efficiency and control, nostalgia for oversimple shortcuts, and denial of messiness prevents the inconvenient "anomaly" that is a chance to see depth. Mechanical, materialistic,

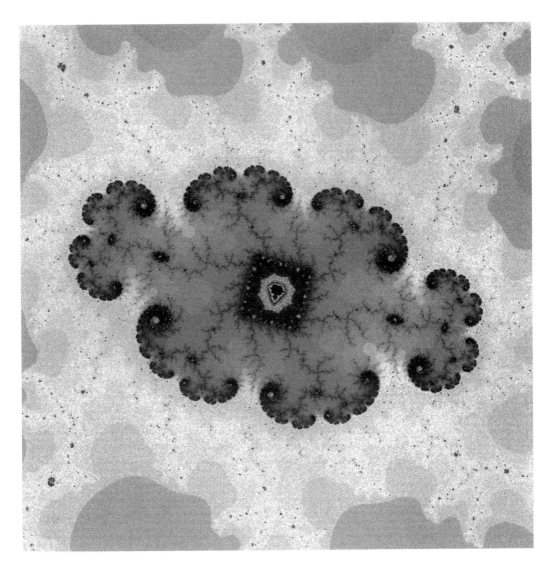

linear-paradigm programs are still in high gear. Technology is ease for horizontal spines, but the living whorl of wildness is basic and keeps intruding.

Mandelbrot set. Courtesy of Michael Frame, Mathematics Dept., Yale University.

    The dysfunctional world's symptoms are in part manifestations of the human attitude that de-souled them—Christian and Cartesian. Descartes did not literally deny the existence of a soul—in fact he said man is divided into mortal body and immortal soul. That soul is the thinking process in man, the ability to cogitate in a mathematical mode[85]—which looks at the world as if it's dead, soulless. "Having denied the soul in things, having said to things, with Descartes, 'You don't have souls,' things have turned around and said, 'Just you watch what kind of a soul I have.' "[86] Man does not live by his head alone. Descartes was a man (one who looked like an honest Dutch merchant, according to Balzac in *Illusions perdues*); men are mortal, and proceed timewise by logic-light. But even Descartes posited the pituitary gland as a sort of a gateway between the realms of mind and body.[87] He wrote his *Meditations* as a philosophical basis for a new mathematical physics "which would be acceptable and attractive to the Church."[88] He succeeded. But now many see the need to balance his kind of thinking with a kind which pays more attention to the meaning of nature's elusive wholeness and the human life within it.

What Way of Culture Shall We Iterate?

For humans to live a balanced life in society, and to find fulfillment, requires a holistic practice of work, worship, wisdom. As Jung wrote, "Necessities exist in ourselves: Nature and culture. We cannot only be ourselves, we must also be related to others. Hence a way must be found that is not a mere rational compromise; it must also be a state or process that wholly corresponds with the living being. it must be a *semita et via sancta,* as the prophet says, a *via directa ita ut stulti non errant per eam* ("A path and a holy way"; "a straight way so that fools shall not err therein."—Isaias 35:8)."[89] The three together—dedicated action, spiritual love, and intuitive wisdom—make for an integrative spirituality. It is a "straight way" in that it is an auspicious direction in a world of endless change and uncertainty. The triple way is a main road, with dynamic feedback loops, junctions, and cloverleafs when needed, for pilgrims on a long journey. This is a time-honored answer to the question of how culture can best relate to nature.

In our encounters with the world, Jung reminds us, the psyche plays a crucial part. As Jung suggests, civilization is never merely a reaction to environment. The soul gives its own special reply, and more than half of what ensues is due to that responsiveness of the psyche. The psyche is the crucible of creativity where nature's creative power acts intensively. "The psychic depths are nature and nature is creative life."[90] Jung wrote that such things as making money, social existence, family, and posterity "are nothing but plain nature" and are not culture. In his view, "Culture lies beyond the purpose of nature," and producing genuine culture is the task and privilege of maturity.[91] What, besides the ability to use a part of the brain to think rationally, differentiates man from animal? Jung answers this question in the following way:

> No one makes history who does not dare to risk everything for it, even his own skin, for he carries through the experiment, which is his own life, to the bitter end; and in so doing he interprets his life, not as a continuation but as a beginning. Continuation is a business already provided for in the animal, but to initiate is the prerogative of man, the one thing of which he can boast that transcends the animal.[92]

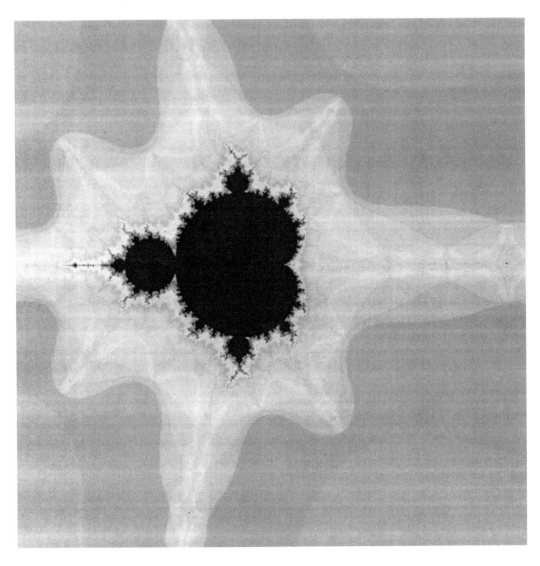

So as our electric lights and electronic devices keep us awake, disturbing circadian rhythms (much of the modern world suffers sleep disorders), we must remember this: We can never separate blood from clay, men from mountains and rivers, eyes from sun, or reality from feeling. Nature is us. Culture evolves. Psyche lives. Ralph Waldo Emerson wrote, "A friend may well be reckoned the masterpiece of nature,"[93] for life—of physical nature and man's psyche, as Heraclitus said long ago—"is an everlasting fire," and human life can glow with a wonderful light when conditions are right. We have much to be humble about, yet we are parts of an intelligence which transcends time and flows with endless creativity. We flow with fractal-like creativity, therefore we are.

To ask "What way of life shall I iterate?" is to inquire into destiny, our character, and our consciousness. A passage from a

Mandelbrot set. Courtesy of Michael Frame, Mathematics Dept., Yale University.

remarkable book by Gilles Deleuze, *Difference and Repetition,* suggests philosophically some of the fractal-like situations involved in the reiterations of our lives. Deleuze asks us to consider the experiences which we call "repetition" in life, especially in spiritual life. A series of presents follow one after another, encroaching upon each other. And yet no matter how strong the incoherence or the contrasts of the successive presents, we get the impression that each one of these presents is playing out the same life "at different levels." Deleuze says that it is this that we call "destiny." He notes that destiny does not consist in step-by-step deterministic relations between presents succeeding one another in the chronologically linear order of time. Instead it implies non-localisable links, subtly connecting successive presents, relationships acting at a distance, "systems of replay, resonance and echoes, objective chances, signs, signals and roles which transcend spatial locations and temporal successions." These nonlinear destiny-expressing presents always appear to play out the same thing, to be displays of the same story, only they express the same theme at different levels and have different degrees of intensity and relaxation, different styles and so on. (I find this to suggest a rather fractal-like pattern: character is destiny expressed in a variety of self-similar experiences.) Deleuze suggests that because of this, destiny is never in full agreement with a deterministic scheme but agrees well with freedom. He asserts that freedom lies in the personal choices of the levels. Because of this freedom the succession of presents manifests something which is actually more profound: the manner in which each successive present continues the whole life, but on a different level or a different degree in comparison to the preceding one, since the various levels and degrees of our successive experiences coexist and offer themselves for our personal choice based on a past time which was never present in a plain and simple way. "What we call the empirical character of the presents which make us up is constituted by the relations of succession and simultaneity between them, their relations of contiguity, causality, resemblance and even opposition. What we call their noumenal character is constituted by the relations of virtual coexistence between the levels of a pure past, each present being no more than the actualisation or representation of one of these levels." Thus Deleuze observes that we experience our lives empirically as a succession of continually different presents, yet from the viewpoint of active synthesis our life is also *"the ever-increasing coexistence of levels of the past within passive synthesis."* Deleuze explains that each present we experience contracts a level of the whole, and reminds us that this level is already one of relaxation or contraction. In his view, "the sign of the present is a *passage* to the limit, a maximal contraction which comes to sanction the

Anyway All

Start anywhere it's always a fractal
down in the waters above or the sky below
The same thing expands in the facets of crystals

and it's usually hidden with some kind of veil
not seeing its orders we think hey it's just so
but start anywhere you'll be led to a fractal

go to pasts caught in life's simplest cell
delicate temples in frost and in snow
the same (what?) expands in the facets of crystal

chains within chains linked into spirals
for centuries only a few almost knew
now start anywhere and find all these cracked fractals

it's too much to live just at one level
knowing unknowing, our dreaming's a flow
the strange thing expands, facets in crystals

Constant, yet tricky as laughter and jackals
loopy and lawful behind the wild show
start anywhere it's always some fractal
the same thing expands in the facets of crystals

Poem and collage by the author.

choice of a particular level as such, which is in itself contracted or relaxed among an infinity of other possible levels. Moreover, what we say of a life may be said of several lives." Since each life is a passing present, Deleuze argues, it is possible for one life to replay another at a different level, "as if the philosopher and the pig, the criminal and the saint" and all the other lives played out the same past on different levels of a gigantic cone, embodying a vast spiral of possibilities. Each living being chooses his or her pitch or his or her tone, perhaps even his or her lyrics, but the tune still remains the same in all these variations, and underneath the different lyrics the same tra-la-la is singing the common song in a multitude of tones and pitches.[94]

This description reaches to convey a fractal sensibility without having at its command the vocabulary which fractal geometry makes available. It points, as many profound observations do, toward a sense of oneness. There is a sameness or rather a self-similarity to our features and traits within the wholeness of our lives. Over a lifetime one person, first as an infant, then in kindergarten, then as a schoolchild, then as an adult, then as middle-aged, then as an elder, lives out many self-reflective aspects of a whole life. Each whole life has many self-reflective qualities.

STRAND SEVEN

ENVOY

Child of Oneness

Child All Awe and Law

This strand starts with some playful reflections exploring the paradoxes of wholeness; so expect to encounter the strangeness which paradox entails. Then it settles into examining some traditional visions of the One, and the history of the idea of natural law.

The ins and outs of the theme of oneness and partness extend as far as one can pursue them. Metaphysics, thinking about the world as a whole, attracts both mystics and scientists.[3] Whatever is deep seems to sing; whatever is real smacks of paradox. So in these breezy reflections on the One we should expect some musical conundrums to flow and some odd-looking prose (which is the way I like it) to unfold. A gnostic named Hippolytus once said that knowledge of the whole person is hard to grasp and the soul is hard to comprehend, "for knowledge of man is the beginning of wholeness, but knowledge of God is perfect wholeness."[4] To awaken the conscious self to the principle of the whole or Tao one needs to forget oneself, so that in knowing one *unknows*. (Does the timelessness of primordial depth make sense to the busy little bee of hurrying ego? Not unless it's willing to have its mind blown and take a laid-back approach to the issue of control.) Loss and finding are both involved in becoming one person; the individuation process seeks well-nuanced oneness. To come out of a trial, illness, challenge, disaster, soul trauma as a real human being is all anyone can ask for—that's life's true achievement, to be an authentic person. True success, the main thing for the life of a human being, in the view of traditional worldviews using different symbol systems, is to reach the true Self of Universal Intelligence. We all seek oneness in a cracked world, spiritual teachers have said again and again.[5] Each one craves the One, mystics such as Plotinus have said. Oneness is not just an abstraction—psyches realize it in images, such as mandalas, leading to integrative experiences.[6] But to consider the One may take many steps.

Is it possible to consider the One by freely traveling among many scales and topics in relation to the unity that connects them? (How do we get stuck in this position—taking on the Atlas task of trying to talk about Wholeness? Of course every poet, artist, and lover does this constantly.) Can we approach the One as if it were a child—say, the child Dionysus, fluid, supple, containing contrasts in dynamic wholeness? (As Heraclitus noted, the One, in differing, ultimately agrees with itself—dynamic process makes a backward-turning connection, as the string of a bow or lyre bends it around—opposites, rebellions, contraries work in one process.) Can we be light and quick, glancing at Atman, Tao, Allah, Plotinus, Yahweh, yet glancing at life, with curve of spiral, fern frond, architecture's arches, clustered notes of pulsing music, precise as peas in a pod, all as aspects of the One? Can we explore the One as vitally paradoxical, with qualities both fluid and changeless, male and female, living and dying? Can we hold on to the essential point that it is not two separate parts but both together as one?

The One is always paradoxical, and one is always initiated into the One, reborn to it as a child again, from disillusioned immaturity. Shamanic trance, yogic *samadhi* (the highest attainable state of consciousness), mystery ritual, mystic intuitions, Buddhist philosophies, participation mystiques, birth, death—all are about the One. Daytime consciousness with ego rationality dissociates itself from the all-one "contamination continuum" (Jung's term for the unconscious, where everything leaks into everything else) by labeling things in the mixed-up undifferentiated aesthetic continuum "oceanic consciousness." The unconscious is free-flowing, using this for that—a serpent with its tail in its mouth, time trapped in space, and vice versa, the big inextricable from the small.

Dreams are windows on this wholeness, ice on waves, and the profound may seem shallow to a shallow glare. The unconscious is able to unify; the One comes up with its own answers, often in concise images, weird and dynamic, to stand for One, which rational scrutiny can't quite understand no matter how hard it tries. A dream deer speaking for your Self might tell you, "I'm your child and mother, I'm a connecting animal, linking people, animals, stones with one another when I enter them. When I appear I redeem you from the meaningless hazards of life. The same fire burning in me burns in the whole of nature. If a man loses it, what does it matter if he gains the world—he's lonely, weak, sad, lost."[7] "Lost" is a word for feeling Oneless. A magical animal of instinct, an uncarved block, a crystal stone just so; all can stand for the One. Mount Kailas, sexy Goddess, Krishna, Buddha, Christ—all these are images of soul, to activate and individuate "wholicipants" of the whole. For God is copula (link among parts) and so is soul.[8] "One of the most remarkable features of the unconscious: *it is, as it were, present before our eyes in all its parts,* and is accessible to observation at any time. The reason for this paradoxical quality is that the unconscious, in so far as it is activated in any way by small amounts of energy, is projected upon certain more or less suitable objects," as Jung wrote.[9] Deep images reflect wholeness to beckon us to a depth beyond us which can heal us as well as bewilder us.

Along the way there are illusions of not-wholeness—Zen Buddhism's story of the princess who claimed she lost her eyes, and couldn't see; tied to a pillar and shown her face in a mirror, she saw. Koan struggles are paradoxical, like fish in the ocean seeking to know water, one with one, learning to go with the grain. Losing sleep in *zazen* meditation to awake to One, when one is emptiness, *ku* or *sunyata*. One as recovery of nakedness, reality, love, health, inborn intelligent energy,[10] instinct and natural harmony. Many views from various visions of, comments on, and insights into the One and about losing the One, and finding the One, will flow toward us in waves as we consider the One. The One takes many forms: wise old Proteus, god of the sea, could take on different shapes. Seekers coming to him for answers to their questions had to catch him, then hold him tight and not be fooled by any form he took—animal, plant, or whatever. An explosion billions of years ago is how the universe started, science says—original unity blew apart and has been trying to be healed ever since. Who has never felt some longing to belong? Proteus may appear as a dolphin, a palm tree with a spiderweb shimmering in the sun, at any point a glint of loneliness rocking on the waves, flashing image after image. The One is not confined but is a unified mystery of open possibilities.

> O western wind, when wilt thou blow
> So the small rain down can rain,
> Christ, that my love were in my arms
> and we in our bed again.

Loss and longing crave original wholeness. When oneness is there and we are in its embrace, obliviously in relationships of belonging with it, we may know or say little of it, but that is because we *are* it. But when it's lost, we feel bereft and spend a lifetime in disciplined or confused seeking—David Bohm on the track of quantum wholeness, Charles Manson doing harm, and everyone in between hoping in their own ways to find again the One . . .

Death and sex and One, loss of self, transformation of self are among the deepest enduring themes for all people.[11] The divine Child of Energy[12] at play, free in the wide, wide world, seems innocently or wisely unaware of any not-oneness. One can't know the One by ignorance, just as one can't get to heaven on roller skates or a feather bed. We all seek and depend, for which one of us is whole or needs no healing? Wholeness is the union of conscious and unconscious, and so wholeness is always beyond the ego's consciousness; it is immeasurable and both older and younger than consciousness. If we identify with the archetypal Child, ancient and new, the boy who rides the dolphin, the boy with wings, a lyre, or Hercules' club of power, we can go anywhere. "A child shall lead them" is an ever-hopeful teaching in Judaism. The Child is the image of undifferentiated possibilities, undecided omnipotentiality.[13]

Because everything relates to the One, we can go directly to the core, following freely, within the overall fractal organization of parts, any of the interrelated aspects. (By "fractal organization" I mean that parts of existence at various scales—a dream, an artwork, or an act of kindness—reflect the whole.) Or maybe it is better to suggest the oblivion, the self-forgetfulness involved in music, as a way of experiencing the One. In any freeing, intuitive, experimental, playful-yet-substantive fling at the One we know the unpredictable complexity of play (a basketball game, an ensemble improvising jazz, or debate and conversation, for example). Play involves dynamic ideas that are graceful and viable, workable within the rules. Play works with homemade original ideas arising from practice and soul, ideas which lead and succeed and make the player shine like a star. This does not happen through mere luck—usually chance works against us—for to win takes persistence, unflagging ideas or inspirations, energetic carry-through. Fulfillment demands struggle to succeed, giving

The enigmatic child Krishna: innocent child yet knower of all, very small yet all-encompassing, infantile yet full of cosmic power. Painting by an anonymous artist during India's colonial period. Photo of poster courtesy of Subramanyam Ramachandran.

In-Verse Map of the Mandelbrot Set

The hierarchical jaggedness in branches of lightning
becomes a mountain range with trees and clover
until one ladybug's spots suddenly take off flying

to star whorls being born, and black holes of dying
and intermittent turbulence of fractal cascade lovers
with hierarchic jaggedness in branches of lightning

like devil's staircase steps in steps of steps declining
into a garden where ladybugs, ovals in larger ovals,
zoom inward forever and then one and all go flying

making mooncurves, arcs of spirals, stars in eye cells
squaredancing skies, each one whirling into others'
hierarchic jaggedness, branches forked with lightning

till cracked egg sunrise always hurting and inspiring
beyond five rolling hills above dark flowing rivers
smooth rounded ladybugs take off, their dots flying

at the sound of wailing babies with fractals of crying
calling for concentric nipples of their sweet mother
hierarchical jaggedness cries of branching lightning
becoming six butterflies of zigzaggy whimsical flying

Inverse Mandelbrot set. Image courtesy of Clifford
Pickover, *The Pattern Book: Fractals, Art, and Nature*
(Singapore: World Scientific, 1995).

one's all. The Child is "all that is abandoned and exposed and at the same time divinely powerful: the insignificant beginning, and the triumphal end; the 'eternal child' in man is an indescribable experience, an incongruity, a handicap, and a divine prerogative; an imponderable that determines the ultimate worth or worthlessness of a personality."[14]

The seeking of wholeness is discernible in the behavior of people whose families have suffered unexpected tragedies. For example, survivors of a killing may seek to learn details of how it happened, the people and objects involved, as if to fill in gaps and make a whole of parts that cohere because of the disjunction, discordant discomfort of broken senseless loss. Disjunction needs closure—wholeness. The psyche abhors a vacuum of sudden breaks which reveal no pattern of meaning. Massiveness is overwhelming, intimidating, ugly. Start small, and a tiny bit of healing knits together more and more. There are many threads you can pick up on to weave yourself back into the whole. Be like a water molecule, at home in so many conditions.

"Thou shouldst unite things whole and not whole, that which tends to unite and that which tends to separate, the harmonious with the discordant; from all things arises the One, and from the One all things arise," as a Greek philosopher of dynamic flow, Heraclitus (535–475 B.C.E.) wrote.[15] Heraclitus wrote that "the universe speaks to us in patterns." It speaks in hidden wholeness, with patterns like invisible fractal processes of soul relations. Going from one to many a tree grows from one seed, a trunk branching to many; going from many to one, a war becomes an argument, a conversation, a music, a Child.

Child of Wonder Oneness

> Eternity is a child at play, playing draughts; the kingdom is a child's. —Heraclitus[16]

> Like a child begging for "both," he must declare that Reality or the sum of all things is both at once. —Plato[17]

Think of the One all you want—as many thoughts as grains of sand—as Vedic seers, Lao-tzu, prophets, Plato, Aristotle, Plotinus, Buddha, Shankara, Aquinas, Kepler, Newton, Einstein . . . you're still a child playing, measuring sand and water with seashells on an infinite shore. Looking at stars, standing on sand. Better to keep this fluid freedom and self-awareness than to decide you are empowered to be the one who knows the only One, authorizing you to impose your oneness on all, to pave with one cement this shore in the name of a dogmatized other shore, sanctioned by words you forget are words, with your soul nowhere, lost, high and dry.

Childlike in the imaginative exuberance of his characters and his flourishes of language, Shakespeare wrote abundantly, brought his dramatic stories alive with the colors of a Dionysian fertile mind for the Globe. Shakespeare—we hear his words and feel we know his soul—yet he is unknown. The One is a secret open and closed. "It is not we who have secrets, it is the real secrets that have us."[18] You find the key to unlock them in your heart, in dreams, and in the ecosystem. And then there are the naive who use the reality of oneness as an excuse, saying since we're part of nature whatever we do is part of nature, too—strip-mining, spilling oil, melting down nuclear cores, building nuclear bombs. As logic-wielding humans we are free to use the concept or language of oneness to excuse despicable exploits, which we later learn to regret.

The Child Dionysus is "the Undivided," the Child who guides souls; Gopal, Govinda, Goswami are names of Krishna, the youthful cowherd Lord who leads the cattle with love; Christ is the shepherd boy who rescues lost sheep, wherever they may wander. Tammuz was also a shepherd, and in ancient times the weepers for Tammuz melted in their grief and became one with the dying rising life they celebrated.

The Child loves the whole playground of scales, loves miniature worlds in playthings. Culture is the world in art and fantasy and the textures and style of everyday life. Chuang-tzu's supple child dance, which takes place on many levels at once, is a moving dance to reconcile and unite opposites, to guide the soul into these swirls and move through this fractal healing process. ("Fractal" and "healing" because both words have to do with wholeness.) Dionysus plays on the strings, making music at various levels, twining them together to hold things in place. How do things happen in so orderly a way, with rhythms coming and going at so many levels—why are all events not at once in time, and all bunched up in space—why is there beauty, order, symmetry, meaning, glory—the joyous Child's play spread out like fractal patterns? Kokopelli, the humpbacked flute player, keeps wandering the One's landscapes with quirky song and eros rampant.

If the Child is there (Lao-tzu calls himself "only a glorious infant still nursing at the breast"[19]) how far away can the Mother Goddess be? Poet Gary Snyder notes that "it is clear that the empirically observable interconnectedness of nature is but a corner of the vast 'jewelled net' which moves from without to within. The spiral (think of nebulae) and spiral conch (vulva/womb) is a symbol of the Great Goddess. It is charming to note that physical properties of spiral conches approximate the Indian notion of the world-creating dance, 'expanding form.' "[20]

Another Divine Child story is told in old Christian traditions.

> There was once a giant named Offero who lived in the old country of Canaan who was huge and strong and ugly. Offero was so proud of his might that he vowed to serve only those stronger than himself. He served a king for some time and then observed that the king trembled at the name of Satan. So he found Satan, a terrible being at the head of a great demonic host, and served him. In time he saw that the devil feared the crucifix. "I will serve the one on the cross then," he vowed. Next he met a hermit priest and asked him the way to the crucified one. "Christ? I will tell you," said the hermit, and tried to teach Offero about Jesus and how to fast and pray. "I can't do that—I don't understand it," Offero told the hermit. So the hermit told him to wait for Christ at a place where travelers crossed a river. "Use your strength to carry the weak ones over the swollen stream," his teacher told him. "I can do that," Offero said, and he built a hut of boughs, and lived there listening for travelers to help. He carried many different travelers across using a palm tree for a staff to steady his feet. One dark stormy night a child's voice called—"I need help! Carry me." (Why is he out in the storm? "The Son of Man has no place to rest his head"; therefore all places are his. The Child in this legend is said to be "smaller than small and bigger than big," like Tao or the Atman able to be at all scales.) Offero searched with his lantern and found the lone lost child on the shore. He lifted the child up onto his shoulders and waded into the waves of the "endragoned" waters as the winds raged; he had to walk slower and slower, for the weight grew heavier and heavier. In the middle of the rushing river it seemed he was carrying the whole universe. "Will I ever get to the other shore?" he wondered. And the child said, "You are carrying the weight of the origin of the earth, and I've accepted your service." Offero then realized this was none other than the Christ child and he was forgiven his sins and found the way to salvation open. On the other shore Offero planted his staff and it sprouted leaves and grew fruit. The child vanished, and Offero knelt and prayed. His name became Christopher, meaning "the one who carried Christ."

The Child carrying the world was carried across a raging stream by an almost monstrous subhuman giant, a task which required superhuman skill of muscle and balance, courage and endurance. Moreover, brute force submitted to the higher principle, the sacred. This careful carrying of the Child who was Carrier of All made Christopher into an archetype of protection, the refuge of the God in Nature, the One in the many. The Child held the whole origin of all the parts and is pictured by artists as holding a small globe, as the giant holds the child. The giant became himself, did what he could do, held the all in his docile hands. Traditions aver that each person carries the sacred origin within, and that consciousness is the light of the world. Determined to serve the greatest, Offero faced crises and realized his own spirituality in the midst of the struggles of the turbulent world.[21]

Owen Barfield suggests the parts of the cosmos held by the whole in each make up a fractal-like dynamics of metaphor. He illuminates the intention of the Christopher story in this passage:

> We cannot comprehend nature without first having grasped that the whole may be "in" each part, besides being composed *of* all its parts. We cannot comprehend imagination, or revelation, in literature without first having grasped that that very fact provides the distinction between a symbol and a metaphor. We cannot understand the Old Testament, for we cannot comprehend any significant historical record, without first having grasped the fact that particular events, or particular stretches of history, may themselves be symbols of the whole. And we cannot comprehend the New Testament, unless we have also understood that we are confronted with the paradigm of all symbol both in space and in time, when not merely *natura naturans* becomes manifest to the understanding and the senses as *natura naturata*—which was and is happening all the time and everywhere—but also the one voluntary origin of *natura naturans* itself become manifest as *natura naturata* in the body of a single human being.[22]

This dynamic of the cosmic image is true not only of Jesus for Christians, but of Krishna for Hindus, of Buddha for Buddhists, and of other figures for other faiths: their symbolic life holds the whole and provides access to it.[23] To be a true archetype, an image must unite opposites, mediating the conscious and unconscious. The Child is also the "biggest boy," the High God, Zeus, for the "Primordial Child [is the] . . . monotone that consists of all notes at once, the Leitmotif that develops into all the other divine 'figures.' " The cosmic One includes all, like one vast fractal.[24] The One includes us yet looms beyond us, immeasurable, a Being of beings.

Traipsing through the One in any direction or dimension is fine with agile Chuang-tzu, for he is a most adaptable "old boy," always ready to revel in mindboggling perspectives. In ancient Chinese tales, the sage is often pictured as supple as a child. Chuang-tzu provides a good introduction to fractals because he fluidly considers many sizes without the usual prejudices. His talk of scales, which makes all seem rather interchangeable, allows us to zoom in to the tiny and see how the small equals the vast. Any scale is enough and more—it is all you can handle; it will occupy you for the time being. Each scale is equal to any others in intricacy—it has its own net of structures and relations, its own rhythms and nature. Usual standards fail when we are faced with Chuang-tzu's vision. He says, "You've heard men's music but not the music of earth; you may have heard earth's music, but not

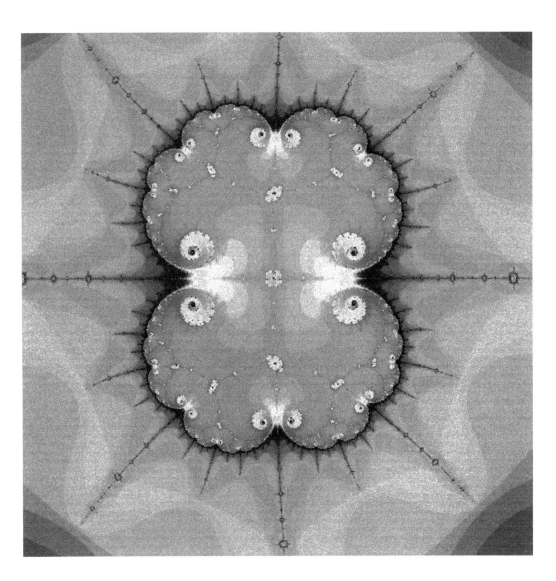

Symmetrical fractal image. Courtesy of Michael Frame, Mathematics Dept., Yale University.

heaven's; heaven's is vaster, deeper, longer played. Hear thunder and river wind as music."[25] The vast shows some scope of the One beyond our conventional human-sized view of things.

The childlike sage Chuang-tzu revels in Zen-like paradoxes as if unbound by usual standards of perception. "Under heaven there is nothing greater than a feather, and the T'ai mountain is small. There is no one more long-lived than a child who dies prematurely, and P'eng Tsu did not live out his time. Heaven, earth, and I were produced together and all things and I are one. Since they are one, can there be speech about them?"[26] How can these contradictions be true? A tare seed is greater than a mountain—don't get fixed in your view, be flexible enough to give the tare seed close attention and it will seem like a mountain. Chuang-tzu writes, "The white colt leaps over the crevice and vanishes; this is the life of man."[27] The synapse fires, the subtle charge registers, the flashing colt gallops on. The free play among scales gives the mobile imagination liberating visions of cosmic freedom, all within One.[28]

The Child holds the principle of ambivalence; there the Dionysian dance takes its steps, not just this or that, here or there, but playing with ambidextrous possibilities: "wherever ambivalence appears there is a possibility for Dionysian consciousness."[29] If one is ambivalent about ambivalence, one is one-sided. The One is not one-sided but full of endless possibilities, both pandemonium days and nights of atonement and peace.

The Child is the hard-to-attain treasure, the jewel, the pearl, the flower, the chalice, the golden egg, and the perfect circle. Writers seek to make a perfect text, but every text is flawed. Yet we may console ourselves with the thought of the Navaho weaving custom—the weaver always leaves a "flaw thread," a mistake, so the design is not perfect. That way spirit can enter—passing through an escape hatch, a loophole in the law, means to transcend what is here and discover truth for oneself. Freedom! Fair enough—you are welcome to that. Flaw makes it all the better; soul needs things to work on, work out, get involved in, then find a way out of. In other words, since this is a mystery we're talking about I don't have to write the final word, the exact perfect dogmatic explanation—I can suggest, I can cite, I can evoke and celebrate and gently indicate. Especially since the topic is an ineffable mystery which you experience as an eternal Child, life's flow forward, tomorrow's hope, the Child Savior promised to those who wait and watch, the sphere of wholeness which is the self and a shapeshifter that can be friend or fiend.[30]

Hidden in the Layers of Scale from DNA to Stretchmark Galaxies

> I had come forth on purpose to look for them, but did not expect to find them so soon. Such is the difference between looking for a thing and waiting for it to attract your attention. In the last case you are not interested at all about it, and probably will never see it. —Henry David Thoreau[31]

> Every individual is a spark of the effulgence of God; God is dancing in every cell of every being. —Sathya Sai Baba[32]

> But as no one can appreciate the beauty of a poem unless his vision embraces it as a whole, so no one can see the beauty of the orderly governance of creation unless he has an integral view of it. —Bonaventure[33]

It was in the vital interests of mystics to see signs and wonders of Oneness in direct observations and in the image-forming un-

The fractal-like aspects of the thirteenth-century Castel del Monte, built in southeastern Italy under Arabic influence, are discussed in Heinz Gotze, *Castel del Monte: Geometric Marvel of the Middle Ages*, trans. Mary Schäfer (Munich: Prestel, 1998).

conscious. Otherwise they could find no meaning for what felt momentous. Everything deep is to some degree accessible but is typically hidden. Some orders are hidden by their seeming simplicity—a rough-barked tree, for example. We oversimplify when we consider them to be merely rough textures rather than seeing their "patterned chaos." Some things appear to be so complex that it seems pointless to us to try to sort out their haphazard tangles. Gnostics saw ignorance as a cloud covering over truth, as did the Buddhists. Hinduism's *maya* is the veil, the spinning dancer, creating illusion by stimulating unconscious projections.

Images of hiddenness: A jewel in a dunghill, a king masked in weeds, a diamond in the rough. The Tao, according to Lao-tzu, is said to be the "host barely appearing to exist, yet existing the most."[34] Water beneath the pond-scum and moss. The man-lion in the pillar, an incarnation of Vishnu. A proverbial sage in the melon patch (for Taoists say the sage takes refuge in everyday things). Beneath the surface of solidity, the emptiness of matter. The eighteen or thirty-six hidden pillars, righteous men holding up the world. Wisdom hidden, disguised, the stink of enlightenment wiped off. The links of unity, connections not understood until perceived. Hidden enmity and hidden amity. Dawn locked

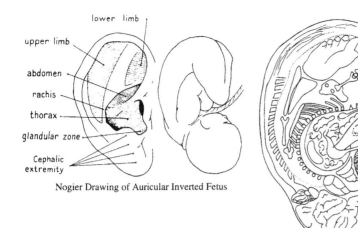

lower limb

upper limb

abdomen

rachis

thorax

glandular zone

Cephalic extremity

Nogier Drawing of Auricular Inverted Fetus

Nogier Drawing of Somatotopic Ear

The auricular microsystem of the ear is used in acupuncture. The human ear is shaped like an upside-down fetus: the lobe like the head, the inner fold like the spine, and so forth. During the development of the embryo, three layers of tissue evolve—ectoderm, mesoderm, endoderm—and the ear functions as an opening into all three. Courtesy of Terry Oleson, *Auriculotherapy Manual: Chinese and Western Systems of Ear Acupuncture* (Los Angeles: Health Care Alternatives, 1998).

up in a cave of a mountain. Mysterious splendor; fractals were there but not obvious—from Euclid till now, who knew?

The One is the kind of background that allows, sets the conditions of being, making possible the dynamic and chaotic processes, the emergence of galaxies—stars and black holes, beauty and destruction. For the last few decades, science has been telling us that our linear intuitions about the need for order in very complex systems have been wrong—vast order abounds for future selection. Complexity can emerge from reiterated simplicity. Self-similarity often appears in dynamics of generation, change, and growth.[35]

How can we integrally appreciate nature unless the whole is available in some sense in many of the parts? The cosmos likes to repeat itself at various scales. Those who reflect on earth and life note the similar saltiness and consistency of ocean and blood, the shining strands of cosmic light and twining coils of life.[36] That the very large and the very small share some aspects may surprise many who read the reports of new research, but to the ancient traditions there are homologies or reflections like diminishing echoes on various levels. Wise observers from all cultures—grandmothers, alert children, poets—have always intuited hidden correspondences.

In some traditions, the universe is a temple enshrining the sacred on a vast scale, and the heavens are replicated in the configurations of homes and villages. African settlements contain

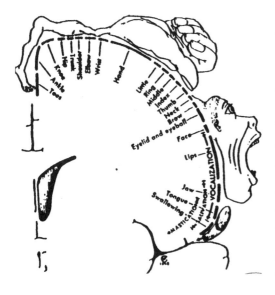

circles within circles, for example.[37] The body is also a temple, a microcosm enshrining the sacred—tradition arrayed everyday necessities to remind man and woman of this continuity.

Today it inspires awe that the physical world, so vast and intricate, works with such well-patterned strands, from supergalaxies to the vast coded information in DNA. But whatever we uncover, there is more that is hidden, in the microscopic as well as in the astronomic. There are far more galaxies than people used to think. In 1996, it was estimated there are 50 billion galaxies, each with 50 billion to 100 billion stars, five times more than previously estimated. It will be up to future scientists to explore possible self-similarities among the constituents of the levels of existence—atoms, sand grains, and stars.[38]

The homunculus helps us to consider how "the whole is in the parts." This schematic representation of the motor organization of the precentral gyrus in the human brain is a detail from Wilder Penfield and Theodore Rasmussen, *The Cerebral Cortex of Man: A Clinical Study of Localization of Function* (New York: Macmillan, 1950).

Interweaving Strands

Every level of the universe is fundamental, from vast to miniscule. All are strands of the fabric, or bits of the cosmic systems, whether we think of pinwheel galaxies or inner-space synapses. Know it or not, we are intimately involved in light. The smallest level imaginable involves (in current scientific thinking) atoms composed of fermions (which include quarks and leptons) and bosons (including photons, gluons, and gravitons). Superstring theory involves tiny one-dimensional strings vibrating in ten-dimensional space. (Space and time do not allow us to consider the integrating speculations of M theory here.)[39]

There are 3 or 4 billion units of DNA at the heart of every human cell (there are 6 billion humans alive at present). This DNA is like the history of life on earth writ small, a kind of language in a secret code of patterns on a very small scale. The Human Genome Project is working to decode the units. Each human brain holds 100 billion neurons, each in touch with others via thousands of dendrites. Their signals can, potentially, travel in more paths than there are atoms in the universe. But unless one feeds on rich ideas and experiences, delighting in creativity, one is in a rut and the world seems like a static boring place.

Rivers and winds are also flows through space, strands of energy, and mountain ranges are strands. There are strands in the "poor, bare, forked" strand that is man, who can fold his hands and often does so when he finds himself caught in the simple twists of fate. There are strands in the ganglia of the brain. And there are strands entwined in momentous adventures—sword and cross intertwined. Traditions of twining-serpent images, such as the caduceus and kundalini, show an archetypal vision of existence. Life as twists made up of twists, dynamic strands of sky and earth, moon and sun. Mandala cells and fractal organs, all reflect the One.[40]

Thousands of galaxies, "assembled" in sky congregations worthy of a Dante, evolved into a supergalaxy—a stream-of-light strand maybe a billion light years across. A long filament in one end of the constellation Aquarius, astronomers say, seems to have over 100,000 galaxies that collapse into a circular pattern. There are fourteen clusters of bright galaxies, each with at least fifty galaxies of stars. The rest, 100,000 dimmer galaxies, could be linked to another filament of galaxies about 300 million light years long. The universe may be composed on a mind-stunningly vast scale as a web of these filaments and voids in series, on scales of several hundred million light years, according to scientists. Scientists understand that structures like the ones now being observed can come about as a result of gravity, but they admit they do not have enough data and understanding to know much about the specific kinds of flows and conditions which bring them about. Hence they are still trying to learn more about their formation and their far-flung filament pattern. Parts of the outer forms are near, but the wholeness remains elusive.[41]

The scales are all interrelated and each has its own integrity and all relate to the One. Wholeness seems too large, its mesh too wide; but it is the "net that nothing slips through" because its mesh is so fine—this is a paradox of simple oneness and endless detail which fractals begin to help us to elucidate. We can imagine possible configurations in which the parts are not distinct from the whole in which they inhere.

But how to get to the center of the One? One answer, which is ancient and also given today for new reasons: Know you already are the center of the One. "Thou art That" is the message of Vedanta. Self is the center of consciousness. Brian Swimme also writes eloquently of how even modern science arrives at the realization that each person lives at the center of the cosmos, each being inseparable from the universe's origin, spirals in spirals of spirals.[42]

Riddles of Early Taoist Vision: "Pao I"

The Chinese wisdom text *Tao Te Ching* speaks of the One in several of its eighty-one chapters. Its teaching is to "embrace the One."[43] The One is heaven, the womb of the universe, the source of being for all and toward which all beings make their pilgrimage. The source has no form but is the seed of all. The One is of extremely small origin, bordering between being and nonbeing.[44] The sage embraces the One and becomes a model of the world. ("Pao I" means to embrace the one, or "to live the vision of the round.")[45]

When the great creative forces, which are themselves nuances of the One, attain the One, they attain their fulfillment: heaven becomes clear; earth becomes peaceful, spirits become efficacious; valleys become replenished; ten thousand rulers become exalted. Without finding fulfillment in what the One gives, each of these is deficient, inadequate, lacking. Therefore, the exalted are rooted in humbleness, the high has a low foundation, and the most famous has no fame—so don't tinkle, Lao-tzu advises, resound—go deep, become one with One.[46] Tao works by return, recursiveness; transformative cycles in time.

"The great fashioner does no splitting,"[47] appreciating the original oneness. Separating things and feeling alienated are splitting activities; freezing is also a kind of cutting, conceiving of that which is changing as fixed, reduced something fluid to a static unliving state. While the style of the *Tao Te Ching* often employs paradoxical proverbs and the One is riddled with mystery, the values here are clear. Depth calls to depth, kindred evokes kindred. Know the One, embrace it, and don't break away, follow Tao naturally, know your similarity to it, and don't be brittle and shatter. Pow!

Eka: *Vedic-Upanishadic Vision: See and Become the One Consciousness*

In Sanskrit *eka* means one; it is an essential image of the divine in the Vedas.

Questions and answers make up some Vedic hymns: "Who . . . is the One in the form of the Unborn, who props up in their place the six universal regions? . . . Seers call in many ways that which is One."[48] "The One is lord over all things, fixed or moving, walking or flying—this whole multiform creation. . . . From afar I perceive the Ancient One, the Father of mighty power, the Generator, our connection, singing the praises of whom the Gods, stationed on their own broad pathway, go about their business."[49] "Only One is the Fire,[50] enkindled in numerous ways; only One is the Sun, pervading this whole universe; only One is the Dawn, illuminating all things. In very truth, the One has become the whole world!"[51]

One is fire, sun, dawn, the cosmic bird: "By their words the inspired sages impart manifold forms to that Bird which is the

One."[52] "He is the One, the Onefold, the only One. In him all the Gods became unified."[53]

A famous dialogue in the *Brihadaranyaka Upanishad* shows the multiscaled whole quality of the divine: How many *devas* are there? The topic being asked about is complex, so the answer is not overly simple. There are three hundred and three *devas,* but it could also be said there are three thousand and three. There are thirty-three, from another view. There are six if one considers the question from another perspective. Or three. Or two. Or one and one-half. Or one. Each of these numbers can stand for the number of deities the mind can grasp to some extent, depending on one's viewpoint. The text goes on to explain them. There are only thirty-three *devas,* but the three hundred three and the three thousand three are their powers. Two means matter and the breath of life. One and one-half depicts the One who blows the air—in him all this has developed. There are various scales and perspectives—the One can be pictured in a variety of ways from various views, and still it can be whole. The One God is Life Breath, Brahman, That.[54] The One consciousness, *atman* Self, exists in all beings, making its form manifold; the wise find it in themselves and find endless joy.[55] One who knows the One that's in fire, heart, and sun attains the Oneness of the One.[56]

One hymn records a vision of the One: "Vena [the seer] has seen the Supreme, hidden in the cave wherein all things assume one single form."[57] The One is not an abstract principle, not a God far away, but the guest of human beings, their guide, and so the expansive Vedic tradition is to offer hospitality, follow the One on one's path.[58] Not dual, One, because our intellect and will strive to move beyond duality; our entire being cannot fully be until it reaches the fullness of unity with Being's Oneness. What about the many? Pluralism is no competitor of the One; rather, it enhances the One's "effective oneness," allowing for "a free interplay among all the tensions of existence" without dissolving the polarity of the real into irreconcilable parties with no connections among them, bridging and bonding them together. "It discovers a dynamism in the very heart of the One, which itself longs to be many." This is the reason for the deep coincidence found in the expressions of many mystics, a common experience of correspondences among the levels—divine, cosmic, human.[59]

At the conclusion of a passage which narrates the origin of everything, the *Brihadaranyaka Upanishad* explains the human being's relationship with the world. This relationship has a fractal quality, Raimundo Panikkar suggests:

Man [is seen in the Upanishads] not as a mere spectator of the universe, or even as a part of it in more or less mystical or mythical participation, but as an image, a mirror, an expression of the whole of the universe, as the whole reality not exactly in miniature (microcosm) but in reflection. . . . It is not that the body of Man is the whole universe or that the whole of reality is present in every conscious and free, that is, personal, beam of it. The specular conception of reality does not make of Man the center of the universe; it makes of him an image, a reflection, of the entire reality.[60]

Again, the wholeness found reflected in the part is not an exact mirror image, but is an integral factor in the psyche. Thus, realization, self-fulfillment, involves experiencing the One in the heart, discovering the whole reality and finding in it the role of humans.

An important statement of the Upanishads which is reminiscent of the relations of fractal parts and fractal whole is "That (the consciousness pervading all) is fullness, this is fullness; from fullness comes fullness, when fullness is taken from fullness fullness remains."[61] One could paraphrase the idea: Oneness there, oneness here, from oneness other onenesses come fractalling out, but when oneness with self-similar parts is generated by oneness, the original one fractally remains. *Eka,* the One, has been called "the crown jewel of the Upanishads."[62] The model of the ultimate One being found in all the beings generated, at various scales of recognition, seems to have fractal-like aspects.

Ehad: *Listen to the One God, One and Only, Only Reality*

Traditionally, *"Hashem ehad"* ("The Lord is one") is considered "probably the most significant and revolutionary phrase in the lexicon of Jewish thought."[63] It is part of the Shema: "Hear, O Israel, the Lord is our God, the Lord is one." The Shema is the "most fundamental verse in the Torah,"[64] which has been recited for centuries by Jewish martyrs (and many other pious Jews as well) at the time of death. In this verse, the word *ehad,* meaning "one," has meant a number of things to different interpreters who elaborate on the nuances which concern them most.

For those with an eschatological outlook, looking toward the future with a Messianic longing, *ehad* means that "the Lord will be one" among all people. A second view holds comprehensiveness as most important. This is the view of the One as all and only. This view sees the One without distinction between present and future but upholds the sovereignty and unity of God at all times. God's demand for exclusive devotion, to be the only God, to be loved with all one's heart, is crucial to this view. A third view is kabbalistic and mystical. In this view the mundane world is illusory, and Ein Soph, God in utter transcendence, is all that really exists. Humans ascend mentally or spiritually toward the greater holiness, approaching the empyrean heights of existence.[65]

Moses Maimonides believed that the unity of God's nature is reflected in the world's unitary nature. The world of being is one vast "individual" existence; "the sphere of the outermost heaven with everything in it is one" individual existence. The One has created one being. The force controlling the whole, setting into motion its first and principal parts—that force is the Supreme Being. The cosmos is made like a large organism, therefore the creator is one. Maimonides draws an analogy from nature to show how One can be the author of many—unity of existence and unity of Creator reflect each other. The process of life involves integration in life-affirming peace (*shalom*), continuously being lost, longed for, and restored. Most of modern science now agrees with the intuition of Maimonides regarding the unity of the universe.[66]

In the prophetic religions, the first letter of the alphabet has often been associated with the One. After that everything becomes more and more split up. Hence Sufi poets, for example, speak of learning only the *alif* (the "A"), the One. *Alif* is a symbol of *tawhid,* "divine Oneness." The One, the First, is enough. "A personal experience of the central mystery of Islam, that of Tawhid," was the essential meaning of early Sufism.[67]

The book of Genesis symbolically depicts the harmony of plant and animal, man and God in the garden of Eden before the psyche split up through the activity of knowing good and evil.[68] ("Good and evil are . . . principles. The world 'principle' comes from *prius,* that which is 'first' or 'in the beginning.' The ultimate principle we can conceive of is God. . . . Good and evil are principles of our ethical judgment, but reduced to their ontological roots, they are 'beginnings,' aspects of God, names for God.")[69] The worldwide themes found in the spiritual traditions of humanity form a varied fractal or family of forms, composed of the ways people seek and respond to the holy or ultimate. If scholars would look at the great traditions as members of the same species and see what each specializes in, as the various kinds of mammals specialize, we might see neglected lessons of wholeness, just as scientists do when they explore using Goethe's mode and move beyond studying isolated mammals. The dynamic gestalt vision Goethe practiced (to which we will return for a more extensive discussion below) enables a "living perception . . . as flexible as the example [nature or life] sets for us."[70] A separatist and static view of religions suffers from inadequate holism. It lacks contexts—the shared underlying human experiences, the similarities in concepts of origins that unify universal forces, and the disciplines of sublimation of the ego in the sacred.

Plotinus: Ascending to the One's Presence, Living an Inspired Dance around the One

Why did mystics such as Plotinus and Lao-tzu care about the One while most moderns don't? They were trying to attain it, they noticed whole patterns with their intuition, and they loved the whole with an acute sense of relationship to and involvement in it. Moderns are trying to break away from the past, to do something original, accomplish something with ease (power), make a short-term gain to satisfy their impulses, desires. Lao-tzu says that with desire only the surface is seen—the externals of the parts of the One. With calm vision and consciousness of depth we experience the expansive innerness of the One, vast wholeness. Mystics are introverted naturally and they interiorize, returning to origin, to one, to womb, to moods reflecting the freshness of childhood, finding the depth, energy, and subtle order deep within.

Plotinus, like Lao-tzu speaking of Tao, describes the One as transcendent, ineffable, mystery. "Awareness of the One comes to us neither by knowing nor by the pure thought that discovers the other intelligible things, but by a presence transcending knowledge."[71] The soul involved in knowing things becomes a participant in the many and loses Unity. To know the One one must renounce knowing, even beauty. (As an anonymous fourteenth-century mystic would write, one must enter a "Cloud of Unknowing.") Plotinus quotes Plato: "It [the One] can neither be spoken nor written about." To say things about it (as Plotinus does) is just to indicate (like Buddhism's "finger pointing toward the moon"). Visionaries and contemplatives who are aware of the transcendent experience closeness to the One, like the rapture of love or light. Paradoxically, the One is ever-present and ever-absent—if one doesn't tune in to it, one misses it.[72] Religious traditions often affirm that each one is a self-reflective offspring of that ultimate One, even though that level of existence is not always apparent.

"The One, the source of all things is simple. It is above even the highest in the world of being." The One is "the awesome existent above," the nameless, the difficult to know. "The One is the greatest, not physically but dynamically. Hence it is indivisible, not physically but dynamically." The mysteries of its unity are mind-boggling. It is the cause of good, therefore it is not called the Good, yet it is the Good above all. The soul knows by way of self-knowledge that its own natural motion is circular—it moves around its center, its source; it clings to, relates to, and communes with it. When the soul withdraws from it, it degenerates, becomes a fragmented creature of wandering and alienation, a selfish lost human, or an animal.[73]

The Stoic philosopher Marcus Aurelius (121–180) wrote, "O Universe, all that is in tune with you is in tune with me! Every note of your harmony resonates in my innermost being. For me nothing is early and nothing is late, if it is timely for you. O Nature, all that your seasons bring is fruit for me. From thee come all things; in thee do all things live and grow; and to thee do all things return."[74] This passage celebrates the mutuality and the agreeable similarities of part and whole.

Plotinus wrote that "The One does not aspire to us, to move around us; we aspire to it, to move around it." We always circle this core, though we do not always pay attention. When we look upon it our desires rest, our discords dissolve, and we dance an inspired dance around it. "The soul gazes on the Source of life, Intelligence, Being, Good, the Root of the soul's existence. All these entities emanate from the One without any lessening, for it is not a material mass,"[75] but elusive wholeness.

The wise use makeshift images, hints and riddles about how divinity might be experienced. Greek sages tell stories, Zen masters use koans. Plotinus, for example, wrote, "If someone is able to turn around . . . he will see God and himself and the All; at first he will not see *as* the All but then, when he has nowhere to set himself and determine how far he himself goes, he will stop marking himself off from all being and will come to the All without going anywhere, but remaining there where the All is set firm."[76] Elsewhere he instructed: "To see the Supreme . . . Cut away everything."[77] Ultimately "like alone joins like" when the soul and One join. "Look upon yourself in this state, you find yourself an image of the One": a self-similar part of the encompassing whole, not just a *part*icipant, but a "wholicipant" in the One. "A flight of the lone to the Alone," the lonely to the Only,[78] a flow from chaos to fractal. The Child whirls around, to listen to the piper and dance, to dissolve, to solve all the devolving with love, "total love," as Bob Marley said.

Goethe's Mode: The Wholeness of Nature, Meaning's Self-Revelation

Some who hear of a kind of science that is not the prevailing one say it must be of no use, as if man doesn't need a way of looking at life with any other goal than short-term gain; as if purposive linear thinking entails no problems, inadequacies, side effects. Goethe's mode is a way of looking at the wholeness we experience when we know that the universe we encounter as fractals is a way of looking at things, a further perspective that reveals ignored relations among isolated kindred members of a group. True scientists try things out in experiments before drawing conclusions.

Goethe believed that "through the contemplation of an ever creating nature, we should make ourselves worthy of spiritual participation in her productions." This requires a shift of focus. The One's infinite generativity is an expansive, pervasive vitality. To understand a living organism or a living tradition requires more than a rigid instrument. "The non-reductionist perspective is simply seeing the dimension of One instead of the empirical dimension of many. Here the One and the many are not exclusive, as they are numerically, because they are in fact the very same. Thus we do not attempt to reduce the many to the One, as is so often said, but instead we see that the many are One. The effect of this non-reductionist perspective is that of looking into a dimension within One itself. Compared with this dimension of One, the notion of 'unity in multiplicity' appears as the Flatland attempt to understand unity."[79]

In Goethe's view, metaphysics is unnecessary; the ancient philosophers of China and India intuited that subtle consciousness is context, the hidden background of Wholeness, allowing all to exist and glow. His method leads to "the coalescence of the researcher with the phenomenon."[80] Goethe's research on colors and on plants illustrates what the conventional approach leaves out. Similarly, Wolfgang Schad's study of mammals and human beings, entitled *Man and Mammal,* based on Goethe's and Rudolf Steiner's work (which carried Goethe's forward), uses actual comparisons of organisms to illustrate how this method works.

A way of characterizing Goethe's contribution is to say that other approaches are usually "extrinsic explanations of isolated parts, while Goethe's explanation is intrinsic to the phenomena themselves"; his perspective explores multiplicity in unity. Goethe's view is not of underlying reality behind appearances but of the intensive depth of the phenomenon itself, "a seeing embedded in the fullness of phenomena, not a theory abstracted from the phenomena."[81] His mode involves the whole person, not just the head; it is intuitive, if intuitive means being receptive to meanings and patterns of wholeness. Goethe thought that the greatest achievement in the study of nature would be to understand that everything factual is, in a certain sense, already its own theory and has its own inner logic and contextual reality. The universe around us is already resonant with meaning; humans need to learn to listen more, and they need to learn to read the phenomena of nature in terms of their own participation in the wholeness of nature. In this view awareness of fractals can offer conceptual entries into this mode of approach, ways to see hidden structures in the universe.

Natural Law and Self-Similarity: Fractal Process Structures

Architecture has been called frozen music —a metaphor that works well in some instances. (Law also is a kind of architecture, a vital structure wrought by generations, an order intended to give certain refuge to the living in their uncertainties.) Why is there so much self-similarity in so many architectural works? Why do we think of smaller replicas while looking at the whole or while seeing one view of the whole, so that even if we see only a part we see the whole idea? And why do architects usually seek structures similar to those already existing near the site of a new work and in the surrounding natural world if not to join, harmonize, unify, seeking wholeness so that elements in space may be at home, in a way of life? Why do they design self-similar structures but to convey a sense of the building's unity from a variety of perspectives?

Line drawing of the Kandariya temple in Khajuraho, India. The spires and other details, like peaks of a mountain, are self-similar to each other.

The German philosopher and theologian Friedrich Schleiermacher (1768–1834) wrote with an almost fractal sensibility that music is like religion—it is one vast whole of parts which are whole,

> a special, a self-contained revelation of the world. Yet the music of each people is a whole by itself, which again is divided into different characteristic forms till we come to the genius and style of the individual. Each actual instance of this inner revelation in the individual contains all these unities. Yet while nothing is possible for a musician, except through the unity of the music of his people, and the unity of music generally, he presents it in the charm of sound with all the pleasure and joyousness of boundless caprice, according as his life stirs in him, and the world.[82]

We could say much the same about the architecture of each nation. Each people has an architecture, and as music is said to help the soul circle its source as pilgrims circle a shrine,[83] architecture gives people an atmosphere of home. Each people also has a body of laws. The form of shrines dedicated to the sacred reveals the particular worldview of the tradition, its symbol system or way of visualizing the One, and the forms of the home and of official buildings reveal the needs and aspirations, the style of life and concerns, of a people: their worldview. Similarly, the laws, too, embody the worldview. Generations reiterate the time-honored revelation of a place venerated by a people, such as Mecca, Benares, Rome, or Jerusalem, periodically pilgrimaging there to glimpse the sacred vision.[84] Law also speaks to the overall outlook sustained by a people over generations. Some of the same issues—disputes over rights and ownership, crimes and outrages—arise in society century after century, though fashions and technologies change, and need to be resolved with civility.

Law must speak for the order of the all. Many things which are composed—made up of smaller pieces—have some fractal-like quality in their order.[85] Why? Composed materials come in many forms: Particles aggregated make brick or stone; stones placed together make walls, walls together make the whole of the building. Vibrations make up notes, notes combined make up phrases, and phrases woven together make up melodies, movements, symphonies. Letters make up words, words make up sentences. Sentences and paragraphs, organized coherently, spell out the principles of law in its wholeness. The hierarchical structures of organization, with their components branching downward, involve a oneness rooted in smaller and smaller parts, each one and each part of one, building up a fractal quality which many composed things share.

In its childhood,[86] the Western theory of "natural law" was based on ideas intuited by philosophers who were considering beauty and regularity in the workings of nature and noting their insights about the observable order of the universe.[87] Two fragments of Heraclitus' teaching may help introduce the topic of law and fractals. (1) "Understanding is common to all [humans]. It is necessary for those who speak with intelligence to hold fast to the common element of all, as a city holds fast to law, and much more strongly. For all human laws are nourished by one which is divine, and it has power so much as it will; and it suffices for all things and more than suffices." In this view, the divine law is the order already in the universe, the deepest "given" of our circumstances, the sacred unity which is discernable in patterns and principles, processes and forms, which share similarity. (2) "Graspings, that is to say groups holding together, apprehensions bringing things together; these are wholes and not wholes; they characterize a system which is convergent, divergent, structured by cooperation and by conflict; this system is consonant, dissonant, held together by harmony and discord alike; from all its components a unity emerges, and from this unity all things emerge."[88] A wholeness emerges in this view, with a dynamism involving polar symmetries, rights and duties, kindnesses and crimes, legitimate and illegitimate behavior. Some Greek thinkers intuited that the universe is like a vast mind. Some who were attracted to the possibilities in math and logic intuited in the mysterious depths of universal order a Mind that was often rational and mathematical in its operations; a mental ability self-similar to the Mind of the cosmos seemed to be the most divine aspect shared by humans. Pythagoras believed that the universe is numbers; Anaxagoras, that

Mind rules heaven and earth; and Plato, that the perfect idea or archetype of justice is in heaven, while approximate forms of it can be found on earth. His book *The Republic* influenced European thought in many ways, including in the area of natural law. Aristotle reiterated this view and carried it forward in his *Nicomachean Ethics.*

The Stoics in ancient Rome sought a mode of life in conformance with nature's ways, believing all men possess a share of divine reason and therefore all deserve a measure of respect.[89] They believed all legal systems shared a common core of natural law. They compared the various systems they knew as well as they were able, looking for patterns of similarity within the system of the divine master plan. They had a vision of perfect justice in the law of nature, a sense of wholeness emerging through seeing connections within a larger whole. Because reason was respected, the law of Rome could be adjusted when necessary; it could be improved by reasoning jurists who fathomed deep unchanging principles and from them developed law in continuity with the abiding essentials of the ideal whole natural law. As Rome colonized outlying regions, the laws of the conquered regions and tribes were valued as specific diverse embodiments of universal principles of natural law. Jurists called the similarity, the common element found in the varied cultures, *jus gentium,* or law of nations; sometimes the concept has been used interchangeably with *jus naturale,* natural law, though it is not exactly equivalent.[90]

Early Christian thought sought to identify natural law with the divine law revealed in the Bible and to make secular law conform to such biblical injunctions as the Ten Commandments.[91] Augustine and other church fathers tried to link natural law to revelation even if it did not exactly fit. Later, Aquinas (c. 1224–1274) drew on the persuasive arguments of Aristotle and saw reason, not just revelation, as capable of arriving at truth. He systematized legal theory and presented natural law coherently. His work influenced many later authorities. Aquinas, like Plato, saw reason as one with the power in heaven and on earth, in the realm of ideas and in nature. Eternal law is God's eternal mind, the reason with which "God determines Himself."[92] This divine reason governs existence, and the laws of all life stem from it. For Aquinas, law meant "an ordinance of reason," promulgated by reason and received by reason—in other words, similar relations among a reasoning God and rational beings. Aquinas saw natural law as knowledge of the Mind of God; an Aristotelian, he believed in deductive geometrical reasoning. He deduced the nature and nuanced forms of natural law from a few simple self-evident axioms, such as "a person should do what reason tells him is right." From such an unarguable axiom he derived the right to preserve life and the duty to respect life. Aquinas arrived at abiding generalities; only the large-grain principles of natural law could be unchanging—the rules derived always depend on circumstances and need flexibility. Hugo Grotius (1583–1685) asserted, "even if there were no God, Natural Law would still hold," putting natural law on a par with math and laws of nature. This assertion suggests that Western presuppositions about the God implied by observed order are not crucial to exploring that order. (This is the direction of science that was emerging; now new possibilities about the source of order are in play.)[93]

Sixteenth-century legislators and rulers used natural law theory to justify their legal systems. Sixteenth- and seventeenth-century thinkers (such as Spinoza, as we shall see) and justice-seekers used natural law theory to oppose governmental oppression and assert individual rights. Natural law theory has been important for many reasons. It taught Roman law to seek the general in the particular and vice versa, fostering approaches to the whole and the parts in many activities.

Natural law methods and maxims in theory and practice deeply influenced Anglo-American common law, which is often more flexible than European civil law. Each century seems to host its own rediscoveries of the logic of mutuality and wholeness, with new needs to voice conditions we must be aware of to pursue the common good.

Since 1850, discussions of natural law have largely been omitted in American courts, perhaps because its fruits are taken for granted as a *fait accompli* in the Constitution. In a sense, the bases of natural law have been thrown into the collective unconscious that is history. The human right of self-preservation is the basic first rule of natural law; thus natural law continues to be meaningful in discussions of minority and women's rights. Humanism without a basis in natural law sometimes seems out of touch with the basic realities of the order in the universe and the organic principles which might help prioritize issues.

No human can exist in isolation from the order of the cosmos. If natural law theory, with its roots in the nature of the universe and the deepest consensus of past human experiences, is the most natural foundation for human rights, the new understanding arising from science, which is now developing a deeper sense of the dynamic complexity and the wholistic nature of reality, will have an effect on old notions of what is reasonable, and new standards and statements will emerge. Universals in nature, patterns newly uncovered by chaos science, and complex adaptive systems studies can expand from Euclid's geometric axioms of linearity to more dynamic and diversified Mandelbrot fractal images of dynamic paradox and infinite wholeness. Perhaps human rights need a "heavenly strongbox"[94]—a treasury that can't be plundered—to be rooted and righted in the deepest patterns of the flow of the cosmos. The justice required must be based on our nature and the nature of the universe we live in—our shared similarity with the One, our recursiveness, our infinity, our scaling within the cosmic whole. Our actual size is vast (Mind) and minuscule (the parts and codes we hold); hence humans are the "meso-creatures" or "middle people," the psyche creatures in between and spread throughout, and our privileges and rights are tied to keeping that perspective.[95]

As we have seen, English and American "civil society" and individual rights spring from old sources: spiritual visions. How should theorists of law adjust and update the legal theory of individual rights to be commensurate with this century's deepened knowledge of genetics, psychology, ecology, literature, and history? Are there dried and forgotten riverbeds in the human psyche which may flow with new water in humanity's future?

Let us consider another historical strand of thought on this theme. Benedict Spinoza, born in Amsterdam in 1632, outgrew some of the limits of orthodox Judaism's teaching, as well as some of René Descartes's philosophy, and dedicated his life to freedom of thought. He wrote *Tractatus Theologico-Politicus*, published in 1670, to voice opposition to the narrow theologians of his day who choked philosophical inquiry and to plead for freedom of thought and speech. The *Tractatus*, a reasoned argument for human rights, argues that a real respect for universal freedom of conscience needs a completely secular framework. It made a great impact, influencing pilgrims who were setting out for America and thinkers such as John Locke who influenced the writers of the American constitution.

It also aroused condemnation among orthodox clergy. In this time of intolerance (some of Spinoza's close friends were persecuted and murdered by mobs, and he was vilified as an amoral atheist), the book was eventually banned. His views were actually rooted in Jewish theology. For example, the idea that God's essential work involves justice for all, and consequently democracy, not theocracy, is the political structure more in harmony with divine order, derives from Judaism. Like earlier philosophers, Spinoza believes that life and the search for wisdom are the same thing, a "gradual expression of God, the infinite in the finite," through reason and love. The universe is rational and the nature of the mind is to know this order.[96] By "reason" Spinoza means not merely the deductive method, with its rather mechanical rigid paths of axiomatic geometrical thought (which he used well in his book on ethics)—his thinking often riffs beyond the ironclad structures, flowing more freely in his prefaces, appendixes, and excursions. "Reason" means to him the whole inner life of human beings. The spirit in its wholeness helps humans interpret the universe; the spirit found in abstract logic is only one aspect.

For Spinoza, as for Gregory Bateson later, mind is active everywhere, not only in humans; Spinoza criticizes the view that humans are unique as a kind of anthropomorphism. For him, both matter and consciousness express God's essential nature. His view that God is present in all existence is transformative—humans participate in divinity by being alive, and this has implications for mediating institutions. Each member of a political community should be considered as an equal manifestation of the presence of God; from this basic view, democracy naturally derives. The importance of considering existing beings in the context of wholeness inspired Spinoza: "Always as we come to understand a thing we see it in relation to wider and wider perspectives until finally we glimpse it as belonging to the very essence of the whole of things, or as eternal." A snowflake melts fast; our understanding its existence involves knowing its links with infinite events of natural laws expressing the nature of the universe as a whole.[97] There is a paradox here, seen already in Taoism, the Atman vision of India, and Plotinus, who spoke of the One as "a fountain always aflow"—Spinoza notes God's indivisible yet pouring-out creative activity.[98] Spinoza believes that we truly see things when we look from the vantage point of eternity. Time distorts our view as it plays out in finite imagination, and we do not see existing things as modes of the whole. Modernity's short memory and fast-paced concerns and fashions may often neglect this, but Spinoza's view (like that of Vaclav Havel) still offers a useful way of drawing on belief to form a politics of reciprocity or respectful mutuality.

There is a long tradition of rediscovering these truths. Like Havel, Spinoza hopes for political awakening through a religious coming of age. Spinoza is concerned with the expression of the human being's essential nature. When one sees and knows with unifying love and reason, one attains the synthesis of imagination and science which is philosophy. A Spinoza scholar puts it this way: "In philosophy one sees the common properties as living in the particulars which are in no way lost sight of. We see the whole in the parts and the parts in the whole. As Spinoza says, 'as each person therefore becomes stronger in this kind of knowledge, the more he is conscious of himself and of God, of himself that is in God, and of God as in himself.'"[99] Humans become established in their true selves through creative thought, and things can be really known in the whole, with the wisdom of the eternal present. This view, which is elaborated in Spinoza's work, shares much with other mystical traditions East and West. In this view the whole person's faculties, coordinated by creative thought, find liberation from cramped confines in the nature of love.

In 1909, John Chipman Gray used fractal-like imagery to begin thinking about international law (which was then only in its gestation, not even its infancy). He suggested that relations among civilized modern nations are similar to those among "a horde of savages composed of organisms" (that is, a horde of family units, each with its rules and law). Each nation, like each savage family, is an organized unit, but the nations do not together form a larger organized body—there is a dissonance of beliefs, yet there is a wholeness of humanity. Rules governing the relations of such nations constitute the law of nations. Gray asked if international law really was law and noted the "slow differentiation from positive morality to positive law."[100] In our age of unprecedented need to realize our interdependence and cultivate compassion with humane mutuality, we continue to ask such questions.

The flexibility of law, which by definition must be regular enough to be reasonably predictable yet must flow with time, is a fortunate trait. Naive scientific views that assumed that all the secret laws of nature would soon be known and that each aspect of nature would be predictable have been proven by chaos science to have been misreadings of the actual situation. The laws of the universe, which are similar to natural law and common law, are dynamically flexible—a fractal-like network, such as the image of Indra's net, lifelike, not rigid and predetermined. Self-organization is the rule, not the exception. Thus, rather than a preset mechanism or exact blueprint, there is "only a set of laws with an inbuilt facility for making interesting things happen."[101] Thus, cosmic process is a dynamical graceful improvisation with the givens within already working rhythms and flows of existence. Chaos science reveals, as Taoism did long before, that chaos harbors all kinds of orders, so chance—"God's dice"—may not be as terrifying as Einstein feared. That intelligence which makes mandalas everywhere, that sacred unity or original order, the source of "order for free," may also be called a strange attractor, or Providence shepherding the whole fractal universe (the whole reflected in the parts), the reason for and meaning of patterns of consciousness.[102]

The "Uncracked One" (to use a Taoist image of the "uncarved block" of original Being) breaks into fractals; undifferentiated energy becomes definite shapes. To find oneself in this context is a healing along fractal-like lines, finding again a semblance of the One. As perennial philosophy has always said, when we contemplate calmly, when we "chill," we realize the hidden order, know the one consciousness of sacred unity in our depths. "Our task is to realize the higher, hidden order of the fractal, to bring out a continuity of consciousness in our very being,"[103] as one writer puts it. How can we ensure that our demands of self-assertion and self-transcendence are fair—a source of new reverence and legal direction ("rights")? We need to begin by knowing to what we most belong. What is a person and what is the place of a person in regard to civilization and nature? What is right and compassionate; what values do the whole realms of which we are similar parts in life demand of us?

Greeks and Stoics, Spinoza and others found openings in ideas through which to know the deep principles' nuances capable of further development. We still seek clarity and order today. We debate our allegiance to humans and to other forms of life. As scientific findings change our perceptions, we consider the rights of amiable apes, faithful dogs, compassionate and wisely humorous elephants, expressive dolphins, and musical whales. We may depend on other creatures more than we now know—animal enzymes are used in medicines, for example. If all sentient beings share the right to not feel needless suffering, should all have equal consideration? If "rights" is not the right term for these concerns, what is? On what basis do we assert the rights of tribal people, such as (at the very least) the right to be themselves? How can they be themselves when civilization's hand reaches them? What are the universal rights of adolescents, ill and elderly folk, the disabled? No one knows exactly what we owe to future generations, what we owe to rainforests and oceans and the sky, what we owe to our children, but in a sense we *are* them. We are not entirely other from them—we are inseparable—mutual parts of a whole continuum. Scales are sometimes confused in the legal system; for example, under American law, a corporation is a person. How is that not an absurdity? Yet because it is the corporation that is a "person," actual persons who are officers in the corporation may not be held culpable for corporate misdeeds. New thinking about human partness in social, ecological, and cosmic wholes may benefit from fractal diagrams combined with the thinking of philosophers such as John Rawls.

The rights of the future may sound sinister to vested interests of today. Thinking which is concerned with considering and forming new laws must again ask questions about human uniqueness and human unities with nature. What makes humans "differ" from nature may be what makes nature in the long run be herself—soul consciousness, unrecognized self-similarity within a larger cosmic whole. The whole cosmos can know itself through this part— humanity. Perhaps that's what makes humans unique: they are the parts of the universe that allow it to know itself through experiencing the vast—which is what makes them able to realize the One. Thus, paradoxically, humans are unique because they're the same as all else in nature, only more so. What is the basis for respect? Reason? Some great human beings may not have had reason as their main virtue. Is it an ability to live with conscience? The usual arguments that humans are other than nature assume that there is nothing spiritual in nature, no sacred unifying reason commensurate to what makes humans unique. But when they survey millennia of evolution with new knowledge, many people find signs that a Universal Intelligence does exist within and also outside of humanity. Thus we are called to stop underestimating nature. In microcosmic energy patterns studied by quantum physicists and macrocosmic galaxies known to today's astronomers there are orders, laws akin to a cosmic psyche's archetypes, ethical "conscious" patterns of organization, order attractors. Humans almost uniquely embody finely nuanced, deeper aspects of a nature which is itself full of universal intelligence.[104]

The human ego makes people feel as if they are different. But when we survey designs and structures of life-forms, it is obvious that nature out-imagines man in all her varieties and inventivenesses. No part of nature feels shame, feels self-loathing, feels conflicts of duty, or commits overkill as humans do, and Plotinus noted that no other part of nature has the ability to go astray and then rejoin nature, reharmonize by means of wisdom. But that's because other forms don't need to reconcile themselves with nature. Their meanings correspond with their function and performance since they naturally express the idea of their identity. Nature is transient, but it stems from the eternal; historically man has known he's mortal but has often thought of himself as having an immortal soul.[105] Understanding oneness and partness anew inevitably affects our legal systems and personal acts. While this summary doesn't pretend to make a breakthrough in law, it may help show the depth and rationale of Vaclav Havel's ideas (discussed in the introduction) about our need to rediscover cosmic order. People need to genuinely know the depths of the context of their lives to have a sound basis for identity and life together; a false sense of isolation breeds illusions.

If you think this exploration of natural law's basis has no clout, I invite you to delve into the question of a basic human value agreeable to all, help discover for our time (the Age of Dissonance?) a concept that would carry the needed clout. Everything is still unfolding, and we don't yet fully know what it really means to be "human." We need a Gandhian sense of humanity's oneness, as true to life as natural fractals are in their structure and function.

Envoy to the Envoy

There is in human life a natural quest for wholeness and meaning—so much that is in a person drives toward that even when the ego is busy avoiding it—and this comes out in dreams. Comprehension (understanding of meaning) and comprehensiveness (wholeness of the One) are intertwined. From one confused point of time and space you see nebulous randomly scattered stars; from another point you can see spirals of stellar orders—nebulae.

Paradoxes tease us: "The closer you get to infinity the farther away it seems." The vastness and strength of Tao work by smallness and weakness, and vice versa. "You can't get close to it, can't keep it at arm's length." Emily Dickinson knew, and said in one of her verses, that wholes aren't found here on earth (except maybe in dreams). Fractals can help still and calm the mind, allowing it to grow clear, empty of self (worries, desires, fears, agitations), so that it can enter into the One, swimming among the fractal waves, dreaming, seeing wholes . . . What terrorist aware of *tawhid* (the One in Islamic theology) would murder innocent children of the One God? What business aware of the One would poison the environment?

One may think of oneness as a small abstract topic, but like the soul, it is an endless depth. There are so many threads of the One to follow up. One needs inspiration from the One, so one can complete one's reflections on the One. A clue from the Whole suggests an idea: pick up on small points, each whole in itself. Fractals can enable an opening; as Blake sang and Huxley echoed, if the senses are cleansed, one can see all as it really is—infinite. Fractals sometimes enable that seeing of infinity. Fractals, like music, can be a potent stimulus to the creative and ordering imagination. Contemplate them as Tibetan Buddhists contemplate mandalas, watch them unfold, explore them, and fractals reveal possibilities in the One. Dust and straw are many, the sacred is one. Far-off nebula lights are many, their spiral is one. "Brains" is plural. ("Do you have enough brains?") Heart is singular—One. ("You gotta have heart! Miles and miles and miles of heart!" even if the bluffing tough guys realize it only when it's almost too late.)

The psyche, depth psychologists tell us, craves an expression that will embrace and express its whole nature. To enjoy spiritual connectivity is the *exalted* melancholy of our fate. To have the freedom to play out our parts creatively within the necessities of our responsibilities is "the exalted melancholy of our *fate*," to use a phrase used by Martin Buber in his book *I and Thou*.[106]

Michelangelo's sculpture of the slain Christ on the lap of Mary, the great white marble *Pietà*, is, in my opinion, probably the greatest work of art the Western world has produced. Its philosophical implications are quite profound. It is a cosmic image expressive of the whole psyche: the son is the innocent victim, whose burst heart, like the original fireball, floods space with love and light. The mother is nature, the blue sea who gave life (with all its vulnerabilities) a start. If you join the mother and son with your own heart's compassion you support blue-gened life, cradle it, rock with it and roll; you do not crucify it. You join the fractal of cosmic unity and cradle life (for our lives are cradled even as we cradle life) as the lotus cradles the dewdrop. The twelve-faced dodecahedron[107] enshrines the ever-living spiral. A Zen koan asks, "When the many are reduced to the one, to what shall we reduce the one?" This returns us to a question we considered already: If time cooks all things, what cooks time? If the cosmos is a game, who plays the Child? Why are both creature and parent, and their interface or relationship, so mysterious and so obvious?[108]

Or, as a Sufi poet long ago asked and answered, "Am I the one within the many? No, I am the one with the many in me."[109] Who is varied? I, for one. The Child plays on, incorporating the horizon. The horizon is the aspect of the whole which we can begin to comprehend at once, that taste of the Tao or Atman which at any given time we can experience; the figure and configuration opens questions and gathers answers. The horizon opens, as we understand more, to reality ever beyond us and yet within us.

As the *Tao Te Ching*'s first page asserts, the secret innards and outer surfaces of existence are known by different modes of thought, but ultimately they form one synchronistic whole. The world of physics and the world of psyche are interlinked by a mysterious consciousness, or, as Thoreau calls it, Universal Intelligence. Jung suggested we study the most fundamental of mathematical axioms, infinite series of numbers, geometrical continuums, which today's fractals help embody and extend. This area of math promotes the scientific exploration of the structure of mind, both conscious (which calculates so well) and unconscious (which gives rise to mathematical and other ideas). Numbers and shapes offer a tangible link between matter and psyche. Patterns of wholeness, such as mandalas, of which many fractals would seem to be archetypal variations, constitute the kind of geometrical continuum which intrigued Jung and seemed to him promising for future understanding.[110]

Envoy to the envoy to the envoy: All these human visions of the One show how deep the sense of a Whole holding all has been for people. A fractal sensibility (awareness of wholeness in the parts) may help us extend wisely in the other direction. Because psychological health is not all oneness, James Hillman envisions

Tibetan drawing of the Buddha in a circle of Mandelbrot sets. "The core of every core, the kernel of every kernel, an almond held in itself, deepening in sweetness: all of this, everything, right up to the stars, and the meat around your stone. Accept my bow . . . high, high above, your own suns are growing immense and they glow as they wheel around. Yet something has already started to live in you that will live longer than the suns." Rainer Maria Rilke, "Buddha inside the Light," in *Selected Poems of Rainer Maria Rilke,* trans. Robert Bly (New York: Harper and Row, 1981), 151. Collage by the author.

what we might call the "fractalizing" of consciousness: fractal sensibility allows the parts to exist and allows us to value their particularities, their character.

> Like knows like. If the world is a messy many, then the definition of consciousness follows one proposed early in the 20th century by the French philosopher Henri Bergson: "qualitative multiplicity." . . . Consciousness would no longer be conceived as a clear light hovering over the face of the deep, observing each thing in its kind. Rather, the light would fracture, fluctuate, show variegations that reflect the characteristics of the world, our consciousness replying to its character. We would conceive of consciousness to be as multitudinous as the world, a microcosm of the macrocosm: as without, so within ourselves . . . the multiple images of the world.[111]

We return in summing up our reflections to a point made by Vaclav Havel: "We must discover a new respect for what transcends us: for the universe, for the earth, for nature, for life, and for reality. Our respect for other people . . . for other cultures can only grow from a humble respect for the cosmic order and from an awareness that we are a part of it."[112] I believe fractals can help us

return again and again to this recognition of particularity within a web which holds in oneness. In my view it is possible to contemplate fractal patterns to visually conceptualize various kinds of connectedness. Fractals are about oneness, visualizing how the One has parts in an often invisible order and exquisite interrelatedness. Fractals bespeak the "sacred unity" Gregory Bateson discerned in his careful thoughts about how the parts of the universe form a whole.

The relations of infinite mutuality, like Indra's net, are imaginable as fractal-like processes of interweaving life. Sometimes disasters reveal them. Perhaps all that I have been trying to suggest in this strand about the One is most strikingly articulated by Rabbi Irwin Kula in a discussion about the effect of the events of September 11, 2001 on his spiritual outlook:

> For me, that there's something "out there" and that I'm here no longer meant anything, because every time I thought there was something out there, it turns into inevitably something opposed to me. Something I have to define myself against, whether that's God, or whether that's a Christian, or whether that's a Muslim, or whether that's a Buddhist. And that's not my experience.
>
> My genuine experience of life is that there is nothing "out there." This is all there is. And when you see the seamlessness of it all, that's

what I mean by "God." Every tradition has that. Every morning, three times a day since I'm five or six years old, I've been saying, "Hear O Israel, the Lord is our God, the Lord is One." Right? It's one of our few creedal statements, the Shema. Three times a day, since I'm six years old.

If you ask me what 9/11 really did, it made me understand the truth of that, "Everything is one." Not that there's some guy hanging out there who has it all together, who we call "One," but that it is all one. We all know it deep down. We've all had those experiences, whether it's looking at our child in a crib or whether it's looking at our lover or looking at a mountaintop, or looking at a sunset. Right? We've all had those experiences. And we recognize, "Whoa. I'm much more connected here."

That's what those firemen had. They recognized; they didn't even think about it, right? Because actually, if you think about it, you begin to create separations. They didn't think about it. All they knew is we're absolutely connected. We're absolutely connected to the 86th floor. Well, that's where God is. That's not where God is. God isn't anywhere. That's what we mean when we say "God." And yet these insights of connectedness and oneness which make us feel so at home in the world are so difficult to hold on to, so we end up living lives of isolation and loneliness.

Perhaps Rabbi Kula sums it up best when he says, "The real Torah, the real wisdom, the real religious tradition, the real experience behind religion, is about love. It is about connection, and it is no more complicated than that."[113]

CONCLUSION

Unfoldings without a Finale

Fractal images have led to a growing contemplation of our reality as a place made up of folded worlds within self-similar worlds—that is, worlds folded in between dimensions.   —John Briggs[1]

Something Fractal This Way Comes! (Why Are There Fractals in Culture?)

I recently heard a radio talk show featuring an expert who was designing a program that would model the vulnerabilities of a system. A caller asked how it would handle catastrophes, such as terrorist strikes on a city: whether it would be like a Mandelbrot set in depicting multiple possible outcomes with their relative likelihood. The expert answered no, but I suspected that the caller was making a suggestion, rather than expecting to hear that a fractal visualization was already part of the analysis. It is interesting that a visual paradigm of fractal geometry came to the listener's mind. We never know what is possible until we try. Probably more and more fractal applications will be tried in future years.

Fractals pervade the world around us and are an integral part of our own physical being. Each time we sniff to recognize an odor we compare and sort memories by means of fractal-structured processes in the brain. Each moment of vision, whether waking or dreaming, involves fractals in corneal vascularization and other ocular structures. Human physiology is predisposed to appreciate certain forms because the human body's systems share certain configurations in their own makeup with the patterns they perceive. Organisms with networks of nerves and cells evolved in a world of branching trees and fractal river basins. Not only clouds and lightning, but also patterns of investment on Wall Street can be analyzed for fractal patterns.[2] Computer designers use fractals to expand computer memories and researchers seeking to condense information for long-range communication also use fractal configurations. If you want to flexibly play with scale, fractals are your vehicle. Origami folders, Hollywood filmmakers, architects and design artists, and other creative and inventive people today are learning new possibilities in their various fields by studying fractals.[3] This book is full of many other examples of places in nature and culture where we encounter these fascinating forms of scale invariance, showing self-similarity or self-affinity despite expansion or contraction. These examples depict the orders of chaos, the infinite in the finite, and meanings related to wholeness.

We can see how fractal-like perceptions—the ability to notice or employ qualities such as self-similarity or a union of recursions, which are now associated with fractal patterns—were sometimes prefigured in compositions of literature and visual arts, in poetry, myth, and philosophy. What are some typical functions of fractal-like images in the humanities? When are such patterns evoked, constructed, and described—how are fractals used in the humanities, and for what purposes?

In terms of space, fractals help us extend our vision far beyond our usual primary standard, which is our own embodied individual self. Fractal-like images serve to expand and indefinitely extend the conceptual space of vision, yet still keep it as part of possible experience here and now. In architecture, painting, poetry, literature, and law, for example, fractals traditionally function to suggest infinity and unity through graphic symbolism. Fractals work well when one needs to dynamically conceptualize the finite as part of the infinite, the part as counterpart to the whole, parts as counterparts of each other—so many reflective pearls of the same all-stringing consciousness, or in Taoist symbolism, similar "chips off the old block." Besides this structure's use in creation, which consists of a union formed of various scaled self-replications (and all metaphors or "reflectaphors" are arguably fractal-nuanced[4]) there is also the art of hiding fractal patterns, so they will not be too obvious, so they exist on an unconscious level.

In terms of time, there are various focal points which involve our lives in fractal processes: "strange attractors," which so often typify chaotic[5] dynamics, trace repeated variations through "phase space" and thus iterate fractal images. "The strange attractor provides the stability and at the same time allows the system to respond dynamically."[6] Powerful images, such as the archetypes of the collective unconscious, function in peoples' lives as "strange attractors."[7] They provide model scenarios, organizing principles, themes with implications growing beyond themselves, inspiring loops of activity which elaborate themselves and return to their root. Inevitable irresistible archetypes in psyches and universal patterns in cultures can be considered strange attractors, and the dynamics iterated in these processes of the psyche are said to be fractal. They are repeated and active in individuals, society, and culture at varying scales. Throughout the ages, archetypes and patterns of the One/many in cosmic myth and abstract images have been able to configure life's many poignant situations into a variety of imaginable forms. Such cosmic images have a maximum power to extend and contain, attract and transform. Attractive images program and channel the energies of our lives in religious, patriotic, or secular enthusiasms, hip or square, sensual or intellectual, male or female, old-fashioned, postmodern, or whatever.

In their abiding presence archetypes are like river channels[8] which under the right conditions fill with the waters of psychic interest energies. They are great basins of attraction. In their creative/destructive power they are like lava. Lava destroys things in its path, and creates—generating new land. Today with videotape and helicopters we are able to view the process from above: the stream of lava's cloudy red-hot flow, the newly forming crust cracking violently apart, earth's innards bursting her seams. Lava solidifies to make new landforms, and green grows through the debris. It shows the planet is "alive" with dynamism from core to crust. The volcano's dynamic eruption is an image of creativity that involves, according to some scientists, the conditions which served as the cauldron of life's origins: the mix of hydrogen, methane, ammonium, carbonic gases, and steam from which the first cells emerged. We can also see green growth in the gray ash and lava rubble—a new landmass accumulating, able to support forms of life.

If we assume organism is fundamental, endurance is the resultant property of evolution, as Whitehead wisely said.[9] The whole of existence is a process involving an organic evolving dynamic: Matter self-organizes. Planets and stars, planetary systems and galaxies self-organize. On planet Earth, under the right conditions, life emerges and evolves. When evolution is the paradigm then organicism is the *modus operandi*; because of this in some fashion or other there are similarities among the levels, each having its own organic structure and all together having an organic integrity.

Fractals are common in nature and underlie important cultural products perhaps in part because they may be a natural strategy, something like a default mode. They offer the path of least

M. C. Escher's "Whirlpools" depicts self-similar fishes of two colors swirling into and out of infinity. Courtesy of Cordon Art, The Netherlands.

H E A V E N ' S   F R A C T A L   N E T

resistance—they are patterns easy to reiterate because already existing, repeated the same throughout but in different sizes, to make a structure or system that is complex, unified, expansive, and detailed. Architectural structures with blatantly repeated motifs are examples of this conservatism, which is why Mandelbrot said a rather too obvious fractal style is not the highest artistic accomplishment possible. In the greatest works the principles are more subtle, hidden like the order in tree bark, or complicated with inspiration beyond mere rigidly simple repetition (of the same arch or spire in a couple of different sizes, for example). A satisfying artwork contains nuanced details and harmonies at all scales.[10] Music is like this too—the best is not too programmatic and mechanical, but, as with painting and literature, more subtle and surprising. Vital richness seems related to shapes and textures hauntingly both more simple and more complex—traits associated with the Mandelbrot set.

We, like the Austrian botanist Gregor Mendel (1822–1884) and other reductionists, simplify to see plainly and live efficiently; in so doing we oversimplify, we reduce and leave out inconvenient anomalies. Fractals and chaos theory help us live with complexity. Psychological readiness is required to realize the need to account for complicated relations and to accept and delight in the pervasive patterns (fractal and nonfractal) in the universe and ourselves. Fractals enhance our vocabulary of concepts, and every well-educated person in the twenty-first century will eventually know something about them. Why? Because they uniquely help us appreciate and consider life's processes, including culture.

Wherever there are deep patterns of order, the human being can potentially get in touch with the forces that generated and lie behind those patterns. Perhaps the way light pinwheels, playing like square-dancers do-si-do-ing through the cells of the eye, is like a built-in operating manual to the secrets of the cosmos. With a double spiral life swirls into existence and swirls out. Existence dances together in cycles on all levels, large and small. One can tune in to harmony's source, "thank heaven" for beauty's gift of well-knit elegant clarity, and refresh one's soul at the spring of grace. The artist's unconscious depths and the luck of inspiration and craft are combined in the creative process to help the patterns emerge. Those involved in the humanities contemplate what it is to be human, and they help the patterns be realized in fractal wholeness, finding fulfillment in the vision of the cosmic in various aspects of the experienced details.

Fractals can be a way to keep in mind larger wholenesses in which we are involved—the real but elusive unity. Fractals at the same time help us to keep track of, to not lose sight of, the process of flow and diversity, the beauty of the rough and nonuniform.

Fractals, like the Alps and the clouds, cascades and lightning, depict the chaos/order dynamic with an elegance which involves repetition but also freedom and uniqueness. Thus fractals help creatively convey both unity of parts and uniqueness of parts—the cosmic and the local, the social and the personal, the zoom out and the zoom in. They are a potential, not a guarantee; people may apply them in different ways—a night watchman uses a flashlight to protect, a burglar uses it to rob. They can be inspiring, in their beauty and implications for learning about nature's secrets, but as with all things human, much depends on using wisely that which has been given.

Images of infinite holding and generating can present compact programs, recursive diagrams of adaptation to earth's life in human psyches.[11] They depict the mystery of participation in larger wholes, and show in an inspiring way paradoxes of transcendence—"the beyond within."[12] They elicit and even seem to celebrate (with their rhythmic harmonies) cosmic reality and our belonging—we are each ourselves, yet we are harmoniously integral.

Fractals visually illuminate patterns in diagrammatic maps (just as music does audibly), artfully conveying, distilling, and projecting. (This is especially vivid when we zoom in on animated fractals in the Mandelbrot set.) Thus fractals enliven our sense of the possibilities in our givens, our taken-for-granted relationships. They project a template for our imaginations to picture opportunities in the promising future of life. They are more in tune with actuality than are too-linear forms. Fractals sometimes seem able not only to present an image accurately depicting natural or cultural life-relations in harmony (knowledge) but to nurture new understanding of hidden depths (wisdom). They may help link us and our age to the wisdom of the whole in honored traditions.

Vedantic philosophers and Taoists, if they were to use contemporary terms, might say that "something fractal" abides in the nature of the consciousness which we humans share with the deepest, most ancient, all-pervasive ground of Being. The individual psyche, like the transcendent "Oversoul" (or universal intelligence, Mind, Spirit, Tao, God, etc.) inevitably makes and sees exquisite wholes, configuring fractal patterns; and that "something fractal" hides its traces. Once you open this fractal package you're home—in the cosmic context of infinity's vast and minuscule systems, riding the waves of the reiterating rhythms which are the echoes of life, involved in the oneness of the multiscaled levels of existence, the complexity/simplicity of consciousness. If we go along with the traditional insights of mystics worldwide we might arrive at a summary of experiencing "something fractal" in the humanities.

Rudolf Steiner suggested that in each person there is a light that is constructively reiterating or weaving, and there is a weaving of fractal networks that strengthens, and there is a strength that has the power to enlighten.[13] Fractals, when approached in the most fulfilling ways, seem vital with the breath of life, and bright with the strength of light. Culture reflects nature's intricately pulsating life. The humanities help fulfill the human wish for wisdom. Fractals inevitably play their part in this whole interwoven (and interweaving) process. Something fractal this way comes, something fractal that way goes. Zoom either way and you find both yourself (subjective part) and the cosmos (objective whole). Fractals are mirrorlike in their possibilities, reflecting whatever approaches are made by persons who would potentially learn from them, but, as I have been saying, they are not a panacea. Those who know the limits of fractals are best equipped to say what fractals cannot do; that is beyond the scope of my work here.

Fractals are cool, because they represent a universal geometrical concept, an abstract intelligence. Fractals are hot, because they dramatically show "sexy" (attractive) polarities in dynamic interactions, the push and pull of vitality. Fractals are just right, because they offer us a positive vision to help the creative processes of our age to keep improvising onward.

Nothing New (and All Things New)

While it is true that "there's nothing new under the sun" and also nothing that lasts eternally under the sun, the "difference that makes a difference" or the newness of the fractal vision presented here can be considered in several ways. To make connections between principles in geometry and nature on the one hand, and artifacts, images, and processes in psychology and culture which were not previously labeled fractal on the other hand, does constitute a new step. Awareness of fractal patterns provides a key to how traditional symbols function to represent and evoke such elusive dimensions as wholeness, complexity/simplicity, infinity, paradox, self-similarity, and recursiveness in time and space. Identifying things as fractals or associating them with fractal-like qualities allows and prepares us to consider aspects which might otherwise be ignored. Fractals can open new doors to the creative contemplation of oneness and manyness—the many illustrations I have presented help demonstrate this cosmic quality, and aspects of fractals' rich possibilities help the reader recognize patterns. I can affirm that the many examples I have gathered here are only a smattering—those with an eye for fractals will discern many more. Obviously a student of comparative religion such as I am is not a mathematician with a new formula—that's what Benoit Mandelbrot is. A comparativist is someone who makes connections, sees relations, and is concerned with wholeness and underlying unity, with seeing the pattern that connects. In terms of comparative religion, philosophy, art, and history, fractals lead us into a reexploration of consciousness as overall context. They help us think about the nature of Mind, whether in the sense of Buddha Mind or Bateson's vision of Mind in the evolutionary process. Fractals and images of recursion in general help reopen the discussion of Self in culture, Self as a reflexivity or consciousness that is expansive, inclusive, reflective. In many traditions in the past—shamanism, mysticism, yoga, and so on—people contemplated the spiritual reality in all; the One in the all-one soul of humanity becomes again a possible experience, to be considered. Fractals can help us visualize varieties of patterns, see basics again, neglected depths. This has the potential in receptive minds to change attitudes, reorient stances, and develop wisdom regarding interconnectedness. We are faced, in a new century, with a new twist on the theme of religion and philosophy: how vast Mind is part of us and/or we are part of it. Fractals also help us consider questions about social psychology and about processes of the wrinkle-folded brain, as we saw in Strand Two, in the discussion of J. Richard Eiser's book *Attitudes, Chaos, and the Connectionist Mind.*

Benoit Mandelbrot demonstrated how fractal phenomena of nature occur in the cracks of difference in the three dimensions—length, width, and height (represented by line, plane, solid).[14] A crumpled-up sheet of paper has a texture that is complex, somewhere between two and three dimensions. In its wrinkles, dimensions are compressed—this crinkled ball of paper is rough like many textures in nature. This rumpled plane of complexity can be said to possess a shape that "passes through vastly many more mathematical points on the surface of a plane than does a single straight line."[15] Coastlines and rivers, trees and lungs, the texture of the rough bark of a tree and recursive arabesques are like the crumpled paper. The fractals in images of culture also depict depths, anomalous complexities of relationships among parts, parts of wholes which exceed and collapse the usual dimensions of the perceptions. The Self, according to wisdom traditions, is the simple unity of depth, allowing the interrelated complexity or richness of experience. The flatness, linearness, and smoothness of surface, to which we reduce complexity for convenience's sake, is sometimes quite useful. It can also be problematic, like the isolation we employ until we forget to reintegrate with wholeness (and so suffer), fixating on the part as if it were all. The Self is ultimately of the same depth as the Oneness discovered and referred to by the sages of wisdom traditions—Heraclitus, Plotinus, Vedantins, Zen Buddhists, Native Americans, and so forth. Invisibly it bespeaks cosmic nesting, cosmos within cosmos, system interlaced with system, dream condensing situations of waking, waking enacting impulses of fantasy, impulses of imaginative creativity in attractive images. Consider the griffin, for example, a mythological creature with the head and wings of a great eagle and the body, legs, and tail of a lion. Why a conglomerate or medley, a hybrid monster? This anomaly, this freakish dragonlike cross between a lion and an eagle, represents the anomaly of Christ—a mixture of heaven and earth, man and God, flesh and angel, justice and mercy—and Christ is a name for the higher Self found potentially in all. It represents a unity more intricate than simple pragmatic conscious everyday calculations can take in, beauty more mysterious than theories can account for, and it is represented in other inclusive cosmic images as well—the Way, the Vine, the Tree of Life. Fractals behind the roughness of nature—tangled vines and roots, mountains cracked with ridges slanting the same way—as Briggs and Peat write, "emerge from a holistic chaotic process whereby countless 'parts' are subtly interconnected—true chaos as opposed to mathematical simulation produced by repeating an algorithm. Consequently, natural fractals have an individuality, spontaneity, depth, and quality of mystery that no algorithm— even a nonlinear one—can reproduce."[16] So do cosmic images from the cultural traditions of the world—they resonate in the psyche with individual vitality and mystery because the Self is inseparable from the whole.

"Nature makes its fractal forms out of matter and energy," as Briggs and Peat suggest.[17] With "order for free," energy forms systems of matter, and the possibilities inherent in matter inform the configurations of energy processes. Comparing the processes of nature with human creativity, Briggs and Peat observe that artistic works are made from the combinations of perceptions, concepts, language, and experience. Through creatively combining such categories, artists impart to their works dynamic vitality—contrasts, polarities, upsets of balance, suspense and resolution. "The concords and discords form patterns that are always surprisingly and significantly self-similar and self-different from each other, reflecting the curious mystery of our being in the world."[18] Art's truth is in some way or other a fractal-like reflection with fidelity to some aspects of existence with its levels of intelligent organization— levels such as conscious and unconscious, cellular, symbolic, social, ecological, and cosmic.

Perhaps the experience of fractals should be seen as a seed vision which you swallow—and then it unfolds you, crumples your linear thought, tosses you into the water so you'll learn to swim in a different element beyond the usual cliches. Briggs and Peat suggest that "Fractals and chaos allow us to add the rule-

The unconscious is an ocean of images. Anonymous (Sufi?) ink drawing.

breaking Dionysius into our idea of what it means to be reasonable. If to logic we add harmony and to harmony we add dissonance, then to be rational is to be creative."[19] We need a new reasonableness—not "nothing but," but "both/and." Emotional intelligence needs to be part of our repertoire, a depth detector, a love dimension, a sense of Self and Sacred, Self as Sacred, also known as spirituality. The dynamics of affinity, rough-and-tumble, play of smooth and ribbed, that which turns back in upon itself, that which spirals again and again around and out of itself, that with its eyes on a prize beyond. "The sensual self-similarity and difference of nature and art provide an inspiration to be more alive."[20] Love opens new possibilities, breezes through old boundaries, unfolds new unknown dimensions. Fractals are like the hidden sound track, the graphics, the eloquent geometry of some of Self's mysterious life processes.

Chaos theory (and fractals have been called the patterns of chaos) is as much about aesthetics as about science. Briggs and Peat write that chaos theory points us in a direction, as art does— toward "the direction we find in the healing images of nature, the direction in which lies our effort to contact the secret ingredient of the Universe we call spirit."[21] Wholeness has to do with psyche, consciousness, beauty, and the sacred—fractals are a key to discovering ways these dimensions intersect. Fractals usher us closer to a sense of the Self of Unity, the One, paradox and open secret of the cosmos. The principle of the whole, Tao, Buddha Nature, Ein Soph of mystical Judaism, *tawhid* of Islam, *chit* or pure consciousness of the Upanishads, "Grandfather" of the Native Americans. Science and art both depend on pattern recognition. Poets, philosophers, writers, and composers discover and display patterns, arrange patterns, play among the patterns, to delight others who need pointers, reminders, to see what's already there. Starbursts on cacti, mazes of branches, configurations of the Self's shadows. In this spirit, Walt Whitman, in a poem which riffs on the image of unfolding, suggested human genetic fractals, selfsimilarities of excellent traits of human life replicating:

> Unfolded out of the folds of the woman man comes unfolded,
> and is always to come unfolded,
> Unfolded only out of the super-best woman of the earth
> is to come the super-best man of the earth,
> Unfolded out of the friendliest woman is to come the friendliest man,
> Unfolded only out of the perfect body of a woman
> can a man be form'd of perfect body,
> Unfolded only out of the inimitable poems of woman can come
> the poems of man (only thence have my poems come),
> Unfolded out of the strong and arrogant woman I love,
> only thence can appear the strong and arrogant man I love,
> Unfolded by brawny embraces from the well-muscled woman I love,
> only thence come the brawny embraces of the man,
> Unfolded out of the folds of the woman's brain come all the folds
> of the man's brain, duly obedient,
> Unfolded out of the justice of the woman all justice is unfolded,
> Unfolded out of the sympathy of the woman is all sympathy.
> A man is a great thing upon the earth and through eternity,
> but every jot of the greatness of man is unfolded out of woman.
> First the man is shaped in the woman, he can then be shaped in
>   himself.[22]

Such a fractal-like pattern of thought helps us riff onward, improvising our sense of our part in the dynamism of existence. We go on, expanding our sense of consciousness from interstices.

We go on: Unfolded out of the egg, unfolded out of the DNA, unfolded out of the folded brain, unfolded out of the folds of woman, unfolded out of the fold of childhood, unfolded out of the folds of culture's blanket with patterns of stories, images, rituals woven so skillfully. We go on: Unfolded out of the folds of dreams, unfolded out of the streets of society, unfolded out of the turns and twists of fate, unfolded out of the knots of *maya* and karma, ignorance and passion, out of the knitted brow. We grow on, unfolded out of the hidden cracks and wrinkles, branching between polar forces, unfolded out of the simple which grows complex, unfolded out of the origami-animal energies of hopes and dreams. We go on unfolding from crevices to canyons of potentiality, unfolding the long message closely creased in its small envelope. We are unfolding the codes in the crinkles and cracks between dimensions; unfolding the paths of fractal complexity which cannot be reduced to linear style; unfolding the secret patterns behind the ridges and stubble, the options amidst the trouble; unfolding the clarity of the grain already in wood and agate; unfolding the basic situation we've grown blind to, in dreams that unfold in magic wisdom realism; unfolding the future from the densely packed seeds of the viable past.[23]

Fractals have taught us to approach with respect the strange, the anomalous, the untimely and unfitting for the revelations of a larger pattern they involve. Scales of space and rates of time cycles are integral to human relevance. Fractals have taught us to value and utilize the creative tension, to learn to soothe the fracas between science and religion, rationalism and poetry, technology and humanities. Discernible and applicable in many realms, they give us scope to see the big picture.

Fractals, resonant with the complexities of the deeply simple, suggest many meanings and values and uses, not just one. Fractals open up ways to affirm self-transcendence, showing the wisdom of the old images that depict our situation—from sufis, Zen masters, Hasidic rabbis, yogis, mystics. They offer ways to discuss hidden worlds, the mysterious, the sacred, the infinite, the life-giving; dimensions which are by nature elusive. This reaffirming helps us imagine better, unpack for consideration, notice nuances, implications, complexities. Fractals are part of a new impetus and language to allow us to see patterns, notice relations in many conditions and situations. If we approach deep matters with only a surface awareness and expectations, we will miss the profound. Using linear means, we miss the systems, cosms of consciousness. If our only tool is a hammer, every problem looks like a nail. Fractals, though not a panacea, expand the possibilities of response with conceptual models. Fractals demonstrate and enable further unfoldings, helping us keep the necessary creative tension between self-assertion and self-transcendence. As Plotinus wrote, "the Soul of the All and also the individual soul is a principle of no small importance; with this we must weave all things to-gether."[24] Fractals are visual reflections of psyche which does this weaving, as close as the visual comes to resembling music. Fractal and recursive images of various sorts can be openings into the archetype of cosmic abundance, splendid extensiveness, the precious generative power of "order for free."

Getting Cracking: The Proof of the Principle Is in the Practice

> I folded myself into one piece.
>
> —Virginia Hamilton Adair[25]

Practice is the dynamic ingredient in vital systems—how they work. How do you apply something that claims to be useful or necessary to life? How is it life-supportive? How does one apply in life the fractal implications of all we have been considering; how do we relate to them in actual praxis? If fractals are an idea whose time has come, as I claim, they will continue to emerge in many attitudes and behaviors, fields and creative processes. It is as an answer to our quests and questions that fractals are emerging in our time. "There are periods when a particular idea holds sway in many different fields. The great question is why?" asks Gerald Holton, a historian and physicist at Harvard.[26] Why? I would suggest the Zeitgeist has something to do with it, and another reason is the conscious and unconscious desire for a vision and experience that will correct the predominant one-sided take. It starts with starvation in some aspect of psychic activity, experienced lack; in this case, a lack of larger visions of whole contexts, a lack of deep interconnectedness, a hunger for a view that includes these two things and shows them as inevitably more real than a part that is isolated. The unbalance sets the process in motion; it tips the level so that gravity's pull makes things come one's way. In our present time, when atomization has become rampant, when alienation and isolation pervade, we are rediscovering how all is interconnected in quantum physics and ecology. A corrective helps us regain balance; fractals may

"Life and Death." When this picture is scrutinized, sometimes the background and foreground flip, exchanging places. What shall we call the aspect of consciousness involved when we shift perspectives? What processes are involved in noticing fractal wholeness? Currier and Ives engraving.

Mandelbrot set
C6PTLM11.PNG.
Courtesy of Paul W.
Carlson, *Mind-
Boggling Fractals* CD-
ROM.

be seen as a sign of natural and spiritual resilience because they visualize wholeness in new ways.

In *The Quark and the Jaguar,* Murray Gell-Mann writes that specialization, although a necessary feature of our civilization, needs to be supplemented by integrated thought across disciplines. "We need to celebrate the vital contribution of those who dare to take what I call a crude look at the whole."[27] Fractals might be seen by modern people as a sign of the One in the depths. Jung wrote of the soul's qualities, "the most unpleasant dreams can best bring us near to the blood relationship of humanity and can most effectively reduce the arrogance which goes with lack of instinct. Even if a whole world is out of joint, the all-embracingness of the dark soul can never break to pieces, and the wider and more numerous become the cracks in the surface, the greater grows the strength of the one in the depths."[28] Thinkers who study consciousness, whether in terms of psychology or physiology, are likely to gain insights from exploring fractals. Whether they speak in terms of neurons and attitudes, of networks and attractors, or of the emergent self and social construction, they would do well to include a discussion of fractal patterns.[29] Fractals are a conceptual tool which may help us refine many a "crude look at the whole."

How do we use fractals to fold ourselves into one piece? There are neural nets in the brain—the nervous system is a net to catch the mesh of the rest of the cosmos in perceptions and concepts. The net of the meta-patterning that connects all is found in all the reflective societies, in their cultures that help them see. The net in Dante's masterpiece becomes the ladder of light, which is also known as the great chain of being in medieval worldviews. In other cultures there are other expressions of the unity of interrelated coexistence. Fractals help us unpack the infinite from dust, pollen, spores, seeds, grain; they help us unpack the germinating force where it is locked and hidden and folded. Fractals help us picture mutuality—parts recognizing kinship within larger wholes.

To see beauty around us is a subtle skill honed by spiritual discipline. As those who have had the experience say, "There is something abundantly and compellingly energizing in those moments when we see the interconnectedness—what Plotinus calls the unity—of the universe and the consanguinity of living beings."[30] One lesson we learn from fractals is that it is possible to find relations of whole and parts in larger and larger networks. Where we set the limits of self is determined by our own vision. Plotinus noted that there is no legitimate place to draw a limit, to say "this and no further is I." A person's primary identity is with the universe, a finely textured relationship of parts to whole in which none of the parts could exist without the whole.[31] Fractals, as visualized patterns and as images in the humanities, can illustrate this, helping us imagine our interdependence, our wholeness and our partness.

Fractals help us see with our imaginations the lines of relation and the realms of existence which exist in what often seem like nearly invisible cracks. Folded between the genes from the mother and the genes from the father, the individual. The humanities' fractal-like patterns open up the split between us and our ancestors, revealing the worlds in there. That is, they reveal human experience to the imagination through the disciplines of history, philosophy, literature, and the arts; they invite us to consider the many worlds which exist in human life. The worlds between the time you set the clock and the time you go to sleep. The worlds between the two involved in lovemaking, the whole work of muscles and the aurora borealis of climax. The worlds in the twilight, the moment between waking and sleeping, the worlds in dreams, the worlds in deep sleep, the worlds in repair of your whole body and psyche, the worlds in groggy waking in the middle of the night and again in the morning. The dimensions between your zigzagging fingers, the folds of your brain, the branches of your lungs, the spirals of your eyes. Wholeness is the meta-stability which self-heals the breaks. The dimensions smaller than the space between hairs on your head, the worlds between the crow's feet of your eyes, the dimensions of the dimple you were born with, and the big gaps that grew in your land, like the Grand Canyon. Fractals help us imagine dimensions that are betwixt and between—exfoliating from fertile crevices—self-reflective worlds within worlds. They display suggestions of the modus operandi of consciousness—self expanding, self refreshing, self returning to the One after self-exhausting among the many. Literature and the arts are like fractals (which exist between dimensions) in that they guide us into the dimensions between realms—between personal and social, between agony and ecstasy. The humanities have to do with that which makes us human; they portray and discuss that which all humanity shares. The humanities, with their studies of literature, history, religion, philosophy, and law, embody understandings of how unities are fractalized among us. Because fractals open the conditions that encourage new contemplation of ignored possibilities, I believe they can serve as an impetus to creative understanding. Contemplation promotes new approaches, and it gives us freedom to mull issues receptively. It is more open-ended than deliberate; purposive thought is more predetermined to find what it seeks. Overly purposive thought ignores the enfolded hidden realms of nuance, contradiction, and depth as unnecessary, inconvenient. Contemplation involves freedom from having to explain away anomalies; it deepens understanding, allowing us to admit the inherent weirdness and wildness which reductionism denies. The order of fractals allows for the existence of dynamic chaotic processes and thus fractals help contemplation to unconvolute the compressed and repressed contortions in actual situations. They help us understand the way things are and solve the puzzles of world and psyche. I will provide an example of this from the thinking of one observer of knowledge in our times. French thinker Jean-François Lyotard draws the following conclusion from a study of fractals and related research:

> The continuous differentiable function is losing its preeminence as a paradigm of knowledge and prediction. Postmodern science—by concerning itself with such things as undecidables, the limits of precise control, conflicts characterized by incomplete information, fractal catastrophes, and pragmatic paradoxes—is theorizing its own evolution as discontinuous, catastrophic, nonrectifiable, and paradoxical. It is changing the meaning of the word knowledge, while expressing how such a change can take place. It is producing not the known, but the unknown. And it suggests a model of legitimation that has nothing to do with maximized performance, but has as its basis difference understood as paralogy. . . . any sophisticated theory is useful . . . as a generator of ideas.[32]

Probably only by creatively entering into the ways of fractals personally, following a natural fascination, exploring playfully,

will you really see what I mean about their potential. Your contemplative involvement would begin to reveal how fractals can unfold possible understandings of wholeness, because fractals show boundaries in existence and also dissolve differences in integrating them into larger wholes. Fractals reveal the possibility of seeing units, parts, elements, individuality's assertions, and also the larger actualities of wholeness, unfolding self-transcendence in the One, the "meta-fractal" that connects the scales and dimensions of existence. So many explorations are underway, from visual arts, music, and dance, to scientific writings about "fractal thinking" and "the philosophy of fractals," that it seems premature to conclude much about the unfolding future possibilities.[33] This series of reflections has been an improvisation on my part to suggest a few points which I hope others will be interested in and will pursue further in their own various ways. Pursuing fractal connections, in math, in nature, and in the contemplation of patterns, begins to reveal some of their amazing potential. Exploring fractals can tap their usefulness as dynamic models of relationships, templates of possibilities, and generative stimulators of ideas.

"Rippled Surface." Linocut by M.C. Escher. A detail of this image appears on the title page. Courtesy of Cordon Art, The Netherlands.

NOTES

INTRODUCTORY REFLECTIONS

1. Thomas Merton, "Hagia Sophia," in *A Thomas Merton Reader,* ed. Thomas P. McDonnell (Garden City, N.Y.: Image, 1974), 506.

2. *Psychological Reflections: An Anthology of the Writings of C. G. Jung,* ed. Jolande Jacobi (New York: Harper and Row, 1961), 204–205.

3. The term "fractal" was coined by Benoit Mandelbrot in 1975. His pioneering book *The Fractal Geometry of Nature* (New York: W. H. Freeman, 1982) remains the classic on the subject. For basic introductions to fractals, see also Linda Garcia, *The Fractal Explorer* (Santa Cruz: Dynamic, 1991), and Michael McGuire, *An Eye for Fractals: A Graphic and Photographic Essay* (Redwood City, Calif.: Addison-Wesley, 1991). These are useful entry points for anyone with or without a mathematical background, rich with images and insightful discussions as well as bibliographies.

4. Fractals have been found useful in the study of heartbeat patterns and brainwaves, river discharges and earthquakes, traffic and boundary analysis, branching crystals and the shape of instant coffee particles, for example. "Trees, clouds, rivers, mountains, bronchi, the vascular system and so forth can be similarly represented by fractals, because they are unions of rescaled copies of themselves. . . . The excitement over fractals . . . is over a paradigm shift. Fractal geometry is fundamentally a new language for describing and analyzing the complex forms of nature, a new language that supplants the traditional language of Euclidian geometry." Gerald J. G. Junevicus, "Chaos and Fractals: Paradigms Lost," *Choice* (September 1996): 73–90. This article is an excellent bibliographic introduction to the topic.

5. See, for example, the essays in Gerald A. Edgar, ed., *Classics on Fractals* (Reading, Mass.: Addison-Wesley, 1993).

6. See John D. Barrow, *The Artful Universe* (Oxford: Oxford University Press, 1995), 62. Besides their usefulness in maximizing surfaces, fractals and fractal-like structures (which I sometimes call "semi-fractals" in this book) may afford durability as well. A hexagon made of hexagons, for example, is a tough structure that can withstand pressure; it has strength through and through, though divided, since each unit shares an indomitable solidarity with the others.

7. Mac Wellman, "Werewolves, Fractals, and Forbidden Knowledge," interview by Dawn-Marie Garrett, *Theatre* (Washington, D.C.) 27, nos. 2–3 (1997).

8. Ron Eglash, *African Fractals: Modern Computing and Indigenous Design* (New Brunswick, N.J.: Rutgers University Press, 1999) is a fine example of a study of fractals in the cultures of a particular continent.

9. I find early Taoist thought and the vision of Vedanta, Buddhist philosophy, and Christian spirituality equally inspiring. If asked to label what I do, I must say I am an essayist or writer. I work in the field of comparative religion in the discipline of history, and I am concerned with soul (psychology) and love of wisdom (philosophy); involved in these, I make commentaries on culture.

10. Jung, *Psychological Reflections,* 298.

11. "Metaphysics is in essence a systematic way of attempting to say something relevant about *all.*" David Bohm, *On Creativity,* ed. Lee Nichol (London: Routledge, 1998), 89.

12. On the topic of traditional religious and philosophical views of the order found in the natural world see Seyyed Hossein Nasr, *Religion and the Order of Nature* (New York: Oxford University Press, 1996).

13. Italo Calvino, *Six Memos for the Next Millennium* (Cambridge, Mass.: Harvard Uni-

versity Press, 1988). Calvino wrote a lecture for each of the five values I list, but died before writing about the projected sixth value, consistency. Had he lived, he might have found a fractal model useful in conceptualizing how consistency is possible in a time of multiplicity.

14. Toby Cole, ed., *Playwrights on Playwriting* (New York: Hill and Wang, 1961), 241.

15. Norman O. Brown's *Love's Body* (New York: Vintage, 1966) is an example of this kind of intertextual work, and Ralph Waldo Emerson's essays, each one composed as a mosaic of passages, may be considered another.

16. Examples are as varied as the oneness implicit in the views of primal shamans and the love in Buddhism and Christianity.

17. Barrow, *The Artful Universe,* 245.

18. Those interested in the methods of applying this idea should see Henri Bortoft's work, such as *The Wholeness of Nature: Goethe's Way toward a Science of Conscious Participation in Nature* (Hudson, N.Y.: Lindisfarne, 1996).

19. Gregory Bateson's exploration of what he calls "ecology of mind" (found in his book *Steps to an Ecology of Mind* [1972; reprint, New York: Ballantine, 1990]) suggests a new way to consider the nature of order in living systems; it encompasses modes which discover patterns common to many disciplines. His work proposes approaching the world of evolution, thought, adaptation, genetics, and embryology with an integrated meta-science, using a method of multiple description to discover underlying (fractal-like) patterns which develop and survive. Bateson envisioned and began to practice an epistemology that compared thought, evolution, and epigenesis. He called this epistemology the "bonus." His work strove to "propose a sacred unity of the biosphere that will contain fewer epistemological errors than the versions of that sacred unity which the various religions of history have offered." He proposed this, not to rival any institutional religious traditions, but out of need—the need for clarity in human understanding. His epistemology glimpses a higher order, overlapping patterns of necessity, archetypal thought, and evolution; because these things are systemic, they share a pattern which connects. Gregory Bateson, *A Sacred Unity: Further Steps to an Ecology of Mind,* ed. Rodney E. Donaldson (New York: HarperCollins, 1991), xiii.

20. Craig Holdrege, *Genetics and the Ma-nipulation of Life: The Forgotten Factor of Context* (Hudson, N.Y.: Lindisfarne, 1996).

21. The rigidly linear hyper-rational mind may be hostile to nonlinearity, with its paradoxes and expansion of the rules of the game. But is overly purposive rationality an operation, a calibration, a procedure, or is it something sacred, the highest core and standard by which all else in the universe must be judged and ordered? We all appreciate the bright side of reason and could not do without it. But we dare not gloss over the night side of rationality. Being chained to inescapable logic can make for a life of fulfillment, as in French chemist Louis Pasteur's case, or for a life of soul-emptiness, as in Nazi Adolf Eichmann's.

22. Arthur Koestler, *The Act of Creation* (London: Pan, 1970).

23. Lieh-tzu, *The Yellow Emperor,* quoted in John Briggs and F. David Peat, *Turbulent Mirror: An Illustrated Guide to Chaos Theory and the Science of Wholeness* (New York: Harper and Row, 1989), 119.

24. Paul Valéry, *Seashells,* trans. Ralph Manheim (Boston: Beacon, 1998) (previously published as Paul Valéry, "Man and the Sea Shell," in *Aesthetics,* trans. Ralph Manheim [New York: Pantheon, 1964], 30); Mihaly Cziksentmihalyi, *Creativity: Flow and the Psychology of Discovery* (New York: Harper, 1997).

25. Mandelbrot, *Fractal Geometry,* 1, 18.

26. Long-term fitness often goes unnoticed in the food chain. For 250 million years dragonflies have been eating about 300 mosquitoes a day; dragonflies in turn are eaten by trout and frogs, which are eaten by humans.

27. Physicist Wolfgang Pauli has said that the deepest pleasure in science comes from finding an "instantiation, a home, for some deeply felt, deeply held image." Quoted in Stuart A. Kauffman, *The Origins of Order: Self-Organization and Selection in Evolution* (New York: Oxford University Press, 1993), vii. Perhaps my own exploration of fractals owes its origins to zigzag swirls of infancy's vision and heavenly days in Vermont, glimpses of subtle light tessellating across the excitable cells of my eyes and producing wonder, the entoptic geometry of the rods and cones experiencing the extraordinary and familiar. I recently found a fractal-like linoleum block print I made thirty-five years ago, a whirl of whirling

stars. The vivid, haunting patterns of Mandelbrot's fractals reawakened my wonder at this.

28. Just as a quiltmaker or mosaic maker improvises, so does a collagist, playing off the found pieces, performing solos taking off from them. Much of the life of the mind in our age has to do with collaging the data one finds, colliding and interweaving symmetries just as a shifting kaleidoscope does. I am the first to admit, then, that this book is a gingerly sideways slide of material synthesized together, themes sidling up to us clumped by affinities, a series of fractal puddles, reflecting light refracted by the sky.

29. I hope those allergic to new words will forgive me a little word coinage. We "wholicipate," not just participate, because we interexist, all in all. I consider the net a fractal image because within the sections, in a net of diamond-shaped units, one can imagine larger and smaller composite diamond shapes, and so on.

30. Fritjof Capra, *The Web of Life: A New Scientific Understanding of Living Systems* (New York: Anchor, 1996). The entire book demonstrates Capra's statement.

31. F. David Peat, *The Blackwinged Night: Creativity in Nature and Mind* (Cambridge, Mass.: Perseus, 2000), discusses eloquently how quantum physics depicts this point.

32. Riff: Once we in the Western world needed to hear of the happenings at the Sea of Galilee. Then we needed to see what Galileo could see. Now we need to know of the seas of galaxies. (If there are, in the universe, billions of stars for each individual on earth, doesn't that provide a humbling cosmic perspective on the claims of humanity's various belief systems to exclusive rightness? I feel that it does, and that it suggests implications about our belonging to our own planetary home, Gaia.)

33. The phrase is associated with Kauffman's *Origins of Order.* Just as "self-organizing," a term used in systems theory, has a rather democratic association, though it applies to stars, ecosystems, cells, and so forth, "order for free" bespeaks a modern sensibility of not expecting order, not knowing how to account for it—it turns up without any investment on our part. The ancients seemed less surprised to find deep patterns instead of randomness. Perhaps nineteenth-century science helps explain the difference in viewpoint between us and them.

34. For more on this, see Brian Swimme and Thomas Berry, *The Universe Story: From the Primordial Flaring Forth to the Ecozoic Era* (San Francisco: HarperSanFrancisco, 1992), chapter 1; and F. David Peat, *The Blackwinged Night,* 59–88.

35. The term "big bang" seems unconsciously anthropocentric, evoking images of a dynamite blast, weapon discharge, bomb detonation. The theory of the big bang was arrived at through a gradual process, from all the scientific educated guesses: it holds that 15 billion years ago everything began, and for 300,000 years there was a thick haze of swarming subatomic particles, like a channel of static on TV, and then atoms formed. Later, stars and galaxies evolved, and four and a half billion years ago, life began on earth. The powerful opening of existence evolved all "microcosms" and "macrocosms." I occasionally use the term "cosms" to stand for systems.

36. What might a prayer to this One sacred origin sound like? "Our fireball who wert in heaven, glorious is thy flame and hallowed be thy flare. Thy kingdoms are self-similar, thy spiritual mark of Mind is everywhere. Give us this day our daily symbiosis, and bless us while we speciate, and forgive us our entropies, as we forgive those who devolve against us, and lead us not into genocide or speciescide or omnicide, for thine is the chaos and the order for ever and ever, Amen." (I mean this to be taken lightly, but not entirely in jest.) Traditional religions teach in various ways that it is ennobling to identify with the vast spirit, the Mind behind all, and to sacrifice and sublimate the lower self, the small ego, for the higher spiritual reality which we share. Consider the likely alternative riff: "I believe in my ego, separate forever, creator of society and culture, and in technological strength, its offspring, lording it over world markets and systems, with freedom to enjoy all its exploitative gains in splendid isolation. Deliver us from any other social systems and bless our pure individualism forever, world without end, Amen."

37. A. and E. Keary, *The Heroes of Asgard: Tales from Scandinavian Mythology* (London: Macmillan, 1923). The subtlety of the elves is like the work of the ants who befriend the two brothers in the Mayan myth *Popol Vuh.* See *Popol Vuh: The Mayan Book of the Dawn of Life,* trans. Dennis Tedlock (New York: Simon and Schuster, 1996), 96, 140–141.

38. For a cultural-historical overview of the concept of infinity, see Eli Maor, *To Infinity and Beyond: A Cultural History of the Infinite* (Boston: Birkhauser, 1987). See also James P. Carse, *Finite and Infinite Games* (New York: Free, 1986). In Carse's book, the "Infinite Game" is the ongoing religious quest to affirm life.

39. For an interesting introduction to the philosophical implications of fractals, see John Briggs and F. David Peat, *Seven Life Lessons of Chaos* (New York: HarperCollins, 1999), especially chapters 4–7. For a book-length study of fractals in African culture, see Eglash, *African Fractals*. For a sense of how fractal images and principles can stimulate a developing art and craft, see Peter Engel, *Origami from Angelfish to Zen* (New York: Dover, 1994). See also Diego Uribe, *Fractal Cuts: Exploring the Magic of Fractals with Pop-up Designs* (Norfolk, England: Tarquin, 1993).

40. Vaclav Havel, "Civilization's Thin Veneer," *Harvard Magazine,* July–August 1995, 32ff.

STRAND ONE

Part of this chapter appeared as "Indra's Net in the Postmodern Waters," *Benares Hindu University Journal of Scientific Research* 47 (1997): 103–124. Some of its main ideas were discussed in "Heaven's Fractal Net: A Religious Image" (paper presented at the annual conference of the American Academy of Religion, Midwest Region, Chicago, April 1, 1995).

1. *Psychological Reflections: An Anthology of the Writings of C. G. Jung,* ed. Jolande Jacobi (New York: Harper and Row, 1961), 224. Rabindranath Tagore also seemed to believe "the two great religions [Christianity and Buddhism] represent the highest expectation of man—the truth of love . . . [and] the truth of peace." Amiya Chakravarty, ed., *A Tagore Reader* (Boston: Beacon, 1966), 273.

2. Others who have addressed the issue include Alfred North Whitehead, *Science and the Modern World* (New York: Macmillan, 1959); C. G. Jung, "Mind and Earth," in *Civilization in Transition,* trans. R. F. C. Hull, vol. 10 of *The Collected Works of C. G. Jung,* ed. Herbert Read, Michael Fordham, and Gerhard Adler (New York: Pantheon, 1964); Aldo Leopold, *A Sand County Almanac* (1970; reprint, New York: Oxford University Press, 1989); Rachel Carson, *The House of Life* (Boston: Houghton Mifflin, 1972) and *Silent Spring* (1962; Boston: Houghton Mifflin, 1987); Lynn Townsend White, *Dynamo and Virgin Reconsidered: Essays in the Dynamism of Western Culture* (Cambridge, Mass.: MIT Press, 1971); Ian G. Barbour, *Religion in an Age of Science* (San Francisco: Harper and Row, 1990); and Ian G. Barbour, ed., *Western Man and Environmental Ethics: Attitudes toward Nature and Technology* (Reading, Mass.: Addison-Wesley, 1973). See also Theodore Roszak, *The Voice of the Earth: An Exploration in Ecopsychology* (New York: Simon and Schuster, 1992) and a wide variety of philosophers, anthropologists, and ecologists.

3. Gregory Bateson, *Steps to an Ecology of Mind* (1972; reprint, New York: Ballantine, 1990), 483, and *A Sacred Unity: Further Steps to an Ecology of Mind,* ed. Rodney E. Donaldson (New York: HarperCollins, 1991), 313. In Bateson's view, we live in a world of two levels: human-level conscious learning and a larger level of evolution. Though we live much in the first, we are creatures also of the second. "We have lost a wholeness of being. . . . The damage is the taking apart. The sacredness is the coming together. The sacred is the hook up. [The sacred is] the total hook up and not the product of the split." In his view, art, poetry, rhythmic prayer are discoveries, or "uncoveries of that which one knew before. Then sacredness has something to do with this covering and uncovering deeper components." In our crises hope lies in retrieving links. *A Sacred Unity,* 280, 301–303.

4. Gregory Bateson uses this phrase throughout *Mind and Nature: A Necessary Unity* (New York: Dutton, 1979).

5. Igor Aleksander, quoted in Clive Davidson, "I Process Therefore I Am," *New Scientist,* March 27, 1993, 23. Aleksander uses the term "consciousness" to mean "human thought processes"; it does not have here the more expansive meaning found in Hinduism, Taoism, and various mystical traditions. Education, learning, and understanding can gain much from fractal models of wholeness. Without a sense of connection, proportion, wholeness, one assumes the wrong things and guesses wrong. When one is unaware of relating to larger wholes, one becomes closed, alienated. Fractals are a better model of reality because they enable us to visualize wholeness

in describing or picturing processes of life. I would argue that learning is fractal and is improvisational play. The hermeneutical circle involves a growing reiteration of grasps at wholes and parts—trying things out in a spirit of exploration, fluid creativity, exploring series of possibilities.

6. In many parts of the world, rational grids have been used to divide up land. In Cambodia, for example, the Pol Pot regime imposed such grids without concern for natural, dynamic parts of the terrain, such as water tables.

7. See Stanislav Grof, *The Holotropic Mind* (San Francisco: Harper, 1990), and Michael Talbot, *The Holographic Universe* (New York: Harper, 1991). Ken Wilbur assesses this model in *Eye to Eye* (Boston: Shambhala, 1996) and raises important issues. Wilbur rightly notes that an oversimplification of complex levels of existence into a hologram model would result in reductionism and confusion. Nevertheless, with new findings in the study of complexity, chaos, and fractal geometry making their impact, scientists and engineers are belatedly (and sometimes while being dragged kicking and screaming into postmodern paradigms and sensibilities) beginning to do more justice to the patterns that connect, discerning subtle unities and interfaces in living processes, cycles in behavior, the elusive roughness and organic orders of nature. These studies offer fruitful metaphors for thinking about, visualizing, and describing the processes found in religious traditions, if we have the humility to learn from nature.

8. Ivars Peterson, "Fractals Past, Fractals Future," *Science News* 151, no. 9 (March 1, 1997), S13.

9. Riff on Benoit Mandelbrot: In the World War II era, Mandelbrot was a young man whose approach to math did not easily fit into the way the subject was conventionally studied in France; he had the ability to visualize algebra in images, solving problems intuitively. He never learned the linear order of the letters in the alphabet, so he has difficulty finding something in an alphabetical list, needing to scan the whole. In his geometric thinking he stuck with the incontrovertible fact that nature is largely non-Euclidean—"Clouds are not spheres, mountains are not cones, coastlines are not circles and bark is not smooth, nor does lightning travel in a straight line." His

diverse interests and discoveries converged in his uncovering the principles of fractal forms in nature. For more on his life and thought see John Briggs and F. David Peat, *Turbulent Mirror: An Illustrated Guide to Chaos Theory and the Science of Wholeness* (New York: Harper and Row, 1989), 89–96.

10. Riff on how gaps can be theoretically filled by assuming that various parts of the whole share the same nature: An artist, knowing the textures of bark and the configurations of leaves, can "fill in" a sketch of the whole tree even if he can see only parts; similarly, a mandala or a song with a traditional structure can be completed by traditional people knowing the gist of the gestalt. Through intuition of likely self-similarity, one improvises a compatible fulfillment of the whole. Now that's an interesting process, with clues for those interested in creative processes of innovation.

11. Leon O. Chua, editor of the *International Journal of Bifurcation and Chaos,* in the journal's inaugural editorial, vol. 1, no. 1 (1991), 1. I suggest that this forfeiture of knowing is related to the forfeiture involved in denying one is part of nature.

12. Riff on grace: Grace in this sense is the process of becoming one, reconciling the broken parts—for example, the conscious with the unconscious. Grace provides the whole person with a sense of peace; the goal of the "ultimatropic" drive in the psychic core or spine of each being is to relate to wholeness, on one level or another. (As "phototropic" means moving toward light, "ultimatropic" means seeking the ultimate, realizing one's potential depending on one's nature and capacity for spiritual consciousness. Grace is the sacred attractor.) If this attempt to refurbish the term "grace" seems too vague, read further.

13. This is poetically as well as prosaically true—music's sound patterns in time can be represented visually by computer imaging, and Julia sets look like flowing symphonies of elaborated motifs depicting relations of parts to whole. Fractals, like great music, can wrap dramatic diversity in elegantly unified packages. See examples in Arthur C. Clarke, *Fractals: The Colors of Infinity* (Princeton, N.J.: Films for the Humanities and Sciences, 1994, videotape), or other colored animations of fractal processes. The following Web sites present useful information on and images of fractals: <http://classes.yale.edu/99-99-00/math190a/welcome

.html>, <http://www.home.inreach.com/kfar rell/fractals.html>, and <http://library.think quest.org/26242> (accessed October 14, 2002).

14. David Bohm uses the term "implicate" in this way—the implicate order of wholeness. See his *Wholeness and the Implicate Order* (Boston: Routledge and Kegan Paul, 1981).

15. F. David Peat, *The Philosopher's Stone: Chaos, Synchronicity, and the Hidden Order of the World* (New York: Bantam, 1991), 224.

16. By this I mean the structures of those relations and processes that are larger than us, which we participate in and find a larger reality in knowing. Another way of saying this is that it is natural for people to consider and practice ways to realize their deeper consciousness, and fractals may be helpful in doing so.

17. Benoit Mandelbrot states that fractals are not a panacea in *The Fractal Geometry of Nature* (New York: W. H. Freeman, 1982), 3, 418.

18. J. C. Smuts, *Holism and Evolution* (New York: Macmillan, 1926); Arthur Koestler, *Janus: A Summing Up* (New York: Random House, 1978); Lewis Thomas, *Lives of a Cell* (New York: Bantam, 1974); and Bateson, *Mind and Nature* come to mind.

19. James Gleick, *Chaos: Making a New Science* (New York: Penguin, 1988); Manfred Schroeder, *Fractals, Chaos, Power Laws: Minutes from an Infinite Paradise* (New York: W. H. Freeman, 1991); Heinz-Otto Peitgen and P. H. Richter, *The Beauty of Fractals: Images of Complex Dynamical Systems* (Berlin: Springer-Verlag, 1986); John Briggs, *Fractals, the Patterns of Chaos: A New Aesthetic of Art, Science, and Nature* (New York: Simon and Schuster, 1992); Peat, *The Philosopher's Stone;* and Michael McGuire, *An Eye for Fractals: A Graphic and Photographic Essay* (Redwood City, Calif.: Addison-Wesley, 1991).

20. For a discussion of Mandelbrot's re-luctance to narrow the definition of "fractal," see his *Multifractals and 1/f Noise: Wild Self-Affinity in Physics (1963–1976)* (New York: Springer-Verlag, 1999), 14–15. There Mandel-brot gives reasoned and well-documented arguments for leaving the definition more loosely open than strict and narrow. The na-ture of the principles involved can be better grasped and further discovered with a flexible approach that is open and responsive than with one that imposes a preconceived notion too rigidly. Mandelbrot wisely says that if fractal geometry proves useful enough to survive, the question of what it is will become superfluous.

21. McGuire, *An Eye for Fractals,* 21, 155.

22. Dietrich Stauffer, *From Newton to Mandelbrot: A Primer in Theoretical Physics* (New York: Springer-Verlag, 1990), 187.

23. Emerson writes of "dislocations, which apprize us that "this surface on which we now stand is not fixed but sliding." "Cir-cles," in *The Selected Writings of Ralph Waldo Emerson,* ed. Brooks Atkinson (New York: Modern Library, 1968), 268. A. E. Housman, "Reveille," in *The Collected Poems* (New York: Holt, Rinehart and Winston, 1965), 14.

24. Murray Gell-Mann, quoted in Horace Freeland Judson, *The Search for Solutions* (New York: Holt, Rinehart and Winston, 1980), 22.

25. "Cosmic" denotes something that re-lates to the context of the vast universe around us rather than to the earth alone. "Cosmos" means "order" as found in galaxies, planetary systems, and all the organic levels of existence.

26. The *Rig Veda* is available in, among other forms, *The Hymns of the Rigveda,* trans. Ralph T. H. Griffith (Delhi: Motilal Banarsi-dass, 1986). The text here is a paraphrase of Griffith's translation of mandala 2, hymn 28, verse 5 (page 149).

27. Knots, knitted string, and woven threads began to be used thirty to fifty thou-sand years ago. The physical evidence for this consists of impressions of woven cordage in the clay floors of huts from that time. Early humans probably used netting in capturing small game such as jackrabbits in game drives. Heather Pringle, "New Women of the Ice Age," *Discover,* April 1998, 62–69. There is also in-direct evidence from "Venus" figurines from around twenty-five thousand years ago; some seem to have woven hair nets.

28. For a recent example, see James Burke, *The Knowledge Web: From Electronic Agents to Stonehenge and Back—and Other Journeys through Knowledge* (New York: Simon and Schuster, 1999), *Connections* (Boston: Lit-tle, Brown, 1978), and *Pinball Effect* (Boston: Little, Brown, 1996). For an interesting explo-ration of ways that "life is a network" of intel-ligence on many levels, see Frank T. Vertosick, *The Genius Within: Discovering the Intelligence of Every Living Thing* (New York: Harcourt, 2002).

29. Lao-tzu, *Tao Te Ching: A New English Version,* trans. Stephen Mitchell (New York:

Harper and Row, 1988), chapter 73. This line long ago became a common proverb in China, and it is still current today.

30. *The Atharva Veda,* trans. Devi Chand (New Delhi: Munshiram Manoharlal, 1982), book 8, hymn 8, verses 7–8; and *Hymns of the Atharvaveda,* trans. R. T. H. Griffith (New Delhi: Munshiram Manoharlal, 1985). This verse sounds as if it was invoked to get power over opponents. In the *Atharvashastra* one of the seven means of approaching an enemy is the Indrajala, a tactical network of injury using conjuring, jugglery, magic, tricks, and illusion deployed in war to confuse the enemy. Which came first—the veil of *maya* (illusion) or the net of Indra? See Heinrich Zimmer, *Philosophies of India* (New York: Meridian, 1957), 123. Another use of the image of the cosmic net is found in the *Svetasvatara Upanishad:* "The non-dual Ensnarer [*jala* or net of *maya*] . . . rules . . . all the worlds." *The Upanishads,* trans. Swami Nikhilananda (New York: Harper and Row, 1964), 131.

31. *Rig Veda,* VI.47.18; see *Hymns of the Rigveda,* trans. Griffith, 313.

32. *Brihadaranyaka Upanishad,* chapter 3, 9, in *Upanisads,* trans. Patrick Olivelle (New York: Oxford University Press, 1996). Emily Dickinson's sense of the mind as of skylike and Godlike dimensions is seen in poem 126 of her *Collected Poems:*

> The brain is wider than the sky,
> for, put them side by side,
> the one the other will include with ease,
> and you beside.
> The brain is deeper than the sea,
> for, hold them, blue to blue,
> the one the other will absorb,
> as sponges, buckets do.
> The brain is just the weight of God,
> for, lift them, pound for pound,
> and they will differ, if they do,
> as syllable from sound!

The Collected Poems of Emily Dickinson, ed. Martha Dickinson Bianchi and Alfred Leete Hampson (New York: Barnes and Noble, 1997), 67.

33. Allen Ginsberg, *Collected Poems, 1947–1980* (New York: HarperCollins, 1988), 542.

34. Bill Porter, *Road to Heaven* (San Francisco: Mercury House, 1993), 156.

35. Quoted in David Loy, "Indra's Postmodern Net," *Philosophy East and West* 43, no. 3 (July 1993): 481. Net imagery in postmodern literature is touched upon by Italo Calvino, *Six Memos for the Next Millennium* (Cambridge, Mass.: Harvard University Press, 1988). The last chapter, on multiplicity, briefly follows the "infinite net" metaphor and sensibility in postmodern fiction. Calvino also discusses traditions (such as those of Ovid, Lucretius, Cabala, Raymond Lully, Galileo, etc.) involving the infinite system of relationships among existing things, and threads of interconnected systems (26).

36. David Mumford, Caroline Series, and David Wright, *Indra's Pearls: The Vision of Felix Klein* (Cambridge: Cambridge University Press, 2002).

37. Francis H. Cook, in *Hua-Yen Buddhism: The Jewel Net of Indra* (1977; reprint, Delhi: Sri Satguru, 1994), argues that the new element in Buddhist thought is the conception of "the universe as the infinitely repeated identity and interdependence of all phenomena" (35). The Chinese words *ch'ung ch'ung wu-chin* mean "infinitely repeated or reiterated." In this view, any object is simultaneously both primary (*chu*) and secondary (*pan*). The idea is that things are not merely visually alike—though that likeness may offer a clue—but their nature is intrinsically empty of lasting traits, all in all, all as all, all with all.

38. Bukkyo Dendo Kyokai, *The Teaching of Buddha* (Tokyo: Buddhist Promotion Foundation, 1966), 80.

39. Gary Snyder, *Earth House Hold* (San Francisco: City Lights, 1969), 92.

40. Riff or rant on limits which prohibit: Of course, if those entrenched in rigid ego get a small glimmer of this fully developed Buddhist vision, there is a chance they will feel envy, anger, resentment, or fear that this is a conspiracy to recruit members for a Buddhist cult, damage their own interests, and so forth. This is a vision which opens the wonder of worlds within worlds for those who marvel disinterestedly. To those with a vested interest in self-importance, self-aggrandizement, or empire-building it appears as a threat—an anti-Western Buddhist plot. The individualist venture of ego empire-building requires ignoring the depth dimension of nature's interconnectedness, the ramifications and implications of reality's undeniable unity. An Ayn Rand

would bristle at the net, because the individualist viewpoint emphasizes solitariness, not solidarity.

41. Albert Furtwangler, *Answering Chief Seattle* (Seattle: University of Washington Press, 1997), 16. The words in brackets are Furtwangler's; he discusses what is involved when white intermediaries make an English text for white readers from a Native American's speech. The speech is thought to have been given in 1854. Chief Seattle lived from 1786 to 1866.

42. Matthew 13:47. In the Old Testament, net imagery is used, for example, in Ezekiel: "My net shall I spread for him," Ezekiel 12:13 and 17:20.

43. James Baldwin, *Collected Essays* (New York: Library of America, 1998), 828–829. The strand of this vision of mutuality in American culture includes Emerson's philosophy of the Oversoul, Whitman's identification with a vast Self, the lines near the end of John Steinbeck's *Grapes of Wrath* (New York: Viking, 1967) where Tom Joad speaks about people not having separate souls but being part of a larger soul (434, 436), and the lines spoken by Eva Marie Saint in *On the Waterfront* about everybody being "a part of everybody else." These are only a few examples.

44. John Muir, *Nature Writings* (New York: Library of America, 1997).

45. Riff by Thomas Mann: "The world hath many centres, one for each created being, and about each one it lieth in its own circle. Thou standest but an ell from me, yet about thee lieth a universe whose centre I am not but thou art. . . . And I, on the other hand, stand in the centre of mine. For our universes are not far from each other so that they do not touch; rather hath God pushed them and interwoven deep into each other, so that you . . . do indeed journey quite independently and according to your own ends, whither you will, but besides that you are the means and end too, in our interwovenness, that I arrive at my goal." Thomas Mann, *Joseph in Egypt*, trans. H. T. Lowe-Porter (New York: A. A. Knopf, 1938), vol. 1, 4.

46. Bonaventure, in the prologue to his *Breviloquium*, wrote, "as no one can appreciate the beauty of a poem unless his vision embraces it as a whole, so no one can see the beauty of the orderly governance of creation unless he has an integral view of it." R. J.

Schoeck, *Intertextuality and Renaissance Texts* (Bamberg: H. Kaiser-Verlag, 1984), 83.

47. Loy, "Indra's Postmodern Net," 482. D. T. Suzuki also analyzed the symbolism of Maitreya's tower in the *Gandhavyuha Sutra* (*Essays in Zen Buddhism: First Series* [London: Luzac, 1949]). For further discussion of Indra's net see Douglas R. Hofstadter, *Gödel, Escher, Bach: An Eternal Golden Braid* (New York: Basic, 1979), 258.

48. Augustine used the image of statues holding up a temple, each able to see one aspect only, in his treatise *The City of God*.

49. *A Zen Harvest: Japanese Folk Zen Sayings,* compiled and translated by Soiku Shigematsu (San Francisco: North Point, 1988), 78.

50. Ibid., 34.

51. D. T. Suzuki, *Sengai: The Zen of Ink and Paper* (Boston: Shambhala, 1999), 49.

52. *A Zen Forest: Sayings of the Masters,* trans. Soiku Shigematsu (New York: Weatherhill, 1981), 122, #1230.

53. Ibid., 37, #37.

54. Ibid., 75, #570.

55. Phillip Kapleau, *Three Pillars of Zen* (New York: Bantam Doubleday Dell, 1965).

56. *The Concise Yoga Vasistha,* ed. and trans. Swami Venkatesananda (Albany: State University of New York Press, 1984). See also *Yogavasishtha,* trans. Hari Prasad Shastri (London: Favil, 1937).

57. Brian Swimme, *The Universe Is a Green Dragon: A Cosmic Creation Story* (Santa Fe, N.M.: Bear, 1984), 32.

58. Aristotle, *Physics,* ed. and trans. Hippocrates G. Apostle (Grinnell, Iowa: Peripatetic, 1980).

59. Origen, *An Exhortation to Martyrdom, Prayer, First Principles: book IV, Prologue to the Commentary on the Song of Songs, Homily XXVII on Numbers,* trans. Rowan A. Greer (New York: Paulist, 1979), 198–200. Origen wrote of man as a little world, as did the German Romantic philosopher-poet Novalis (1772–1801) and others.

60. Daniel Kealey, *Revisioning Environmental Ethics* (Albany: State University of New York Press, 1990), 70.

61. "The Ascetic and Theological Teaching of Gregory Palamas," trans. B. Krivosheine, *The Eastern Churches Quarterly,* no. 4 (1938): 3. Reprint.

62. Cf. Henry David Thoreau, *In the Maine Woods,* ed. Joseph J. Moldenhauer

(Princeton, N.J.: Princeton University Press, 1972).

63. Blaise Pascal, *Pensées: Thoughts on Religion and Other Subjects,* trans. W. F. Trotter (New York: Washington Square, 1965), #72, 19–25.

64. Ibid., #267, 83.

65. See Brian Greene, *The Elegant Universe: Superstrings, Hidden Dimensions, and the Quest for the Ultimate Theory* (New York: W. W. Norton, 1999), for more on superstring theory. This theory is currently being debated and refined. It posits that the universe is made of little loops of vibrating strings, or as Greene puts it, "dancing filaments of energy."

66. Interestingly, just as DNA molecules are made of strand-shaped twists, which are in turn made of smaller twisting strands, etc., polymers are chemical compounds consisting of repeated structural units. Polymers are made up of a structural shape like "a string of pearls," yet inside each pearl is a polymer structure much like the overall shape—a fractal. T. Gregory Dewey, *Fractals in Molecular Biophysics* (Oxford: Oxford University Press, 1997), 25.

67. Jeffrey Burton Russell, *A History of Heaven: The Singing Silence* (Princeton, N.J.: Princeton University Press, 1997), 17.

68. Various thinkers have written about the importance of valuing ideas such as heaven among children. See Robert Coles, *The Moral Intelligence of Children* (New York: Random House, 1997). High hopes, meanings, orientations are tied in with such metaphysical imagination.

69. Thomas Patrick Hughes, *A Dictionary of Islam* (Clifton, N.J.: Reference Desk, 1965), 256. The entry on the Kaaba is also available at <http://www.bible.ca/islam/library/islam-quotes-hughes.htm>. See also <http://almadinah.org/Fazailaamaal/fazailehajj3.htm> and <http://answering-islam.org/Responses/Saifullah/aqsa.htm> (accessed January 6, 2003).

70. Martin Buber, *The Legend of the Baal-Shem* (New York: Schocken, 1969), 19.

71. Maltbie Babcock, *Presbyterian School Hymnal* (Richmond: Presbyterian, 1929).

72. Luca Signorelli (c. 1450–1553) painted a masterpiece in the hilltop cathedral in Orvieto, Italy, which rivals Dante's depiction of the afterlife. One writer said that at the world's end the church in which it is painted will be transported directly to heaven, and be right at home there.

73. Dante Alighieri, *Inferno,* in *the Divine Comedy,* trans. John Ciardi (New York: W.W. Norton, 1977), translator's note to XXXIV:143.

74. Dante Alighieri, *Inferno,* XXXIV, in *The Divine Comedy: A New Prose Translation,* ed. and trans. H. R. Huse (New York: Holt, Rinehart and Winston, 1966), 166.

75. Dante Alighieri, *Purgatorio,* XXXIII, in ibid., 326.

76. Dante Alighieri, *Paradiso,* XXXIII, in ibid., 481.

77. "The movement of the imaginal ego should be conceived less as a development than as a circular pattern. . . . the psyche insists on repetition. . . . Work, ritual, remembrance and style return to the same ground again and again. . . . The purgatory of faithful repetition of the same mistakes is also their redemption into individual style." James Hillman, *The Myth of Analysis: Three Essays in Archetypal Psychology* (Evanston, Ill.: Northwestern University Press, 1997), 184–186. Plato (d. 347 B.C.E.) wrote of the round shape of the universe, copied in the spherical shape of the head, which contains soul circles; and also the circles in the dynamism of the world soul (the soul extends throughout the body of the world, from center to circumference, communicating its motions through the whole). Francis M. Corford, *Plato's Cosmology: The Timaeus of Plato* (New York: Harcourt Brace, 1937), 150, 72–93. Plotinus (d. 270 C.E.) also mentioned the soul's circular motion long before Dante wrote.

78. Dante Alighieri, *The Inferno,* trans. John Ciardi, XXVIII:143.

79. Dante Alighieri, *Purgatorio,* trans. John Ciardi, (New York: New American Library, 1962), xxiii. There are many precedents for ideas of the soul's circularity. Plato said the soul is a circle, though Aristotle taught that this view of Plato's should not be taken too literally; Rumi wrote of the soul's circular path around God; and so forth.

80. Dante Alighieri, *Paradiso,* in *The Divine Comedy,* trans. Lawrence Grant White (New York: Pantheon, 1948), VIII:16–21.

81. Dante Alighieri, *Paradiso,* in ibid., XXVII:106–111.

82. For a smart reflective riff exploring roundness, see Natalie Angier, *Woman: An Intimate Geography* (Boston: Houghton Mifflin,

1999). She begins, "Plato called the psyche a sphere. Jung said that the circle symbolizes the self. The circular mandala signified the unity of the conscious and unconscious minds . . ." (139–140) and goes on to consider rose windows, domes, wedding rings, the faces, eyes, and breasts that babies first see, and fruits and nuts, the sun and moon and other roundnesses which mean much to humans. Jung writes of Paracelsus, "The animate world is the larger circle, man is . . . the smaller circle . . . the microcosm. Consequently, everything without is within, everything above is below. Between all things in the larger and smaller circles reigns 'correspondence' . . . a notion that culminates in Swedenborg's *homo maximus* as a gigantic anthropomorphization of the universe." C. G. Jung, *The Spirit in Man, Art, and Literature*, trans. R. F. C. Hull, vol. 15 of *The Collected Works of C. G. Jung*, ed. Herbert Read, Michael Fordham, and Gerhard Adler (New York: Pantheon, 1971), 9. Ralph Waldo Emerson introduces his essay "Nature" with a verse including the couplet "A subtle chain of countless rings / The next unto the farthest brings." *The Selected Writings of Ralph Waldo Emerson*, ed. Atkinson, 2.

83. I am told that Swami Veda of the Shri Vidya tradition (in the lineage of the great Indian sages Shankara [eighth century?] and Vidyaranya [fourteenth century]) considers Dante's *Paradiso* to be *Vidya*, an expression of highest spiritual wisdom, and that he notes a counterpart to Beatrice in the goddess Tripurasundari, whose name means "beauty of the three worlds." For a comparative study of *The Divine Comedy* and *Savitri*, the epic poem by Sri Aurobindo, see Prema Nandakumar, *Dante and Sri Aurobindo* (Madras: Affiliated East-West, 1981).

84. Dolores Dyer Lucas, *Emily Dickinson and Riddle* (DeKalb: Northern Illinois University Press, 1969), #280, 128.

85. Blake's verse at the beginning of "Auguries of Innocence" presents a vision of interconnective levels in a series of infinitives: "To see a World in a Grain of Sand / And a Heaven in a Wild Flower, / Hold Infinity in the palm of your hand / And Eternity in an hour." The rest of the poem (128 lines) declares implications of these interconnected infinities; the vast is in the small, all is together, so the treatment of one part by another—for instance, men's treatment of creatures—if cruel or violent, will have repercussions. To kill a butterfly or moth or fly incurs a debt. Human flaws transform into externals—envy becomes snake venom, miserly greed creates the luxuries of royalty and the sufferings of poverty. The small earthly disturbance of beggar rags fluttering tears heaven's sky to rags. Blake says what is to blame for the way adult life is in disarray. He tells us to see for ourselves, to guard against a loss of kindness and compassion, to resist corruption, insensitivity, and too much abstraction. *The Portable Blake*, ed. Alfred Kazin (New York: Viking, 1962), 150–154.

86. Jorge Luis Borges, *Labyrinths* (New York: New Directions, 1964), 171–172. In my view the structure of human consciousness is religious, and the structure of the universe inspires religious awe (e.g., wonder at stars in the night sky) and raises philosophical questions about the meaning of one's life cycle and matters that seem beyond one. Such circumstances generate behavior, in the form of religious orientation, even if one thinks one has left religion behind. For example, one centers one's life on something transcendent: the power of reason, the importance of human life, or another point held sacred. Even in secular lives there are structures of consciousness and behavior similar to those in more traditional religious lives. Secular rituals, beliefs, and hopes function much like the religious ones they are unconsciously similar to, in the net which none elude. John Donne wrote of Kepler's scientific discoveries, celebrating man's power, "Man hath weaved out a net and this net is throwne / Upon the Heavens, and now they are his owne." "An Anatomy of the World—The First Anniversary," in John Donne, *Selected Poetry*, ed. John Carey (New York: Oxford University Press, 1996), 165. This seems rather arrogant today, as if the Strategic Air Command can really control the heavens, or as if the Internet or "anthro-net" of electronic media can be the ultimate "nestwork" (the world, creation, is our home, our nest)—as if it can be a human home for life, holding all reality. Today the human-fabricated vastness of cyberspace and electronic media, "the noise machine," if that is all there is to the noosphere, might seem like a sinister noose controlled by evil forces. One in a paranoid mood senses only crude fascist fractals of manipulation (whole environments of harshly controlled groups and members) and conspiratorial horror, the future

seems nightmarish, as films such as *The Matrix* illustrate. The view of a vast cosmic consciousness beyond human control, of which all intelligence is a reflection or distortion, with *maya* as the illusory veil of mind-projected desires and fears, is very different. There are some humans who desire to control; there is an imprisoned splendor; to confuse the levels too simplistically makes a hopeless tangle of *maya*.

87. On a more mundane yet self-similar note, a broken man on skid row may characterize his life as "a failure within a failure within a failure," as Ted Edwards did in David Irsay and Harvey Wang's *Flophouse: Life on the Bowery* (New York: Random House, 2000).

88. Margaret Trawick, *Notes on Love in A Tamil Family* (Berkeley and Los Angeles: University of California Press, 1990), 11.

89. Gregory Bateson, *Steps to an Ecology of Mind* (1972; reprint, New York: Ballantine Books, 1990). In the exquisite "nestwork" (if I may be forgiven for coining a word which describes the world, creation, as our home, our nest) of existence, organism and environment form a network of mutual survival in which the organism incorporates and reflects the environment—interacting with the seams or features of the environment shapes creatures' sinews; thus the environment is a fabric of given strands interlaced. As Brian Swimme and Thomas Berry explain, a community takes a new species into itself in a process of mutual interaction. The species newly migrated first takes the community of life in its new location into itself. In many ways it does this, in ways which are reflected in its phenotype, and also in its gene pool. Swimme and Berry observe that this intimate internal relatedness explains why most species will die out if merely plucked from their environment and plopped down in some other biome. The extracted and inserted creatures are not able to recognize anyone, to relate to familiar supports of life. The ancient relationships that the ages of adaptation have worked into their exteriors and into their brains are no longer able to activate them; because of this they die. Swimme and Berry marvel at how the amazing complexity of a whole mountain community of life gradually is brought into the very heart of a newly arriving woodpecker's reality. Because of this process the bird's former identity dissolves, and instead what is alive there is the whole mountain-ecosystem-as-woodpecker. Swimme and Berry

assert that this dynamic of interrelatedness involving adaptation and natural selection is an inevitable pressure, at all times and places, making for a deeply interwoven intimacy. This interactive dynamic in living creatures and their communities is deep, entering into the shaping of the very structure of the organism's genes, its body, and its mind. They submit that this dynamic mocks the foolish modern view in which a community is made up of discrete individuals; they argue that to be alive inevitably involves finding one's identity entwined in the living together of the whole community. Brian Swimme and Thomas Berry, *The Universe Story* (San Francisco: Harper SanFrancisco, 1992), 134. In the electronic techno-info age there are new visions of nets: "We straddle two competing life-forms: the data-net and the flesh-net. Which is real? The data-net as an auto-defense for the human species, an electronic shield that we have constructed to absorb the shock-waves of technological change for a human species that has gone into a shell turtle-like? Or the flesh-net as an artificial construct designed by the electronic kingdom to experience feelings for the baby body of the information net, while it comes to maturity? The data-net as an externalization of the human nervous system (McLuhan)? Or the flesh-net as a simulacrum of information?" Arthur Kroker and Michael A. Weinstein, *Data Trash: The Theory of the Virtual Class* (New York: St. Martin's Press, 1994), 104.

90. Margaret Mead, *And Keep Your Powder Dry: An Anthropologist Looks at America* (New York: William Morrow, 1942), 21.

91. Trawick, *Notes on Love in a Tamil Family*, 11.

92. Douglas Hofstadter writes,

the elusive sense for patterns which we humans inherit from our genes involves all the mechanisms of representation of knowledge, including nested contexts, conceptual skeletons and conceptual mapping, slippability, descriptions and meta-descriptions and their interactions, fission and fusion of symbols, multiple representations (along different dimensions and different levels of abstraction), default expectations, and more. . . . the explanations of "emergent" phenomena in our brains—for instance, ideas, hopes, analogies, and finally consciousness and free will—are based on a kind of Strange Loop, an interaction between levels in which the top level reaches back down towards the bottom level and influences it, while at the same time being itself determined by the bottom level. There is a self-re-inforcing "resonance" between the different levels. Memory, resonance, repetition, tradition. (Douglas R. Hofstadter, *Metamagical Themas: Questing for the Essence of Mind and Pattern* [New York: Bantam, 1986], 674)

93. Trawick, *Notes on Love in A Tamil Family*, 185. *Kolam* or *rangoli* patterns are auspicious ornaments yet express traditional wisdom. Created with an awareness of the hurry and confusion of the day, the marketplace noise and the flux and dust of *samsara's* distractions, the *kolam* posits a hope, a choice, a signifying for order. See Vijaya Nagarajan, "Hosting the Divine: The Kolam as Ritual, Art, and Ecology in Tamil Nadu, India" (Ph.D. diss., University of California, Berkeley, 1998). Some *kolams* exhibit fractal qualities because the rules used to draw them are applied at a number of different scales. See P. Prusinkiewicz and J. Harlan, *Lindenmayer Systems, Fractals and Plants* (New York: Springer-Verlag, 1989).

94. Peat, *The Philosopher's Stone,* 171.

95. Herbert Guenther, *Ecstatic Spontaneity: Saraha's Three Cycles of Doha* (Berkeley: Asian Humanities, 1993), 18–45. He notes that "meanings are grasped by aisthesis, the capacity for perceiving wholes and wholeness . . . a capacity rooted in our spiritual nature" (19). As another writer puts it,

> The existence of wholes, in which parts take appointed places in mutual harmony consonant with the total pattern and task, is an established fact of nature, not a privileged property and invention of the human mind. . . . If nature were atomized and inherently chaotic, only creative mind could see and carve into it and from it those patterns of higher order to which we concede consistency and beauty. But nature is not atomized. Its patterning is inherent and primary, and the order underlying beauty is demonstrably there; what is more, human mind can perceive it only

> because it is itself part and parcel of that order. (Paul A. Weiss, *Within the Gates of Science and Beyond: Science in Its Cultural Commitments* [New York: Hafner, 1971], 199–200.)

96. It is redundant to say that the *universe* is one, that the cosmos is an order of orders. Yet it is necessary to remind ourselves of this when prevailing fashions emphasize only a newly discovered relativism of differences. When rushing from a recently held presumption of universals in one's own parochial image, it does not help to rush into the arms of an equally unbalanced parochial view that there can be no unity or order in the universe. The implications of the simplest universal possible (e.g., Being) would keep one busy, if one followed them up instead of denying them. Asserting that there can be no unity, order, non-imposed universals is being overconfident of one's own grasp of reality while on the rebound. Historians tell us that the belief in the absoluteness of scientific truth espoused by thinkers of the Enlightenment is the offspring of the older Christian belief in exclusive claim to total truth. Such brittle views have an all-or-nothing quality. If a different view appears, it causes true believers to doubt their own system: "If only one way can be right, it must be the Christian way. If faith is lost in that, all religions must be false." So goes the train of thought. But the coherence of the cosmos does not go away just because the disenchanted ignore it. Signs of the self-harmonious unity of the whole are visible all over—approximate parallels, resemblances, reminiscent echoes, haunting and elusive likenesses, the ways of water and flame and leaf, galaxy and flower and seed, fir and snowflake and arrowhead, eyes and petals and lips. There is a kind of loose consistency, a constancy among levels, dimensions, aspects of the whole; there are undeniable kinships in nature. To understand nature is to harmonize. To simply comply with the rhythms of nature—to ply with the Tao or the Spirit behind the universe, to agree with the overall system's consistency—this sanity brings out similarity, symmetry, connective patterning of metaphors. The Shakers sang,

> 'Tis a gift to be simple,'tis a gift to be free,
> 'tis a gift to come down where we ought
>   to be,

and when we find ourselves in the place just right,
it will be in the valley of love and delight.

When true simplicity is gained,
to bow and to bend we shan't be ashamed;
to turn, to turn will be our delight
till by turning, turning we come round right.

It is a matter not of superficial over-simplification but of experiencing the deep simplicity, the sweet correspondence of order, as one does when sleeping deeply or discovering an answer to a problem. As the wandering Baul singers of Bengal put it, "The simple has its thirty million strings whose mingled symphony ever sounds. . . . Take all the creatures of the world into yourself. Drown yourself in that eternal music," almost evoking a fractal sensibility of multitudes held together in wholeness.

97. This 1966 statement by Richard Feynman is quoted by John L. Hitchcock in *Atoms, Snowflakes, and God: The Convergence of Science and Religion* (Wheaton, Ill.: Theosophical Publishing House, 1986), 40.

98. See Bohm, *Wholeness and the Implicate Order.*

99. *The Art and Thought of Heraclitus: An Edition of the Fragments with Translation and Commentary,* trans. Charles H. Kahn (Cambridge: Cambridge University Press, 1979), fragment 54, p. 55.

100. Mary Catherine Bateson, *With a Daughter's Eye* (New York: Morrow, 1984), 185.

101. Gregory Bateson and Mary Catherine Bateson, *Angels Fear: Towards an Epistemology of the Sacred* (New York, Macmillan, 1987), 30.

102. Poet Rabindranath Tagore used this phrase in "Religion of the Artist," in *A Tagore Reader,* ed. Amiya Chakravarty (Boston: Beacon, 1966), 238.

103. Johann Wolfgang von Goethe, "Spirit Song over the Waters," in *Selected Poems,* ed. Christopher Middleton (Boston: Suhrkamp/Insel, 1983), 71.

104. Quoted by Gary Snyder in "Blue Mountains Constantly Walking" from *The Practice of the Wild* (San Francisco: North Point, 1990), 107–109, 114.

105. Riff by Rumi:

Every form you see has its archetype in the placeless world; If the form perished, no matter, since its original is everlasting. Every fair shape you have seen, every deep saying you have heard, Be not cast down that it perished; for that is not so. Whereas the spring-head is undying, its branch gives water continually; Since neither can cease, why are you lamenting? Conceive the Soul as a fountain, and these created things as rivers: While the fountain flows, the rivers run from it. Put grief out of your head and keep quaffing this river-water; Do not think of the water failing; for this water is without end. from the moment you came into the world of being, a ladder was placed before you that you might escape. First you were mineral, later you turned to plant, Then you became animal: how should this be a secret to you? Afterwards you were made man, with knowledge, reason, faith; Behold the body, which is a portion of the dust-pit, how perfect it has grown! When you have travelled on from man, you will doubtless become an angel; After that you are done with earth: your station is in heaven. Pass again even from angelhood: enter that ocean, That your drop may become a sea which is a hundred seas of Oman. Leave this 'Son,' say ever 'One' with all your soul; If your body has aged, what matter, when the soul is young? (Rumi, *Divani Shamsi Tabriz,* trans. Reynold A. Nicholson [San Francisco: Rainbow Bridge, 1973], 40–41.)

106. Thomas Cleary, trans., *The Essential Tao: An Initiation into the Heart of Taoism through the Authentic* Tao Te Ching *and the Inner Teachings of Chuang-Tzu* (San Francisco: HarperSanFrancisco, 1992), 63.

107. Chuang-tzu, *Chuang Tzu: Genius of the Absurd,* arranged from the work of James Legge by Clae Waltham (New York: Ace, 1971), 198.

108. Ibid., 194.

109. Lao-tzu, *The Wisdom of Laotse,* ed. and trans. and with an introduction and notes by Lin Yutang (New York: Modern Library, 1948), 50–51, 170–171.

110. Kuang-Ming Wu, *The Butterfly as Companion: Meditation on the First Three Chap-*

ters of the Chuang Tzu (Albany: State University of New York Press, 1990), 379.

111. Ibid., 234.

112. Swimme and Berry, The Universe Story, 71.

113. For an in-depth study of experiences of "the zone," "flow," "harmony," "the Zen moment," creative processes of full concentration immersed in the energy of consciousness, see the work of psychologist Mihaly Csikszentmihalyi, such as Flow: The Psychology of Optimal Experience (Chicago: University of Chicago Press, 1991), and Creativity: Flow and the Psychology of Discovery and Invention (New York: Harper, 1997).

114. Peat, The Philosopher's Stone, 204.

115. I'm being facetious in using this term, but there is some truth in it. Again, my apologies to those with a phobia of new words.

116. Some people will ask for evidence of infancy's natural freshness, as if the babies they have seen have been hardened, stale, rigid, bored, and jaded. They will pretend they have no prior evidence of infants' suppleness, sensitivity to sensory input, or curiosity and ability to learn through play. Nevertheless, the neural networks of the brain activated before age two (even those networks later used to deny this) constitute a vast ability to develop; if this is not brought into play, potentials harden and shrink. Seeing everything for the first time, infants know a more undifferentiated wholeness of "oceanic consciousness," as Freud called this state, which shares qualities with mystical experience. See William B. Parsons, The Enigma of the Oceanic Feeling: Revisioning the Psychoanalytic Theory of Mysticism (New York: Oxford University Press, 1999); Anthony Starr, Freud: A Very Short Introduction (New York: Oxford University Press, 2001), 113–114.

117. On interest in fractals see Michael Frame and Benoit Mandelbrot, Fractals, Graphics, and Mathematics Education (Washington, D.C.: Mathematical Association of America, 2002). Water, which I used as a metaphor just now, has long been used in China as a symbolic medium for meditating on Tao and the realization of natural wisdom. The Taoist philosophy expressed in the Tao Te Ching is a worldview with the mission of pointing out natural patterns, rhythms of nature, wisdom related to the systemic nature of what is already here. Water is used as a primary system, a universal element to illustrate many ideas. It is a symbol complex so simple that it's all one fluid thing, but able to inform, symbolize, and serve as a comparative system for other processes of nature, including human life. Water seeks its own level; lowly and humble. it serves as it goes, as humans could; it returns again and again. It is patient; it wears away the hard rocks. On the surface it is reflective, showing the ripple effect of any impact; dropping through space it cascades, and it runs underground secretly. The Grand Canyon began as a rivulet; water has a memory, and returns where it went before. It seeks a path of least resistance. "Still waters run deep" as equanimity. Water germinates seeds, revives living things ("Just add water"). Water takes different forms depending on conditions—it can be ice, mist, steam. If roiled up then left alone, water clarifies itself, like consciousness. It is self-purifying—brooks and creeks, rivers and lakes. Water does not contend. Tao-like, water is the mediator of the cosmos's desire to care for the earth's many needs.

118. James McGrath wrote this verse for the PBS program on Indian artist Helen Hardin, and it is found in Jay Scott, Changing Woman: The Life and Art of Helen Hardin (Flagstaff, Ariz.: Northland, 1993), 152.

119. Loren Eiseley, The Unexpected Universe (San Diego: Harcourt Brace Jovanovich, 1985), 146.

120. We go way back—not a few decades, but to the fireball at the origin of the cosmos. We exist with all else as a net of allurements, as cosmologist Brian Swimme calls them, strands drawn to each other, psyche-physiques bonded with ancient embraces of love. The stars emerge from their response to allurement and in turn stimulate others in the web of being to pulse, evoking others' existence in a net of affinities, self-organizing along lines of most allurement and least resistance. The sun, Our Star, Surya of the Hindus, Ra of the Egyptians, Grandfather of the Native Americans, made of the fireball's creations, burns with a creative flair of its own, like all stars. Like all stars, Our Star is burning itself out through continual self-sacrifice, consuming many tons of hydrogen each second, rays flowing into other orders, bestowing energies and elements on the networks of existence. To traditional people the burning of the sun often means something, such as a continual process of self-sacrifice, or

the journey of time and change. To secular moderns it is a matter of gravity and nuclear forces, and worries about wearing enough sunscreen. To poets the properties of organic life bespeak Mind, tugging the net of interrelated inherent order patterns. In us, as Brian Swimme writes, "this supreme dynamic of love, of allurement and evocation, in action since the beginning of the universe, after billions of years becomes aware of itself." Swimme, *Green Dragon*, 61. The net of love, knotted by affinities, relations, correspondences, renews itself and grows in depth and self-awareness through human awareness and love. We don't even know what powers are within us until allurements call on us and we respond, turned on. For the cosmological points in this paragraph and elsewhere, I am indebted to Brian Swimme and Thomas Berry for their treatment of the nature of the universe.

121. David Steenberg, "Chaos at the Marriage of Heaven and Hell," *Harvard Theological Review* 84, no. 4 (Oct. 1991): 447–466. See also a response in *Harvard Theological Review* 86, no. 4 (Oct. 1993): 455–469, and Steenberg's reply in the same issue, 471–476. See also C. Dyke, "Strange Attraction, Curious Liaison: Clio Meets Chaos," *The Philosophical Forum* 21, no. 4 (summer 1990): 369–392; and Sofia Diaz, "Bharata Natyam: A Hindu Fractal," *Anthropology of Consciousness* 1, nos. 3–4 (Oct.–Dec. 1990): 19–23. This paper uses the frame of fractals to explore some representative aspects of Indian classical dance as indicative of the whole culture, though fractals are only referred to at the beginning and end. Charles D. Minahen, *Vortex/t: The Poetics of Turbulence* (University Park: Pennsylvania State University Press, 1992) explores symbolic turbulence, in the shape of a chaotic whirl, in ancient works such as the Bible and the Odyssey, the writings of Plato and Lucretius, and those of Dante, Descartes, and Blake, Poe and Mallarme. For chaos in ancient Greek stories see Joseph Eddy Fontenrose, *Python: A Study of Delphic Myth and Its Origins* (Berkeley and Los Angeles: University of California Press, 1959).

122. See Fritjof Capra and David Steindl-Rast, with Thomas Matus, *Belonging to the Universe: Explorations on the Frontiers of Science and Spirituality* (San Francisco: HarperSanFrancisco, 1991). Pages xi–xv summarize major shifts in scientific thinking and parallel shifts in new theological thinking, including the shift to network imagery and an embracing of mystery. Brian Swimme speaks eloquently of belonging in the third lecture of his *Canticle to the Cosmos* series (6 audiocassettes, Sounds True Audio, 1995). The gist is something like this: Our world is an interpenetrating symphony of consciousnesses, in which each one flows into the others, and only in this flow of consciousness can the fullness of consciousness be approached. Reality can only show itself in the community of consciousness shared by conscious beings. Why did the fireball develop into this? Because an infinite number of centers of consciousness were required to show the fullness which was there, and joy comes about when they reflect in one another. Thus we enter a cascading symphony of interrelating sounds, we dive into experience, and "reality" (as a multivalent mysterious treasure) surfaces out of (or within) that relationship. We activate parts of reality through our encounters.

123. Claude Lévi-Strauss, *The Raw and the Cooked* (New York: Penguin, 1992), 15.

124. Johannes Kepler, *The Harmony of the World*, trans. with an introduction and notes by E. J. Aiton, A. M. Duncan, and J. V. Field (Philadelphia: American Philosophical Society, 1997).

125. Brian A. Lynn, "The Fractal Geometry of Music," *Concerto* (Cambridge, Mass.) 1, no. 1 (summer 1983), 8.

126. James Hillman, *A Blue Fire: Selected Writings*, introd. and ed. by Thomas Moore in collaboration with James Hillman (New York: HarperCollins, 1991), 162.

127. "Rent" of course means "rended" or "ripped, torn." William Butler Yeats, "Crazy Jane: Talks with the Bishop," in Donald Hall, *To Read a Poem* (New York: Harcourt Brace, 1992), 367.

128. This point is suggested by Mandelbrot in his introduction to photographer Michael McGuire's book, *An Eye for Fractals.*

129. Pablo Neruda, *Canto General*, trans. Jack Schmitt (Berkeley and Los Angeles: University of California Press, 1991), 361.

STRAND TWO

1. Blaise Pascal, *Pensées: Thoughts on Religion and Other Subjects,* trans. W. F. Trotter (New York: Washington Square, 1965), 11,

#29. The idea that nature speaks in a language of meaning is found also among Islamic mystics and European philosophers. Henri Bortoft discusses the point in *The Wholeness of Nature: Goethe's Way toward a Science of Conscious Participation in Nature* (Hudson, N.Y.: Lindisfarne, 1996).

2. See Michael McGuire, *An Eye for Fractals: A Graphic and Photographic Essay* (Redwood City, Calif.: Addison-Wesley, 1991).

3. Forgive me for making verbs of the names of people who express patterns of infinity exquisitely and unforgettably.

4. The Zen master Dogen wrote these words in "Keisei Sanshoku" (Sound of the valley, form of the mountain), a chapter of his *Shobogenzo;* they are quoted in Joan Halifax in *The Fruitful Darkness* (San Francisco: Harper, 1993), 56–57.

5. Ibid.

6. D'Arcy Wentworth Thompson, quoted in Gary Snyder, "Poetry and the Primitive: Notes on Poetry as an Ecological Survival Technique," in *Symposium of the Whole: A Range of Discourse toward an Ethnopoetics,* ed. Jerome Rothenberg and Diane Rothenberg (Berkeley and Los Angeles: University of California Press, 1983), 98.

7. Dennis L. Sepper, "Goethe against Newton . . ." in *Goethe and the Sciences,* ed. Frederick Amrine, Frank J. Zucker, and Harvey Wheeler (Boston: D. Reidel, 1987), 187. Also in Dennis L. Sepper, *Goethe contra Newton* (Cambridge: Cambridge University Press, 1988).

8. James Gleick, *Chaos: Making a New Science* (New York: Penguin, 1988), 240.

9. Thomas Traherne, *Centuries, Poems, and Thanksgivings,* ed. H. M. Margoliouth (Oxford: Clarendon Press, 1958), vol. 1, 15–16, #31.

10. See Ernest McClain, *The Myth of Invariance* (New York: Nicolas Hays, 1976).

11. Quoted in Deepak Chopra, *Creating Health* (Boston: Houghton Mifflin, 1987), 210.

12. William Blake, *The Portable Blake,* ed. Alfred Kazin (New York: Viking, 1962), 549–550.

13. Manfred Schroeder, *Fractals, Chaos, Power Laws: Minutes from an Infinite Paradise* (New York: W. H. Freeman, 1991). In my life, an interest in fractals beginning around 1993 marked a reawakening of interest in observing nature and respecting the power of that which

is lifelike, such as realism in art, acting, and writing—that which is concerned with copying real-life configurations, gestures, talk, etc. In this case it is a seeking of truth in living organisms and processes of nature, learning from the way things happen, basing art on that. Fractals can kindle a focus on the patterns in trees, leaves, and seeds, mountains, winds, and waters—direct observation of them, noticing and noting specific features. I admire Thoreau for his accurate observations in such works as *Faith in a Seed: The Dispersion of Seeds and Other Late Natural History Writings,* ed. Bradley P. Dean (Washington, D.C.: Island Press for Shearwater Books, 1993). Aristotle also was a keen observer of nature.

14. Schroeder, *Fractals, Chaos, Power Laws,* xiii.

15. "Depth" here refers to the concept through which Gregory Bateson inquired into the meaning and interconnectedness of levels.

16. Schroeder, *Fractals, Chaos, Power Laws,* 70.

17. John Briggs, *Fractals, The Patterns of Chaos: A New Aesthetic of Art, Science, and Nature* (New York: Simon and Schuster, 1992), 71.

18. Paul Valéry, "Man and the Sea Shell," in *Aesthetics,* trans. Ralph Manheim (New York: Pantheon, 1964), 3–30.

19. John Allen Paulos, *Beyond Numeracy: Ruminations of a Numbers Man* (New York: Vintage, 1992), 92.

20. N. Katherine Hayles discusses this in her article "Chaos as Orderly Disorder: Shifting Ground in Contemporary Literature and Science," *New Literary History* 20, no. 2 (winter 1989): 305–322. "The movement from scale-invariant models to scale-dependent paradigms has an obvious correspondence to the movement in critical theory away from totalizing theories. . . . Lyotard argues that 'paralogy' (an umbrella term under which he groups such diverse theories as fractal geometry, quantum mechanics, and Gödel's Theorem) provides corroborating evidence from within the physical sciences that will let us 'wage a war on totality' [actually on totalizing theories]." Presumably this is because fractals are decentralizing, distributing the whole to all the parts. Hayles urges caution in interpreting the shift, suggesting that scientific theories are not social programs and stating that Lyotard's "apparent conviction that fractal geometry can

combat totalitarianism is a modern version of social Darwinism" (310–311). Time will tell whose grasp of the implications of fractal geometry is more accurate.

21. Briggs, *Fractals*, 30.

22. Benoit B. Mandelbrot, *The Fractal Geometry of Nature* (New York: W. H. Freeman, 1982), 150.

23. Walter Ong's *Ramus, Method, and the Decay of Dialogue* (Cambridge, Mass.: Harvard University Press, 1983) discusses Western civilization's habit, going back to Greek philosophy, of privileging vision in understanding.

24. J. Richard Eiser, *Attitudes, Chaos, and the Connectionist Mind* (Oxford: Blackwell, 1994), 179–180, 182.

25. McGuire, *An Eye for Fractals*, 124.

26. Briggs, *Fractals*, 25.

27. Stuart A. Kauffman, *The Origins of Order: Self-Organization and Selection in Evolution* (New York: Oxford University Press, 1993), 407.

28. Riff on wholeness: What is it that makes a "whole" thing "complete"? Is it that we can imagine everything else about its context or story—even though it's only a sentence or a person? (How is a sentence like a person? Each is whole.) Then what is deep mystery—that we can't imagine an unknown amount of it, but are awed by a sense of its greater unknown wholeness? A haiku is whole. A villanelle or a sonnet is whole.

Consciousness has at least this sense of wholeness. Rumi helps us reconceptualize our self as embedded in wholeness. "The center clears. Knowing comes / The body is not singular like a corpse / but singular like a salt grain / still in the side of the mountain." Rumi, *Unseen Rain: Quatrains of Rumi*, trans. John Moyne and Coleman Barks (Boston: Shambhala, 2001), 1. A chip off the old block. This relationship implies that the whole is expressed in its constituent parts. Whatever a writer writes before he dies is complete, they say. Why? Because writing is a fractal-like process of expression—if he lived longer he would write more of the same whole. There is a Chinese saying: "See Tao in the morning, die peacefully at night." Like the proverb "See Naples in the morning and die," it means that nothing would be missed; the wholeness of the experience is there in some form or other to be tasted. A spore of fungus, a branch of sphagnum—the bit contains the original whole.

What is wholeness in relation to ideas? Brainwaves, synapses, and whole units—a quality of a whole glimpse of relations—are extendable by adding on more, yet each is also whole in itself.

29. Briggs, *Fractals*, 25.

30. Bortoft, *The Wholeness of Nature*.

31. Heisenberg's indeterminacy principle applies at the level of subatomic particles, but scholars in psychology and other fields also realize that the observer affects the observed, and is not perfectly objective.

32. See Ron Eglash, *African Fractals: Modern Computing and Indigenous Design* (New Brunswick, N.J.: Rutgers University Press, 1999).

33. *Rock and Hawk: A Selection of Shorter Poems by Robinson Jeffers*, ed. Robert Hass (New York: Random House, 1987), 265.

34. Riff on awe, by Brian Swimme:

The beginning and the end of human existence is awe. We have that in common with all those countless humans before us who became mesmerized by the night's beauty. Our ancestors had their ways of explaining what it all meant. And now we too have a way, a new way, of explaining what is there. But in all cases awe is primordial. And if the explanation is a good one the awe will only deepen. The primary purpose of our explanations is not to remove the awe but to bring us to a more intimate understanding of these mysteries enveloping us and thus carrying us still deeper into the ocean of beauty in which we find ourselves. During the modern period, we became so puffed up with our sense of superiority concerning science's explanations of the universe we did not even notice that we stopped wondering over the stars. It seemed reasonable to stop paying attention to the cosmos. Why wonder about something when we were convinced it was only a machine? Why pay attention to something when we had the mathematics that explained it? We regarded a scientific explanation as something that removed the mystery, so that in time we tricked ourselves into thinking that the mathematical explanations of phenomena were more significant than the phenomena! (Brian Swimme, *The Hidden Heart of the Cosmos: Humanity and the*

New Story [Maryknoll, N.Y.: Orbis, 1996], 47–48.)

35. In the *Mahabharata,* the epic of ancient India, Indra meets the Garuda, the Cosmic Bird. A myth tells that before Garuda can steal *soma* (the nectar of immortality) from the *deva*s and serpents who guard it, he must first multiply and then reduce his size (in the fire of the battle Garuda develops ninety times ninety mouths to drink rivers to extinguish fire; then he takes on a tiny body, golden like "bundled sunbeams") to enter (as a river enters the sea) the place where the *soma* is kept. Garuda finds there an iron wheel, with sharp blades revolving bright as fire and the sun, guarding the *soma.* He begins to revolve in time with the wheel (becoming similar to it) and, becoming smaller, he darts between the spokes, where he finds two shimmering snakes with tongues darting like lightning, fierce and venomous. He flings dust in their eyes, cuts through them, and takes the *soma,* becoming bright. The sun is now dark. Indra hits Garuda with his thunderbolt and Garuda laughs—a feather falls like zigzag lightning. And Garuda proclaims, "One of my feathers is more than you could ever explore, Indra." *The Mahabharata,* trans. J. A. B. van Buitenen (Chicago: University of Chicago Press, 1978), book 1, chapter 5, part 30, verse 6. Indra realizes this must be the famous "fair-winged" cosmic bird, and tells Garuda he wants to be friends, because Garuda can easily "carry with the quill of one feather" all the worlds. In the *Rig Veda,* IV.27, Agni in the womb is said to envision all the generations of gods in order and become a falcon. A reference to a feather falling from the great bird as it flies precedes verses describing the shining *soma* drink. Mushrooms were thought by Vedic people to grow from lightning strikes. The Firebird's "falling feather" is a way of imagining the awe-inspiring power and meaning of lightning.

36. The theme of cosmic holding is not limited to divine figures and what is beyond one, but is found also in religious practices envisioning the spiritual structure of the human being. In tantric and many other religious worldviews the human body contains the cosmos. Mircea Eliade, *Yoga: Immortality and Freedom* (Princeton, N.J.: Princeton University Press, 1970).

37. Annamacharya, *Adhyatma sankirtan-* alu (Tirupati: Tirumala Tirupathi Devasthanam, 1951), vol. 7, 96, 265; vol. 8, 87, 116. *Hiranyagarbha* is the cosmic golden egg-shaped universe in Hinduism.

38. See, for example, Russian dolls: egg-shaped figurines of mothers nested within mothers. The recursive mother images in psyche and culture are universal. Jung writes,

the mother is an archetypal experience; she is experienced by the more or less unconscious child not as a definite, individual feminine personality but as the mother, an archetype charged with an immensity of possible meanings. As life proceeds the primordial image fades and is replaced by a conscious, relatively individual image, which is assumed to be the only mother-image we have. But in the unconscious the mother always remains a powerful primordial image, coloring and even determining throughout life our relations to woman, to society, to the world of feeling and fact, yet in so subtle a way that as a rule, there is no conscious perception of the process. We think all this is only a metaphor. But it becomes a very concrete fact when a man marries a wife only because in some way she resembles his mother, or else because she very definitely does not. Mother Germania is for Germans, like *la belle France* for the French . . . The all-embracing womb of Mother Church is anything but a metaphor, and the same is true of Mother Earth, Mother Nature, and "matter in general. (C. G. Jung, *Civilization in Transition,* trans. R. F. C. Hull, vol. 10 of *The Collected Works of C. G. Jung,* ed. Herbert Read, Michael Fordham, and Gerhard Adler [New York: Pantheon, 1964], 35.)

39. *The Poems of Tukaram,* trans. J. Nelson Fraser and K. B. Marathe (Delhi: Motilal Banarsidass, 1991), 78. Tukaram also sings, "In every hair of Thy body unnumbered worlds arise and pass away," 84.

40. Tulsidas, *Ramacarit-manas, or The Ramayana of Tulsi Das,* trans. F. S. Growse (Allahabad: Ram Narain Lal, 1937). See book 1, dohas 27, 29; chaupai 26; doha 42, etc., and book 7, doha 22 and the chaupai that follows it, doha 27, and so forth.

41. For more on Hindu temples, see

http://classes.yale.edu/fractals/panorama/index
.html>, and follow the "Indian Architecture"
link (accessed October 16, 2002).

42. This text is paraphrased from the *Taittiriya Upanishad,* chapter 2, part 8, verses 1–4,
in *Upanisads,* trans. Patrick Olivelle (New
York: Oxford University Press, 1996), 188–
189.

43. *Isha Upanishad* I.1, in *The Upanishads,*
trans. Swami Nikhilananda (New York: Harper
and Row, 1964), 89.

44. Sir Edwin Arnold, trans., *The Light of
Asia, or The Great Renunciation (Mahabhinish-
kramana)* (New York: Thomas Y. Crowell,
1884), 208.

45. See Francis H. Cook, *Hua-yen Buddhism: The Jewel Net of Indra* (1977; reprint,
Delhi: Sri Satguru, 1994), 2ff.

46. Paul Reps, comp., *Zen Flesh, Zen
Bones: A Collection of Zen and Pre-Zen Writing*
(Garden City, N.Y.: Doubleday, 1961), 101.

47. Julian of Norwich, *Showings,* trans.
James Walsh (New York: Paulist, 1978), 130–
131. The second quotation is from *Psychological Reflections: An Anthology of the Writings of
C. G. Jung,* ed. Jolande Jacobi (New York: Harper and Row, 1961), 308.

48. Cook, *Hua-yen Buddhism,* 22. Part of
what I am trying to say in this paragraph is
illustrated by recent findings about cognitive
processes in the research of social psychologist
Richard Nisbett of the University of Michigan.
His studies, "carried out in the United States,
Japan, China and Korea—document a familiar
division. Easterners, the researchers find, appear to think more 'holistically,' paying greater
attention to context and relationship, relying
more on experience-based knowledge than abstract logic and showing more tolerance for
contradiction. Westerners are more 'analytic'
in their thinking, tending to detach objects
from their context, to avoid contradictions and
to rely more heavily on formal logic." Erica
Goode, "How Culture Molds Habits of
Thought," *New York Times,* August 8, 2000,
section D, 1 and 4.

49. Rumi, "Thousands of Rose Gardens,"
in Andrew Harvey, ed., *The Essential Mystics*
(San Francisco: HarperSanFrancisco, 1996),
156.

50. Theodore Roszak, *The Voice of the
Earth: An Exploration in Ecopsychology* (New
York: Simon and Schuster, 1992), 162.

51. Ibid., 163.

52. Loren Eiseley, *The Immense Journey*
(New York: Random House, 1957). See also
George Sielstadt, *At the Heart of the Web: The
Inevitable Genesis of Intelligent Life* (Boston:
Harcourt Brace Jovanovich, 1989). Others
have also written on this theme of the cosmic
journey. Buckminster Fuller, who coined the
term "spaceship earth," wrote interestingly
about design implications and the idea of the
boat. He explored the fractal-like composite
kinship: "the set-of-all-the-boats called the
race . . . maintaining their relative continuity
with respect to each other externally, as the
individual boats persist as a continuity of internal sets and subsets (to the power of any
number) of synchronized interactions." Buckminster Fuller, *Ideas and Integrities* (New York:
Collins, 1969), 234–235.

53. Robert Graves, *The White Goddess*
(New York: Farrar, Straus and Giroux, 1976),
480.

54. Thomas Moore, in James Hillman, *A
Blue Fire: Selected Writings,* introd. and ed. by
Thomas Moore in collaboration with James
Hillman (New York: HarperCollins, 1991),
240.

55. Jacqueline Simpson, *Icelandic Folktales and Legends* (Berkeley and Los Angeles:
University of California Press, 1972), 72. Almost half a million men—497,664—are sharing the pieces of sealskin. The interested reader
may delve into the symbolic associations of all
those twelves.

56. Quoted in Eli Maor, *To Infinity and
Beyond: A Cultural History of the Infinite* (Bos-
ton: Birkhauser, 1987), 164. See also James P.
Carse, *Finite and Infinite Games* (New York:
Free, 1986).

57. "Hymn for the Creation," by Johann
Christoph Friedrich von Schiller (d. 1805), is
translated under the title "The Greatness of
Creation" in *The Poems and Ballads of Schiller,*
trans. Edward Bulwer-Lytton (New York:
Clark and Maynard, 1864).

58. J. D. Memory, "Blake and Fractals," in
Gerald A. Edgar, ed., *Classics on Fractals*
(Reading, Mass.: Addison-Wesley, 1993), 1.

STRAND THREE

1. Nasr said this at "Spirit and Nature," a
conference held at Middlebury College in Middlebury, Vermont, 1991. See Seyyed Hossein
Nasr, "Islam and the Environmental Crisis," in

Spirit and Nature: Why the Environment Is a Religious Issue, ed. Steven C. Rockefeller and John C. Elder (Boston: Beacon, 1992), 83–108.

2. For example, "When man is endowed with this virtue, he becomes divine. Its six facets are: Character, Non-Violence, Compassion, Control over mind, Control over senses, and Nobility. Emulate Sri Rama—evolve into the man supreme. It is because of these six qualities that Sri Rama in human form became divine. The youth of India should cultivate these six virtues." Sathya Sai Baba, Shivaratri Eve Discourse (pamphlet; Prashanti Nilayam, India: Ashram, March 1995).

3. Brian Swimme's works include The Universe Story: From the Primordial Flaring Forth to the Ecozoic Era (with Thomas Berry) (San Francisco: HarperSanFrancisco, 1992), The Hidden Heart of the Cosmos: Humanity and the New Story (Maryknoll, N.Y.: Orbis, 1996), The Universe Is a Green Dragon: A Cosmic Creation Story (Santa Fe, N.M.: Bear, 1984), and a lecture series, Canticle to the Cosmos, 6 audiocassettes, Sounds True Audio, 1995.

4. E. M. Forster's novel A Passage to India (New York: Harcourt Brace and Company, 1952) features fractal-like echoes of confusion, for example, reiterations of sound which change as they pass from voice to ear to voice, and so forth. "If several people talk at once, an overlapping howling noise begins, echoes generate echoes, and the cave is stuffed with a snake composed of small snakes, which writhe independently" (147–148; see also 225).

5. Mircea Eliade, The Sacred and the Profane: The Nature of Religion (New York: Harcourt, Brace and World, 1959), 21.

6. Ibid., 30.

7. Some Reform Jewish thinkers and rabbis seem to have fallen into this trap after World War II. They left out any aspects of Judaism that could not be accounted for with a rational mind, denying there were any teachings about the soul and the afterlife, for example. Seeking answers to such questions, some Jews went to Zen or Tibetan Buddhism or Hinduism to get another view. Within the Western framework other modes have offered a way other than the hyper-rational. For example, Goethe's sometimes misunderstood alternative to isolative, calculative, analytic thinking is discussed in Henri Bortoft, The

Wholeness of Nature: Goethe's Way toward a Science of Conscious Participation in Nature (Hudson, N.Y.: Lindisfarne, 1996).

8. Eliade, The Sacred and the Profane, 43. In this view "traditional" means "nonsecular."

9. Ibid., 47ff.

10. This is one of the basic points of chaos science—the sensitivity of the process to initial conditions. Ancient people's myths, the happenings of the origin, are the archetypal acts which must be symbolically repeated by man to renew creation—at New Year's celebrations, for example. Tribal groups are usually small and preliterate, without a scripture or a missionary urge, usually with a shaman as specialist in the sacred.

11. The term "biospiritual" is used by Brian Swimme in Canticle to the Cosmos.

12. See Brian Swimme and Thomas Berry's discussion of the beginning in The Universe Story, 17–25.

13. Clarissa Pinkola Estes, Women Who Run with the Wolves: Myths and Stories of the Wild Woman Archetype (New York: Ballantine, 1992), 19.

14. Eliade, The Sacred and the Profane, 162–213.

15. Plotinus, Rumi, and other mystics use the imagery of circling the divine center. The arcs made by all that "comes from the center," as Rumi says, and circles it, are fractal-like paths within the whole. This is meant as an imaginable symbolic iterative process, not a mathematically exact formula. The Essential Rumi, trans. Coleman Barks (San Francisco: HarperSanFrancisco, 1995), 279.

16. Lao-tzu, Tao Te Ching: A New English Version, trans. Stephen Mitchell (New York: Harper and Row, 1988), chapter 25.

17. Ibid.

18. Mencius, trans. W. A. C. H. Dobson (Toronto: University of Toronto Press, 1963), book 6, paragraph 20.

19. Ibid., VI.19–20.

20. Ibid., VI.33.

21. Ibid., VI.39.

22. Quoted by Fritjof Capra, The Web of Life: A New Scientific Understanding of Living Systems (New York: Anchor, 1996), 21, a valuable overview which goes a long way toward exploring what it means to be part of "one great harmonious whole."

23. This Being, the ultimate reality of in-

finite eternal consciousness, according to Hindus, is the meaning of "I am who am" in Exodus 3:14. See, for example, Mangala S. Venkataramiah, *Talks with Ramana Maharshi* (Tiruvannamalai: Sri Ramanasramam, 1978), 102.

24. *Satapatha-brahmam According to the Madhyandina School,* trans. Julius Eggeling (Delhi: Motilal Banarsidass, 1972), chapter 7, part 2, section 1, verse 4.

25. *Bhattabhaskaramisra* Taittiriyabrahmanam (Delhi: Motilal Banarsidass, 1985), chapter 1, part 5, section 9, verse 4.

26. *Manava Dharma Shastra* (Delhi: Motilal Banarsidass, 1964).

27. Rockefeller and Elder, *Spirit and Nature,* 119.

28. A young American I met in August 2000, who had recently returned from New Zealand, told me of working at the site of a new stupa being constructed there, and of the smaller stupas of clay, and the inscribed stupas on them. Since it was a traditional stupa, I assume it is not unique.

29. Huston Smith, *The World's Religions: Our Great Wisdom Traditions* (San Francisco: HarperSanFrancisco, 1991), 281. This is a revised edition of *The Religions of Man* (New York: Harper, 1958).

30. In Arthur C. Clarke's *Fractals: The Colors of Infinity* (Princeton, N.J.: Films for the Humanities and Sciences, 1994), one of the scientists who developed a system of fractal compression, Michael Barnsley, marvels at the mystery of how God could create a universe in which there is free will. He saw the fractal nature of existence as the way God accomplished this, in an elegant and brilliant way. How? If each thing, including persons, is endowed with a nature of self-similarity which shares in the intelligence behind and pervading the whole, it also has the ability to be a part, free to participate or to set itself apart. It can turn away in dissonance or harmonize; it can color its individual self in a way that blends or one that contrasts. These are freedoms. The whole system allows for that possibility in the free will of the part, and yet it can be as Barnsley pictures it—a created universe, a system with the sacred at its source.

31. A. Cohen, *Everyman's Talmud* (New York: E. P. Dutton, 1949), 26.

32. Ibid., 22, 210–237.

33. Ibid., 8.

34. Ibid., 60, 211. Compare Jesus's instruction in Matthew 5:48: "Be perfect even as your Father in heaven is perfect."

35. *The Talmud: The Steinsaltz Edition,* with commentary by Adin Steinsaltz, vol. 13, *Tractate Ta'anit, Part 1* (New York: Random House, 1995), chapter 1, 5B, 62.

36. *Pirke Aboth: The Tractate "Fathers," from the Mishnah, Commonly Called "Sayings of the Fathers,"* ed. R. Travers Herford, revised 3rd ed. (New York: Jewish Institute of Religion Press, 1945), chapter 3, part 18, page 87. The German Romantic philosopher and poet Novalis wrote of humans as destined to become God. Thoreau in his journal in 1850 eloquently described the ethos of Western prophetic legacy—man feeling angst, shame, alienation in relation to God. His generalizations have some truth to them, though his knowledge of the whole of Hinduism and Judaism was limited. "The Hindoos are more serenely and thoughtfully religious than the Hebrews. They have perhaps a purer, more independent and impersonal knowledge of God. Their religious books describe the first inquisitive and contemplative access to God; the Hebrew bible a conscientious return, a grosser and more personal repentance. Repentance is not a free and fair highway to God. A wise man will dispense with repentance. It is shocking and passionate. God prefers that you approach him thoughtful, not penitent, though you are the chief of sinners. It is only by forgetting yourself that you draw near to him." *The Heart of Thoreau's Journals,* ed. Odell Shepard (New York: Dover, 1961), 34–35.

37. Cohen, *Everyman's Talmud,* 9.

38. Pinhas Sadeh, *Jewish Folktales,* trans. Hillel Halkin (New York: Doubleday, 1989).

39. Leonard Cohen, "Suzanne," in *Stranger Music: Selected Poems and Songs* (New York: Random House, 1994), 95.

40. In ancient art spirals on different scales and levels of existence often visually suggest the kinship of sea creatures, ocean waves, clouds, curls of hair and beard, and many other natural self-similar whorlings. In Africa, Dogon culture has many spirals. Marcel Griaule, *Conversations with Ogotemmeli* (New York: Oxford University Press, 1965). Karl Marx, approaching some Christian images from a different angle, wrote that the essence

of the value of linen "is manifest in its likeness to gold, just as the sheep nature of the Christian is manifest in his resemblance to the Lamb of God." Quoted in Alphonso Lingis, *Deathbound Subjectivity* (Bloomington: Indiana University Press, 1993), 165. Augustine in *On the Trinity* discusses the exact resemblance between Father and Son, saying God is the "first species," by which all created things are made in their respective species, and God is the form by which all created things possess their forms. The resemblance of Father to Son is special, for Christ as the Word is exemplar of all things. In the traditional Christian view, created beings have similitude to God via participation in the Son.

41. "This foundation, God, . . . can only be recognized by that which is akin to it." as Jung wrote. But to nuance the actual situation further, "Christ can indeed be imitated to the point of stigmatization without the imitator's even remotely approaching the ideal or heeding its meaning; the point here is not a mere imitation that leaves a man unchanged and makes him into an artifact—it is rather a matter of realizing the ideal on one's own account (*Deo concedente*) in the sphere of one's individual life." *Psychological Reflections: An Anthology of the Writings of C. G. Jung,* ed. Jolande Jacobi (New York: Harper and Row, 1961), 279, 302.

42. Thomas à Kempis, *The Imitation of Christ: A Modern Version Based on the English Translation Made by Richard Whiteford around the Year 1530,* trans. Harold C. Gardiner (Garden City, N.Y.: Image, 1955).

43. I Corinthians 11:1.

44. I Corinthians 10–12 describe the mystical body of Christ.

45. Matthew 13:24, 31–33, 44–45, 47, 52.

46. C. G. Jung discusses this in *Psychology and Religion: West and East,* vol. 11 of *The Collected Works of C. G. Jung,* trans. R. F. C. Hull (New York: Pantheon, 1958), 413.

47. Morris A. Inch, *Chaos Paradigm: A Theological Exploration* (Lanham, Md.: University Press of America, 1998), 53–54.

48. In Matthew 18:22, Jesus, asked if one should forgive one's brother seven times, says, "No, seventy times seven." In other words, seven times seven times ten, and more. This is like Judaism's old custom of forgiveness of debts every jubilee year—the forty-ninth year—mentioned in Leviticus.

49. Thomas Traherne, *Centuries* (New York: Harper, 1960), The Third Century, #59, 145.

50. Ibid., The First Century, #39, 19–20.

51. Hermes Mercurius Trismegistus, *His Divine Pymander,* in 17 books, tr. Dr. Everard, London: Printed by J.S. For Thomas Brewster, 1659, pp. 155–156. (Tenth book, paragraphs 125–130.) Available at http://wwwlib.umi.com/eebo/image/42089/85 (accessed March 4, 2003). Spellings have been altered to conform to contemporary English.

52. This need to expand, to open, in order to share in the experience of higher being is emphasized in yoga, Zen, Taoism, and other traditions, although each uses different exercises, therapies, methods to accomplish it.

53. Phillip B. Wagoner, " 'Sultan among Hindu Kings': Dress, Titles, and the Islamicization of Hindu Culture at Vijayanagara," *Journal of Asian Studies* 55, no. 4 (Nov. 1996): 853.

54. Ninian Smart, *Worldviews* (New York: Charles Scribner's Sons, 1983), 121.

55. Brown also quotes Hodgson on the Qur'an: "Almost every element which goes to make up its message is somehow present in any given passage." Brown also remarks here on "Simultaneous totality, as in *Finnegans Wake,* or more generally, in what Umberto Eco called 'The Poetics of the Open Work': 'We can see it as an infinite contained within finiteness. The work therefore has infinite aspects, because each of them, and any moment of it, contains the totality of the work.' " Jorge Luis Borges's story "The Alef" also presents a view of reality in which, as Brown says, "it is all there all the time." Norman O. Brown, "The Apocalypse of Islam," in *Facing Apocalypse,* ed. Valerie Andrews, Robert Bosnak, and Karen Walter Goodwin (Dallas: Spring, 1987), 157–158.

56. Sufis are Muslim mystics on the path of the heart. See Annemarie Schimmel's works, such as *Mystical Dimensions of Islam* (Chapel Hill: University of North Carolina Press, 1975).

57. Rumi, *Divani Shamsi Tabriz,* trans. Reynold A. Nicholson (San Francisco: Rainbow Bridge, 1973), 81.

58. Zlatko Dizdarevic, *Sarajevo: A War Journal* (New York: Fromm International, 1993).

59. In a book by Anthony Loyd, a photojournalist in the Bosnian war, we see that even an atheist who curiously observed a

sniper to see what killing is like finds reasons to value compassion: "Everything I had seen and experienced confirmed my views about the pointlessness of existence, the basic brutality of human life and the godlessness of the universe. But however oblivious to my own death I became, I saw no reason to allow my fellow man to suffer unnecessarily. Retaining a sense of compassion seemed the only inner victory I could possibly achieve against the madness." Anthony Loyd, *My War Gone By, I Miss It So* (New York: Atlantic Monthly, 2000).

60. One can imagine a figure of cosmic consciousness and cosmic suffering witnessing all the tragedies of the human race—Jesus, Buddha, Krishna, etc. Ordinary men are not vast enough to witness, let alone cause, great suffering without great repercussions.

61. Lao-tzu, *Tao Te Ching,* trans. Mitchell, chapter 74.

62. Nathan McCall, "Makes Me Wanna Holler," *Newsweek,* Feb. 7, 1994, 49.

63. Riff on drugs and consciousness: How can we know that consciousness is a fundamental quality associated with Godhead? Those who alter their consciousness through drugs reach states artificially approximating some aspects of pure consciousness through the suspension of attachments and the impairing of thought and nerve function. This allows the abiding, still base of awareness to be rested on, while the chemically relieved mind floats. Temporal and spatial limits appear lifted. But the heart is not steady in these undisciplined shortcuts and those who attempt this cheating or gate-crashing are thrown out of the wedding feast when it's discovered that they are not wearing the appropriate cloak (Matthew 22)— the impurities reduce them to new depths. The imagery of the language of drug users is interesting. Lenny Bruce said he knew he should not shoot up heroin, but that doing so was "like kissing God." He meant he got to enjoy consciousness. An addict who said he felt "unworthy to be in the kingdom of God" felt that with drugs he could experience "being on the threshold." He associated the numbness of mind, temporary peace, with closeness to God. It is the pure, loving heart which authentically and naturally enjoys the feeling of spiritual nearness to the divine. A mere physical manipulation of consciousness can simulate peace, but how much more is attained by the one who has attained through self-

sacrifice an expansiveness of soul. Just as reality is not just the right combination of chemicals in the liver (which is affected by mescaline, changing one's consciousness), so God is not just the body pulsing with a drug. (Allen Ginsberg, inhaling ether, asked "What *can* be possible / in a minor universe / in which you can see / God by sniffing the gas in a cotton?" Allen Ginsberg, "Aether," *Collected Poems, 1947–1980* (New York: HarperCollins, 1988), 242. In a variety of changes of consciousness, including peak experiences in sports and exercise, meditation, and mystical practices, one is oblivious to all but the present moment.

64. John Lamb, "No. 587: A Deathrow Inmate Tells His Own Life Story," interview by David Isay and Stacy Abramson, *New York Times Magazine,* Jan. 2, 2000, 34.

65. Genesis 3:5.

66. John 10:34.

67. *The Simone Weil Reader,* ed. George A. Panichas (New York: David McKay, 1981), 475.

68. James Hillman, *A Blue Fire: Selected Writings,* introd. and ed. by Thomas Moore in collaboration with James Hillman (New York: HarperCollins, 1991), 268–289.

69. One can see the activities of human lovemaking, and also of devotion, as forming fractal-like cycles of time. Caresses, kisses, and so on are of a style and ilk, and each lovemaking is in a different form, with scales of intensity, yet the different instances are self-similar integral parts of a whole. Similarly, in the lives of those who are religious, every day may be of the same order, may involve the same essential, personal way of practicing devotions, worshiping, praying, yet the practices differ in intensity, duration, inspiration, etc., so they are variations at different scales.

70. C. J. Bleeker, "The Opening Address," *Proceedings of the Eleventh International Congress of the History of Religion* (Leiden: E. J. Brill, 1975). Among those who promote the perennialist approach, which Bleeker is decrying, is Fredrick Heiler. See his discussion of "seven areas of unity" in the world religions in "The History of Religions as a Preparation for the Cooperation of Religions," in *The History of Religions: Essays in Methodology,* ed. Mircea Eliade and J. M. Kitagawa (Chicago: University of Chicago Press, 1959), 142–153.

71. Wilfred Cantwell Smith, *The Meaning*

and End of Religion (New York: Mentor, 1964), 15.

72. A. Gordon Melvin, *The New Culture: An Organic Philosophy of Education* (New York: John Day, 1937), 257–264.

73. "A strange attractor is an infinitely detailed global form that controls chaotic motion . . . the global distribution of very subtle information." It is a varied path of reiterated behavior in "phase-space," a pattern showing a state toward which a system is being pulled repeatedly without ever quite attaining it. F. David Peat, *The Philosopher's Stone: Chaos, Synchronicity, and the Hidden Order of the World* (New York: Bantam, 1991), 225.

74. Ralph Waldo Emerson, *English Traits, Representative Men, and Other Essays* (New York: E. P. Dutton, 1927), 161; he also wrote here of how biographers write their own lives in writing of others. There is also a proverb: "It takes one to know one."

75. For example, everyone in the village has transactions and exchanges during the course of the year, with various mutual benefits.

76. Franz Pfeiffer, *Meister Eckhart*, vol. 1, trans. C. de B. Evans (London: John M. Watkins, 1924), 288. Eckhart's writings are also available in *Meister Eckhart: A Modern Translation*, trans. Raymond Bernard Blakney (New York: Harper and Brothers, 1941).

77. W. B. Yeats, "Crazy Jane: Talks with the Bishop," in *To Read a Poem*, 2nd ed., by Donald Hall (New York: Harcourt Brace Jovanovich, 1992), 367.

78. Buddha's statements on beauty are found in the *Samyuta* and the *Digha Nikaya*, discussed by Juan Mascaro in his introduction to his translation of *The Dhammapada: The Path of Perfection* (Harmondsworth: Penguin, 1973), 21.

79. Carl Gustav Jung, *Two Essays* (Princeton, N.J.: Princeton University Press, 1966), 235. "Virtual" has come to mean other things since Jung's time.

80. Herbert V. Guenther, *Wholeness Lost and Wholeness Regained* (Albany: State University of New York Press, 1994), 64.

81. "Vibrancy" is a term used by Brian Swimme in *Canticle to the Cosmos* to emphasize this quality of life fulfillment.

82. Margaret R. Miles, *Plotinus on Body and Beauty: Society, Philosophy, and Religion in Third-Century Rome* (Oxford: Blackwell, 1999), 24.

83. Ibid., 138–139.

84. *Dear Theo: The Autobiography of Vincent Van Gogh*, ed. Irving Stone (New York: New American Library, 1969), 476.

85. The reason it's good to see a retrospective covering all the years of an artist's work rather than just isolated items is simple. Such a retrospective gives us the necessary sense of self-similarities within a whole body of works (each work shares some self-similarities with the others), seeing what's reiterated and what is a significant departure, what is typical of the whole trajectory, what's nuance, contrast, and innovation.

STRAND FOUR

1. Henry James, "The Middle Years," in *The Complete Tales of Henry James,* ed. Leon Edel (Philadelphia: J. B. Lippincott, 1964), vol. 9, 75. The phrase "the madness of art" requires exploration. To the plodding, linear, prosaic mind art is inexplicable: "How'd they do that?" But James is praising as mystery or "madness" that which appears to be sheer self-organizing creativity to the pedestrian literalist and logical materialist. See note 54 below, also.

2. *The Journal of Henry D. Thoreau,* ed. Bradford Torrey and Francis H. Allen (New York: Dover, 1962), vol. 2, 239, and vol. 1, 443.

3. John Muir, *My First Summer in the Sierra* (Boston: Houghton Mifflin, 1911), 211.

4. That kind of short-sighted view is overly linear. It is a great eliminator, reducing the extraneous and selecting the undeniable, but its operations are too linear by themselves to be creative.

5. Albert Einstein's experience is eloquently discussed in Brian Swimme, *The Hidden Heart of the Cosmos: Humanity and the New Story* (Maryknoll, N.Y.: Orbis, 1996), 108.

6. William Irwin Thompson, ed., *Gaia, A Way of Knowing: Political Implications of the New Biology* (Hudson, N.Y.: Lindisfarne, 1987), 8. Thompson begins this passage "Imagination is needed to shape a theory. . . . pure induction could never produce a scientific view of the world. . . . [the] poetic imagination of the ancients is more sensitive to humanity's embeddedness in the biosphere" than

logical linear thinking is. Thompson argues that the imagination is too often misunderstood and denigrated as a source of deception and delusion, when in fact it allows us to sense what we do not know, to intuit what we cannot understand, to be more than our ego consciously knows. We all know rationality's strengths. Its intense scrutiny enables us to survive, communicate, and succeed in much of the business that makes up our lives. It is a tool that empowers us to analyze and strategize. Rationality's blind spot is its self-centered stifling of alternatives out of hand. It can be ignorant of emotional intelligence, and can avoid recognition of the deeper sources of creativity. It is a good servant but a disappointing candidate for the part of absolute master of the cosmos or standard for all values. For that we need a unifying power.

7. Jung wrote that creativity involves "the unconscious activation of an archetypal image, and [the elaboration and shaping of] this image into the finished work." The artist's unquenched thirst seeks the original spring from the cool underground source and knows a vital image when it emerges from the unconscious. The artist senses which image answers the needs of the time and brings it up, puts it in a suitable vessel, and flavors it with values usable by people. Conventional people's mainstream attitudes exclude odd elements of the psyche; the more open artist on the back roads finds and prizes them, bringing them into play. C. G. Jung, *The Spirit in Man, Art, and Literature,* trans. R. F. C. Hull, vol. 15 of *The Collected Works of C. G. Jung,* ed. Herbert Read, Michael Fordham, and Gerhard Adler (New York: Pantheon, 1971), 82–83.

8. Gregory Bateson, *A Sacred Unity: Further Steps to an Ecology of Mind,* ed. Rodney E. Donaldson (New York: HarperCollins, 1991), 263. The importance of beauty is being studied anew these days. See, for example, Elaine Scarry, *On Beauty and Being Just* (Princeton, N.J.: Princeton University Press, 1999). As another example, see "What Dance Has to Say about Beauty," *New York Times,* July 23, 2000, section 2, 26–27, a conversation among fourteen dance professionals. Eric Schoefer, a choreographer, said, "I am drawn to the concept of beauty as an experience—beatific, to beam, to emanate—versus the concept of beauty as an object—form, space and time." Myra Bazell,

also a choreographer, suggested, " 'Beauty' . . . [is] not the right word because what we're striving for is to accept what's honest, what's nature, what's sometimes organic to an extreme, or sometimes inorganic to such an extreme that it moves us. But what I find beautiful are things that are ugly as well as beautiful. We have to invent a new word. Maybe 'creamy,' as in cream of the crop."

9. The poet Petrarch once climbed Mont Ventoux and read there a passage from Augustine: "men go to admire the high mountains, the vast floods of the sea, the huge streams of the rivers, the circumference of the ocean, and the revolutions of the stars—and desert themselves." Petrarch realized then, "I ought to have learned, even from pagan philosophers, that 'nothing is admirable besides the mind; compared to its greatness nothing is great.' " While this shows both thesis (desire to experience mountains) and antithesis (appreciation of human mind), Bateson (like me) is suggesting a synthesis—a vision of Mind which includes both mountains and personal mind, as well as molecular, evolutionary, and galactic scales. Petrarch, "The Ascent of Mont Ventoux," translated in *The Renaissance Philosophy of Man,* ed. Ernst Cassirer, Paul Oskar Kristeller, and John Herman Randall, Jr. (Chicago: University of Chicago Press, 1951), 44.

10. Northrop Frye asserted that beauty "often seeks the goal of reassurance rather than discovery." Northrup Frye, *The Double Vision: Language and Meaning in Religion* (Toronto: University of Toronto Press, 1991), 31. In what situations do we find that to be true? The beauty in a painting may reassure, with a calm landscape, a restful scene, but the statement sounds more like that of a critic at a museum than of an artist in the midst of the struggle and process of creating. Certain kinds of beauty have a kind of comforting stasis. But the experience of beauty in the modern and postmodern world is not so simple, as reality is fraught with paradox, interweaving levels and dimensions, depths and juxtapositions, coincidence and surprise. Artists, story-tellers, and other communicators have to ambush the preoccupied audience with fresh insights to get their attention and often true reassurance is earned only after the dramatic ordeal, the traumatic journey, as a homecoming. Both beauty and belief have the power of totalization over

people. They are metaphoric systems which silently say, "Know this (story, doctrine, gospel, theology) and it suffices, no need to go further," and the satisfying power of a thing of beauty leaves one uninterested in distractions. The wholeness of a work of art can do this, and artworks, or things of beauty, are each self-contained systems, worlds within which one can wander. (A Tamil saying holds that "The artist has to be able to go high and low"—because a world can exist between the high and the low, not at one end of the spectrum only.) The artist labors a lifetime with the constant challenge of discovery—how to make a truly satisfying whole, to evoke the "convulsion" of beauty—beauty being a convulsion of bliss, a knot of relevance, the superimposition of wild imagination and rigorous order. And it is by going through disturbance, change, surprise, laughter, and tears that the relief of untying tension's knots in experiencing beauty can be earned. Not that all art should disturb; both slow, contemplative music and fast dance tunes have their place. To wake people and rivet attention through shock can be a legitimate aim of art. John Cage wrote, "The highest duty of the artist is to hide beauty." Quoted in Lewis Hyde, *Trickster Makes This World* (New York: Farrar, Strauss and Giroux, 1988), 303. William Carlos Williams wrote, "Rigor of beauty is the quest." Quoted in M. L. Rosenthal, *The Poet's Art* (New York: W. W. Norton, 1987). A useful collection on this is Albert Hofstadter and Richard Kuhns, eds., *Philosophies of Art and Beauty: Selected Readings in Aesthetics from Plato to Heidegger* (1964; Chicago: University of Chicago Press, 1976).

11. "The end-virtue of humility comes only after a long train of humiliations; and the chief labour of humbling is the constant, resourceful restoration of ignorance." R. P. Blackmur, "A Critic's Job of Work," in *The Double Agent: Essays in Craft and Elucidation* (New York: Arrow, 1935), 271; reissued as *Language as Gesture* (New York: Harcourt Brace, 1952), 373–374. We realize we don't know, and so we begin to explore and learn—this has been a theme of great thinkers from Socrates to Paul Valéry.

12. Bateson, *A Sacred Unity*, 264. Rabindranath Tagore's thoughts on the process of memory involving an "inner artist" are found in Amiya Chakravarty, ed., *A Tagore Reader* (Boston: Beacon, 1966), 89. See also F. David

Peat's *The Blackwinged Night: Creativity in Nature and Mind* (Cambridge, Mass.: Helix, 2000).

13. David Mamet, *Three Uses of the Knife* (Columbia University Press, 1998), 49.

14. Tom Waits, quoted in Robert Palmer, "Tom Waits, All-Purpose Troubadour," *New York Times*, Nov. 14, 1993, section 2, 1.

15. Ibid.

16. Jung, *The Spirit in Man, Art, and Literature*, 82–83.

A riff on creativity: Creativity is the amazing luxury of not knowing exactly what you are doing. Someone writing a poem or painting a painting does not know exactly how it will turn out, if it will be a success, be appreciated by others, be read now or in a hundred years, be forgotten or gotten, be loved or hated, be ignored or shape a hero or the mother or daughter of a hero. So the work is a series of leaps into the unknown (the English word "play" is rooted in the image of joyful leaps, according to Joan M. Erikson, *Wisdom and the Senses: The Way of Creativity* (New York: W. W. Norton, 1988), 47, trusting the intriguing image that beckons and begins things. James Hillman notes that the creative is an achievement of love marked by imagination and beauty and by connection to tradition and nature as a living body. Love makes it. James Hillman, *A Blue Fire: Selected Writings*, introd. and ed. by Thomas Moore in collaboration with James Hillman (New York: HarperCollins, 1991), 283–285.

17. Colin Martindale, "What Makes Creative People Different," *Psychology Today*, July 1975, 44–50. Arnold M. Ludwig uses what is described as a "fractal analysis" to inquire into creative expression and mental disturbance in "Method and Madness in the Arts and Sciences," *Creativity Research Journal* 11, no. 2 (1998): 93–101. Silja J. A. Talvi discusses the study in "Study Links Angst to Creativity," *Poets and Writers* 27, no. 2 (March/April 1999), 13–14.

18. In conversation with the author in Bellagio, Italy, March 2000.

19. Quoted in Jack Kroil, "When Pablo Met Albert," *Newsweek*, June 20, 1994, 66.

20. Riff—a refreshing rant from Bread and Puppet Theater of Glover, Vermont: "Why cheap art? People have been thinking too long that Art is a privilege of the museums and the rich. Art is not business. It does not belong to

banks and fancy investors. Art is food. You can't eat it but it feeds you. Art has to be cheap and available to everybody. It needs to be everywhere because it is the inside of the world. Art soothes pain, art wakes up sleepers! Art fights against war and stupidity! Art sings Halleluia! Art is for kitchens. Art is like good bread. Art is like green trees. Art is like clouds in the blue sky. Art is cheap! Hurrah!" Poster in the Bread and Puppet Museum, Glover, Vermont. Art is a function of depth, beyond economics in this sense.

21. Carl Andre, quoted in Hyde, *Trickster Makes This World,* 307.

22. C. G. Jung, *Civilization in Transition,* trans. R. F. C. Hull, vol. 10 of *The Collected Works of C. G. Jung,* ed. Herbert Read, Michael Fordham, and Gerhard Adler (New York: Pantheon, 1964), 145.

23. Rainer Maria Rilke, *Ueber Dictung und Kunst,* ed. N. H. Engelhardt (Frankfurt am Main: Suhrkamp, 1974), 41–49.

24. See Lao-tzu, *Tao Te Ching: A New English Version,* trans. Stephen Mitchell (New York: Harper and Row, 1988), chapters 20, 28, 50, and 58, for example. One of the archetypal divine figures celebrated in Rig Vedic hymns is the Child of Energy.

25. Norman O. Brown, *Love's Body* (New York: Vintage, 1966), 67. Also see Earle J. Coleman, *Creativity and Spirituality: Bonds between Art and Religion* (Albany: State University of New York Press, 1998).

26. Claudio Rodriguez, *Poesia Completa (1953–1991)* (Barcelona: Tusquets Editores, 2001). James Gleick, in *Chaos: Making a New Science* (New York: Penguin, 1988), writes eloquently of how orders lurk mixed together in turbulence. Much earlier, Jung also wrote about the deep principle involved in such things. For example, "there is a cosmos in all chaos, secret order in all disorder, unfailing law in all contingency." *Psychological Reflections: An Anthology of the Writings of C. G. Jung,* ed. Jolande Jacobi (New York: Harper and Row, 1961), 254.

27. Benedetto Croce, *Breviaro di estetica,* 9th ed. (Bari: Laterza, 1947), 134.

28. Ibid., 137.

29. Herbert Guenther, *Ecstatic Spontaneity: Saraha's Three Cycles of Doha* (Berkeley: Asian Humanities, 1993), 18–19, 28–29, 37ff. Aristotle said that "The soul is in a manner all things." *Aristotle's "On the Soul,"* trans. Hip-

pocrates G. Apostle (Grinnell, Iowa: Peripatetic, 1981), 7, 14–15.

30. John Dewey, *Art as Experience* (New York: Minton Balch, 1934), 194, quoted in *The Open Work,* by Umberto Eco, trans. Anna Cancogni (Cambridge, Mass.: Harvard University Press, 1989), 25–26.

31. Ibid., 21. Simone Weil's definition of art is worth comparing here. "Art is an attempt to transport into a limited quantity of matter, modeled by man, an image of the infinite beauty of the entire universe. If the attempt succeeds, this portion of matter should not hide the universe, but on the contrary it should reveal its reality to all around." *The Simone Weil Reader,* ed. George A. Panichas (New York: David McKay, 1981), 477.

32. Eco, *The Open Work,* 21.

33. I believe the biologist Edmund Sinnot used this term in *Biology of the Spirit* (New York: Viking, 1957), 101ff.

34. Brian Swimme suggests this example in one of his lectures in his lecture series *Canticle to the Cosmos* (6 audiocassettes, Sounds True Audio, 1995).

35. "Earlier" in evolutionary terms, such as in childhood, where open-ended play is a great teacher of future skills and activities.

36. Brian Swimme elaborates on this point in one of his lectures in *Canticle to the Cosmos.*

37. Thomas Berry, *Creative Energy* (San Francisco: Sierra Club, 1996), 34. Blaise Pascal wrote that man is nobler than the universe which brings his life to an end (the laws of nature with their limits)—nobler "because he knows that he dies and the advantage which the universe has over him; the universe knows nothing of this." *Pensées: Thoughts on Religion and Other Subjects,* trans. W. F. Trotter (New York: Washington Square, 1965), 103, #347.

38. Stuart Kauffman, in his studies of biology, uses this term.

39. See Gregory Bateson, *Mind and Nature: A Necessary Unity* (New York: Dutton, 1979); David Ray Griffin, *Religion and Scientific Naturalism: Overcoming the Conflicts* (Albany: State University of New York Press, 2000). See also the discussion in Fritjof Capra and David Steindl-Rast, with Thomas Matus, *Belonging to the Universe: Explorations on the Frontiers of Science and Spirituality* (San Francisco: HarperSanFrancisco, 1991).

40. For example, in his *Metaphysics,* Ar-

istotle discusses various traditions of the One: "Xenophanes, who was the first among these to speak of the One . . . said nothing clearly, nor does he seem to have touched upon the nature of the One in any of these two senses [as finite formula or infinite matter] but gazing at the whole heaven, he said 'the One is God.' " The Pythagoreans held that "the Finite and Infinite and the One are not to be regarded as being other natures [such as earth, fire, or water] . . . but that the Infinite itself and the One itself are the substances of the thing of which they are predicated, and hence that numbers are the substances of all things." Aristotle finds this idea of things existing by imitating numbers too simple. He cites Plato's view that sensible things exist apart from Ideas and are named according to Ideas—things exist by participating in the Forms (which are the causes of all things); by participation in the One the Forms exist. *Aristotle's Metaphysics,* trans. Hippocrates G. Apostle (Grinnell, Iowa: Peripatetic, 1979), 22–23.

41. See *Coomaraswamy: Selected Papers,* ed. Roger Lipsey, vols. 1 and 2 (Princeton, N.J.: Princeton University Press, 1977).

42. Jung discusses the sun as the first image to become a symbolic bearer of human destiny, climbing from childhood, sacrificing for the fruits of autumn "which are seeds of immortality: in children, in works, in fame, in a new order of things, which in their turn begin and complete the sun's course over again." Jung, *Psychological Reflections,* 295.

43. Quoted by Umberto Eco in *The Open Work,* 40.

44. As Katya Walter puts it, "mattergy"— sounding like the name of a sweet little Hindu goddess, "Mataji." Katya Walter, *Tao of Chaos: Merging East and West* (Rockport, Mass.: Element, 1994).

45. Peat, *The Blackwinged Night,* 172.

46. Ibid., 173. My view is that if we can go to Plato for a wisdom vision to relate to contemporary knowledge, we can also go to the deepest understandings in the *Tao Te Ching* and the Upanishads for clues about Tao or consciousness.

47. Ibid.

48. Peat discusses this on 172–177.

49. F. David Peat, *The Philosopher's Stone: Chaos, Synchronicity, and the Hidden Order of the World* (New York: Bantam, 1991), 204.

Brian Swimme in his *Canticle to the Cosmos* lectures affirms and celebrates this too.

50. Stephen Jay Gould's cautions about the differences between evolution in nature and changes in culture are well founded, as is his criticism of human arrogance. Stephen Jay Gould, *Full House: The Spread of Excellence from Plato to Darwin* (New York: Harmony, 1996), 219.

51. The *Kama Sutra* is the classical Sanskrit manual of lovemaking positions.

52. John Fordham, *Jazz Heroes* (London: Collins and Brown, 1998), 47.

53. Whitney Smith, "Disorder Aided Musician's Development as Conductor," *Indianapolis Star,* April 9, 2000, section 1, 1.

54. Skill, logic, and good intentions are insufficient to make true art and poetry, which require a further inspiration. Socrates praises this madness in Plato's *Ion* and *Phaedo:* "If any man come to the gates of poetry without *the madness of the muses,* persuaded that skill alone will make him a good poet, then shall he and his works of sanity be brought to nought, by the poetry of madness, and behold, their place is nowhere to be found." He also said that "love is . . . a sort of madness, a gift of the gods." The gates of poetry, art and love require some surrender to what's beyond us and our logic. For more on this see Plato's passages on "Artistic Inspiration" in Hofstadter and Kuhns, *Philosophies of Art and Beauty,* 53ff.

55. D. T. Suzuki, *Zen Buddhism: Selected Writings,* ed. William Barrett (Garden City, N.Y.: Doubleday, 1956), 224.

56. Some thinkers, such as Jean Huston, specialize in studying this.

57. Jung wrote that people in the second half of life are engaged in different tasks than people in the first half of their lives. The second half is more suited to the creation of culture, for example. Jung, *Psychological Reflections,* 110–132.

58. Joseph Campbell, *Erotic Irony and Mythic Forms in the Art of Thomas Mann* (San Francisco: Robert Briggs Associates, 1988), 31.

59. See Arthur Koestler, *The Act of Creation* (London: Pan, 1970).

60. Edward Linenthal, *Sacred Ground: Americans and Their Battlefields* (Urbana: University of Illinois Press, 1991), 126n.

61. *Aristotle's Metaphysics,* 18ff.

62. Edward Conze, *Buddhist Wisdom*

Books: *The Diamond Sutra, The Heart Sutra* (New York: Harper and Row, 1972), 84.

63. Jung, *Psychological Reflections,* 270.

64. "Paradox is a characteristic of truth. What *communis opinio* [common opinion] has of truth is surely no more than an elementary deposit of generalizing partial understanding, related to truth even as sulphurous fumes are to lightning." Correspondence of Count Paul Yorck von Wartenburg and Wilhelm Dilthey, quoted as an epigraph to Gershom Scholem, *Sabbatai Sevi* (Princeton, N.J.: Princeton University Press, 1975).

65. Erich Jantsch, *Design for Evolution* (New York: G. Braziller, 1975), 7, 8, 194.

66. Natalie Angier, *The Beauty of the Beastly: New Views on the Nature of Life* (Boston: Houghton Mifflin, 1995), 211. Many artists, writers, and composers with dramatic ups and downs in their lives serve to illustrate this: Van Gogh, Dostoyevsky, Beethoven, Tchaikovsky, Shelley, Melville, and Hemingway, to name just a few.

67. Douglas R. Hofstadter, *Gödel, Escher, Bach: An Eternal Golden Braid* (New York: Basic, 1979), 10.

68. Bateson, *A Sacred Unity,* 263.

69. John Briggs and F. David Peat, *Turbulent Mirror: An Illustrated Guide to Chaos Theory and the Science of Wholeness* (New York: Harper and Row, 1989), 194.

70. Ibid., 195–196.

71. Roger Callois, *Man, Play, and Games,* trans. M. Barash (New York: Free, Macmillan, 1961).

72. Lao-tzu, *Tao Te Ching,* trans. Mitchell, chapters 10, 20, 76.

73. Quoted in Fordham, *Jazz Heroes,* 125.

74. Vonnegut was quoted in a local newspaper, which did not give its source. The ideas on chunking presented here were stimulated by Malcolm Gladwell's excellent article "The Physical Genius," *The New Yorker,* August 2, 1999, 57–65.

75. Plato, Plotinus, Ficino, Novalis, James Hillman, and others write of the relations between soul and beauty in interesting and useful ways.

76. Brian Swimme and Thomas Berry, *The Universe Story: From the Primordial Flaring Forth to the Ecozoic Era* (San Francisco: HarperSanFrancisco, 1992); and Brian Swimme, *The Universe Is a Green Dragon: A Cosmic Creation Story* (Santa Fe, N.M.: Bear, 1984).

Riff on creativity again: Creativity is noticing and following up on creative impulses, being driven by idea spurs. Creativity is giving a fantasy its own space to explore, free rein to create its own world rather than to act out in the common world, therefore allowing it to be at play in its own world, free from constraint, penalties, etc. (When acting out in the common world, one is responsible.) Creativity is immersing oneself in that counterworld of play and freedom to develop, extend, refine, shape, craft artworks. Artists, poets, lovers, drummers, discoverers may seem crazy, as if they can't help but let their unconscious show in different ways. Creativity is valuing what Maya Deren called "those rare occasions whose truth can be stated only by poetry" (*Meshes in the Afternoon,* 1943). Creativity is catching a part of a wave and generating little waves.

Creativity is being a fish in water, or a current:

> the creative process is, at best, not the act of an ego-self, which is then offered to the highest powers, nor even an act of the self in communion with those highest powers, but nondual, which is to say: a manifestation of those powers. This process is no more objective than subjective, for one must be attentive as well as receptive, a state perhaps best described as emptiness. The hallmark of inspiration is this paradoxical synthesis of subjective freedom and objective necessity, both thereby intensified as Nietzsche knew well and described well: "Artists know only too well that it is precisely when they cease to act *voluntarily* and do everything of necessity that their feeling of freedom, subtlety, fullness of power, creative placing, disposing, shaping reaches its height—in short, that necessity and *freedom of will* are then one in them." (David Loy, *Lack and Transcendence* [Atlantic Highlands, N.J.: Humanities, 1996], 128–129.)

Creativity is flying freely with imagination, not getting stuck, or if you get stuck, getting unstuck. "Without climbing the cliff of adversity one cannot arrive at the meadow of happiness," a Tibetan proverb says. And according to Schopenhauer, every child is to a certain extent a genius and every genius to a certain extent is a child, (*The World as Will and Idea,* vol. 2).

77. This point is also made by Brian Swimme, in his first lecture in *Canticle to the Cosmos.*

78. David Bohm perceptively writes, "originality and creativity begin to emerge . . . as a by-product of a mind that is coming to a more nearly normal order of operation," with the flow of natural freedom, rather than reliance on plans and conditioning's mechanical constraints, being crucial. David Bohm, *On Creativity,* ed. Lee Nichol (London: Routledge, 1998), 26.

79. Thomas Szasz, *The Untamed Tongue: A Dissenting Dictionary,* (LaSalle, Ill.: Open Court, 1991), 140.

80. See Simone Weil's essay on beauty, "Forms of the Implicit Love of God," in *The Simone Weil Reader,* ed. Panichas, 469–491.

81. Simone Weil, "The Stars," in ibid., 409.

82. Paul Klee, *Theorie de l'art moderne* (1964; reprint, Paris: Deno'l, 1985), 42–46, quoted in Pierre Hadot, *Philosophy as a Way of Life* (Oxford: Blackwell, 1995), 255.

STRAND FIVE

1. Gertrude Stein, "Composition as Explanation," in *Selected Writings of Gertrude Stein,* ed. Carl Van Vechten (New York: Modern Library, 1962), 516.

2. Karl Krauss, quoted in John D. Barrow, *The Artful Universe* (Oxford: Oxford University Press, 1995), 114.

3. *Bravo Profile,* "Julie Taymor," dir. Bobbie Birleffi, 2000.

4. For example, N. Katherine Hayles, *Chaos Bound: Orderly Disorder in Contemporary Literature and Science* (Ithaca: Cornell University Press, 1990); and Alexander Argyros, *A Blessed Rage for Order: Deconstruction, Evolution, and Chaos* (Ann Arbor: University of Michigan Press, 1991).

5. Gregory Bateson calls it "Mind" in his books *Steps to an Ecology of Mind* (1972; reprint, New York: Ballantine, 1990), *Mind and Nature: A Necessary Unity* (New York: Dutton, 1979), and *Angels Fear: Towards an Epistemology of the Sacred* (New York: Macmillan, 1987)

(with Mary Catherine Bateson). Zen Buddhism calls it "Buddha Mind, Buddha Consciousness," and Vedanta calls it *chit,* pure, formless consciousness. I explore this concept further at many points in this book.

6. *The Selected Writings of Ralph Waldo Emerson,* ed. Brooks Atkinson (New York: Modern Library, 1968), 24–25.

7. This view has been reiterated variously by other writers as well, from classical authors such as Dante, to Native Americans, to creators of popular culture. "The World Is A Circle," a song by Burt Bacharach and Hal David, suggests that the world we live in is a beginningless circle, and that people do not know where it ends. Much in life, the song suggests, depends on one's situation in this beginningless circle. Therefore, if someone thinks he's small that isn't completely true, because just as a small branch seems like a big tree when compared with a tiny twig, to another, even smaller person, the "small" person may seem to be large. These images of different scales in an infinite whole have a rather fractal-like quality.

8. Again, this is Gregory Bateson's language, developed during the current scientific era, though counterparts are found in many traditions and in the experiences of many people from other ages.

9. *Thoreau on Man and Nature,* compiled by Arthur G. Volkman (Mt. Vernon, N.Y.: Peter Pauper, 1960), 18.

10. Ibid., 8. On laws of nature as rooted in the structure of the human nervous system see Todd Siler, *Breaking the Mind Barrier: The Artscience of Neurocosmology* (New York, Simon and Schuster, 1990). See also J. Nigro Sansonese, *The Body of Myth* (Rochester, Vt.: Inner Traditions, 1994).

11. Henry D. Thoreau, *Faith in a Seed: The Dispersion of Seeds and Other Late Natural History Writings,* ed. Bradley P. Dean (Washington, D.C.: Island Press for Shearwater Books, 1993), 164, *Walden and Other Writings* (New York: Modern Library, 1950), 297.

12. *Rock and Hawk: A Selection of Shorter Poems by Robinson Jeffers,* ed. Robert Hass (New York: Random House, 1987), 263–264.

13. Albert C. Todd and Max Hayward, with Daniel Weissbort, eds., *Twentieth Century Russian Poetry: Silver and Steel, An Anthology,* selected, with an introduction, by Yevgeny Yevtushenko (New York: Doubleday, 1993), 422.

14. Far from Africa, the Chinese philosopher and reformer known in the West as Confucius stated the positive side of this: If there is goodness in the heart there is peace in the family; if there is peace in the family there is harmony in the state; if there is harmony in the state there is order in the world.

15. Adam LeFevre, "Villanelle of the Nuclear Physicists," in *Everything All at Once* (Middletown, Conn.: Wesleyan University Press, 1978), 53.

16. Ibid., 11.

17. "A Book for the Hours of Prayer," in *Selected Poems of Rainer Maria Rilke,* trans. Robert Bly (New York: Harper and Row, 1981), 16.

18. Before Rilke, John Ruskin, in his "The Work of Iron," spoke of "the most insignificant pebble" as capable of offering the careful reader a "curious lesson." *The Works of John Ruskin,* ed. E. T. Cook and Alexander Wedderburn (London: George Allen, 1903–1912), vol. 16, 378.

19. Mark Strand, *Blizzard of One* (New York: Alfred A. Knopf, 1998), 20, 44.

20. Paul Lawson, "Any Old Stone," *The New Yorker,* May 17, 1999, 34.

21. Mark Twain, *Innocents Abroad and Roughing It* (New York: Library of America, 1984), 159.

22. Quoted in John Briggs, *Fractals, The Patterns of Chaos: A New Aesthetic of Art, Science, and Nature* (New York: Simon and Schuster, 1992), 93. A similar evocation of hidden potency, Tennyson's "Flower in the Crannied Wall," opens more vistas for those who can see it as a revelation of infinity, "root and all, and all in all." Alfred, Lord Tennyson, available at <http://www.bartleby.com/42/643.html> (accessed January 7, 2003). Rita Dove, in her poem "Maple Valley Branch Library, 1967," writes, "There was so much to discover . . . equations elegant as a French twist, fractal geometry's unwinding maple leaf." Rita Dove, *On the Bus with Rosa Parks* (New York: W. W. Norton, 1999), p. 32.

23. *The Portable Blake,* ed. Alfred Kazin (New York: Viking, 1962), 150; Robert Bly, *Selected Poems* (New York: Harper and Row, 1986), 180. In another poem, "Snowfall in the Afternoon," Bly writes of seeing a world in blades of grass half-covered with snow: "And now the little houses of grass are growing dark." Robert Bly, *Eating the Honey of Words:*

New and Selected Poems (New York: Harper-Collins, 1999), 17.

24. "If My Boundary Stops Here" by Ruth Whitman. The lines are near the end of the poem, carved in granite outside the Back Bay/South End subway station in Boston, Mass.

25. Marie Ponsot, "Roundstone Cove," *The New Yorker,* Feb. 9, 1998, 45.

26. Frank Jones, "Excelsissimus," in *Gary Snyder: Dimensions of a Life,* ed. Jon Halper (San Francisco: Sierra Club, 1991), 288.

27. *Poems of Tennyson,* ed. Jerome H. Buckley (Cambridge: Riverside, 1958), 506.

28. Ch'iu-ti Liu, "A Tree that Travels with its Roots," *Parabola* 17, no. 1 (Feb. 1992): 68–69.

29. Johann Wolfgang von Goethe, "Zahme Xenien," in *Psychological Reflections: An Anthology of the Writings of C. G. Jung,* ed. Jolande Jacobi (New York: Harper and Row, 1961), 141. The thousandfold divided arches exhibit what mathematicians call "translational symmetry" but not scale invariance; the life joy streaming "from everything, from tiniest point to vastest star" is more of a full-fledged fractal.

30. Thomas Traherne, *Centuries, Poems, and Thanksgivings,* ed. H. M. Margoliouth (Oxford: Clarendon Press, 1958), vol. 1, The Third Century, #3, 111.

31. See Martin Buber, *I and Thou,* trans. Walter Kaufmann (New York: Scribner, 1970).

32. Traherne, *Centuries, Poems, and Thanksgivings,* vol. 1, The Second Century, #83, 98.

33. Traherne, *Centuries, Poems, and Thanksgivings,* vol. 1, The Third Century, #3, 111.

34. An eloquent psychologist exploring the background of psychoanalysis reached a similar conclusion. James Hillman, *The Myth of Analysis: Three Essays in Archetypal Psychology* (Evanston, Ill.: Northwestern University Press, 1997), 296. Also, in Islam there is a *hadith* which depicts God as saying, "I was a hidden treasure and wanted to be known," and so creation ensued. In this view the supreme reality must appear to people to be a perfect theophany. A sufi asks, "What is this theophany? The manifestation of Supreme Reality under the form of archetypes." Andrew Harvey, ed., *The Essential Mystics* (San Francisco: HarperSanFrancisco, 1996), 164. This is like

Spinoza's paradoxical view that the Infinite is not infinite until it becomes finite also.

35. Traherne, *Centuries, Poems, and Thanksgivings,* vol. 1, The Third Century, #55, 143. German philosopher-poet Novalis also noted an idea of paradise, which seems similar to Traherne's: "Every beloved object is the focus of a paradise." *Pollen and Fragments: Selected Poetry and Prose of Novalis,* trans. Arthur Versluis (Grand Rapids, Mich.: Phanes, 1989), 30.

36. Frank L. Kersnowski, *Conversations with Robert Graves* (Jackson: University Press of Mississippi, 1989), 103.

37. *The Poems of Emily Dickinson,* ed. Martha Dickinson Bianchi and Alfred Leete Hampson (Boston: Little, Brown, 1935), 332.

38. *Mencius,* trans. W. A. C. H. Dobson (Toronto: University of Toronto Press, 1963), 141–142. Much in chapter 6 of the *Teachings of Mencius* is on this topic; see especially the parable of Bull Mountain, paragraph 20.

39. The first half of this paragraph was inspired by "The Nature of the Human," lecture 8 of Brian Swimme's *Canticle to the Cosmos* (6 audiocassettes, Sounds True Audio, 1995). The second half was inspired by a performance of Margaret Edson's play *W;t.*

40. Oscar Wilde, *The Ballad of Reading Gaol* (London: Collins, 1969), 85–87. Also published in Oscar Wilde, *Poems* (New York: Boni and Liveright, n.d.), 271.

41. Mahmud ibn 'Abd al-Karim Shabistari, *The Secret Rose Garden of Sa'd ud Din Mahmud Shabistari,* trans. Florence Lederer (1920; reprint, Grand Rapids, Mich.: Phanes, 1989), 52–53.

42. There are images of mysterious light and infinity in the Qur'an, for example in sura 24.

43. Riff: The landscape of the Mandelbrot set can be transmuted into a grasshopper's eye or dragonfly's wing, with its rainbow ocean of life; and that ocean is only one of many on the earth mirror, where each waterdrop conceals a hundred more, and many scales glide over, and under, and through each other, yet appear to be a landscape stable enough to bore many cynics.

44. Quoted in Harvey, ed., *The Essential Mystics,* 164–165.

45. St. Teresa of Avila, *The Interior Castle, or, The Mansions,* trans. "A Benedictine of Stanbrook" (London: Thomas Baker, 1946), 23–24.

46. Masao Abe, ed., *A Zen Life: D. T. Suzuki Remembered* (New York: Weatherhill, 1986), 30.

47. "The Zenrin," in *A Zen Forest: Sayings of the Masters,* compiled and translated by Soiku Shigematsu (New York: Weatherhill, 1981), 100, #923.

48. Herbert Guenther, *Ecstatic Spontaneity: Saraha's Three Cycles of Doha* (Berkeley: Asian Humanities, 1993), 41.

49. Kelly Cherry, *God's Loud Hand* (Baton Rouge: Louisiana State University Press, 1993), 46.

50. *The Annie Dillard Reader* (New York: HarperCollins, 1994), 453–454.

51. Charles Wright, "Paesaggio Nottorno," *Negative Blue: Selected Later Poems* (New York: Farrar, Straus and Giroux, 2000), 59.

52. William Aiken, "Fractals," *Poetry* 165, no. 1 (Oct. 1994): 19.

53. Brian Swimme, *The Universe is a Green Dragon: A Cosmic Creation Story* (Santa Fe, N.M.: Bear, 1984), 132, 157.

54. I have heard Jean Houston speak at conferences and in a radio interview on NPR. The ideas in this paragraph are based on my notes on those discussions. Houston has researched and written books on consciousness, creativity, and peacemaking. Jean Houston, *The Possible Human: A Course in Extending Your Mental and Creative Abilities* (Los Angeles: J. P. Tarcher, 1982) and *Life Force: The Psychohistorical Recovery of the Self* (Wheaton, Ill.: Quest, 1993).

55. Natalie Angier, *The Beauty of the Beastly: New Views on the Nature of Life* (Boston: Houghton Mifflin, 1995), 209.

56. A. M. Allchin, ed., *Landscapes of Glory: Daily Readings with Thomas Traherne* (Harrisburg, Pa.: Morehouse, 1989), 57.

57. Italo Calvino, *Invisible Cities,* trans. William Weaver (New York: Harcourt Brace Jovanovitch, 1972), 8.

58. E. M. Forster, *A Passage to India* (New York: Harcourt Brace Jovanovich, 1984), 163.

59. Pinhas Sadeh, *Jewish Folktales,* trans. Hillel Halkin (New York: Doubleday, 1989), 2.

60. David Rothenberg, *Sudden Music: Improvisation, Sound, Nature* (Athens: University of Georgia Press, 2002), 20.

61. Jonathan Swift is famous for the fractal images in his verse on fleas written in 1733: "So, Naturalists, observe, a Flea / Hath smaller

Fleas that on him prey / and these have smaller Fleas to bite 'em, / And so proceed *ad infinitum*." In our century, mathematician Lewis Richardson wrote in 1926, "Big whorls have little whorls, / Which feed on their velocity; / And little whorls have lesser whorls, / And so on to viscosity." These verses are quoted and discussed in Benoit B. Mandelbrot, *The Fractal Geometry of Nature* (New York: W. H. Freeman, 1982), 402.

62. John Allen Paulos, *Beyond Numeracy: Ruminations of a Numbers Man* (New York: Vintage, 1992), 107.

63. Ibid., 110.

64. Dinita Smith, "Fresh Look at a Syntax Skewer," *New York Times,* June 9, 1999, B1, 4.

65. Argyros, *A Blessed Rage for Order,* 316.

66. Steven Johnston, "Strange Attraction," *Lingua Franca* 6, no. 3 (March–April 1996): 50. For the ideas of someone able to see the composer's or writer's "free play as a self-organizing system," see Stephen Nachmanovitch, *Free Play: Improvisation in Life and Art* (Los Angeles: Jeremy P. Tarcher, 1990), 102.

67. Stein, "Composition as Explanation," 513, 516.

68. The South Indian singer-saint Tyagaraja (d. 1847) repeated his Rama mantra for twenty years and attained a vision of Rama. He was inspired to compose masterpieces in praise of Rama, developing the art of variations on the refrain (*pallavi*) of the songs—repetition with gracefully unfolding nuances.

69. To the nursery rhyme Buffy St. Marie, in a song, adds images of a crooked politician and his crooked smile, which he uses to hide a style that is also crooked.

70. Robert Louis Stevenson, *A Child's Garden of Verses* (New York: Crown, 1985), 65.

STRAND SIX

1. Clifford Geertz, "Blurred Genres: The Refiguration of Social Thought," *American Scholar* 49, no. 2 (spring 1980), 165.

2. In both Egyptian and Greek mythology the invention of the lyre is associated with stumbling over a tortoise carapace and discovering the sounds that can be drawn from it.

The art of scrimshaw is also a good example—off-duty sailors created beautiful objects (sometimes representing whales) from the violently won bones of whales, transmuting nature to artifice.

3. Jane Jacobs, *The Nature of Economies* (New York: Modern Library, 2000), is one recent example. Jacobs draws on anthropology, ecology, sociobiology, and the history of economics, seeking a unifying theory by looking at particulars. Michael Pollan explores in a refreshing way how plants manipulate people in *The Botany of Desire: A Plant's Eye View of the World* (New York: Random House, 2001).

4. "In wildness is the preservation of the world. Every tree sends its fibres forth in search of the wild. The cities import it at any price. Men plow and sail for it. From the forests and wilderness come the tonics and barks which brace mankind. Our ancestors were savages. . . . The founders of every State which has risen to eminence have drawn their nourishment and vigor from a . . . wild source." *The Writings of Henry David Thoreau,* vol. 9 (Boston: Riverside, 1906), 534, 539.

5. *The Portable Blake,* ed. Alfred Kazin (New York: Viking, 1962), 602.

6. Noel Boaz discusses White's thought and his own in *Eco Homo* (New York: Basic, 1997), 219.

7. Ibid.

8.. Jürgen Moltmann, *The Future of Creation* (Philadelphia: Fortress, 1977), 129.

9. See, for example, Theodore Roszak, *The Voice of the Earth: An Exploration in Ecopsychology* (New York: Simon and Schuster, 1992).

10. The work of Brian Swimme and Thomas Berry, among others, is remedying this.

11. Indigenous peoples have many ways of relating to earth, with their own often unwritten codes enacted in their lives. Traditional peoples also often have wisdom about the relations of nature to man and earth to culture. *Feng shui* is an ancient Chinese art of harmonizing human life and habitat with nature, sensitive to energy flows, interplay of natural elements, etc. See, for example, Eva Wong, *Feng-Shui* (Boston: Shambhala, 1996). In modern America Wendell Berry, Wes Jackson, and Gary Snyder are among those concerned with these issues.

12. Loren Eiseley wrote about this in his essay "The Cosmic Orphan" in the fifteenth edition of the *Encyclopedia Britannica*, available at <http://www.britannica.com/original/print?content_id=1325> (accessed January 7,

2003). See Gregory Bateson, *Mind and Nature: A Necessary Unity* (New York: Dutton, 1979). Fritjof Capra, *The Web of Life: A New Scientific Understanding of Living Systems* (New York: Anchor, 1996), makes good points about Bateson's accomplishments and limits. See pages 53–56, 273–274, and 305–308.

13. Huston Smith, *Forgotten Truth: The Primordial Tradition* (New York: Harper and Row, 1976), 143. The points Smith made in this book grow more relevant each year.

14. *The Selected Writings of Ralph Waldo Emerson* (New York: Modern Library, 1968), 49. Novalis wrote, "We know only insofar as we make." *Pollen and Fragments: Selected Poetry and Prose of Novalis,* trans. Arthur Versluis (Grand Rapids, Mich.: Phanes, 1989), 65.

15. "Man," in *The Poems of George Herbert* (London: Oxford University Press, 1964), 82.

16. Gary Snyder, "Nature's Writing," in *The True Subject: Writers on Life and Craft,* ed. Kurt Brown (St. Paul: Gray Wolf, 1993), 19.

17. Loren Eiseley, *The Unexpected Universe* (San Diego: Harcourt Brace Jovanovich, 1985), 165.

18. Ibid., 169.

19. Some of the factors in the sympathetic and parasympathetic nervous systems involved in these states are considered by William H. McNeill, *Keeping Together in Time* (Cambridge, Mass.: Harvard University Press, 1995), 6–8.

20. Eiseley, *The Unexpected Universe,* 162–163.

21. George Seielstad, *Cosmic Ecology: The View from the Outside In* (Berkeley and Los Angeles: University of California Press, 1983), 158. Gregory Bateson also discusses this point throughout *Mind and Nature.* As genes are to DNA, "memes" are to culturally learned identities. The term was introduced by Richard Dawkins in *The Selfish Gene* (New York: Oxford University Press, 1976).

22. Riff on fire, flames, and light: The use of fire marked a new stage of life for the human being, the sole creature able to handle fire. Ancient campfires; home fireplaces; altar rituals; artistic portrayals of fire, sun, and lightning; poems on burning energies; all illuminate the human condition. "At the heart of the matter fire is found," the magical flame of life. If we consider what there is to be known about fire, as with Wordsworth's small flower in the cranny, vast meanings are illuminated. Fire's nature, aspects, forms, and symbolic associa-

tions lead us across a gamut from "ordinary" flame, the modern reductionist outlook, which did not exist for archaic man, to the divinity—symbol of ultimate reality—as found in Vedic Agni symbolism and the fire of the Aryans who went into Persia and developed the tradition of Zoroastrianism. Frits Staal's compendium on the Agnicayana ritual develops the Vedic ritual meanings of fire, and the *Katha Upanishad* and the Eleusinian mysteries of Greece reveal deep human spiritual experience in terms of fire. Frits Staal, with C. V. Somayajipad and M. Itti Ravi Nambudiri, *Agni: The Vedic Ritual of the Fire Altar* (Berkeley: Asian Humanities, 1983). Gaston Bachelard's *The Psychoanalysis of Fire* (Boston: Beacon, 1964) illuminates structures of fire's meanings for humans from many cultures.

23. Alfred North Whitehead, *Science and the Modern World* (New York: Macmillan, 1959), 128.

24. Edward O. Wilson, *On Human Nature* (Cambridge, Mass.: Harvard University Press, 1978), 199. See also Dawkins, *The Selfish Gene.* On the differences and similarities between humans and other mammals, see Wolfgang Schad, *Man and Mammals: Toward a Biology of Form,* trans. Carroll Scherer (Garden City, N.Y.: Waldorf, 1977), 276.

25. Edward O. Wilson, *On Human Nature,* 188.

26. Ibid.

27. See William Irwin Thompson, "The Cultural Implications of the New Biology," 11–34; Gregory Bateson, "Men Are Grass: Metaphor and the World of Mental Process," 37–47; Francisco Varella, "Laying Down a Path In Walking," 48–64; and Humberto Maturana, "Everything Is Said by an Observer," 65–82; all in William Irwin Thompson, ed., *Gaia, A Way of Knowing: Political Implications of the New Biology* (Hudson, N.Y.: Lindisfarne, 1987).

28. Edward O. Wilson, *On Human Nature,* 192.

29. Ibid., 176ff.

30. Ibid., 177.

31. Improvisation is important. Only by trying things does life figure out what it can do; and try and try again it does. The wisdom in living organisms is astounding; parts self-organize and sort themselves out: beak cells from a developing chicken injected in the jaw of a mouse become teeth.

32. Jean-François Lyotard, *The Postmod-*

ern Condition: A Report on Knowledge, trans. Geoff Bennington and Brian Massumi (Minneapolis: University of Minnesota Press, 1984), 13, 47–48.

33. Edward O. Wilson, *On Human Nature,* 201.

34. Ibid.

35. Other scientists and thinkers capable of this deeper vision include Teilhard de Chardin, Fritjof Capra, David Bohm, and Ken Wilbur.

36. Whitehead, *Science and the Modern World,* 165.

37. William Irwin Thompson, "The Cultural Implications of the New Biology," in *Gaia, A Way of Knowing: Political Implications of the New Biology,* ed. William Irwin Thompson (Hudson, N.Y.: Lindisfarne, 1987), 11–33.

38. Ibid., 20. For a very useful overview of the contributions of Maturana, Varela, Bateson, and others, see Capra, *The Web of Life.*

39. In his taped lecture series *Canticle to the Cosmos* (6 audiocassettes, Sounds True Audio, 1995), Brian Swimme eloquently brings out some of the deepest implications of scientific discoveries regarding the history and nature of the cosmos; and Henry Stapp, in *Mind, Matter, and Quantum Mechanics* (New York: Springer-Verlag, 1993), delves deeply and responsibly into issue of mind-matter patterns and relationships. See also Pierre Teilhard de Chardin, *Human Energy,* trans. J. M. Cohen (New York: Harcourt Brace Jovanovich, 1971), especially 20–42.

40. Whitehead, *Science and the Modern World,* 176. Whitehead's process philosophy seems to have a fractal-like sensibility at some points, since the whole is in the interconnected parts. See pages 32–33 and 98, for example. "In a certain sense, everything is everywhere at all times. For every location involves an aspect of itself in every other location. Thus every spatio-temporal standpoint mirrors the world." Ibid., 87.

41. Ralph Abraham, *Chaos Gaia Eros* (San Francisco: HarperSanFrancisco, 1994); Stuart A. Kauffman, *The Origins of Order: Self-Organization and Selection in Evolution* (New York: Oxford University Press, 1993); and John Briggs and F. David Peat, *Turbulent Mirror: An Illustrated Guide to Chaos Theory and the Science of Wholeness* (New York: Harper and Row, 1989).

42. The boundary between two or more attractors in a dynamical system acts as a threshold governing various processes; each attractor is said to have a basin, somewhat like a river with a watershed area. Each basin has a boundary within which the attractor is active. For more on this, see James Gleick, *Chaos: Making a New Science* (New York: Penguin, 1988), 233–236.

43. Gleick, *Chaos,* 299. See also Ayal Spitz, "Implementation of the Fractal Reconstructive Memory Model," undergraduate honors thesis, Department of Computer Science, Brandeis University, 1996; J. Richard Eiser, *Attitudes, Chaos, and the Connectionist Mind* (Oxford: Blackwell, 1994), especially 153–213.

44. John Allen Paulos, *Beyond Numeracy: Ruminations of a Numbers Man* (New York: Vintage, 1992), 86.

45. Gleick, *Chaos,* 299–300. Stephen Jay Gould presents an alternative view in *Full House: The Spread of Excellence from Plato to Darwin* (New York: Harmony, 1996). For a brief description of this see Michael Frame's fractals Web site, at <http://classes.yale.edu/math190b/Fractals/Panorama/Nature/Ammonites/Ammonites.html> (accessed November 5, 2002).

46. Quoted in M. L. Rosenthal, *The Poet's Art* (New York: W. W. Norton, 1987), 152.

47. Bateson, *Mind and Nature,* 13.

48. In the glossary of *Mind and Nature,* 230, Bateson defines "stochastic" this way: "(Greek, *stochazein,* to shoot with a bow at a target; that is, to scatter events in a partially random manner, some of which achieve a preferred outcome) If a sequence of events combines a random component with a selective process so that only certain outcomes of the random are allowed to endure, that sequence is said to be *stochastic.*"

49. Bateson, *Mind and Nature,* 21. American poet Robinson Jeffers is a voice for the oneness of human and natural life. In a verse put in the mouth of Orestes, Jeffers wanted to express "the feeling . . . the certitude—that the world, the universe, is one being, a single organism, one great life that includes all life and all things, and is so beautiful it must be loved and reverenced, and in moments of mystical vision we identify ourselves with it." In "Natural Music" he said the sounds of a river, the bombardment of cities, and a young girl's dancing and longing for love and happiness form a single natural music—the cycle of hu-

man history is a sound in the wind—it's all part of one language. *Rock and Hawk: A Selection of Shorter Poems by Robinson Jeffers,* ed. Robert Hass (New York: Random House, 1987), xxxiii, xvii, 3.

50. Bateson, *Mind and Nature,* 48.

51. Ibid., 149.

52. Ibid., 219. Alfred North Whitehead uses the terms "spirit of change" and "spirit of conservation." Whitehead, *Science and the Modern World,* 179.

53. Bateson, *Mind and Nature,* 221.

54. Jonathan Edwards, "Notes on Mind," in *Puritan Sage: Collected Writings of Jonathan Edwards,* ed. Vergilius Ferm (New York: Library, 1953), 26–27.

55. Albert Einstein, "The Religious Spirit of Science," in *Ideas and Opinions* (New York: Crown, 1982), 38.

56. Octavio Paz, *Alternating Current* (New York: Viking, 1973), 62.

57. Gleick, *Chaos,* 261.

58. See Francis H. Cook, *Hua-Yen Buddhism: The Jewel Net of Indra* (1977; reprint, Delhi: Sri Satguru, 1994), 14, 51–55.

59. James Jeans, *The Mysterious Universe* (Cambridge: Cambridge University Press, 1948), 13, 115, 123–124. "The universe begins to look more like a great thought than a great machine" (137). Jeans was not the only one to observe this. English astronomer Sir Arthur Eddington (d. 1944) made a similar remark.

60. Gleick, *Chaos,* 152.

61. Riff on this: Some have excluded themselves from thinking about underlying pattern or meaning, and expect others to do likewise. They take for granted the physical universals, such as the air they breathe and the water they drink, as if doing so were the most rational thing in the world. But what if in human works, in thought and behavior, complexity is integrally woven in simplicity, all held by, and owing existence to, consciousness? What if the shapes of life reveal the flow of time's changes dynamically, like folds in Mt. Olympus and the Himalayas, and the course of flow has longings and laws to fulfill? What if a simple pattern opens a path to ask new questions about the universals which hold all the particulars? The bee's dance of discovery is like the visionary's song, leading to new experience for others. A poet can make suggestions, and a naturalist write essays; one does not need to be a credentialed scientist to remind us that

orange flames and green leaves coincide in their flowpoint shapes, that there are veins of thought, of water, of ore.

62. Thomas Kuhn, *The Structure of Scientific Revolutions* (Chicago: University of Chicago Press, 1974).

63. Gregory Bateson and Mary Catherine Bateson, *Angels Fear: Towards an Epistemology of the Sacred* (New York: Macmillan, 1987), 8. This point is made well in Henri Bortoft, *The Wholeness of Nature: Goethe's Way toward a Science of Conscious Participation in Nature* (Hudson, N.Y.: Lindisfarne, 1996).

64. Roszak, *The Voice of the Earth,* 171.

65. Riff on the signs of the past in the human, all that is in the bones, in the blood, in the cells and DNA: We remember old tropical rhythms in our afternoon energy trough. We recapitulate tides and dawns and dusks, hungers and alarms and excitements. A soul encompassing all creatures, like the ark, meanders through the waters of time. Goethe helps us consider the whole of mammal life which humans represent.

66. Gary Snyder, *No Nature: New and Selected Poems* (New York: Pantheon, 1992), v.

67. Ibid., 381.

68. Charles Peirce, "Issues of Pragmatism," in *Collected Papers of Charles S. Peirce,* ed. Charles Hartshorn and Paul Weiss (Cambridge, Mass.: Harvard University Press, 1934), vol. 5, 505–506.

69. E. L. Grant Watson, *The Mystery of Physical Life* (1964; reprint, Hudson, N.Y.: Lindisfarne, 1992). This book, written before these new ideas about biological processes had begun to be taken seriously, offers ideas on understanding natural processes which are still useful. Watson writes about how gestalt patterns in nature relate to our own subjective tuning-in sensibilities. He gives as examples Melville, Blixen, Darwin, Hardy, and other observers of nature who "By their capacity of observing and awakening senses [were] able to relate the phenomenal with the noumenal as true naturalists should do." Such explorers, in Watson's view, are involved in the "unconscious springs of being," not just the calculative mind, and they "enter into the unconscious of those [living beings in nature] who are to be worked on" (133, 117).

70. Thomas Berry, *Creative Energy* (San Francisco: Sierra Club, 1996), 84–85.

71. M. F. Barnsley, *Fractals Everywhere* (San Francisco: Morgan Kaufmann, 1993).

72. Alexander Argyros, *A Blessed Rage for Order: Deconstruction, Evolution, and Chaos* (Ann Arbor: University of Michigan Press, 1991), 342.

73. J. G. Herder presented his ideas in his 1778 work *Plastik,* recently published in English as *Sculpture: Some Observations on Shape and Form from Pygmalion's Creative Dream,* ed. and trans. Jason Geiger (Chicago: University of Chicago Press, 2002).

74. Burke, *Knowledge Web,* 173.

75. Barry Lopez, from *Arctic Dreams: Imagination and Desire in a Northern Landscape* (New York: Scribner, 1986), excerpted in *A Hunter's Heart: Honest Essays on Blood Sport,* ed. David Petersen (New York: Henry Holt, 1996), 314.

76. Ibid., 313.

77. Ibid. Lopez is paraphrasing Albert Schweitzer. Terry Tempest Williams is another author writing well of landscapes and human lives and how they're intertwined. Terry Tempest Williams, *Desert Quartet: An Erotic Landscape* (New York: Pantheon, 1995), and *Refuge: An Unnatural History of Family and Place* (New York: Vintage, 1992).

78. Robert Bly, "Finding an Old Ant Mansion," in *What Have I Ever Lost by Dying?* (New York: HarperCollins, 1992), 26–27.

79. Will Durant, *The Story of Philosophy: The Lives and Opinions of the Greater Philosophers* (New York: Pocket, 1961), 102, 116, 177, 268, 336.

80. Ibid., 391.

81. John A. Garraty and Peter Gay, eds. *The Columbia History of the World* (New York: Harper and Row, 1972), 716.

82. Descartes is not the only thinker to make intellectual breakthroughs in bedridden isolation. Ignatius Loyola was inspired by readings he undertook while trying to regain his health, Pascal had his aches and pains, Darwin needed the excuse of illness to complete his work, Steven Hawking has his problems—a million people having fun may discover nothing, while a single focused soul in crisis forges a critical insight or evolves a new talent. Humans must have known this for millennia: some ancient hunter-gatherer graves contain full-grown malformed or crippled skeletons, suggesting that the crippled were cared for by the tribe, just as the blind story-teller or mu-sician was. Marcel Proust was a shut-in, a man smoking in bed, following the drift of deep memories and associations. Mark Twain did much of his writing in bed. French mathematician Gaston Julia, a pioneer in the study of iteration with complex numbers, visualized their fractal recursive nature over the course of a year in bed while recuperating from injuries suffered during World War I. Nobel laureate in literature Rabindranath Tagore endured a long confinement indoors while growing up in Calcutta. Asthmatic Jerry Garcia stayed home in bed much of the time as a child, spending more undisturbed time reading there than most children. Martin Scorsese was also kept inside because of asthma, and developed a more intense interior life. Einstein said the best job for a young theoretical scientist would be to work as a lighthouse keeper. Solitude and enhancement of powers by illness is also a perennial shamanic theme. Creativity sometimes thrives in the undisturbed introversion of sickbed solitude. "The isolated part becomes whole"; mysterious powers of a whole self can be activated in subtle unconscious vision, as in the case of idiot savants, or as discoveries are made in dreams. Timothy Leary, *Psychedelic Prayers after the Tao Te Ching* (New Hyde Park, New York: University, 1966), III-6.

83. Charles D. Minahen, *Vortex/t: The Poetics of Turbulence* (University Park: Pennsylvania State University Press, 1992), 71–84. Some say Descartes was told in his dream, by an angel, that the conquest of nature could be accomplished by measure and number. Ralph Abraham, Terence McKenna, and Rupert Sheldrake, *Trialogues at the Edge of the West: Chaos, Creativity, and the Resacralization of the World* (Santa Fe, N.M.: Bear, 1992), 95.

84. Descartes's vortex theory generated many ideas about "the emergence of heavenly bodies from primitive celestial vortices." He imagined the cosmos as pockmarked with unstable whirlpools of energy which could draw some masses of matter into tighter spaces than others. In this turbulence-sensitive view matter originates "as a plasma-like whirlpool, condenses into a furious sun, calms into a jiggling 'terrela' [bright whirligig gas-mass or planet]" then settles into a planetary lump." He envisioned a dynamic system of powerful vortices, producing our planetary system of sun, moon, earth, etc. Gabriel Daniel, a late-seventeenth-century commentator on Descartes, amusingly

speculated that Descartes's death had not been final, but that his spirit had been drawn up into a higher vortex via the swirls of his tobacco smoke. K. L. Cope, "Evolution of the Solar and Planetary Vortices," in *The Pattern Book: Fractals, Art, and Nature,* ed. Clifford Pickover (Singapore: World Scientific, 1995), 3.

85. Bortoft, *The Wholeness of Nature,* 184.

86. James Hillman and Michael Ventura, *We've Had a Hundred Years of Psychotherapy—And the World's Getting Worse* (San Francisco: HarperSanFrancisco, 1993), 4.

87. Similarly, in tantric yoga, there is a *chakra,* a center of higher energy or soul center of consciousness, between and a little above the eyes, which, when activated, is like a "third eye" of wisdom in the yogi.

88. Bortoft, *The Wholeness of Nature,* 375. See also 179–190.

89. C. G. Jung, "The Primordial Images," in *Psychological Reflections: An Anthology of the Writings of C. G. Jung,* ed. Jolande Jacobi (New York: Harper and Row, 1961), 129.

90. Ibid., 125. See also 118.

91. Ibid., 129.

92. Ibid., 131.

93. *The Selected Writings of Ralph Waldo Emerson,* ed. Brooks Atkinson (New York: The Modern Library, 1968), 229.

94. Gilles Deleuze, *Difference and Repetition,* trans. Paul Patton (New York: Columbia University Press, 1994), 83–84.

STRAND SEVEN

1. *Thoreau on Man and Nature,* compiled by Arthur G. Volkman (Mt. Vernon, N.Y.: Peter Pauper, 1960), 18.

2. David Bohm, *On Creativity,* ed. Lee Nichol (London: Routledge, 1998), 61.

3. Bertrand Russell, in his essay "Mysticism and Logic," opens his thoughts on this theme with "Metaphysics, or the attempt to conceive the world as a whole by means of thought, has been developed, from the first, by the union and conflict of two very different human impulses, the one urging men towards mysticism, the other urging them towards science." *Mysticism and Logic, and Other Essays* (New York: Doubleday, 1957), 1.

4. C. G. Jung, *Aion: Researches into the Phenomenology of the Self,* vol. 9, part 2 of *The Collected Works of C. G. Jung,* ed. Herbert Read,

Michael Fordham, and Gerhard Adler (New York: Pantheon, 1959), 222.

5. A Somali proverb emphasizes the cracked quality: "Me and my clan against the world. Me and my family against my clan. Me and my brother against my family. Me against my brother." One can also picture a person divided within himself.

6. The mandalas made by the psyche are symbols of order. "Unity and totality stand at the highest point on the scale of objective values because their symbols can no longer be distinguished from the imago Dei." Jung, *Aion,* 31.

7. Paraphrased from C. G. Jung, *Man and His Symbols* (Garden City, N.Y.: Doubleday, 1964), 207.

8. "Finally the self, on account of its empirical peculiarities, proves to be the *eidos* behind the supreme ideas of unity and totality that are inherent in all monotheistic and monistic systems." Jung, *Aion,* 34.

9. C. G. Jung, *Civilization in Transition,* trans. R. F. C. Hull, vol. 10 of *The Collected Works of C. G. Jung,* ed. Herbert Read, Michael Fordham, and Gerhard Adler (New York: Pantheon, 1964), 25. A dream can be a "little germ of the new which would make [man] at one with the world and himself. . . . All consciousness separates; but in dreams we put on the likeness of that more universal, truer, more eternal man dwelling in the darkness of primordial night. There he is still in the whole, and the whole is in him, indistinguishable from nature and bare of all egohood. It is from these all-uniting depths that the dream arises . . . so flowerlike is it in its candour . . . it makes us blush for the deceitfulness of our lives." Ibid., 144–145.

10. David Bohm makes an interesting point about this, noting that the words "organize" and "energy" are related. The Greek *ergon* comes from the verb "to work." "Energy" means "working within" and if we imagine the movement of life as an organizing energy working within the dynamics of an organism's organs, cells, atoms, elementary particles, and ultimately, Bohm maintains, merging with the universal field movement, this will help us get a sense of what it means to think of flow as the primary activity of this organizing energy of coordinated growth and ongoing life of organisms and evolution's new forms. Bohm, *On Creativity,* 79.

11. The English word "sex" derives from the Latin *secare* "to cut through" and indicates a split in human wholeness; often an illusion or ruse is involved in the dynamics of attraction, driven by unconscious desire to stitch back all to One again—or at least that's one way to contemplate affinities.

12. This is a Vedic image: "All-mover, all-conqueror, conveyer of sacrifice, the Child, ever aiding, he assumes great power. What he meets he grasps, and, newly born, advances vehemently. . . . He is a being of flood and forest who passes aloft." *Rig Veda*, 1.145.3–5, as edited and translated by Raimundo Panikkar, with the collaboration of N. Shanta et al., *The Vedic Experience, Mantramanjari: An Anthology of the Vedas for Modern Man and Contemporary Celebration* (New Delhi: Motilal Banarsidass, 1994), 143.

13. Some of these archetypal images of the Child, who as an archetype unites opposites, are found in Jung's "The Psychology of the Child Archetype," in *Essays on a Science of Mythology*, by C. G. Jung and C. Kerenyi, trans. R. F. C. Hull (Princeton, N.J.: Princeton University Press, 1969), 70–100, esp. 93–97.

14. Ibid., 98.

15. Paraphrased from Charles H. Kahn, *The Art and Thought of Heraclitus: An Edition of the Fragments with Translation and Commentary* (Cambridge: Cambridge University Press, 1979), 85. See also fragment 36, page 45: "Not on my authority, but on that of truth, it is wise for you to accept the fact that all things are one."

16. Andrew Harvey, ed., *The Essential Mystics* (San Francisco: HarperSanFrancisco, 1996), 116. "Draughts" is the game of checkers.

17. Plato, *The Sophist*, 249D, quoted in James Hillman, *The Myth of Analysis: Three Essays in Archetypal Psychology* (Evanston, Ill.: Northwestern University Press, 1997), 263.

18. Jung, *Civilization in Transition*, 465.

19. *The Way of Life According to Laotzu*, trans. Witter Bynner (New York: Capricorn, 1962), 37.

20. Gary Snyder, *Earth House Hold* (San Francisco: City Lights, 1969), 129. The force of life, like the Child, needs nursing, as James Hillman notes in *The Myth of Analysis*, 276.

21. According to legend, en route to being martyred, Christopher (d. 364) prayed that those who looked upon him might not be harmed by storm, fire, or earthquake, and his image became widespread because people believed that any seeing him on that day would "not faint or fail." E. A. Greene, *Saints and Their Symbols* (London: Sir Isaac Pitman and Sons, 1924), 60–61.

22. *A Barfield Reader: Selections from the Writings of Owen Barfield,* ed. G. B. Tennyson (Middletown, Conn.: Wesleyan University Press, 1999), 153.

23. Islam also speaks of God in his most beautiful form as a child. "The Prophet said: I saw my Lord as a beardless youth with curly hair in a green robe." In another *hadith* it is said that God is beautiful and that he likes beauty. The child is free, playful, beautiful, whole—innocent means unharmed and harmless, qualities which seem to make one one with One. Hellmut Ritter, *Das Meer der Seele: Mensch, Welt und Gott in den Geschichten des Furiduddin 'Attar* (Leiden: Brill, 1978), 445ff., quoted in Josef van Ess, *The Youthful God: Anthropomorphism in Early Islam* (Tempe: Arizona State University Press, 1989), 10.

24. Kerenyi, "The Primordial Child in Primordial Times," in Jung and Kerenyi, *Essays on a Science of Mythology*, 67.

25. *Chuang Tzu*, chapter 2, verse 1. My phrasing based on several translations; see, for instance, Chuang-tzu, *Chuang Tzu: Genius of the Absurd,* arranged from the work of James Legge by Clae Waltham (New York: Ace, 1971).

26. *Chuang Tzu*, II.6. My phrasing based on several translations.

27. Chuang-tzu, *Chuang Tzu: Genius of the Absurd*, 253.

28. Jesus also played with scale. A person whose faith is as a grain of mustard seed can move mountains (Matthew 17:20; see also Luke 17:6); the faultfinder sees the mote in another's eye but not the beam in his own (Matthew 7:3); the blind guides strain at the gnat but swallow the camel (Matthew 23:24); etc.

29. Hillman, *The Myth of Analysis*, 275.

30. Some of the images in this paragraph, especially at the beginning and end, are suggested by Jung and Kerenyi, *Essays on a Science of Mythology*, 79, 83.

31. Henry David Thoreau, *Faith in a Seed: The Dispersion of Seeds and Other Late Natural History Writings*, ed. Bradley P. Dean (Washington, D.C.: Island Press for Shearwater Books, 1993), 127.

32. *Sathya Sai Speaks: Discourses of Bhagavan Sri Sathya Sai Baba,* compiled from notes taken by N. Kasturi, vol. 7 (Tustin, Calif.: Sri Sathya Sai Baba Book Center of America, 1975), 186.

33. From Bonaventure's prologue to his *Breviloquium,* quoted in R. J. Schoeck, *Intertextuality and Renaissance Texts* (Bamberg: H. Kaiser-Verlag, 1984), 83.

34. *The Way of Life According to Laotzu,* 47.

35. Avalanches—of snowflakes or sand grains, for example—are scale-free. Chunks fragment down in unpredictable self-similar fragments—5, 50, 500, 5000, 50,000, 500,000: order accrues at a large scale by combination of a multitude of parts, "many chaotic small-scale events that hover on the brink of instability." John D. Barrow, *The Artful Universe* (Oxford: Oxford University Press, 1995), 244.

Life's like that—extinct lives fall out of ecosystems, while complex adaptive systems on the edge of order and chaos, engaged in the best of each, are possibilities that can be selected for trial from the roiling chaos, and determinism's even keel and controlling rudder set a definite trajectory.

36. William Burroughs humorously coined the term "spermament." William S. Burroughs, *Naked Lunch* (New York: Grove Weidenfeld, 1991), 86.

37. See Ron Eglash, *African Fractals: Modern Computing and Indigenous Design* (New Brunswick, N.J.: Rutgers University Press, 1999). It is interesting that aboriginal people of Australia sometimes use ovals within ovals as a motif in their art.

38. The Italian physicist and chemist Amedeo Avogadro (1776–1856) posited that gaseous elements could be composed of molecules with more than one atom. In 1811, he postulated that equal volumes of gas at the same temperature and pressure contain equal numbers of molecules. The number of molecules in a mole of any substance (a mass in grams equal to the substance's atomic weight) is also constant, and this number is called "Avogadro's Constant": 6.02 times 10 to the 23rd power. Benoit Mandelbrot discusses fractal models of galaxy clusters and how diamond mines and stars are distributed in similar clusterings. Benoit B. Mandelbrot, *The Fractal Geometry of Nature* (New York: W. H. Freeman, 1982), 93–94.

39. M theory (in which the M stands for "mystery," "magic," "mother of all theories," or "membrane"—a surface traced out by a string pushed through another dimension), or superstring theory, is a conceptual approach which some theorists think may lead to a "theory of everything" which can include quantum physics and gravity theory. Edward Witten, a well-respected string theorist, in 1995 explained a mega–string theory which shows the connections among various versions of string theory and merges them in a single framework. For a discussion exploring some of these issues see Brian Greene, *The Elegant Universe: Superstrings, Hidden Dimensions, and the Quest for the Ultimate Theory* (New York: W. W. Norton, 1999). Greene, as he says in *The Elegant Universe,* is not a fan of chaos theory.

40. See Ary L. Goldberger, David R. Rigney, and Bruce J. West, "Chaos and Fractals in Human Physiology," *Scientific American* 262, no. 2 (Feb. 1990): 42–49.

41. John Noble Wilford, "Superclusters of Galaxies Shed New Light on Cosmic Architecture," *New York Times,* Jan. 26, 1999, D2.

42. Brian Swimme, *The Hidden Heart of the Cosmos: Humanity and the New Story* (Maryknoll, N.Y.: Orbis, 1996), 112. In 1963 I intuitively realized this and wrote lines at the East River in New York about how each driver over the bridge, each tugboat captain, each seagull, etc. feels like the center of the universe. One as a network of all ones. Riff on the spirals of One: The spirals of One are curving around; the many curve out of the One and curve back into One. The many different spirals twist from One; all the different levels turning and returning are not the same and not separate. All spring from the One and are indeterminate—wrapping around toward fulfillment yet harboring more of the same within, full filaments, the One's infinite potential, "Holy the Firm' "s invisible firmament. The spirals seed more spirals, spores bearing new twisting spores, ideas breeding curling ideas, all One all many at once, curlicuing tendrils, levels of spirals making up spirals making up spirals of DNA. The fluke of creativity, perfectly planned, curls out of itself as if on cue. Riffs of spirals curving round . . .

43. Ellen M. Chen, *The Tao Te Ching: A New Translation with Commentary* (New York: Paragon House, 1989), chapter 10, 78.

44. Ibid., chapter 14, 88–89.

45. Ibid., chapter 22, 112.

46. Ibid., chapter 39, 149–150.

47. Ibid., chapter 28, 124.

48. *Rig Veda*, I.164.6, 46.

49. *Rig Veda*, III.54.8–9.

50. Compare Heraclitus on the subtle fire: "The thunderbolt steers all things," etc. Kahn, *The Art and Thought of Heraclitus,* fragment 119, page 83.

51. *Rig Veda*, VIII.58.2.

52. *Rig Veda*, X.114.5ab.

53. *The Atharva Veda,* trans. Devi Chand (New Delhi: Munshiram Manoharlal, 1982), XIII.4.12–13.

54. *Brihadaranyaka Upanishad,* chapter 3, verse 9, in *Upanisads,* trans. Patrick Olivelle (New York: Oxford University Press, 1996), 3–94.

55. *Katha Upanishad,* chapter 5, verse 12, in ibid., 232–247.

56. *Maitreya Upanishad,* chapter 6, verse 17, *The Upanishads,* trans. Juan Mascaro (London: Penguin, 1988), 101.

57. *Atharva Veda,* II.1.1.

58. Panikkar, *The Vedic Experience,* 666.

59. Ibid., 656–657.

60. Ibid., 658–659; see the *Brihadaranyaka Upanishad,* I.4.17.

61. *Brihadaranyaka Upanishad,* V.1.

62. Madhava-Vidyaranya, *Sankara-Dig-Vijaya: The Traditional Life of Sri Sankaracharya,* trans. Swami Tapasyananda (Madras: Sri Ramakrishna Math, 1986), canto 8.

63. Norman Lamm, *The Shema: Spirituality and Law in Judaism* (Philadelphia: The Jewish Publication Society, 1998), 31.

64. Ibid., 193.

65. Ibid., 31–68.

66. Ibid., 62ff.

67. Annemarie Schimmel, *Mystical Dimensions of Islam* (Chapel Hill: University of North Carolina Press, 1975), 17. See also 418–420. "The Alif is a symbol of the One who alone is, of Him whose Being no being precedeth. Thus the appearance of the Point [for this first letter of the alphabet in Arabic calligraphy] as Alif is what is called 'Firstness'. Before its manifestation it was not so qualified, even as it was not qualified by 'Lastness'. He is the First and the Last and the Outwardly Manifest and the Inwardly Hidden. . . . And as first, last and manifest in all (letters) in between, 'All is Alif.' " Martin Lings, *A Moslem Saint of the Twentieth Century: Shaikh Ahmad al-'Alwai, His Spiritual Heritage and Legacy* (London: Allen and Unwin, 1961), 150f. (Also published as *A Sufi Saint of the Twentieth Century* by the Islamic Texts Society [Cambridge, 1993].)

68. Jung, *Civilization in Transition,* 139.

69. Ibid., 458.

70. Goethe, quoted in Henri Bortoft, *The Wholeness of Nature: Goethe's Way toward a Science of Conscious Participation in Nature* (Hudson, N.Y.: Lindisfarne, 1996), 285.

71. *The Essential Plotinus: Representative Treatises from the Enneads,* trans. Elmer O'Brien (New York: New American Library, 1964), 78.

72. Ibid., 78–79.

73. Ibid., 82–83.

74. Harvey, ed., *The Essential Mystics,* 135.

75. Ibid., 84.

76. Plotinus, *Enneads,* 6.5.7, quoted in Margaret R. Miles, *Plotinus on Body and Beauty: Society, Philosophy, and Religion in Third-Century Rome* (Oxford: Blackwell, 1999), vi.

77. Harvey, *The Essential Mystics,* 135. This direction is found in the writings of mystics around the world, requiring a ripe readiness to seek the One.

78. Ibid., 88.

79. Bortoft, *The Wholeness of Nature,* 260.

80. Ibid., 242.

81. Ibid., 228ff.

82. Friedrich Schleiermacher, *On Religion: Speeches to Its Cultured Despisers,* trans. John Oman (New York: Harper, 1958), 51.

83. Plato, Plotinus, and, later, Rumi all speak of the circling of the soul. "All that comes from the center will circle and circle." *The Essential Rumi,* trans. Coleman Barks (San Francisco: HarperSanFrancisco, 1995), 279.

84. My colleague Professor Raima Larter, of Indiana University–Purdue University at Indianapolis, has discussed this point in conversations with me. She has also discussed it in "Chaos and the Goodness of God," plenary lecture at the Religion and Science Workshop organized by William Durbin, Washington Theological Union, Washington, D.C., June 30, 1999.

85. I am indebted to Benoit Mandelbrot for a telephone conversation in 1999, which got me started in thinking about this aspect.

86. Of course, although to us that time seems like a "childhood," no doubt even at law's origins the customs of law were already

old, the result of rules evolved from necessity, generations of intelligent remembering.

87. It is interesting that this point in law started out as vision, so the inspired mystic was a source of law. J. L. Mehta noted, in a conversation with me at Harvard University in 1978, that in India, Manu and other seers were at the center, not the periphery, of social organization. By 1850 in the Western world mysticism seemed insupportable as a source of law, as rationality found theological views embarrassing. But now in 2000 science is saying, "Wait a minute, boys, this one's not dead." The ancient intuition of subtle unity is now supported by scientific data, providing evidence and reasons to reevaluate. Ecology, quantum physics, and other disciplines point to an interrelatedness, a subtle unity.

Riff on natural law in the form of a villanelle:

In the childhood of the law
watchers watched and made some sense
people looked for what holds all
and they echoed Reason's call
and discerned what order meant.
In the childhood of the law
man resolved to learn from awe
and respect his unknown friends
people looked for what holds all
what could withstand fatal squalls
and what would help hurt make amends
in the childhood of the law
when the human tribe was small
and codes were growing for defense
people looked toward what holds all
the massive intricate and small;
even now we still depend
on the childhood of the law
when people look for what holds all.

88. Kahn, *The Art and Thought of Heraclitus,* 43. Kahn gives this interpretation on page 286.

89. Marcus Aurelius wrote, "Honor the highest thing in the universe; it is the power on which all things depend; it is the light by which all of life is guided. Honor the highest within yourself; for it too is the power on which all things depend, and the light with which all life is guided." *Meditations,* quoted in Harvey, *The Essential Mystics,* 135.

90. This paragraph and several that follow

are deeply indebted to J. Stanley McQuade, "History of the Natural Law Doctrine" in *Jurisfiction,* ed. J. Stanley McQuade (Norcross, Ga.: Harrison, 1982), 236ff. According to the best-known formulation, *jus gentium,* the law of nations, is that law which natural reason has established among all people, equally observed among all nations. See Robert P. George, "Natural Law, the Constitution, and the Theory and Practice of Judicial Review," with responses by James E. Fleming and Joseph W. Koterski, and a rebuttal by George, *Fordham Law Review* 49, no. 6 (May 2001), 2269ff.

91. Deuteronomy 5:7–21.

92. McQuade, "History of the Natural Law Doctrine," 238.

93. Ibid. See also Lawrence Tribe, "The Curvature of Constitutional Space: What Lawyers Can Learn from Modern Physics," *Harvard Law Review* 103 (1989): 1.

94. I am told by Professor Oscar G. Chase, of the New York University School of Law, that legal scholar Ronald Dworkin criticized natural law theory with this term.

95. John Wild, ed., *Spinoza: Selections* (New York: Charles Scribner's Sons, 1958), xxi.

96. Ibid., xxx.

97. Ibid., xxx–xxxiii.

98. James Carroll, "The Forgotten Thinker," *Boston Globe,* July 4, 2000, A11.

99. Wild, *Spinoza,* lii ff.

100. John Chipman Gray, *The Nature and Sources of the Law* (1909; reprint, Boston: Beacon, 1967), 126ff.

101. Paul Davies, *The Cosmic Blueprint* (London: Penguin, 1995).

102. This paragraph and the following one draw some concepts from R. C. L., "Law and Disorder: The New Science of Chaos," chapter 6 of *Laws of Wisdom,* available at the School of Wisdom Web site: http://www.lawsofwisdom.com/LawsofWisdom/chapter6.html (accessed November 7, 2002). Stuart Kauffman, author of *The Origins of Order: Self-Organization and Selection in Evolution* (New York: Oxford University Press, 1993), among other works, uses "order for free" terminology.

103. R. C. L., "Law and Disorder."

104. The human being "experiences in his soul more than the present moment can provide. To a greater degree than any animal, he can learn from past experiences to apply

them fruitfully to the present. And he can plan for the future, thus gaining some mastery over it. Past, present and future are realized simultaneously in the soul of man." Wolfgang Schad, *Man and Mammals: Toward a Biology of Form,* trans. Carroll Scherer (Garden City, N.Y.: Waldorf, 1977), 270. Schad, who works with Goethe's and Steiner's theories, speculates that these unique capacities may be connected with the way the human's three organic systems develop at different times. Hanne Petersen, "Gender and Nature in Comparative Legal Cultures," in *Comparing Legal Cultures,* ed. David Nelken (Brookfield, Vt.: Dartmouth, 1997) calls for a reconsideration of how the legal system treats the presumed difference between man and nature. Thanks to Prof. Oscar Chase of the New York University School of Law for his comments on this.

105. The prophetic traditions have often denied that nonhumans have souls.

106. Martin Buber, *I and Thou* (New York: Charles Scribner's Sons, 1958), 16.

107. For the ancient Greeks, the dodecahedron was a symbol for the universe.

108. The teaching of Jesus, some say, was "Be whole even as your father in heaven," and in healing the infirm he told them, "Be whole."

109. Kaygusuz Abdul, quoted in Harvey, *The Essential Mystics,* 167.

110. Jung, *Man and His Symbols,* 309–310.

111. James Hillman, *The Force of Character* (New York: Random House, 1999), 169. This flexible oscillation between sameness and difference is the way of great mystics such as Lao-tzu and Plotinus. Margaret Miles, who magisterially works with the worldview of Plotinus, advocates such an approach in the study of religion. See her 1999 presidential address to the American Academy of Religion, "Becoming Answerable for What We See," *Journal of the American Academy of Religion* 68, no. 3 (Sept. 2000): 471–485.

112. Vaclav Havel, "Civilization's Thin Veneer," *Harvard Magazine,* July–August 1995, 32ff.

113. Rabbi Irwin Kula discussed this in the *Frontline* documentary "Faith and Doubt at Ground Zero," which was broadcast on PBS September 3, 2002. The text of the interview with Rabbi Kula is available at <http://www.pbs.org/wgbh/pages/frontline/shows/ faith/interviews/kula.html> (accessed November 7, 2002).

CONCLUSION

1. John Briggs, *Fractals: The Patterns of Chaos: A New Aesthetic of Art, Science, and Nature* (New York: Simon and Schuster, 1992), 25.

2. Benoit Mandelbrot, "A Multifractal Walk down Wall Street," *Scientific American,* February 1999, 70. See also Mandelbrot's *Fractals and Scaling in Finance* (Heidelberg: Springer-Verlag, 1997), and *Multifractals and 1/F Noise: Wild Self-Affinity in Physics (1963–1976)* (New York: Springer-Verlag, 1999); Michael Barnsley, with the assistance of Hawley Rising III, *Fractals Everywhere,* 2nd ed., revised (San Francisco: Morgan Kaufmann, 2000); and Walter Freeman, "The Physiology of Perception," *Scientific American* 264, no. 2 (Feb. 1991): 78–85. For an example of the use of fractals in film and the graphic arts, see F. Kenton Musgrave's program MojoWorld, at <http://www.pandromeda.com> (accessed November 7, 2002).

Other examples of fractal applications in various fields include Clifford A. Pickover, ed., *Fractal Horizons: The Future Use of Fractals* (New York: St. Martin's, 1996); Charles Madden, *Fractals in Music: Introductory Mathematics for Musical Analysis* (Salt Lake City: High Art, 1999); Carl Bovill, *Fractal Geometry in Architecture and Design* (Boston: Birkhauser, 1996); Ignacio Rodriguez-Iturbe and Andrea Rinaldo, *Fractal River Basins: Chance and Self-Organization* (Cambridge: Cambridge University Press, 1997); John Lewis Gaddis, *The Landscape of History: How Historians Map the Past* (New York: Oxford University Press, 2002); Myron J. Frankman, "Fractals and the Common Heritage of Humanity," at <http:// www.arts.mcgill.ca/programs/econ/fractal.html and Chip Weston, "Thru Infinity to Unity: The Fractal Connectivity of Consciousness," at <http://www.fractalwisdom.com/Fractal Wisdom/weston.html> (both accessed November 7, 2002).

3. See for example Peter Engel, *Origami from Angelfish to Zen* (New York: Dover, 1994), especially 45–77, for thoughtful reflections on the creative process and discovery of forms. Gary William Flake, in *The Computational*

Beauty of Nature: Fractals, Complex Systems (Cambridge, Mass.: MIT Press, 1998), asserts that the four most interesting computational topics are fractals, chaos, complex systems, and adaptation. Stephan Wolfram's massive book *A New Kind of Science* (Champaign, Ill.: Wolfram Media, 2002) presents an intriguing integration of new scientific trends, including fractal patterns. Considering all processes, those of human effort as well as those occurring spontaneously in nature, as computations, Wolfram suggests a rediscovery of what humans share with the rest of existence, which was already envisioned by shamanism and other views of a spirit pervading man and nature. See pages 845–846.

4. John Briggs and F. David Peat, *Turbulent Mirror: An Illustrated Guide to Chaos Theory and the Science of Wholeness* (New York: Harper and Row, 1989), 191ff. Also see John Briggs, "Reflectaphors: The (Implicate) Universe as a Work of Art," in *Quantum Implications: Essays in Honor of David Bohm,* ed. David Bohm, John Briggs, et al. (London: Routledge and Kegan Paul, 1987), 414ff.

5. Chaos theory and the study of fractals are interrelated: "Fractals are used to describe complex topographies, whether they be temporal or spatial. Chaos, on the other hand, is concerned with the dynamical processes that show an exquisite sensitivity to initial conditions and which can generate complex fractal topographies in phase space. [Often, the trajectories of chaotic systems are drawn to an 'attractor' in phase space that is a fractal.] The language of fractals provides a natural descriptor for chaotic systems." T. Gregory Dewey, *Fractals in Molecular Biophysics,* (Oxford: Oxford University Press, 1997), 241–242.

6. Ibid., 266. As Whitehead notes, "There are two principles inherent in the very nature of things, recurring in some particular embodiments whatever field we explore—the spirit of change, and the spirit of conservation. There can be nothing real without both." Alfred North Whitehead, *Science and The Modern World* (New York: Macmillan, 1959), 179. Gregory Bateson also explored this polar dynamic.

7. Many articles in psychology journals address this. See Michael Butz, "The Fractal Nature of the Development of the Self," *Psychological Reports* 71 (1992): 1043–1063; J. R. Van Eenwyk, "Archetypes: The Strange Attractors of the Psyche," *Journal of Analytical Psychology* 36 (1991): 1–25. See also Robin Robertson and Allan Combs, eds., *Chaos Theory in Psychology and the Life Sciences* (Mahwah, N.J.: Lawrence Erlbaum Associates), 1995.

8. The river channel, of course, is an image used by Jung to characterize archetypes.

9. Whitehead, *Science and the Modern World,* 102. Conversely, we live in a world of change and entropy; if solid matter is fundamental then endurance is an arbitrary fact at the base of the order of nature.

10. Benoit Mandelbrot voiced this idea, that satisfying art is not just active on one scale, but has important elements at all levels of size. See James Gleick, *Chaos: Making a New Science* (New York: Penguin, 1987), 117.

11. For example, Frida Kahlo's painting *The Love Embrace of the Universe, the Earth (Mexico), Me, and Señor Zolotl,* depicting a child held by a mother who is held by a larger mother, held by a larger mother, held by a larger mother, etc. A sketch for this painting is at <http://www.smog.net/artists/kahlo/frida07.php?aID=6> (accessed January 7, 2003).

12. "Beyond within" is Huston Smith's phrase in *The World's Religions: Our Great Wisdom Traditions* (San Francisco: HarperSanFrancisco, 1991), 22.

13. Steiner's verses are quoted near the end of Wolfgang Schad, *Man and Mammals: Toward a Biology of Form,* trans. Carroll Scherer (Garden City, N.Y.: Waldorf, 1977), 276.

14. This is well discussed in John Briggs and F. David Peat, *Seven Life Lessons of Chaos* (New York: HarperCollins, 1999), 108.

15. Ibid.

16. Ibid., 118.

17. Ibid., 119.

18. Ibid.

19. Ibid., 121.

20. Ibid., 124.

21. Ibid.

22. Walt Whitman, "Unfolded out of the Folds," in *Leaves of Grass: The Deathbed Edition* (New York: Book-of-the-Month Club, 1992), 291–292.

23. Rainer Maria Rilke, in a poem in *Das Stundenbuch,* writes, "I want to unfold. / I don't want to stay folded anywhere, / because where I am folded, there I am a lie." *Selected Poems*

of *Rainer Maria Rilke,* trans. Robert Bly (New York: Harper and Row, 1981), 25.

24. Plotinus, *Enneads,* 3.1.8., quoted in Margaret R. Miles, *Plotinus on Body and Beauty: Society, Philosophy, and Religion in Third-Century Rome* (Oxford: Blackwell, 1999), 62.

25. Thus Adair ends her poem "Zazen," which is about going to sit in silence, taking off burdens, hang-ups, accumulated emotional baggage and clutter. It is a dramatic example of modern life's disquieting pressures and the return to ground zero. *New Yorker,* July 20, 1998, 52.

26. Dennis Overbye, "In the New Physics, No Quark Is an Island," *New York Times,* March 20, 2001, section D (Science), 1.

27. Murray Gell-Mann, *The Quark and the Jaguar* (New York: W. H. Freeman, 1994), xiv.

28. *Psychological Reflections: An Anthology of the Writings of C. G. Jung,* ed. Jolande Jacobi (New York: Harper and Row, 1961), 68.

29. For example, see J. Richard Eisner, *Attitudes, Chaos, and the Connectionist Mind* (Oxford, Blackwell, 1994), 121, 174, 178–182, 210–213.

30. Miles, *Plotinus on Body and Beauty,* 182. This may be his great contribution—the vision of how we can find realization by way of the beauty of the One. His sense of the body, like Descartes's, has limited usefulness for the people of our times.

31. Plotinus, *Enneads,* 6.5.7, quoted in Miles, *Plotinus on Body and Beauty,* 181.

32. Jean-François Lyotard, *The Postmodern Condition: A Report on Knowledge,* trans. Geoff Bennington and Brian Massumi (Minneapolis: University of Minnesota Press, 1984), 60.

33. A program by Gabriele Kroos's dance company entitled "Fractalia" was performed in New York in 2001. See Jennifer Dunning's review, "An Incomprehensible Work? How about Some Footnotes?" *New York Times,* January 15, 2001, B10. The Internet has many sites for fractal art and fractal music. Scientific texts include Bruce J. West and Bill Deering, *The Lure of Modern Science: Fractal Thinking* (Singapore: World Scientific, 1995); Dick Oliver, *Fractal Vision: Put Fractals to Work for You* (Carmel, Ind.: SAMS, 1992) has a chapter entitled "The Philosophy of Fractals." See also Midhat J. Gazale, *Gnomon: From Pharaohs to Fractals* (Princeton, N.J.: Princeton University Press, 1999).

Hume, David, 196
Huston, Jean, 156

I and Thou, 236
Illusions perdues, 199–200
Imitation: Christianity and, 95–99; Hinduism and, 92–93; Islam and, 99–101; Judaism and, 93–95; profane, 101–104; and self-similarity in structures of ancient religions, 86–90; in spirituality, 85–86; Taoist, 91–92
Imitation of Christ, The, 97
In the Beginning, 74
Incredible String Band, the, 80
India: architecture of, *227;* art of, *208;* Hinduism of, 30–31, 35–36; infinity of divine beings in, 73–75; interconnected levels of existence in, 47–49, 57; literature of, 158–159, 172–173, 276n35
Indra, 29–31, 57, 159, 265n37, 276n35
Indra's Pearls, 31
Infinite quality of fractals, 4, *111,* 147, 152–166
Interior Castle, The, 154
Invisible Cities, 158
Islam, 40, 99–101, 125, 297n23

James, Henry, 113
Jantsch, Erich, 131
Japan, Zen Buddhism in, 34–35
Jeans, James, 184
Jeffers, Robinson, 72–73, 141–143, 293–294n49
Jones, Frank, 146
Judaism, 40–41, 93–95, 231; literature of, 158–159; oneness in, 222–223
Julian of Norwich, 78
Jung, Carl G., 1, 5, 12, 19, *35,* 97–98, 108, 117, 119, 130, 200, 206, 237, 276n38

Kafka, Franz, 115, 126
Kant, Immanuel, 196
Karma, 93, 102
Kauffman, Stuart, 180, 261n33
Kepler, Johannes, 56, 210
King, Martin Luther, Jr., 177
King, Stephen, 134
Klee, Paul, 136–137
Knight, Etheridge, 113
Koestler, Arthur, 10, 196
Kolam, 47–48
Krauss, Karl, 138
Krishna, 207, *208,* 211, 213
Kuba people, *15*
Kuhn, Thomas, 185
Kula, Irwin, 239–240

Lamb, John, 103
Lao-tzu, 9, 91, 125, 133, 210, 211, 216
Last Year at Marienbad, 160
Laszlo, Ervin, 126
LeFevre, Adam, 143
Leibniz, Gottfried, 196

Lennon, John, 175
Leonardo da Vinci, 118, 119
Leopold, Aldo, 9
Lévi-Strauss, Claude, 56
Lion King, The, 138
Literature (*see also* Poetry): Asian and Indian, 29, 154, 158–159, 172–173, 276n35; beauty in, 138–139; depictions of heaven and hell in, 41–46, 150–151, 237n72; fire imagery in, 175; fractal-like details in, 25–39, 72–76, 158–166; poetic, 45, 139–157; religious, 2, 25–39, 41–46, 72–76, 81, 99–101
Local Knowledge, 175
Locke, John, 195, 231
Look Into It, 239
Lopez, Barry, 9, 191–192
Lord Tennyson, Alfred, 147
Lorenz, Konrad, 9
Love, 103–104, 151–152, 225, 281n69, 286n54; for and by children, 152; risk taking and, 134–137
Loyola, Ignatius, 295n82
Luhmann, Niklas, 53
Luther, Martin, 195
Lyotard, Jean-François, 177, 256, 274–275n20

M theory, 298n39
Mahabharata, 276n35
Maimonides, Moses, 223
Mamet, David, 117
Manava Dharma Shastra, 93, 105
Mandalas, 108, *109,* 110
Mandelbrot, Benoit B., *3, 4,* 10, *16, 17,* 21, 25, 26–27, 48, 56, *58,* 62, *63, 64,* 66, 82, *111,* 132, *141, 189, 199, 209,* 241, 245, 248; on fractal geometry, 264n20; fractal term coined by, 259n3; on the human eye in science, 64–65; mathematical talent of, 263n9; on nomads by choice, 180
Mann, Thomas, 266n45
Manson, Charles, 208
Marxism, 24
Matter, evidences of mind in, 184–188
Maturana, Umberto, 176, 177, 178–179
McCall, Nathan, 102
McCance, Kathryn L., *191*
McGuire, Michael, 68–69
Mead, Margaret, 46–47
Meditations, 200
Melville, Herman, 81
Melvin, A. Gordon, 104, 105
Memory: chunking and, 133–134; evolution and, 180–183
Memory, J. D., 83–84
Mencius, 91–92, 151–152
Mendel, Gregor, 245
Merton, Thomas, 1, 198
Metaphoric relations, 50, 52
Metaphysics, 205–206
Metaphysics, 129–130, 285–286n40
Michelangelo, 236–237
Milton, John, 198

Thoreau, Henry David, 9, 114, 140–141, *157,* 205, 215, 237

Thunder, Johnny, 151

Time, fractals as a process enacted in, 2–3

Towle, Albert, *69*

Traceries in the Void, 116

Tractatus Theologico-Politicus, 231

Traherne, Thomas, 62, 98, 148–152, 156–157

Trawick, Margaret, 46, 47–48, 57, 270n93

Trehan Bahow Mirror, *84*

Trismegistus, Hermes, 99

Tukaram, 74

Tunnel, The, 162

Turbulent Mirror, 132

Twain, Mark, 145

Unconscious, the, 13–14

United Nations, 171

Universe, the: cosmic orphans in, 46; and earth as a ship, 80–84; evolution of, 123–124, 135–136; galaxies of, 219; importance of the observing human eye in, 65–66; interconnectedness within, 28–39, 154–166, 245; interweaving strands of, 218–219; nonlinearity of, 9, 23, 55, 106–107, 115, 260n21; place of human beings in, 151–152, 200–204; as thinking, 185–186; traditional representations of, 217–218, 267n77; units and levels of, 218–219, 298n35

Upanishad, Chandogya, 92–93

Updike, John, 10

Utkin, Iosif, 143

Vaishnavism, 73–74

Valéry, Paul, 9, 10, 65

Vedic-Upanishadic vision, 220–222

Visage of War, 46

Vision of the Sixth Heaven, The, 43

Visual language of fractals, 67–72, 156, 185, *239*

Voice of the Earth, The, 80, 175

Voltaire, François, 195

Vonnegut, Kurt, 133

Waits, Tom, 117

Walden, 141

War, 101

War, The, 160

Weil, Simone, 103, 136

Wellman, Mac, 3

Welty, Eudora, 129

White, Leslie, 169

Whitehead, Alfred North, 15, 109, 175, 178, 179, 243

Whitman, Ruth, 146

Whitman, Walt, 251

Wholeness: art and, 120–126, 236–237; Buddhist vision of, 110; chaos science and, 89; consciousness and, 35–39, 141–148, 220–222; cosmic images of, 60–63, 87–88; defining, 275n28; dreams and, 206–207; expressed by fractals, 28–39, 59, 262–263n5; interweaving strands in, 218–219, 245–246; of nature, 225–226; paradoxes of, 205–210; reflected in self-similarity, 63–72; resonance and, 107–112; sacred space and, 87; thinking in images, 113–119

Wilbur, Ken, 196

Wilde, Oscar, 152

Williams, William Carlos, 181

Wilson, Edward O., 175–180

Winckelmann, Johann Joachim, 190

Wright, David, 31

Yeats, William Butler, 59

Yoga, 198

Yogavasishtha, 35–36, 79

Yogi, Maharishi Mahesh, 63

Yung Ming, 184

Zaire, *15*

Zen Buddhism, 34–35, 186–187, 207, 248; poetry, 50–54

William J. Jackson is Professor of Religious Studies at Indiana University–Purdue University Indianapolis, where he has taught since
1985. He received a B.A. from Lyndon State College in Vermont
in 1975, and a Ph.D. in the comparative study of religion from
Harvard University in 1984. He lived in India for four years and
continues to study culturally creative figures of South India. He is
the author of *Tyagaraja: Life and Lyrics* and *Songs of Three Great
South Indian Saints*.